a moving experience

Holidays on wheels, wings and water

a moving experience

Holidays on wheels, wings and water

PHOTOGRAPHY: GRANT SHEEHAN   *TEXT: SHELLEY-MAREE CASSIDY*

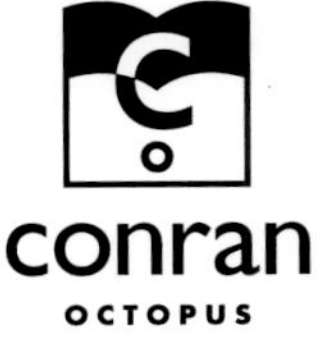

conran
OCTOPUS

Acknowledgements

Much thanks for their assistance and support is due to Fiona Strang, Dieter & Mary Clissmann, Lucette Brehm, Jazzou Jones, Bruce L Jones, Freddie & Kevin Tickell, Frank de Groot, Ali Macareg, Alasdair Cassels, Maureen Camadona, Sophie Dent, Michael Pantich, Dave Lyn & Lauren Madden, Catherine Tondelli, Lucy Hays, David Kleinman, Jan Novak, Katrina Bennett, Elaine & Jean-Pierre Bourbeillon, Alistair Carruthers, Mary Shanahan, Richard Weston, Robert Achten, Lauren Robertson, Wendy Cameron & DAC Productions.

Edited by	Mary Shanahan
Design by	Origin Design, New Zealand
Film stock	Fuji Astia, Velvia, Fuji Press
Cameras	Nikon F Series

Published in 2001 by Conran Octopus Limited, 2–4 Heron Quays, London E14 4JP
www.conran-octopus.co.uk

ISBN 1 84091 195 6

First published by Phantom House Books in 2001

The photograph on page 121 is of a door painting at Hotel Buci Latin, Paris.
Sourced photos Photobank NZ P47, P84; US Submarines P85, 86, 87;
British Airways P90; WAT&G P122, 127; NASA P125.

British Library Cataloguing-in-Publication Data
A catalogue record for this book is available from the British Library
Printed in China

This book is dedicated to Kathy Anderson, Michael Ashe & Charles Dobson, who travelled with us, in spirit.

Contents

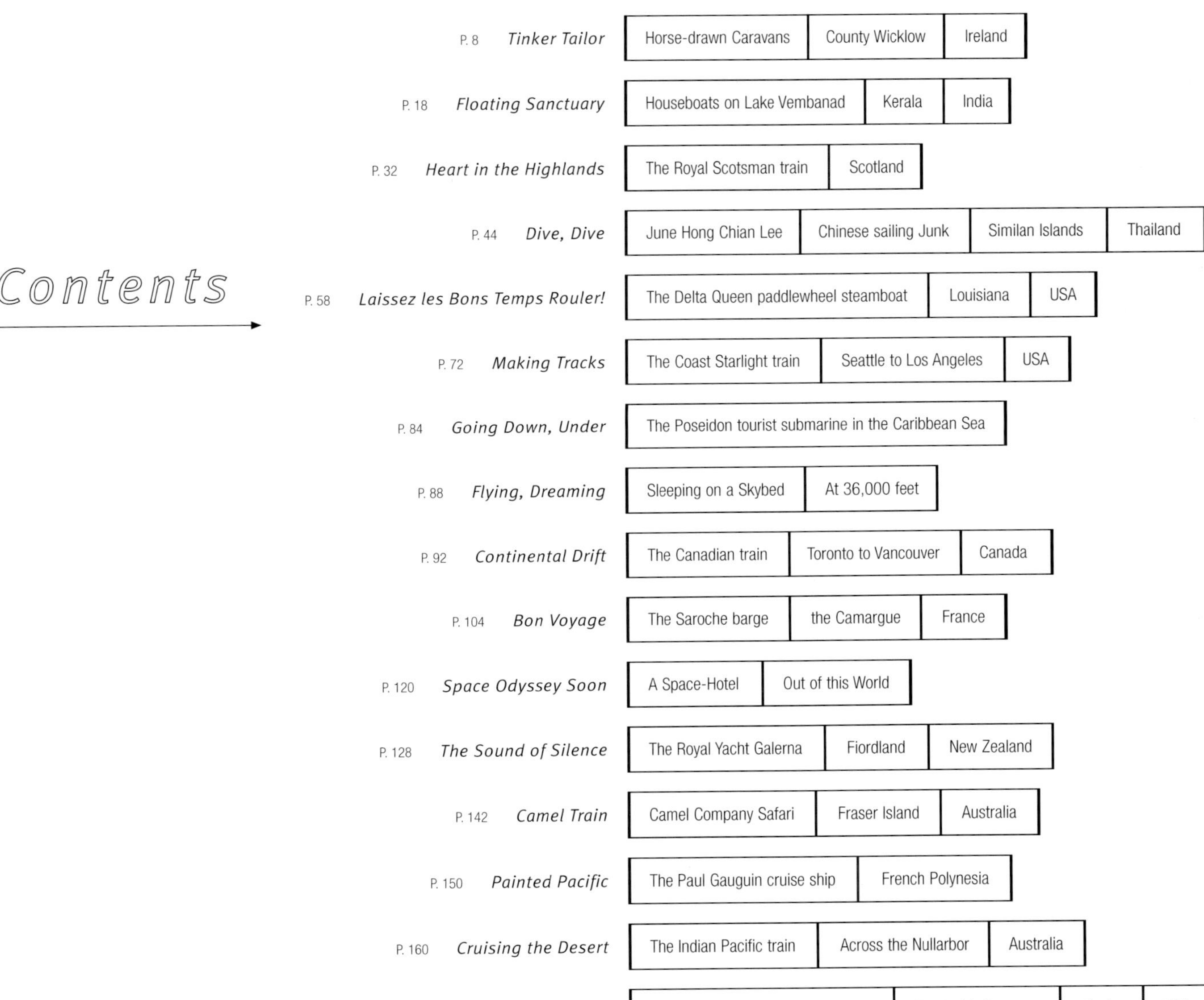

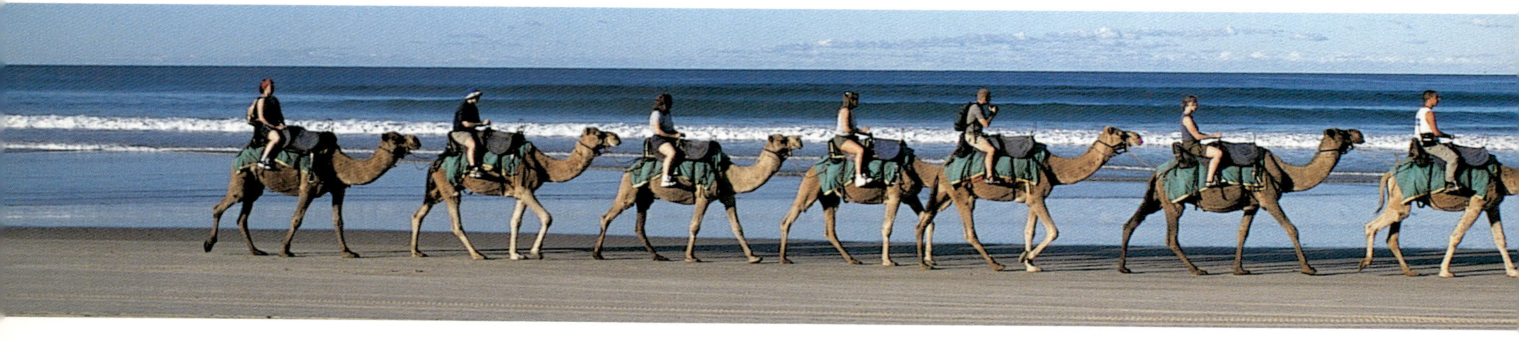

'AND WHAT IS THE USE OF A BOOK,' THOUGHT ALICE,
'WITHOUT PICTURES OR CONVERSATION?'...

from 'Alice in Wonderland' by Lewis Carroll

A Moving Experience...

For most of us, going on holiday, leaving our usual world behind for the new and often unfamiliar starts with the bringing of our suitcases out from storage, and packing for the journey ahead.

Soon that luggage can become a burden, watched over at airports, and anxiously waited for at carousels, then loaded into the transport to reach our next location.

The main disadvantage to visiting several places on a single trip is having to unpack, repack, and settle into a different hotel with every change of location. One of the most agreeable ways to by-pass this bother is to plan a voyage where your accommodation is actually part of your means of transport.

This book is a photographic record and travel journal of places to stay that move, from one location to another. 'Moving hotels', on wheels on water and on wings, from the classic to the unexpected and even the yet to come are shown, and the experience of the trip, the sights and the travellers encountered along the way are described.

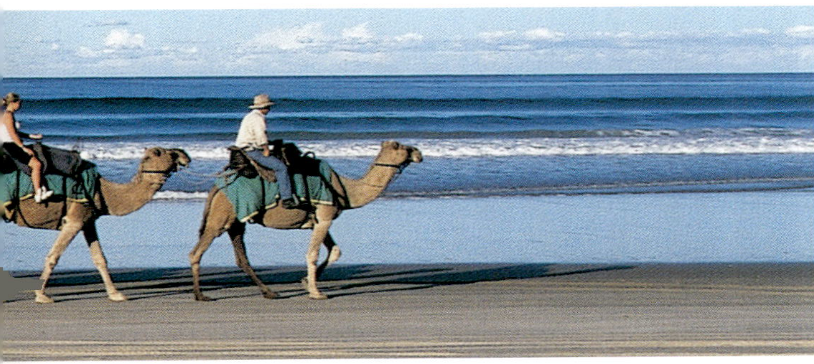

In *A Moving Experience* you will discover a wide range of choices for a hotel room with a constantly changing view, both in this world and out of it. Great train journeys through the highlands of Scotland, across the Australian desert, through the Canadian Rockies and down the coast of California are shown, together with a camel safari, houseboat and barge voyages, grand cruises and more. Whether overland by train and caravan, over water by steamboat and barge, underwater by submarine, or high above the world in a jet liner and soon on a space station, there is a tempting journey for everyone.

As we don't like big stationary hotels, we chose small moving ones. The photographs in most cases were taken from the 'moving hotel' as we travelled, not recaptured on a second visit. At times we had to put up with and work around bad weather. Just like the journey, the weather can't be managed to a schedule. There is always the element of chance, potential for disruption and the need to compromise. Travel is often quite a test of our ability to adapt to and cope with the unexpected events we may meet.

With so many choices, the chief dilemma might be choosing just one. Whichever you choose, we have not shown all there is to see nor told all there is to know.

'TRAVEL, IN THE YOUNGER SORT, IS PART OF EDUCATION; IN THE ELDER, A PART OF EXPERIENCE...'

Francis Bacon

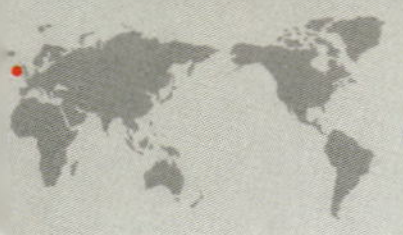

Tinker Tailor...

Horse-drawn caravans, County Wicklow, Ireland

There are few journeys that begin with a lengthy lesson on how to drive your mode of transport. Horsepower is what you will be harnessing in the most literal sense on your caravan trip in Ireland, and horsepower must always be handled with care.

This is a holiday that defies the normal expectation of shuffling off the cares of everyday life. It gives you an extra responsibility – the horse. And in this business, the customer does not come first, the horse does. Fortunately the horses here are good-natured and welltrained, used to their role at the head of the house – the one they pull behind them.

Unlike his temporary handlers probably, the horse has been tested for his temperament, health, road sense and driving skills before being given the job. You may have little experience of horses but luckily the horse has had plenty experience of people.

This may well be a dream holiday for children, travelling in a picturesque caravan, taking time out with parents and with a horse as well. And for the romantic and nomadically inclined this is a taste of a different way of life for a few days, on a summer holiday that is more adventurous than camping.

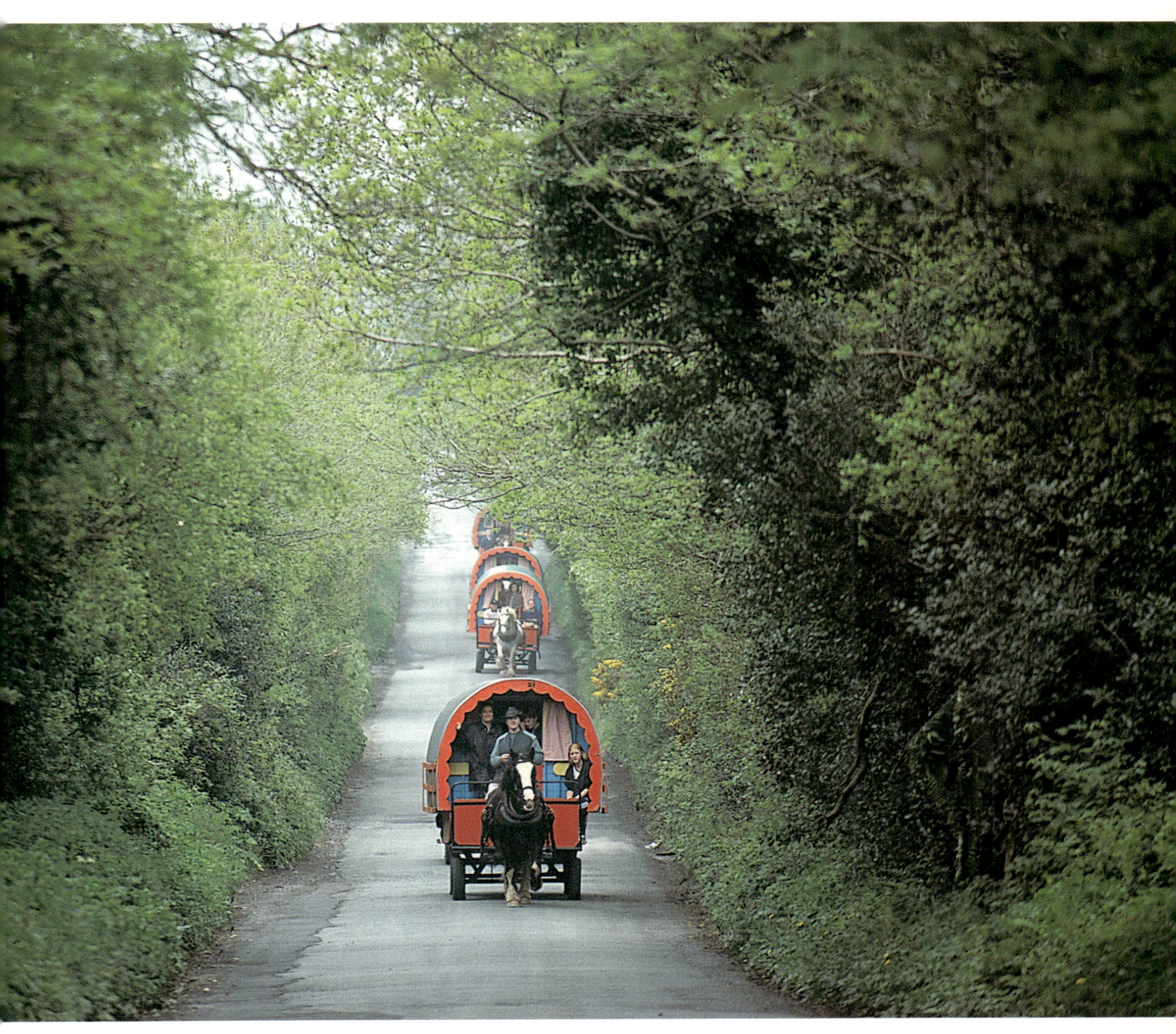

Contemporary nomads journey in convoy in the soft green landscape of the Irish countryside.

The holidaymakers are given a half-day of instructions on the care and handling of the horse, and routes recommended for caravans are mapped out. There is an established network of caravan-friendly farms, where travellers can graze the horse and camp. Or you can roam free and go where the fancy takes you, in your all-terrain vehicle. In addition to designated farmers, many guesthouses and pubs make overnight facilities available for a reasonable fee – at the least providing parking and grass for the horse, and often more, such as meals, fresh farm produce, and hot showers. Horse-drawn caravans have no driving lights, so they must be parked off the road during the hours of darkness.

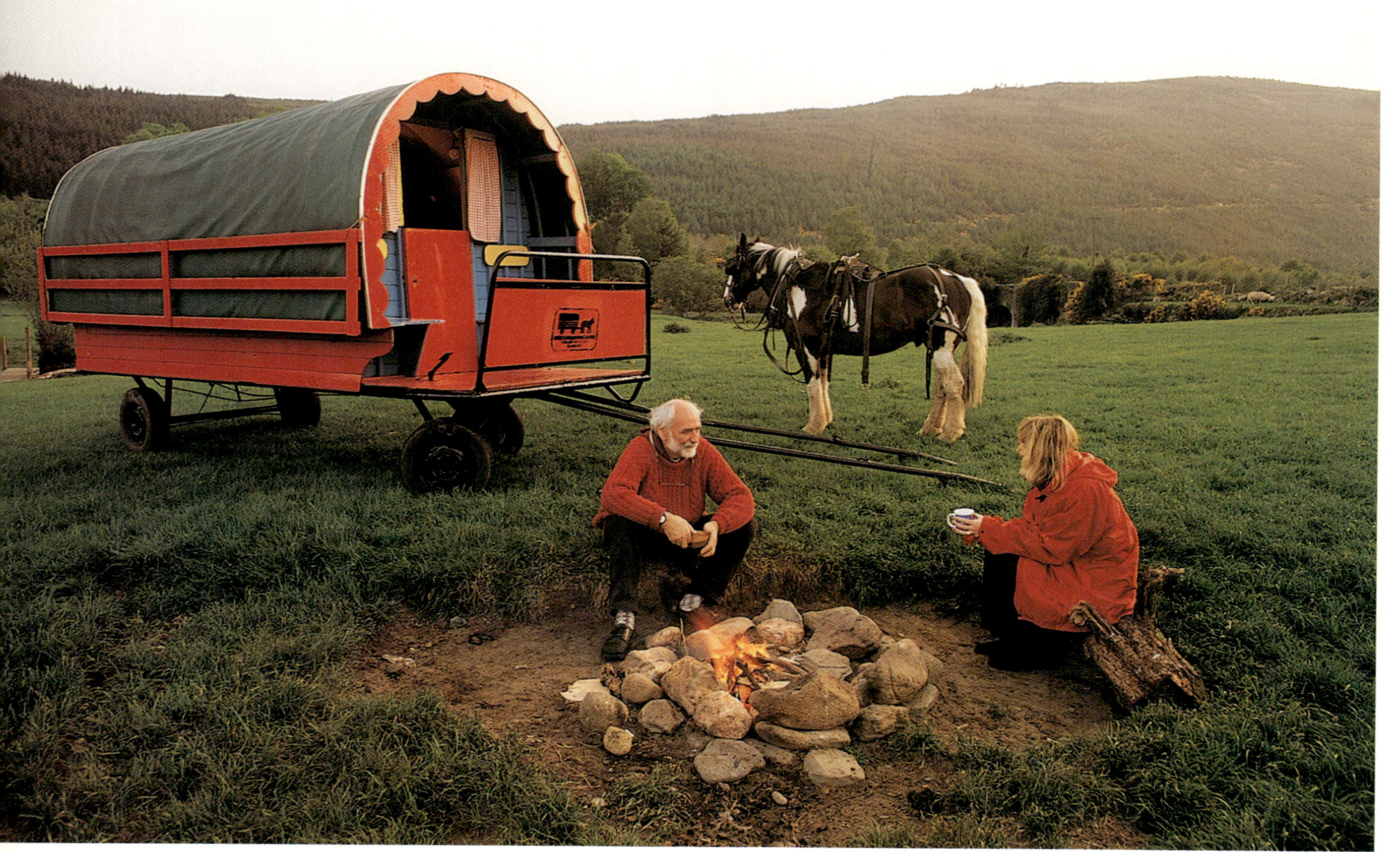

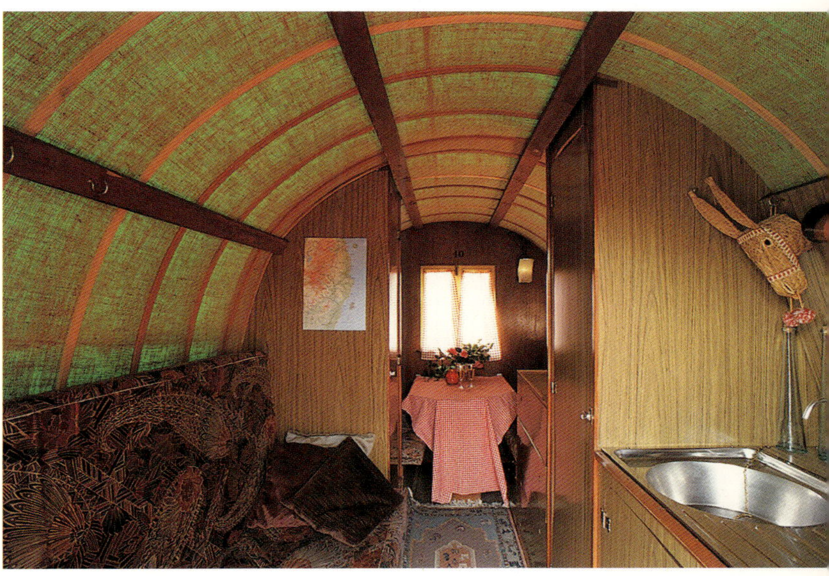

Each caravan has a comfortable simple interior, with four beds – one double – that are seats by day, a well-equipped kitchen, a dining table and plenty of cupboards. The various stops along the way have bathroom facilities and there is often more extensive kitchen and living space in buildings alongside the farmer's field. Gas lamps and candles provide atmospheric lighting. A balcony serves as the entrance to the caravan and the location of the driving seat, wide enough for two or three.

Oats are included for the horse's daily diet, but humans must fend for themselves. Picnic style meals can be made or you can eat at pubs and restaurants along the way. There is no shortage of pubs here.

The caravans are bright bursts of colour as they wander through the green landscape. Reminiscent of the gypsy fables and the covered wagons of American settler days, these are based on the old wooden caravans that the 'travelling people' used to roam around Ireland, sometimes on their own, others in company. This more leisurely use began as a way to go on holiday during World War II, when petrol was rationed or unavailable.

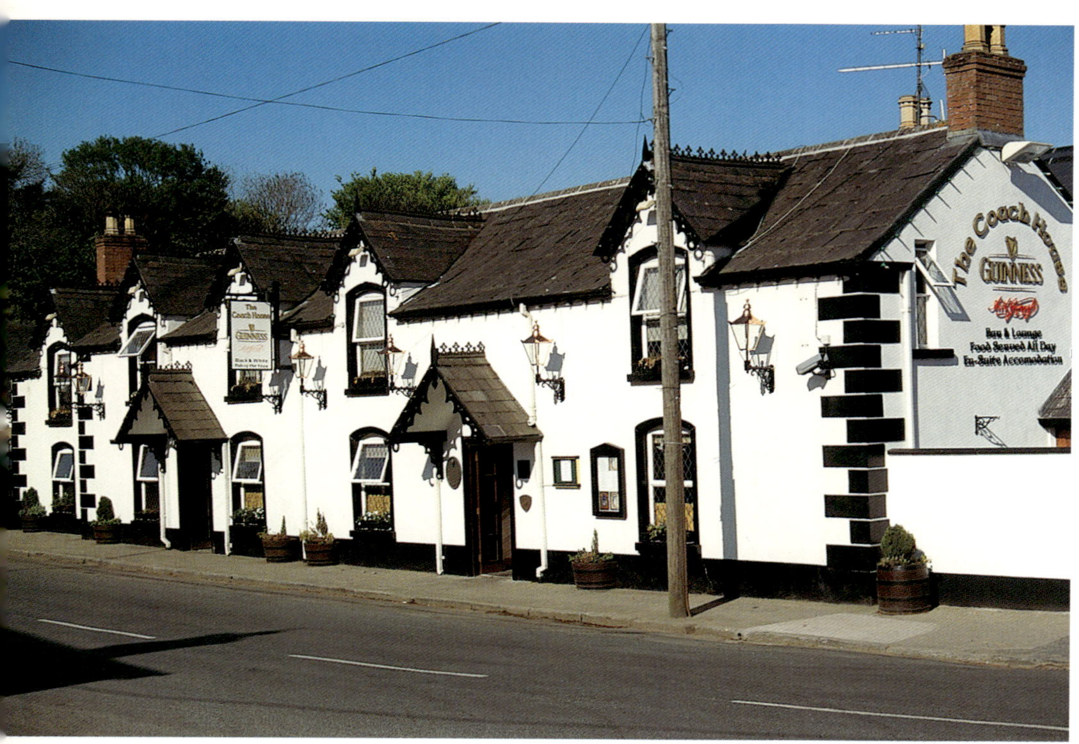

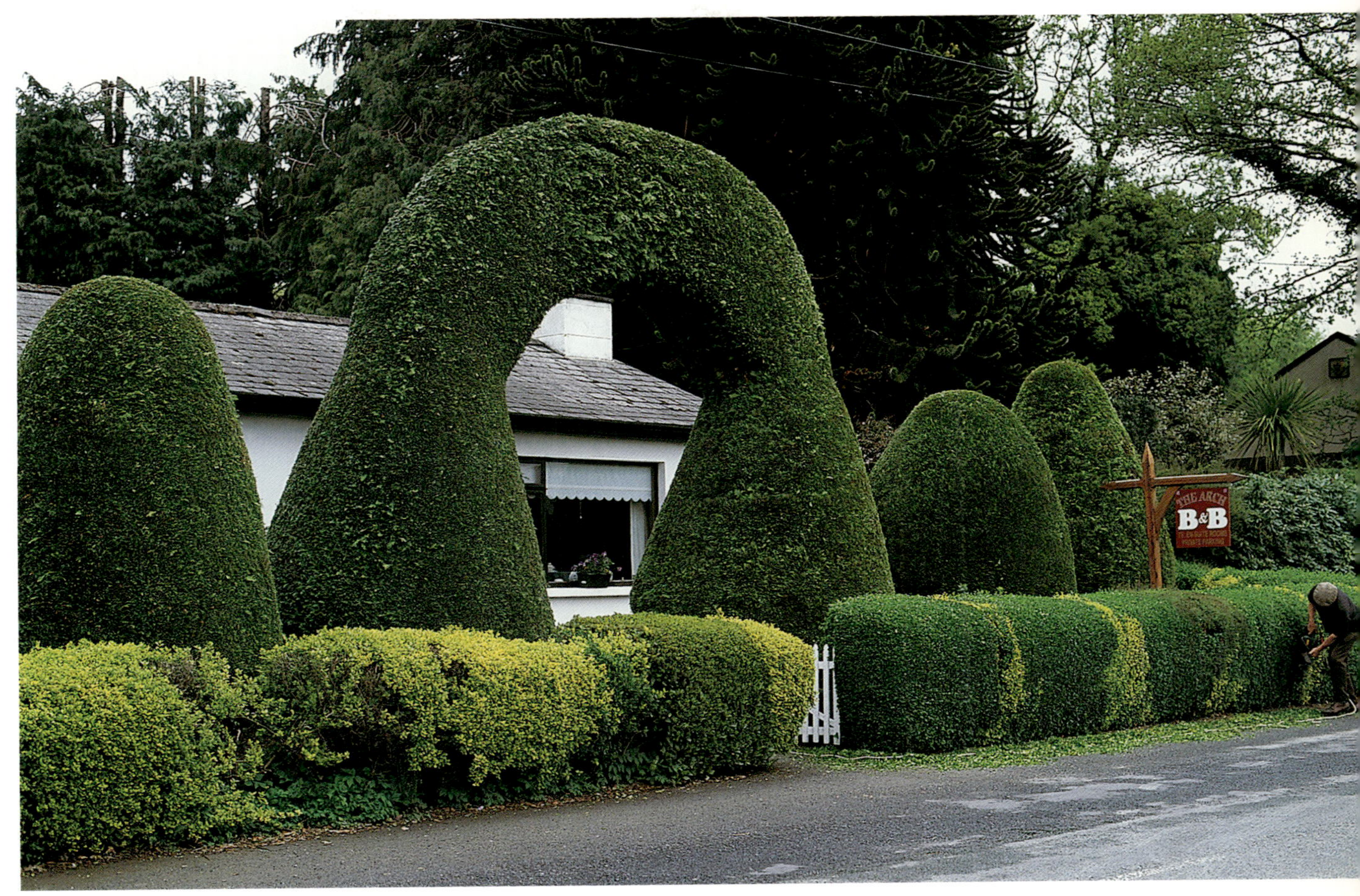

It is comparatively uncrowded here in the centre of County Wicklow, 'the garden of Ireland', only an hour's drive – in a fast car – from Dublin. Travel is through areas patch-worked with farms and dotted with villages. Visiting the towns and villages to shop, to eat at restaurants and cafés or to enjoy a drink and the *craic* (Irish for good times) in the local pub, caravanners can become part of the local life during their holiday. Irish people, world roamers themselves, have a strong tradition of welcoming the stranger; plenty of contact with the locals is characteristic of the caravan holiday. You meet and talk to the farmers at whose farm you park at night; you might ask the way at crossroads, and you travel at a speed – walking pace – that encourages conversation with the people you meet on the road or the man grooming his garden hedge.

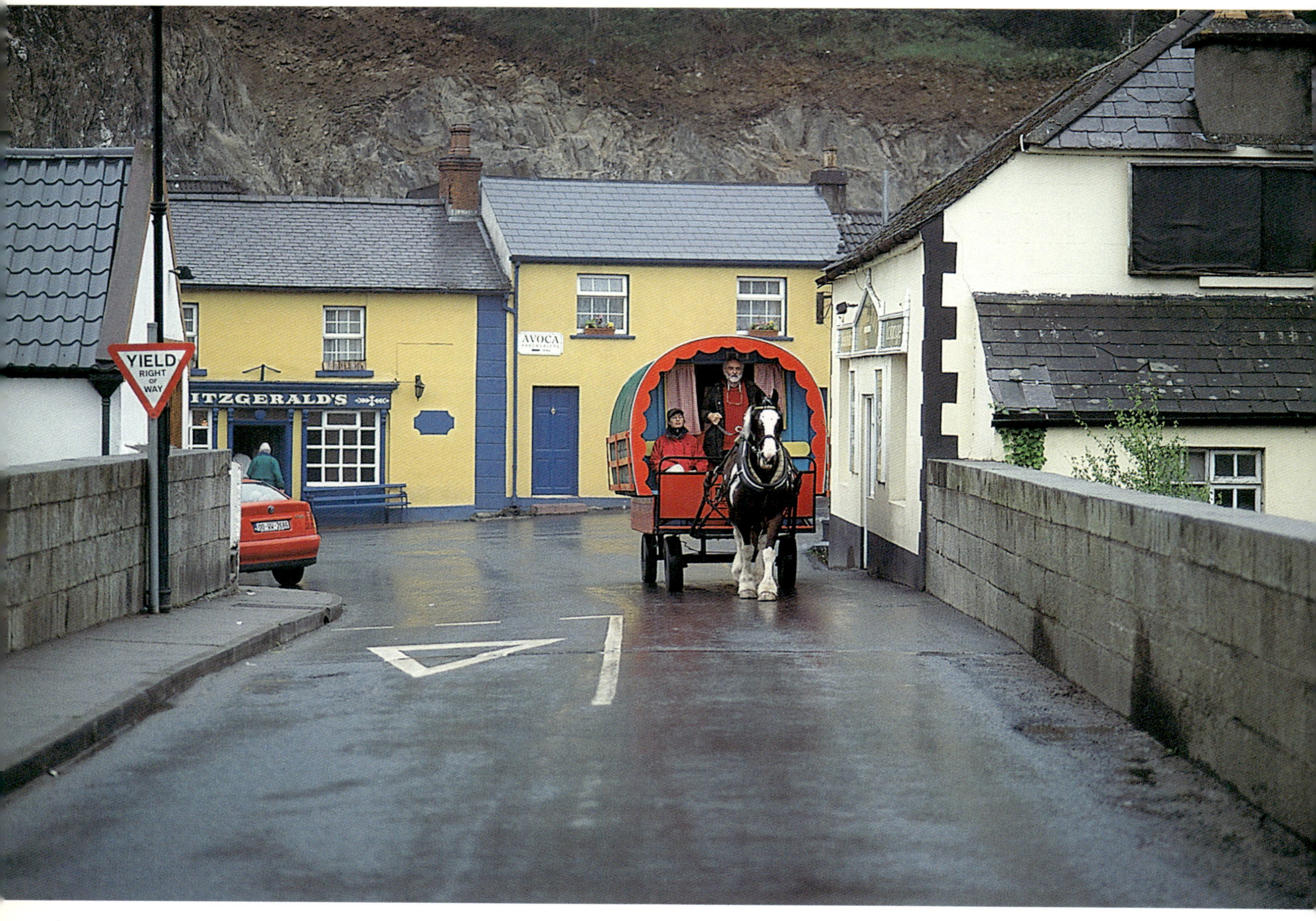

Motorists are surprisingly patient when having to wait for the original horsepower. The sight of the cheerful red and green mobile home often elicits a smile and wave from them as you amble, dawdle even, through the country lanes and villages.

Around seven to twenty kilometres is the usual distance travelled each day, taking between two and five hours depending on the speed of the horse and the number of stops the driver decides to make en route. This is a holiday where you and the horse set the pace.

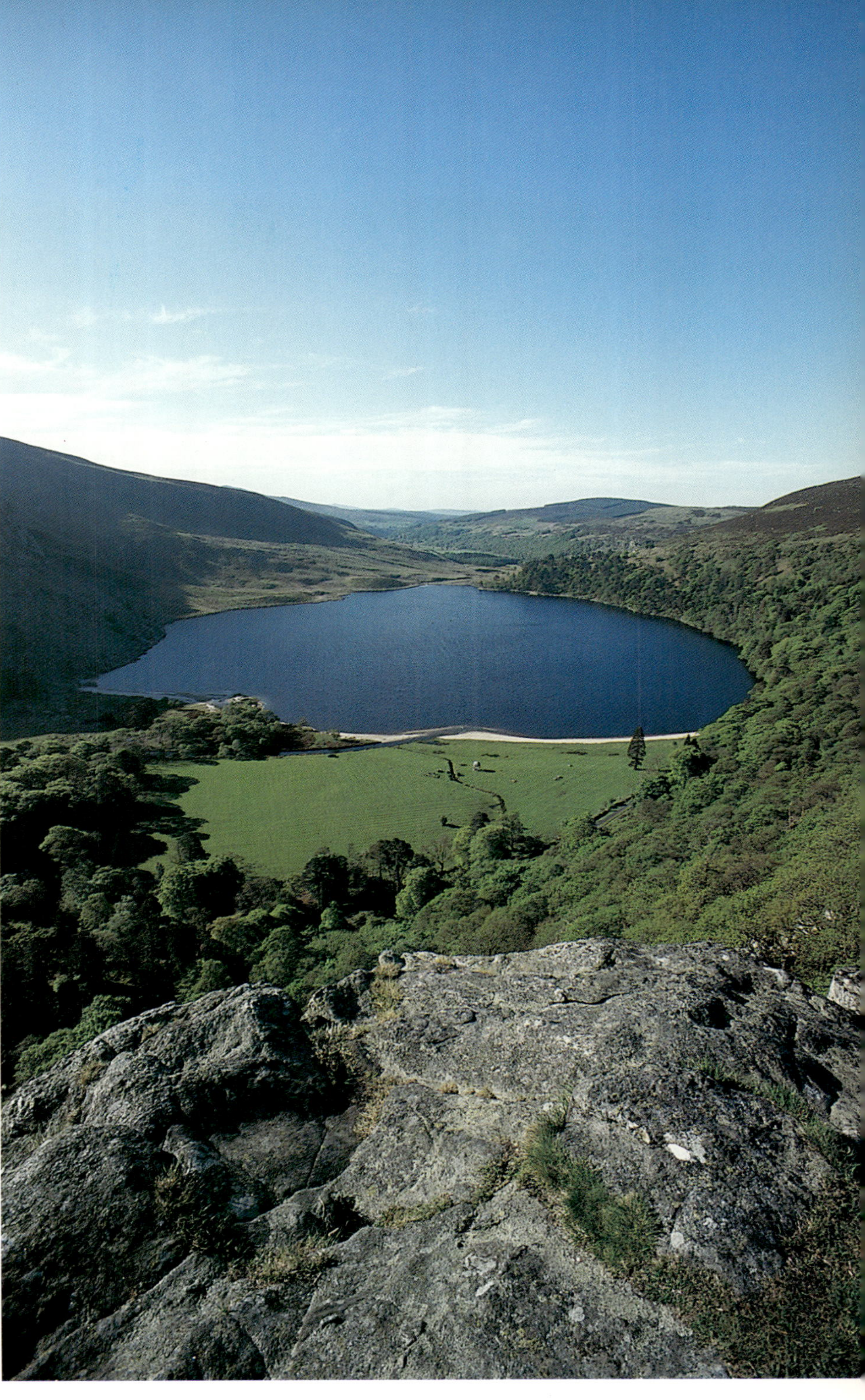

The tranquil waters of Lough Tay, set high in the Wicklow mountains.

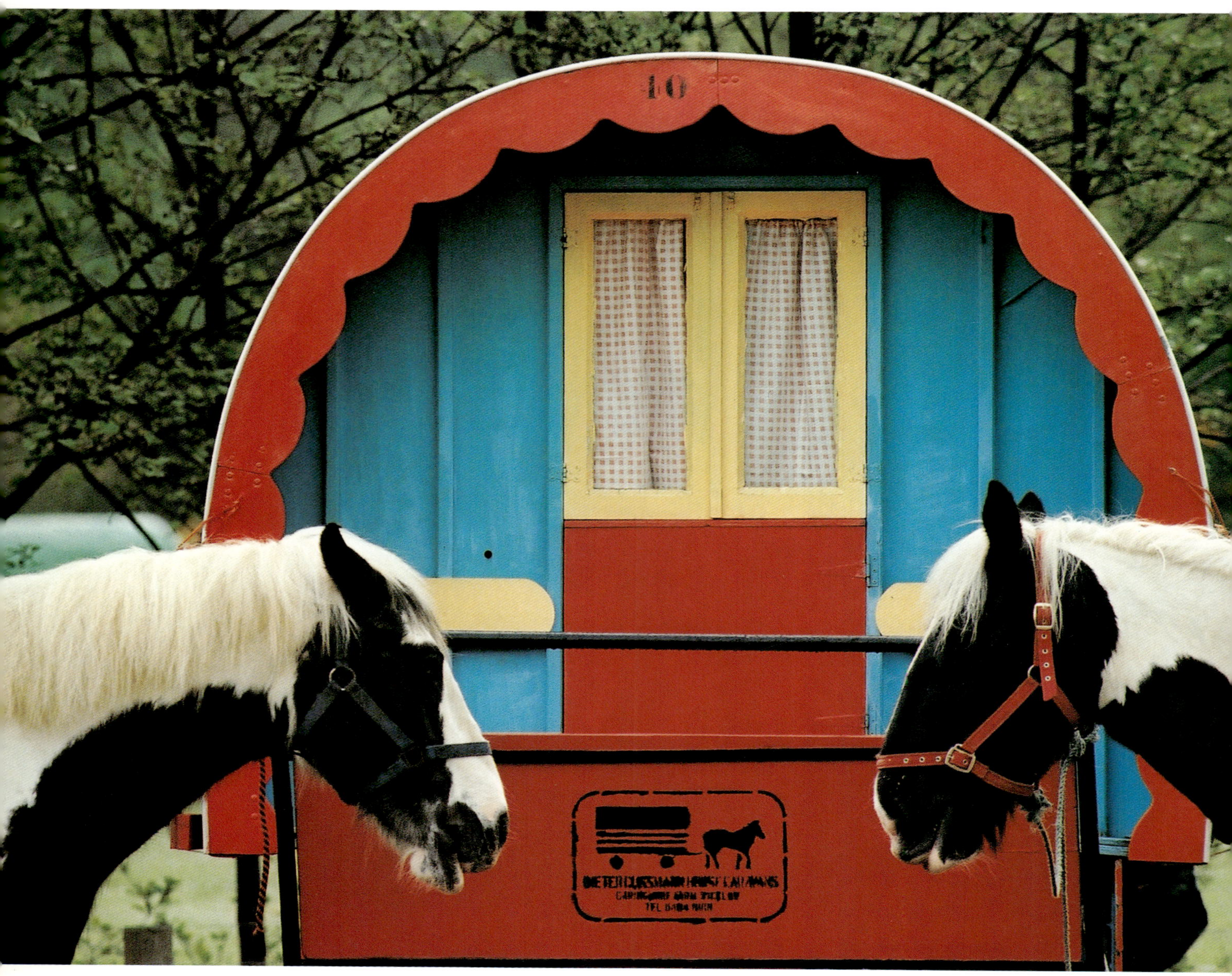
10

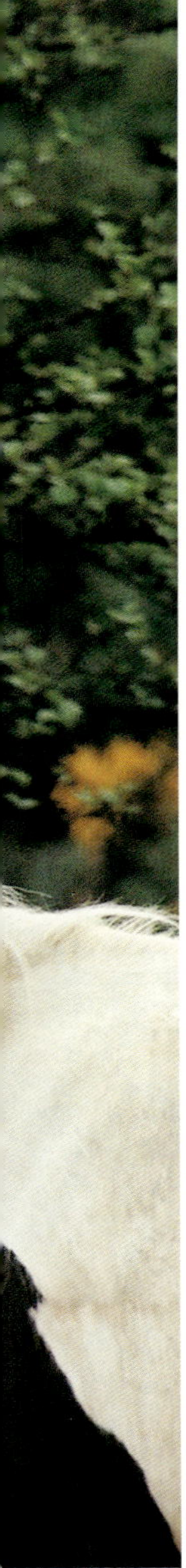

County Wicklow is one of the best-looking areas of Ireland. Heather-covered mountains, deep glens and wooded valleys make for a richly textured landscape. As well, there is a wealth of archaeological sites and monuments. With your mobile home, you can travel where and when you please. In a matter of three horse-hours you can reach sandy beaches that stretch for miles, or head for the valleys, quiet lakes and mountains. The Vale (valley) and picturesque village of Avoca, featured in the popular television series 'Ballykissangel', nestles in a fold of the Wicklow mountains; the road through the Vale of Clara twists alongside the river revealing a new vista at every turn; and the quiet grandeur of the waters in Glendalough, the Valley of the Two Lakes, can all be seen at a leisurely pace. Apart from steep mountain roads, it is all yours for the travelling.

An extra horse can accompany you for riding expeditions, but it must be ridden or led, not tied to the caravan as you travel. Bicycles can be stored on board for pedal powered excursions.

This must be one of the oldest and most traditional of moving experiences, on wheels and behind a horse. And it's perhaps the only holiday where you can try out a pet and return it with no obligation to keep it. The temporary 'travelling people' who return to base after living the gypsy life for a few days quite often want to buy the placid powerful horse that has led them on their journey.

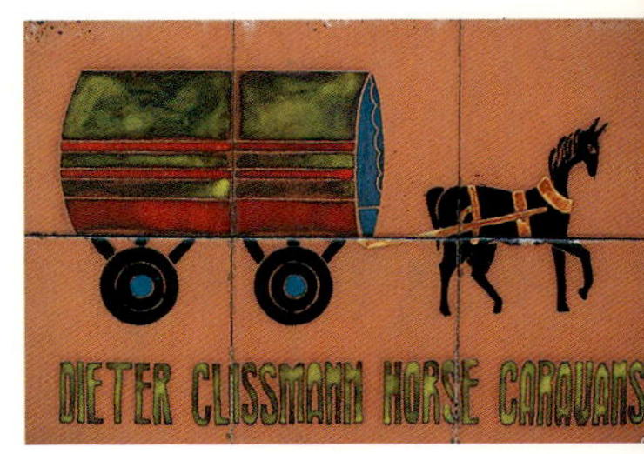

Clissmann Horse Drawn Caravans | *Carrigmore Farm* | *County Wicklow* | *Ireland* | *t: + 353 404 48188* | *f: + 353 404 48288* | *e: clissmann@clissmann.com* | *www.clissmann.com*

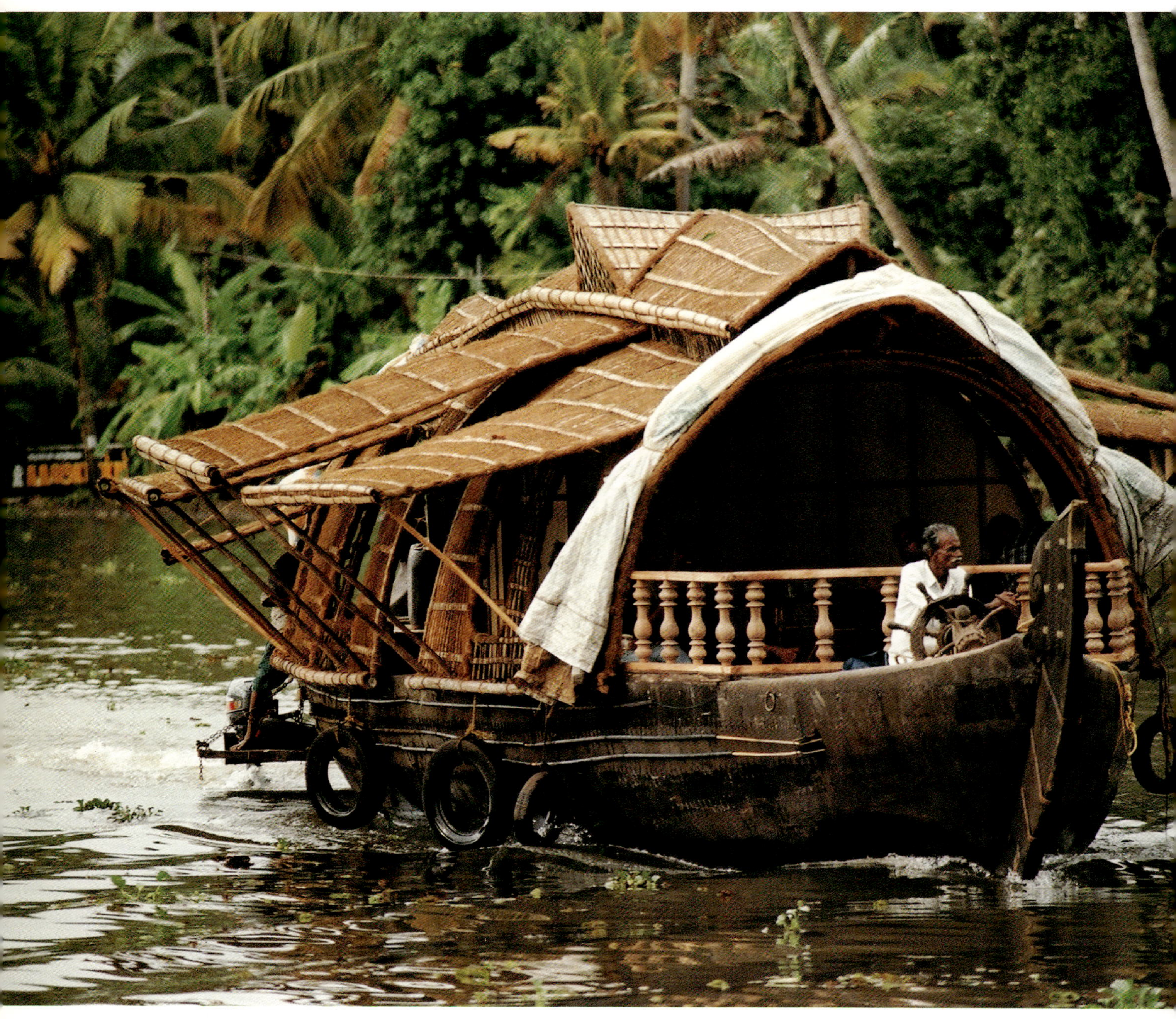

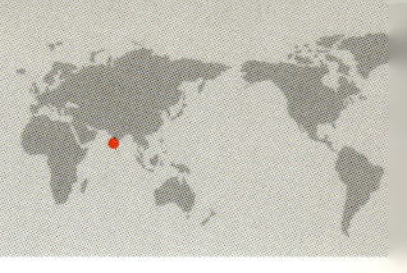

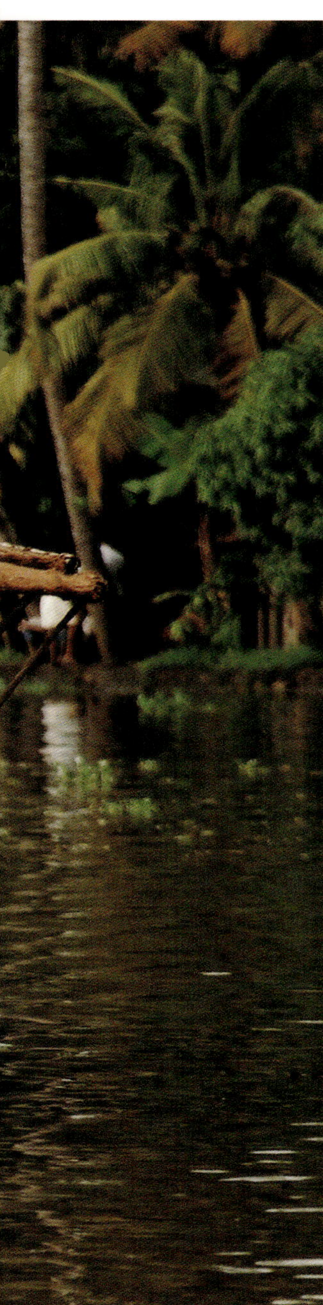

Floating Sanctuary...

Houseboats in Kerala, India

Cocooned in a kettavallam, the traditional houseboat of Kerala, life on the waterways drifts slowly by the curious observer on board.

These graceful canopied boats once carried cargo like coconuts and spices from coast to coast. Some served as picnic boats for wealthy local families. Now trucks are the main freight movers, and the kettavallams carry tourists on overnight expeditions along a picturesque network of rivers and canals in this lush green southern state of India.

Formed by some 40 rivers that flow down from the Cardamon Hills in the Western Ghats, the 1500 kilometres of canals, eight lakes and lagoons leading to the Malabar Coast comprise one of India's most beautiful areas – a vast arterial network for waterborne travel and transportation. This singular journey, through what is known colloquially as the backwaters, is a slow and gentle one. You are a passenger on a meandering journey, seated in a self-contained world from which you can observe rural backwater life flowing placidly by.

One of the most distinctive features of the kettavallam's design is the winged awnings, formed by opening up each side of the arched canopy. These provide for cool air circulation, shade from the hot sun and wider views of the passing scenery. And to some extent, they also shield the passenger within from being clearly seen as a leisurely spectator of the unhurried yet hard life here.

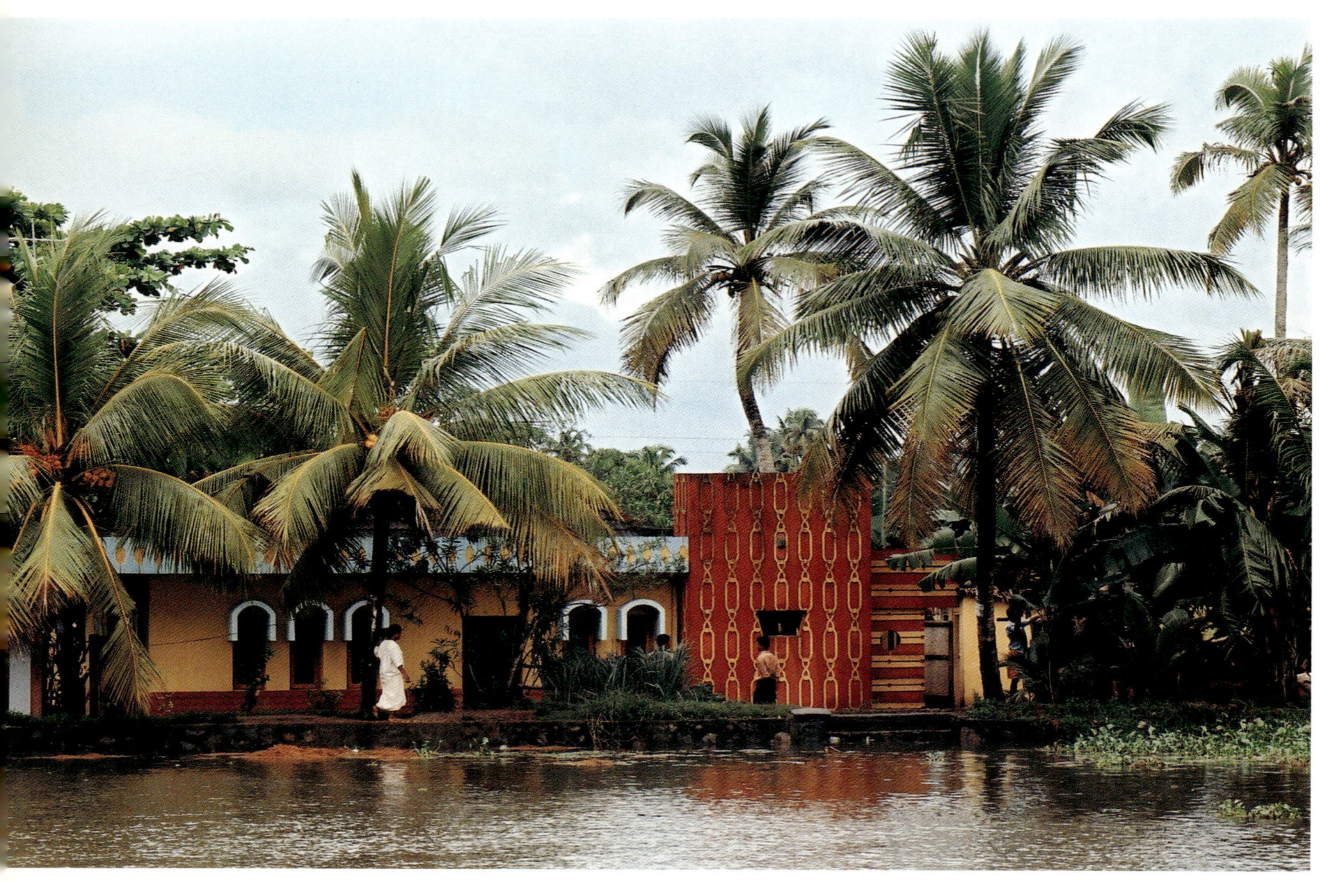

On a pleasantly warm October morning, we embark on our kettavallam cruise, attended by a personal cook and two boatmen, headed into the rural waters. In the language of Kerala the backwaters are apparently known as Kuttanad, meaning the land of the short people. This perhaps refers to the farmers seen working here, who often stand knee-deep in paddy fields. From the houseboat, the expanse of verdant coconut groves and rice paddies seems to stretch endlessly on each side of the canal.

We are overtaken by another kettavallam, still in its traditional use, moving a load of stationery. It is unusual to see a working one now, most have been converted to houseboats. Fat little ferries ply the waters too, full of people going to and from their villages and workplaces along the banks, and fishermen float by in their canoes.

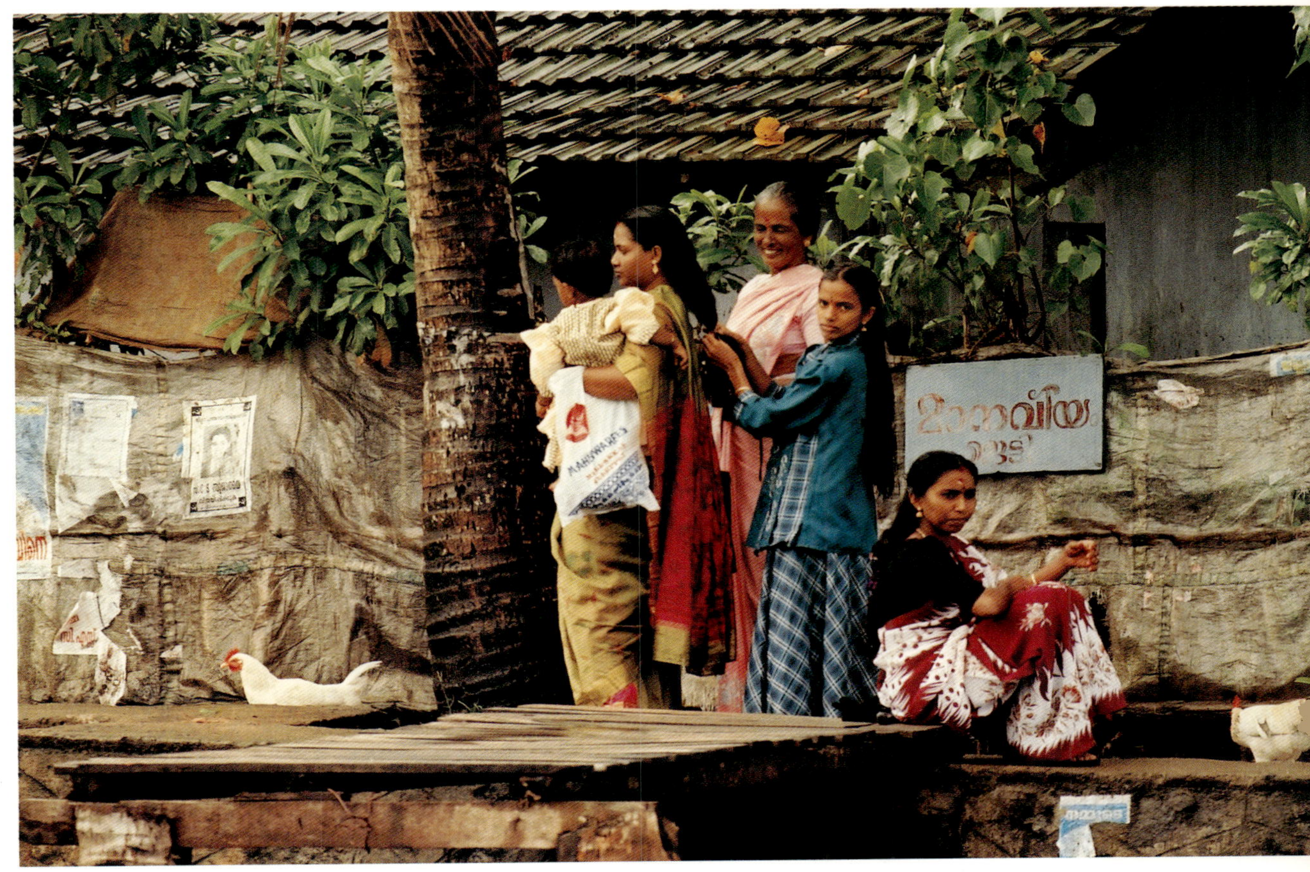

As we slid by at a soothing pace on the first morning of our voyage, delicious aromas drifting on the air alerted our appetites. The cook was preparing our Sunday lunch in his galley at the stern of the boat.

The food served on board is based on the boatmen's traditional diet of fish and vegetables, but a more sumptuous menu is supplied now than would have been standard then. Lunch is a delicious, mouth-watering tomato curry. Mildly spiced, it is served with basmati rice and the best ever chapattis.

Dinner is equally delectable. Pomfret – fried ocean fish – and large local prawns dressed with lime juice and pepper, are served, and a refreshing salad of cucumber, onions and tomatoes. Wedges of watermelon are the juicy dessert. Mineral water, juices and soft drinks are carried on board; any alcohol must be ordered and paid for separately before departure.

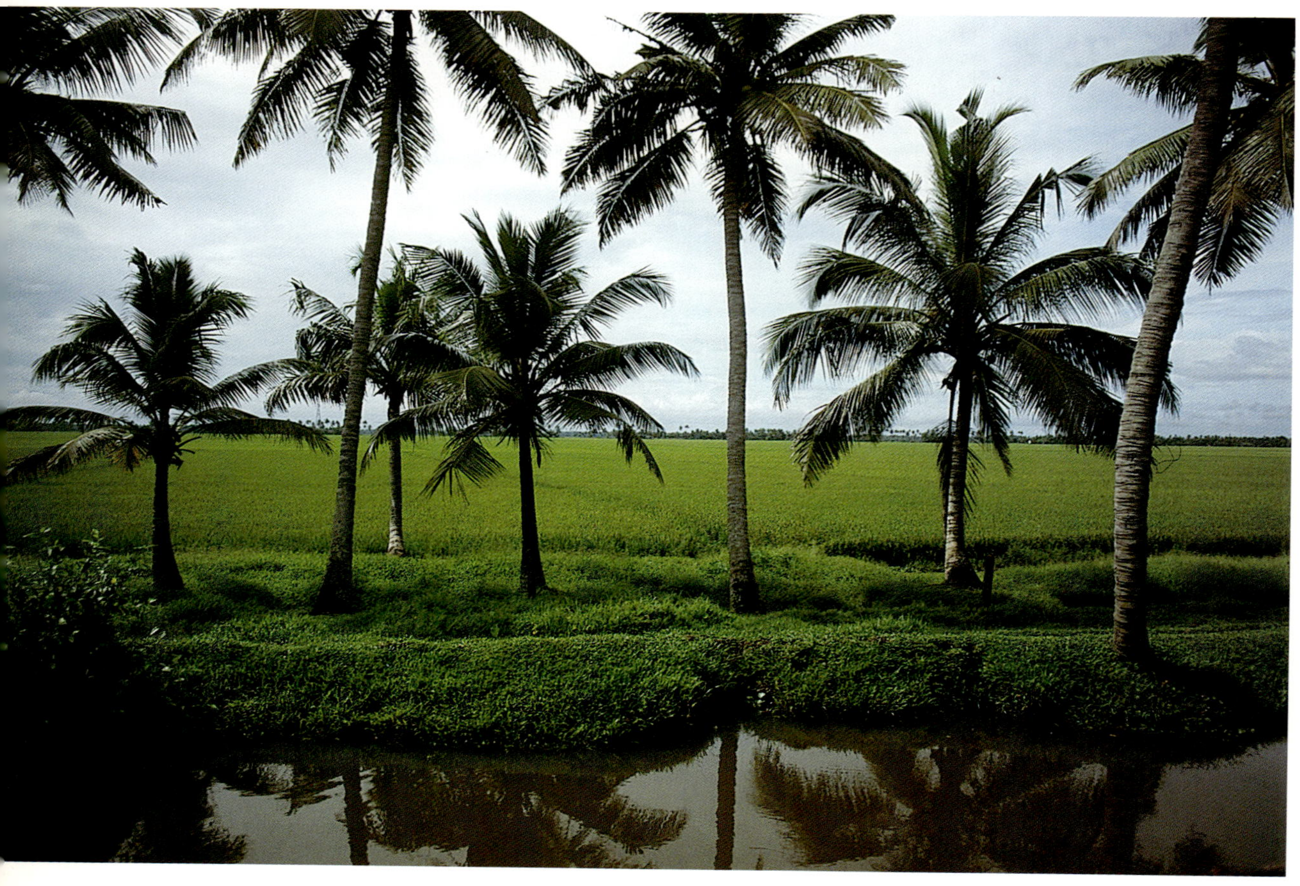

In amongst the rich dark greenery on the banks, there are unexpected splashes of colour. Like exotic birds, women in bright saris suddenly punctuate the foliage. There are giant coloured plants, but as we draw closer we see that some are flowered; others are draped with vivid saris drying in the sun.

People have perched small houses on the narrow ribbons of land bordering the lakes and canals and eke out a living in the watery surroundings. Everywhere there is a fervour of cleaning. Washing is being slapped on bank-side stones, people are busy in the water, washing their hair, cleaning their teeth, and bathing their babies.

The spiritual and the secular are side by side here. The many churches, mostly Roman Catholic, contrast with the propaganda of political posters pasted on tree-trunks and shacks. It is election time and we motor past groups of voters being lectured over deafeningly loud public address systems.

Children run along the bank beside the boat laughing, but with hands held out, entreating us to give them something. 'What do they want?' we ask the boatman. 'They want your pen', he answers, 'so they can learn to write'. We search our bags and give away all but one of our pens, to the delight of those who catch one, and the disappointment of those who miss out. We wish we had more.

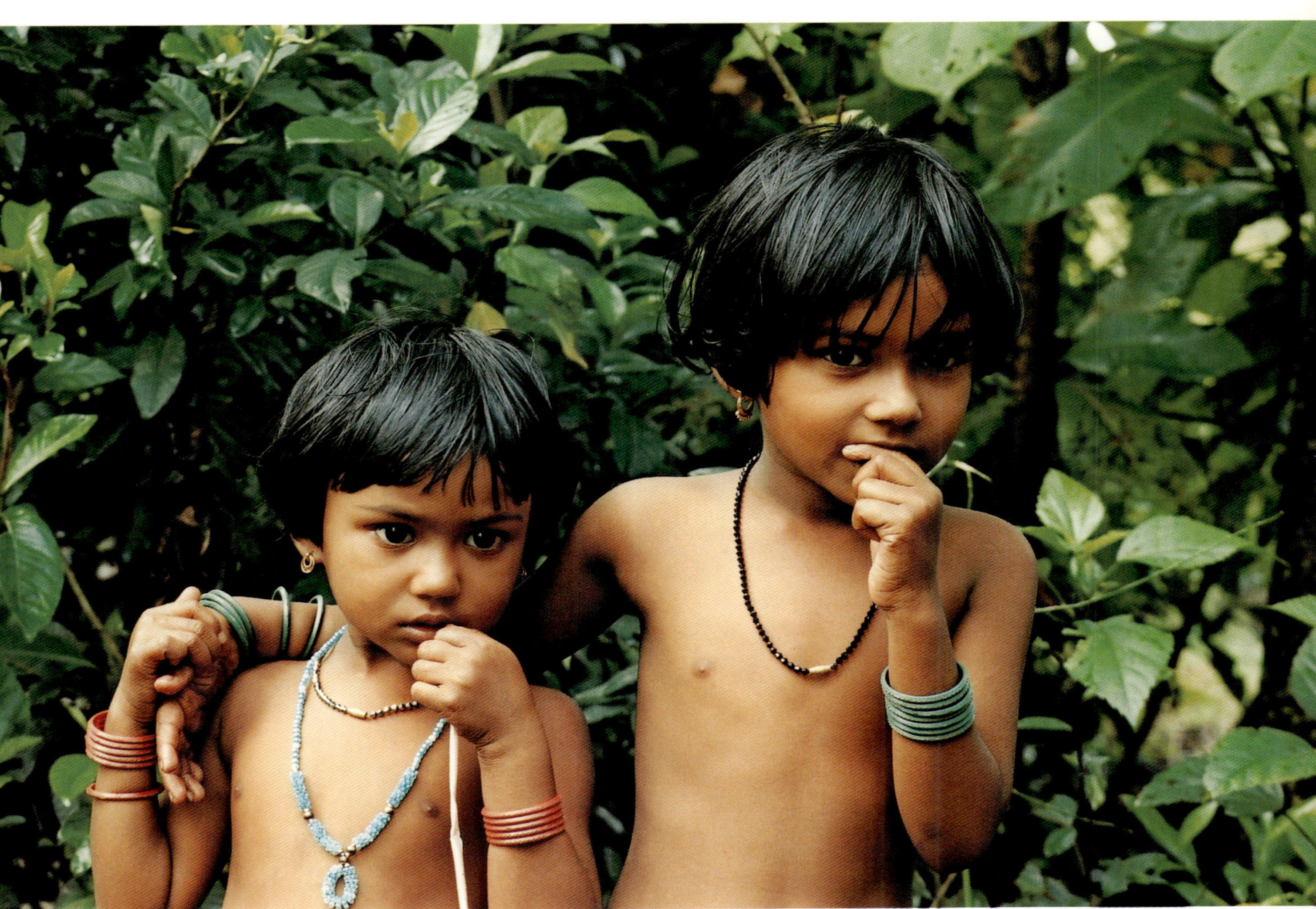

The kettavallam's sitting room is simply furnished with an eclectic mixture of rosewood, mahogany and cane furniture. Comfortable chairs provide viewing places and pull up to the dining table, or you can laze like a marine Maharaja and Maharani on the rolled cushions and mattress on the balustraded sundeck at the bow.

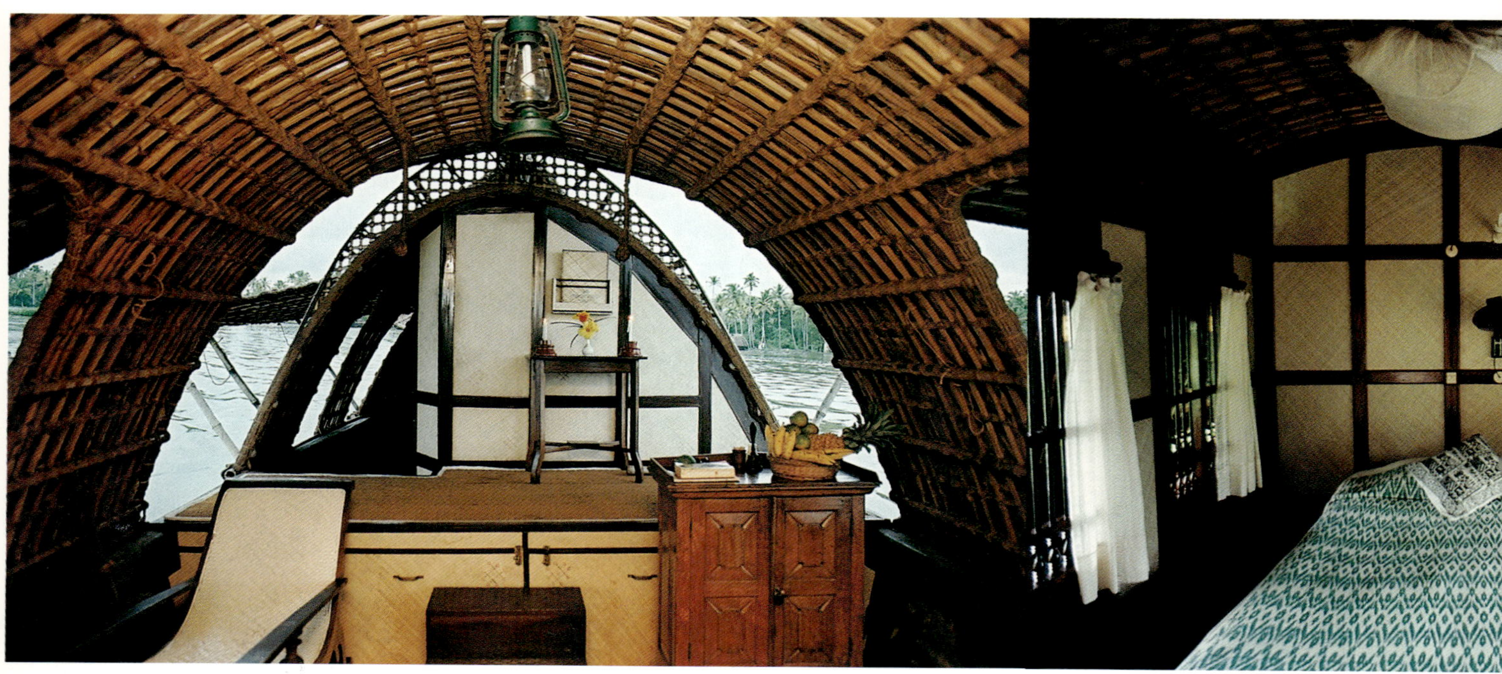

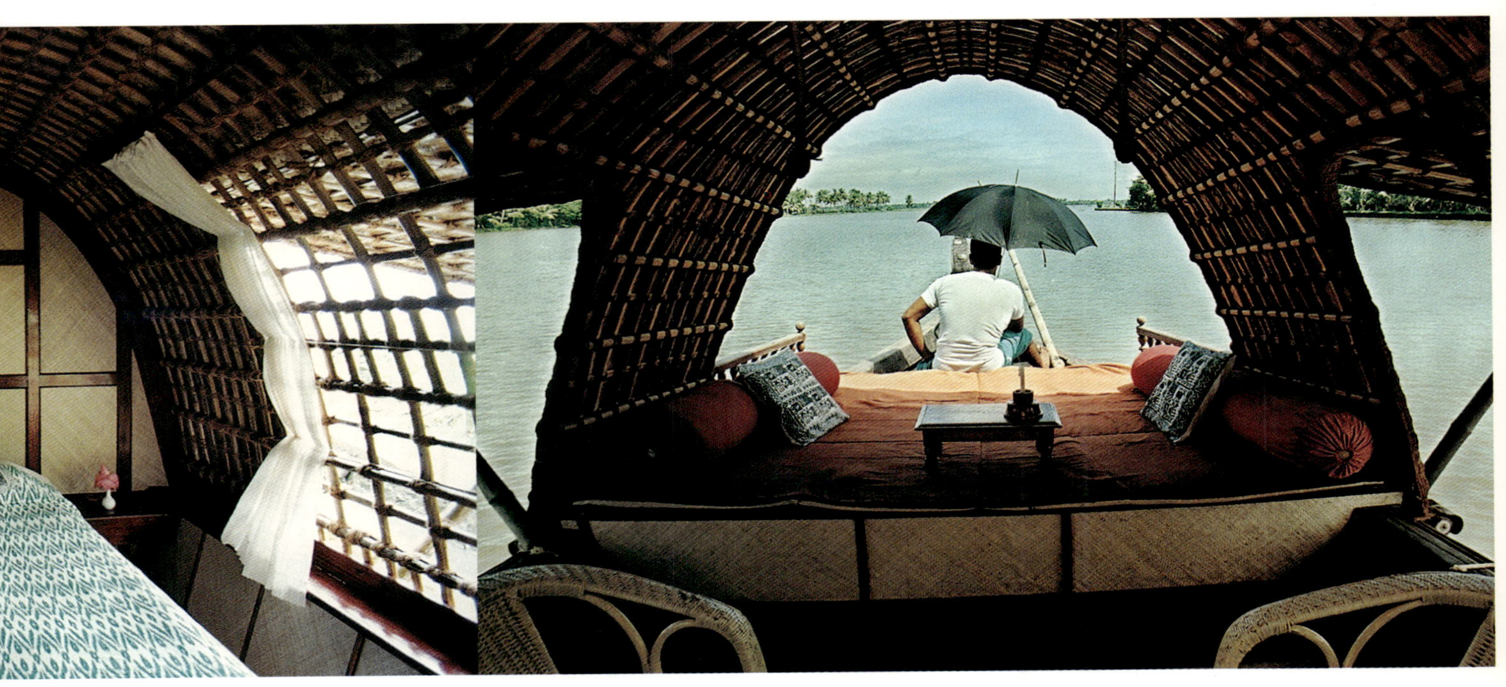

The restful double bedroom has an en suite bathroom, with hot and cold running water, a hand basin and Western style lavatory, but no shower. There is an ample mosquito net draped above the bed, but we didn't see, or more importantly hear, any mosquitoes in our cosy nest. An electric fan adds extra cool air if needed as does the window that opens out so you can see the stars at night.

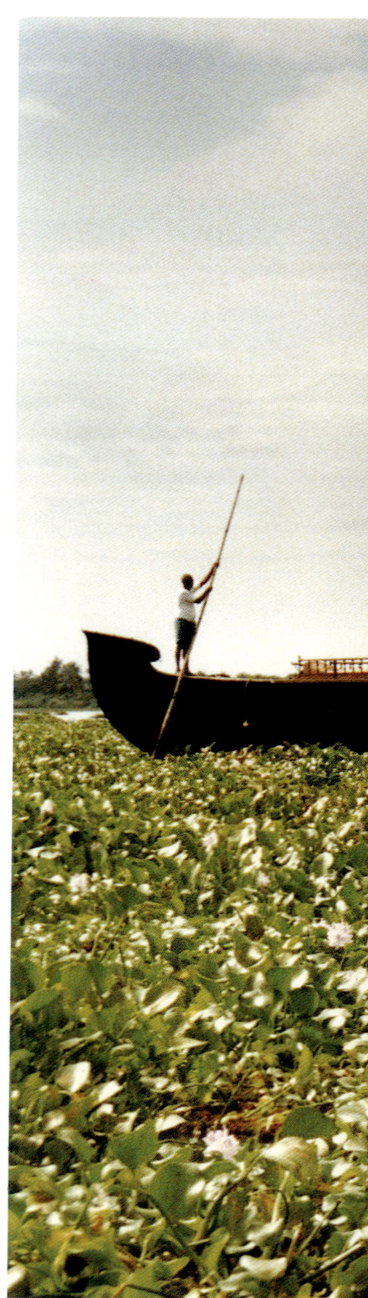

Delicate white birds come swooping in low over the tangle of green vines floating on the water as we anchor for the night in the centre of Lake Vembanad. In the late evening there is only a soft, barely audible, sound of lake water lapping at the sides of the boat, together with the occasional birdcall or a sudden burst of Indian pop music.

Made from planks of the anjili tree fastened by coir rope knots, and covered with palm fronds, the kettavallam is unique to India. Its design allows it to be navigated through the narrowest of canals, propelled from the bow and the stern by two boatmen using punting poles. It does have an outboard motor but is generally sailed and punted through the backwater byways by the sarong-clad boatmen, seemingly suspended above the water.

The boats have either one double bedroom or two, and are around 50–75ft long, 14ft wide and weigh 30–50 tons. The arched ceiling is made of split bamboo, lashed together with coir binding and covered with palm fronds. Woven palm panels cover the walls and coir matting carpets the deck. A coating of sardine oil, or sometimes cashew nut oil, is applied to the surface of the boat to protect and waterproof the wood.

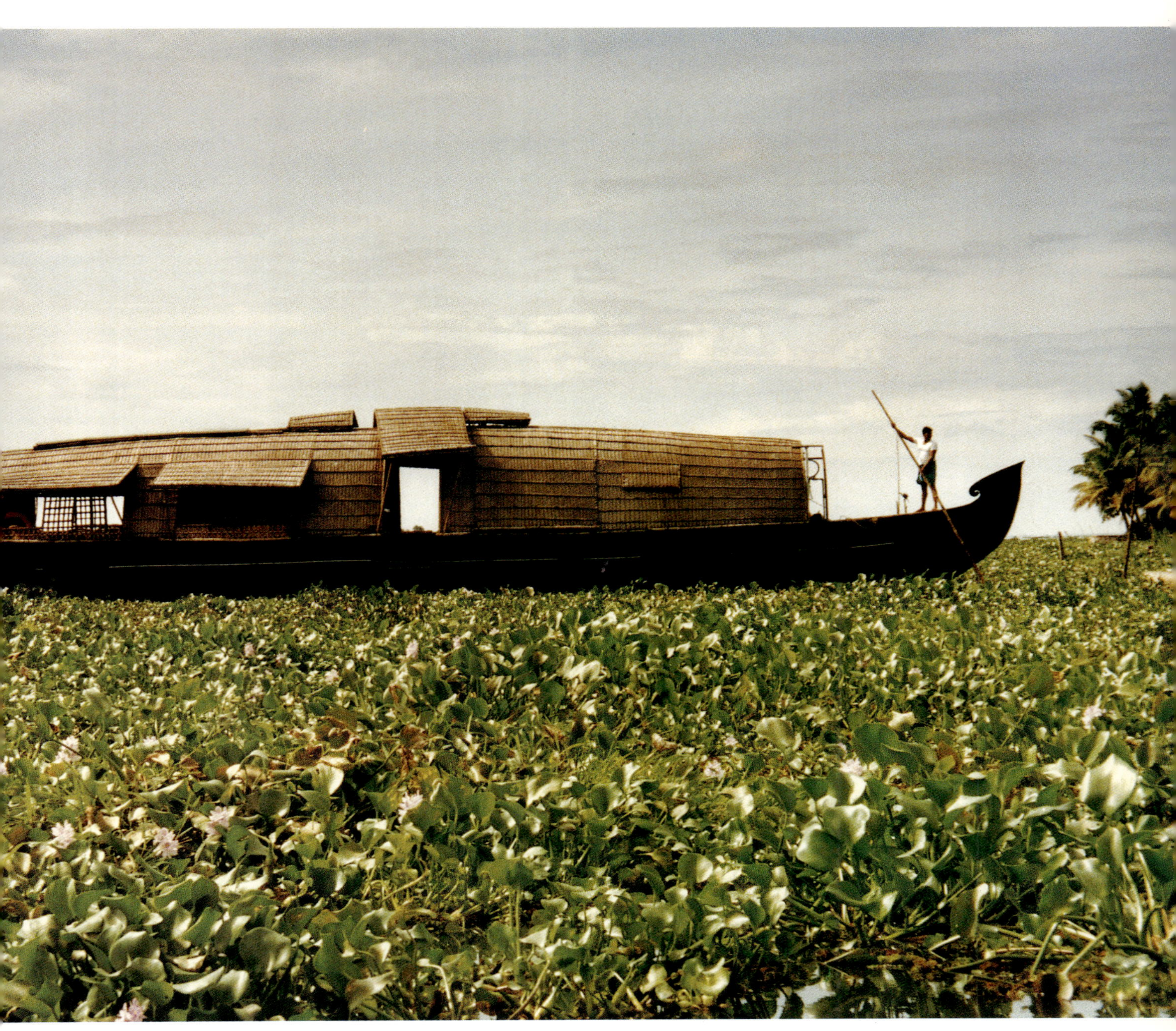

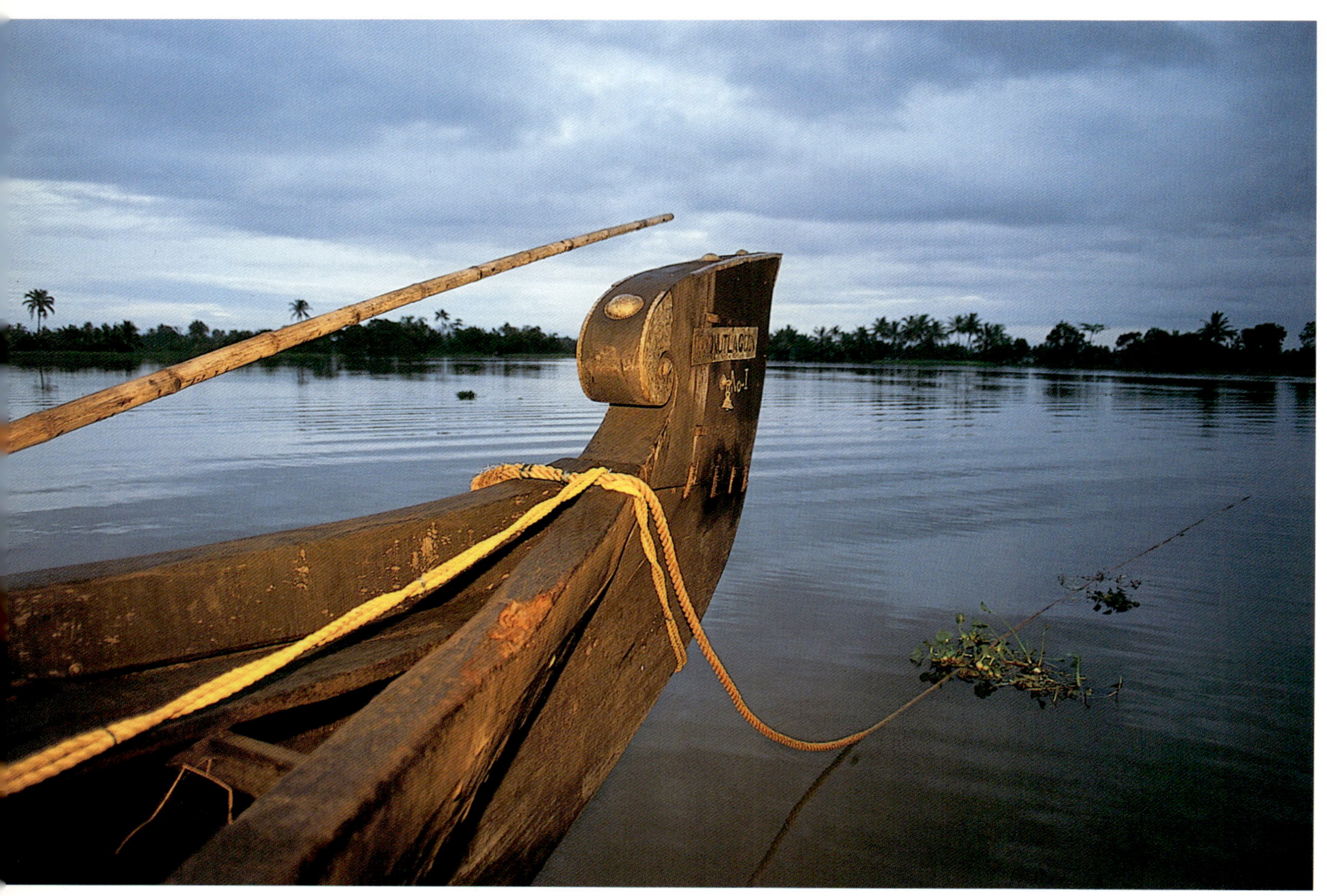

A rooster competition and temple music begin early in the morning. The wake up calls of Kerala travel across the lake to the kettavallam's languid passengers and remind them of the real world. Time to get up, to a breakfast of watermelon juice, masala omelette and a sweet toast, followed by coffee and fresh pineapple. All too soon it is time to end our relaxing cruise and return to our departure point, Kochi (Cochin).

Here we are hit by the bustle of town India, with its cacophony of noise and crowds of people, a sharp contrast with the calm of life on the water.

This is one of India's most interesting cities, with a multi-cultured history. In 1502 Portuguese navigator and explorer Vasco de Gama came to Kochi seeking spices and converts. This was the right place for spices – cinnamon, cardamon, pepper and ginger – which found their way to Europe. However, converts to Roman Catholicism were few; those who were Christian preferred their Syrian brand of Christianity. Portuguese sovereignty was not welcomed either. De Gama died in Kochi in 1524 and was buried in St Francis Church, reputedly the first European church built in Asia. His grave is marked with a plaque, but his remains were repatriated to Portugal.

The port of Kochi was once the coveted prize of three European empires, the Portuguese, Dutch and British. The Portuguese came first, were ousted by the Dutch in 1663, who in turn were overthrown by the British in 1795. Kochi became a centre of Britain's trading interests until 1947, when the Indian flag replaced the British crown. Some of the trading houses from the British Raj days are still there, albeit in name only. Now they are Indian owned, still dealing in spices, rubber, tea and coir.

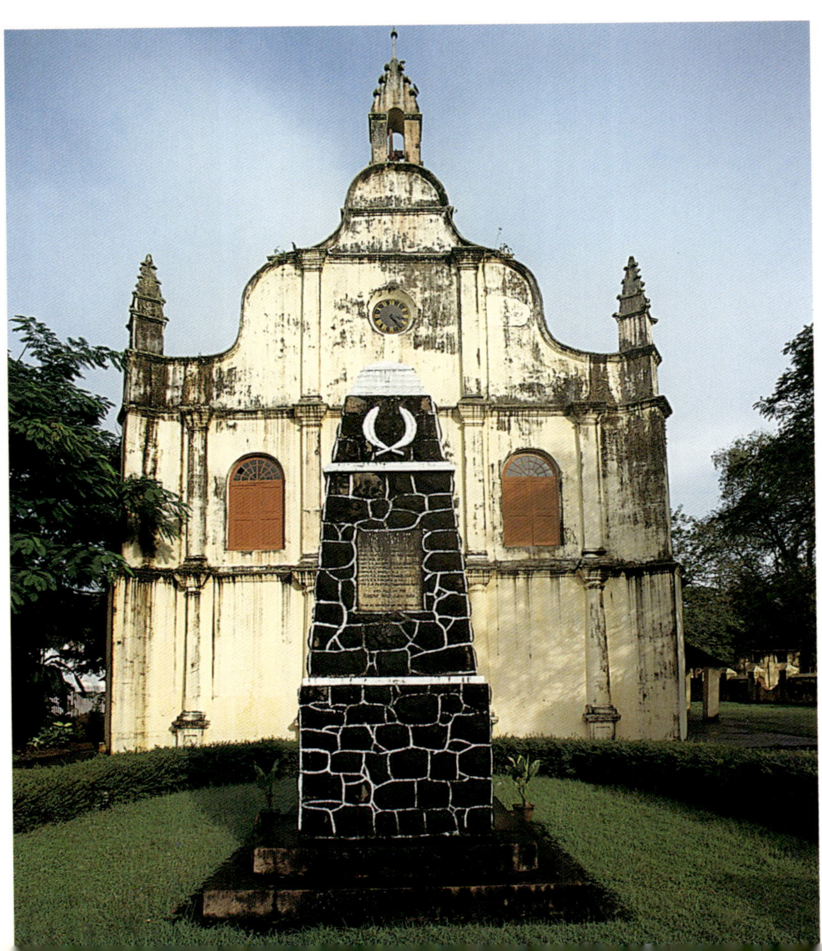

Fishing nets on a grand scale form almost architectural shapes against the night and morning sky, and testify to Kochi's centuries-old association with China. This method of fishing was established during the time of Kubla Khan. Lowered at high tide into the water, the net is like a giant ladle, scooping fish up with it when it is raised. Cantilevered out over the water, these unusual nets are often visible along the backwaters, but these are the most spectacular.

You can begin or end your stay in Kerala with a night or more at the oasis-like Brunton Boatyard Hotel, which is right on the waterfront, virtually next door to the Chinese fishing nets. From the terrace you can watch the fishermen of Kochi travel back and forth in their longboats on their daily expeditions into the Arabian Sea.

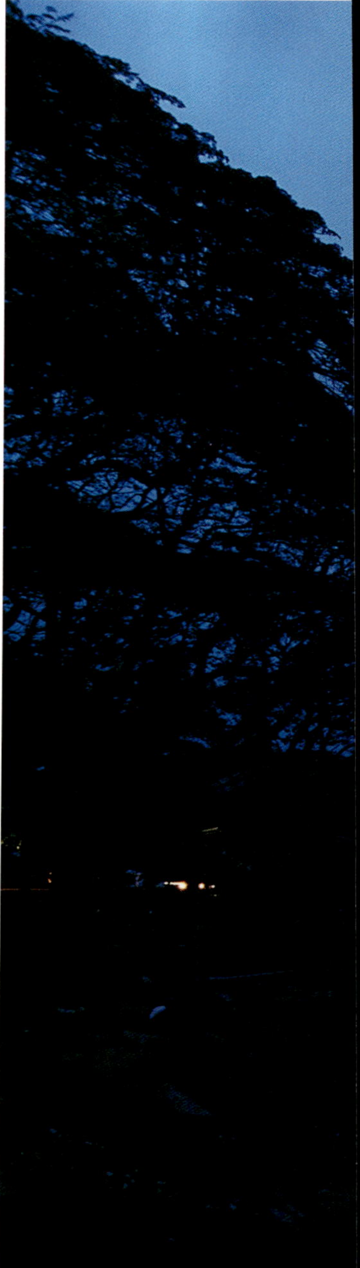

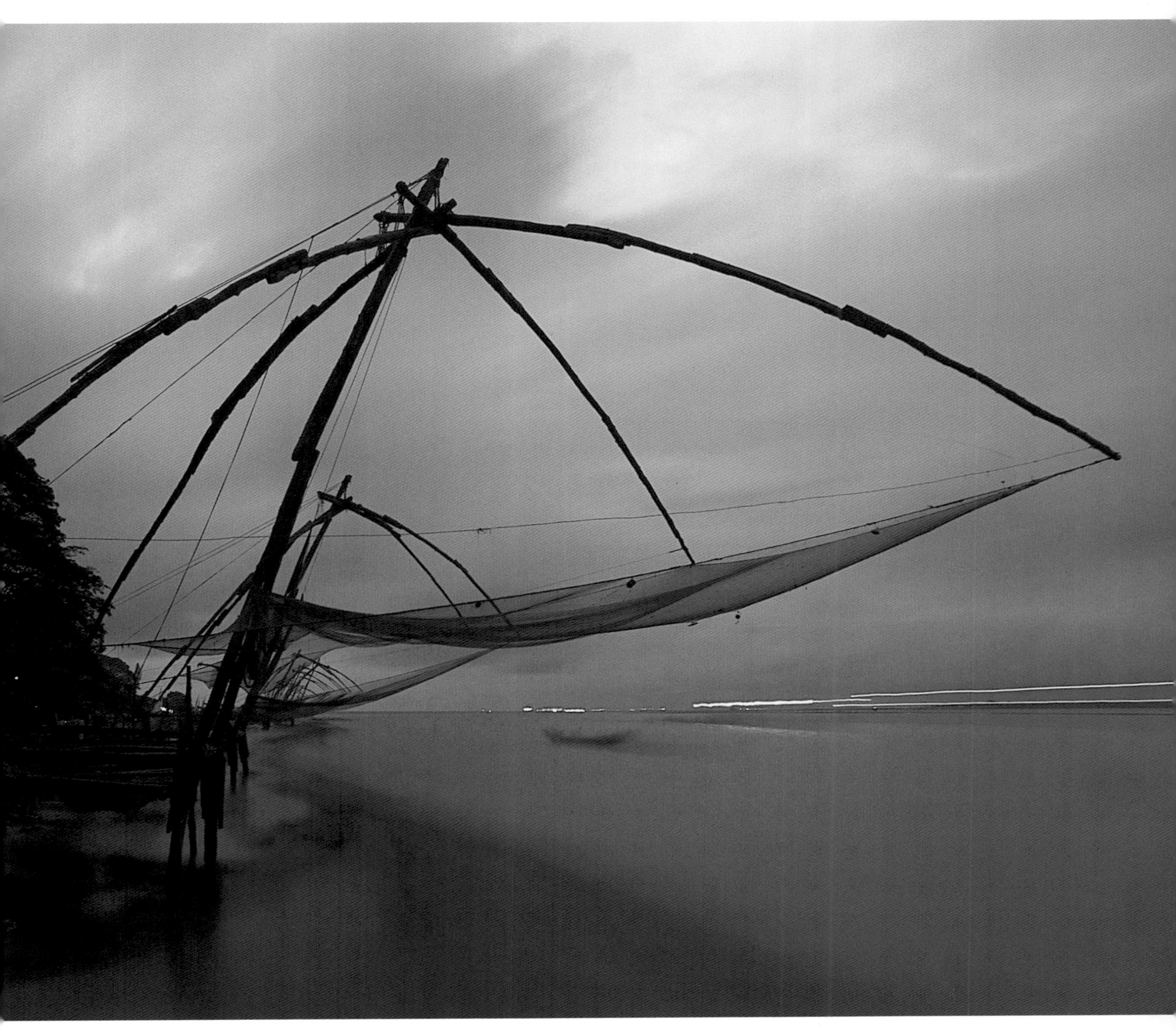

Spice Coast Cruises Reservations	Casino Hotel Group	Cochin	Kerala	India	t: + 91 484 668221	f: + 91 484 668001	e: casino@vsnl.com

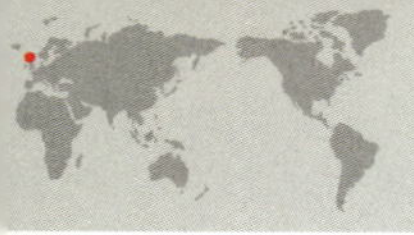

Heart in the Highlands...

The Royal Scotsman train, Scotland

Standing at Edinburgh's Waverley station, inconspicuously, even discreetly on a rear platform is The Royal Scotsman, dressed in burgundy and gold enamel, with no visible outward sign of tartan in its livery. The train and its crew are prepared for the arrival of the passengers. Bagpipes are at the ready. Departure is imminent.

The passengers have gathered in the Palm Lounge at the traditional elegant Balmoral Hotel. When all are present and accounted for, they are transferred literally under the hotel building to the train station by classic taxicab, and driven straight onto the platform to board the train for their journey.

The Great Scottish and Western Railway company is 'engaged in the operation of a luxury touring train in Scotland', and we are embarking on the Classic Tour; four nights and days on board a train that travels through Scotland at the whim of a timetable devised only for the passengers aboard. No concessions are made to stop for newcomers at other stations – once passengers have embarked in Edinburgh there are no additional travellers to be accomodated. For the next four days, the splendid Edwardian carriages of the Royal Scotsman will be the moving residence of just 36 passengers. Mountains and moors, lochs and forests will provide an ever-changing backdrop as the train travels through the contrasting landscape of Scotland.

Along the way there and back, journeying as far north as the isolated and romantic Isle of Skye, we will see and sample many facets of the Scottish country, and its people. And enjoy some of the best cuisine, cooked on board in a space a third or less of the size of a stationary restaurant kitchen.

The train manager and crew, attired in subtle tartan, greet their guests who are then piped aboard. This farewell flourish of the pipes is the only departure announcement we are to hear. We realise later that the days on board were blissfully quiet, no background music or intercom address was to be heard. Silence is a luxury in a constantly noisy world.

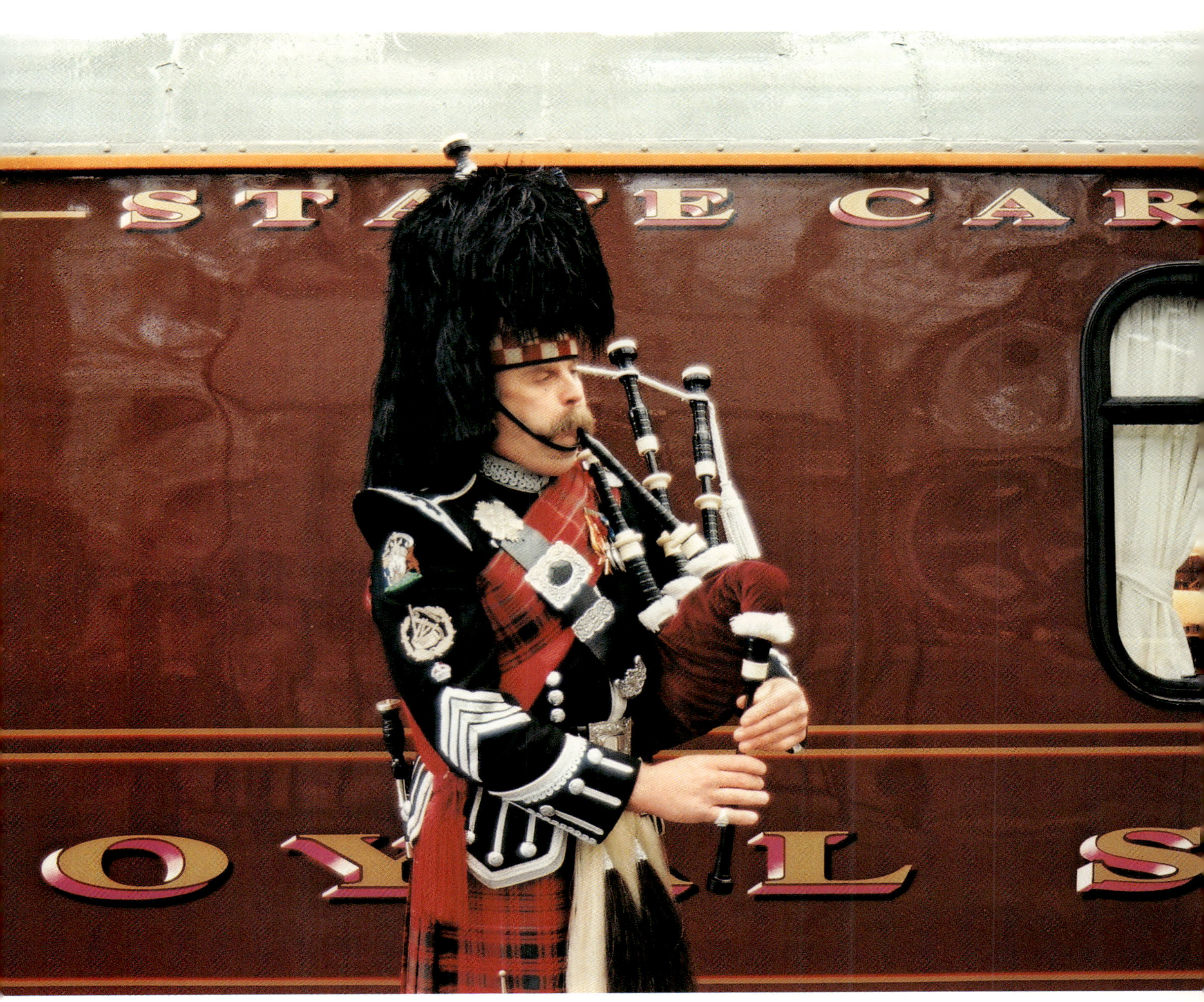

MY HEART'S IN THE HIGHLANDS, WHEREVER I GO...

Robert Burns

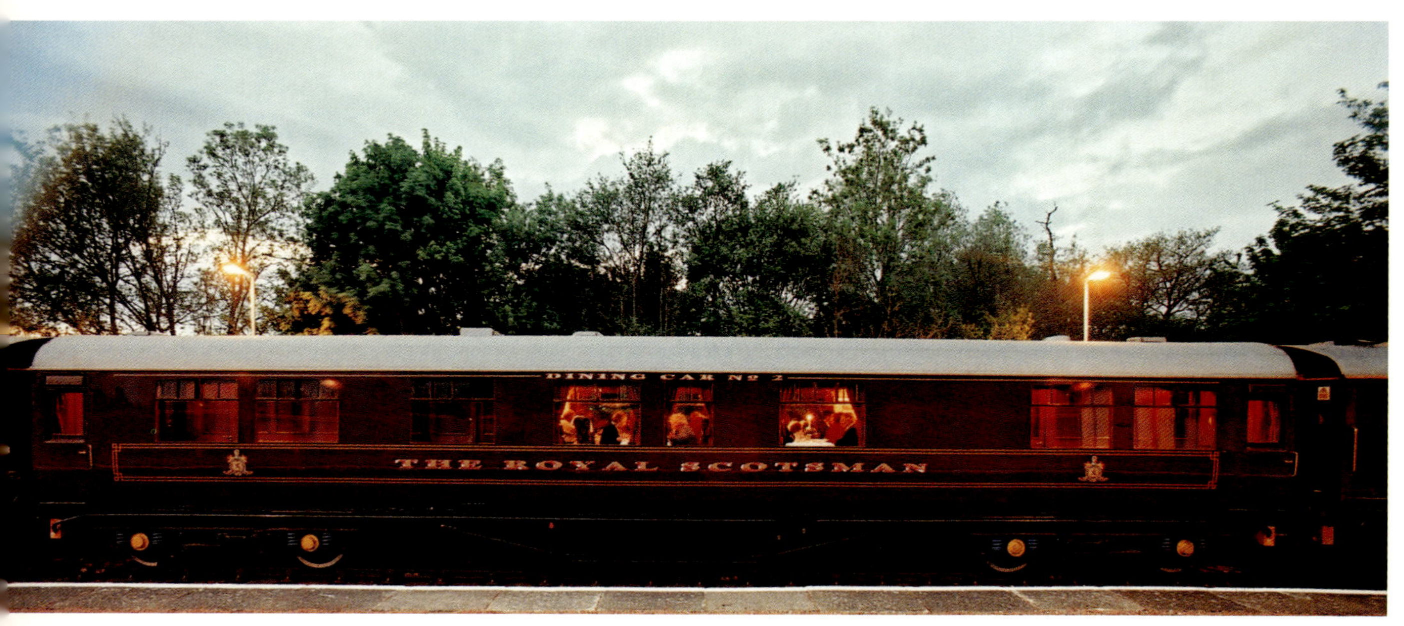

The journey begins in the Observation Car, which will serve as the living room for us all. It instantly appeals, with its subtle soft colours and lively blend of patterns and textures.

Spacious and stylish, the Observation Car provides for separate and combined groupings of passengers with comfortable sofas and armchairs. It is both a meeting place and relaxing room, the social centre of the train. Doors at the end of the carriage lead to an open platform where fresh air fiends or die-hard smokers can stand and watch the view slide past.

As the train leaves Edinburgh station and heads west, we discover that our cabins are a marvel of compressed elegance. Ample storage is cunningly planned, and for those of us who still haven't mastered the art of travelling light, large suitcases can be whisked away to be stored elsewhere on the train. Each cabin is fitted out in rich wood panelling, with comfortable sink – into twin beds, a desk/dressing table, wardrobe, and a well appointed private bathroom – a plus over some other luxury trains where facilities have to be shared. The cabin is a roomy deluxe retreat to stay in during the day if you are so inclined, to read, doze, or look out at the landscape constantly panning past the window. For added comfort, the train is 'stabled overnight' so our sleep is not interrupted by movement on the rails.

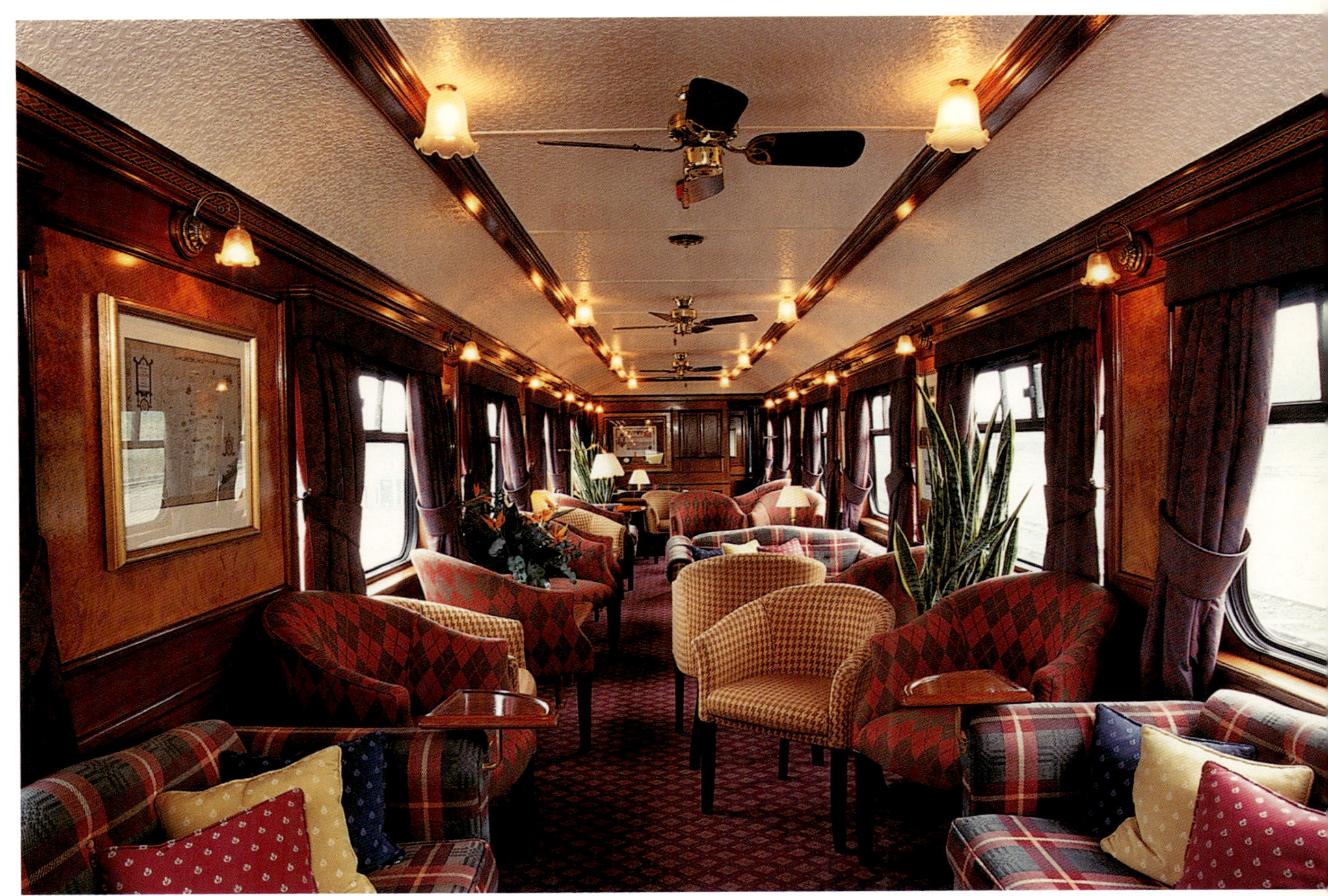

The Observation Car, the social centre of the train.

So what did we see, and taste, in the next four days? Many facets of Scotland were sampled, including its famously changeable weather. Excursions from the train are on offer, a cleverly judged mix of history, food, whisky and a slight measure of shopping. The Royal Scotsman's own motorcoach in matching livery follows the train to transport guests to and from the off-rail tours.

Our first visit was to the Inverawe Smokehouse to see locally caught salmon and trout cured, smoked and sliced. We are then invited to sample it in the owners' riverside home. More of these delicacies are served during our first on board informal dinner, where the high standard of comestibles to come is immediately established.

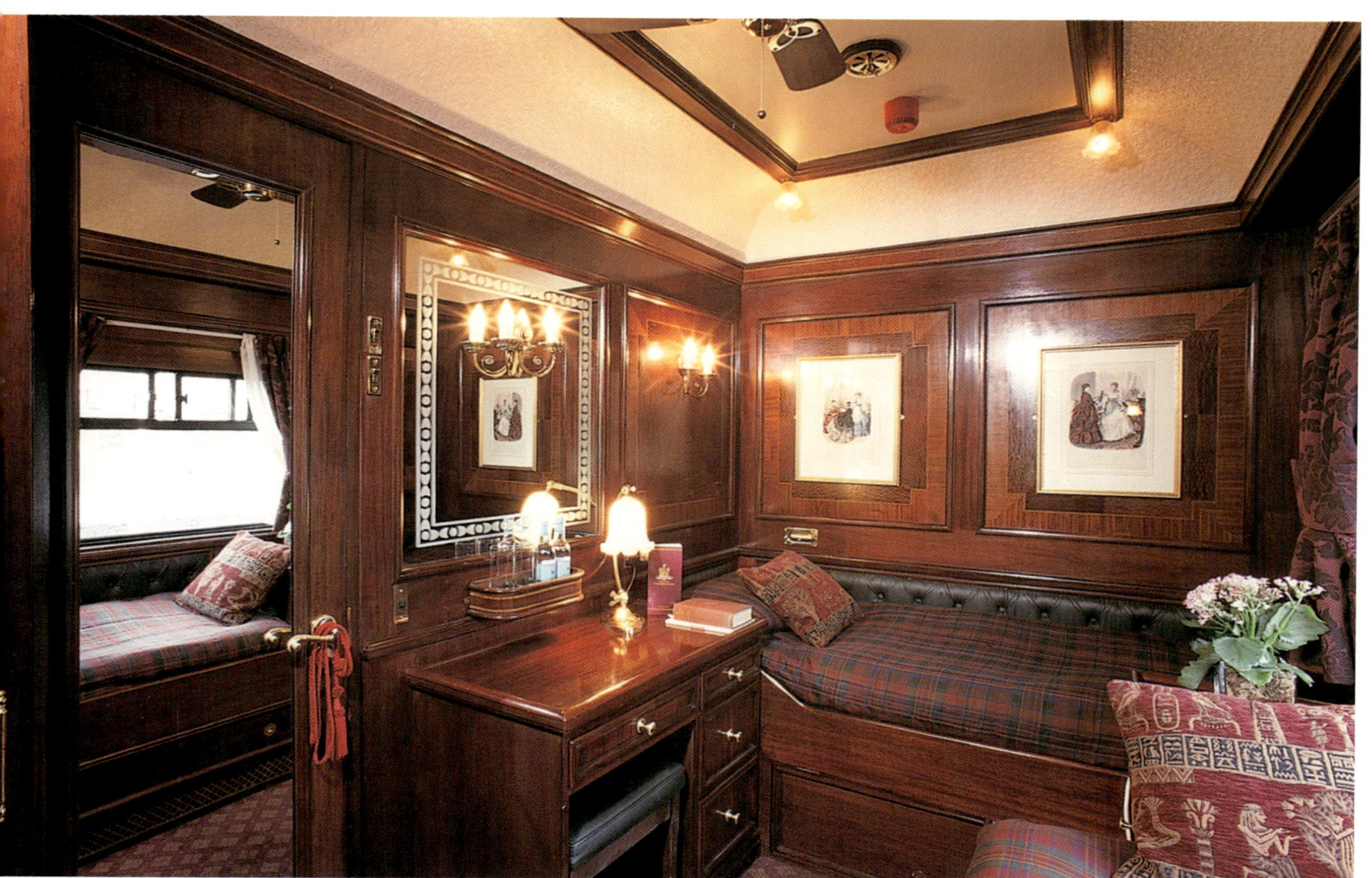

Rich marquetry lines each State Cabin.

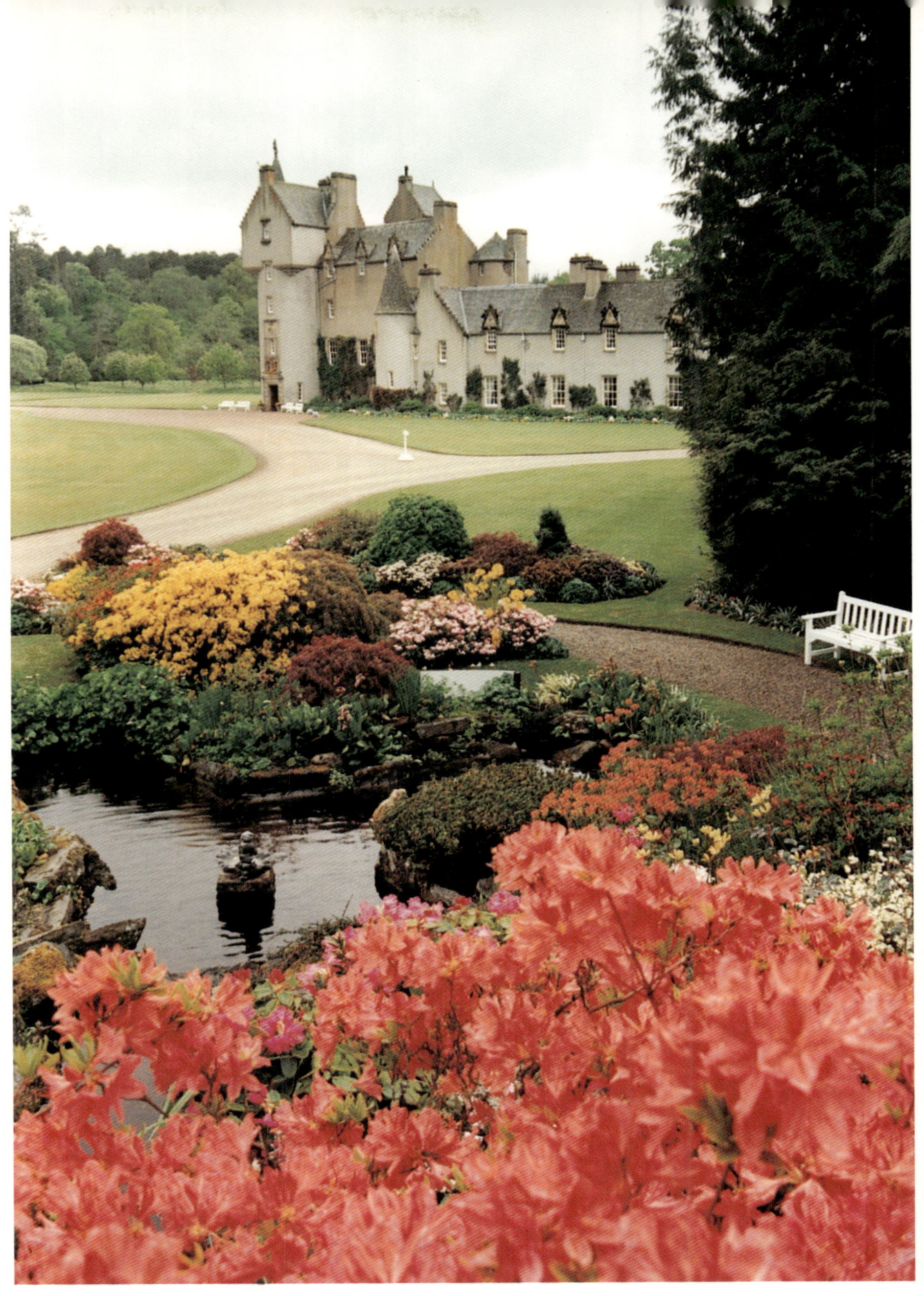

A more romantic destination is Ballindalloch Castle, an elegant and comfortable country house in the Highlands, where we were met and shown around by the owners, the Macpherson-Grants. Over coffee and shortbread, they explained the complicated upkeep of a stately home and garden.

The Royal Scotsman has two dining cars, with non-assigned seating for all meals at tables for two, four, six and eight. A light or hearty breakfast, and a three-course lunch and dinner is served every day. The evening meal is rather like being at a dinner party in a private club atmosphere, with the food, wine and service equivalent to the best restaurants. Formal dress is expected for two of the four dinners, and the elegance of the surroundings befits and encourages dressing up.

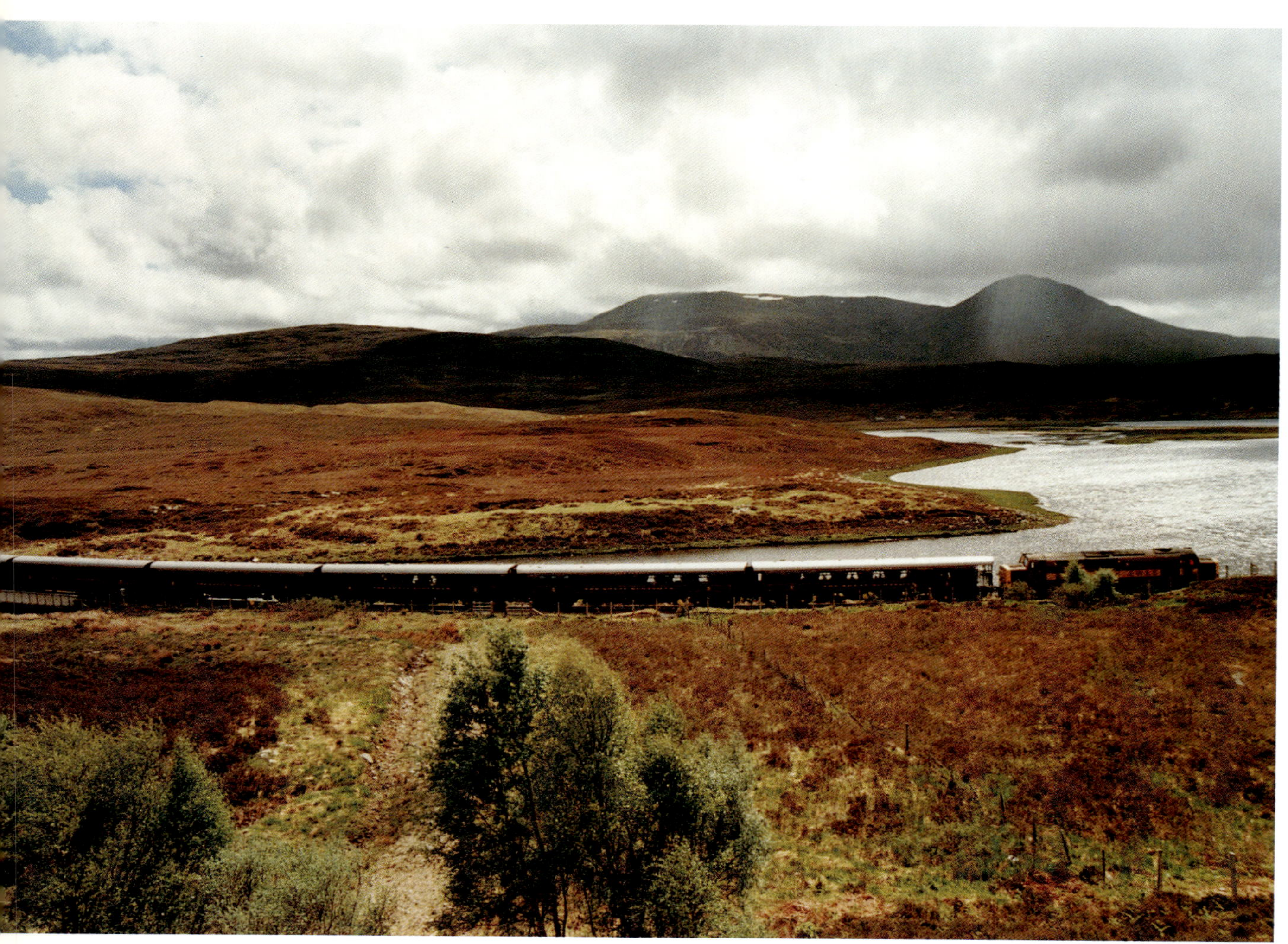

The Royal Scotsman travels north to the Highlands.

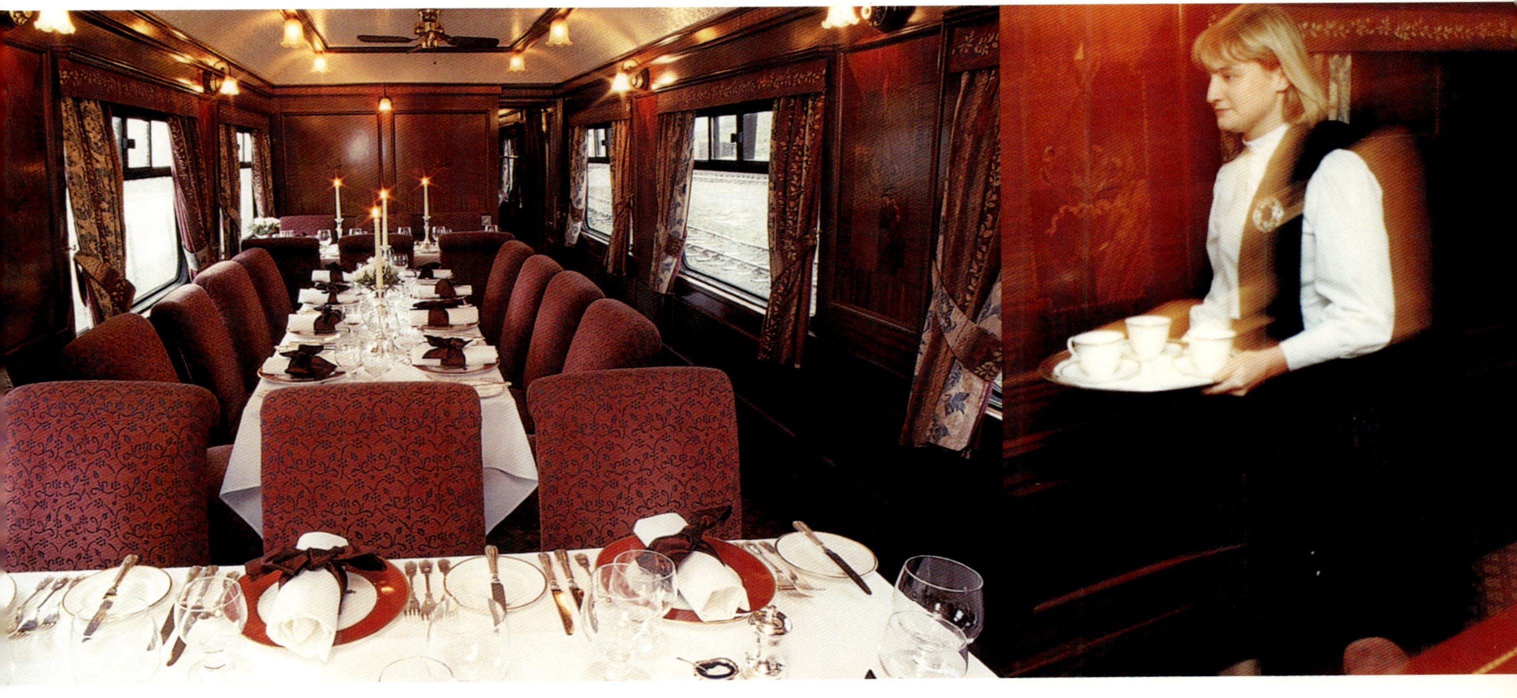

The often-changed menus are carefully planned to suit most tastes and to reflect the season and local produce. Classically based with contemporary twists, the menus are cleverly balanced between the best of traditional and modern cooking. Presentation is simple yet excellent, and the food matched with premium wines selected from the old and new worlds. The next meal is eagerly anticipated to see if it matches or tops the previous one.

Memorable lunch menus included a smoked salmon salad with confit tomatoes, roasted sea bass on an artichoke purée, scallops with sauce vierge, and desserts like sticky toffee pudding and lemon tart.

Dinner delivered more delicious repasts, like lobster tails with salsa sauce, roast saddle of lamb with gnocchi and spring vegetables, and a dessert of baked pineapple. Or courgette and parmesan soup with olive and chilli crostini, breast of guinea fowl with morel sauce, followed by vanilla panacotta with rhubarb compote.

After dinner on most nights, there is entertainment with a very Scottish flavour. A local musician sings traditional airs to the accompaniment of the clarsach, an unusual sounding instrument that is likely an acquired taste; a kilted accordionist plays familiar tunes; and a traditional ceilidh (dance) is held in a private hunting lodge exclusively for the train's passengers.

A popular visit is to a traditional working Highland whisky distillery – the luxuriously appointed Strathisla Distillery. Founded in 1786, this is the home of the luxury Scotch whisky Chivas Regal, and the luscious liqueur Lochan Ora. A comprehensive tasting and purchasing of the products follows a tour around the headily perfumed distillery.

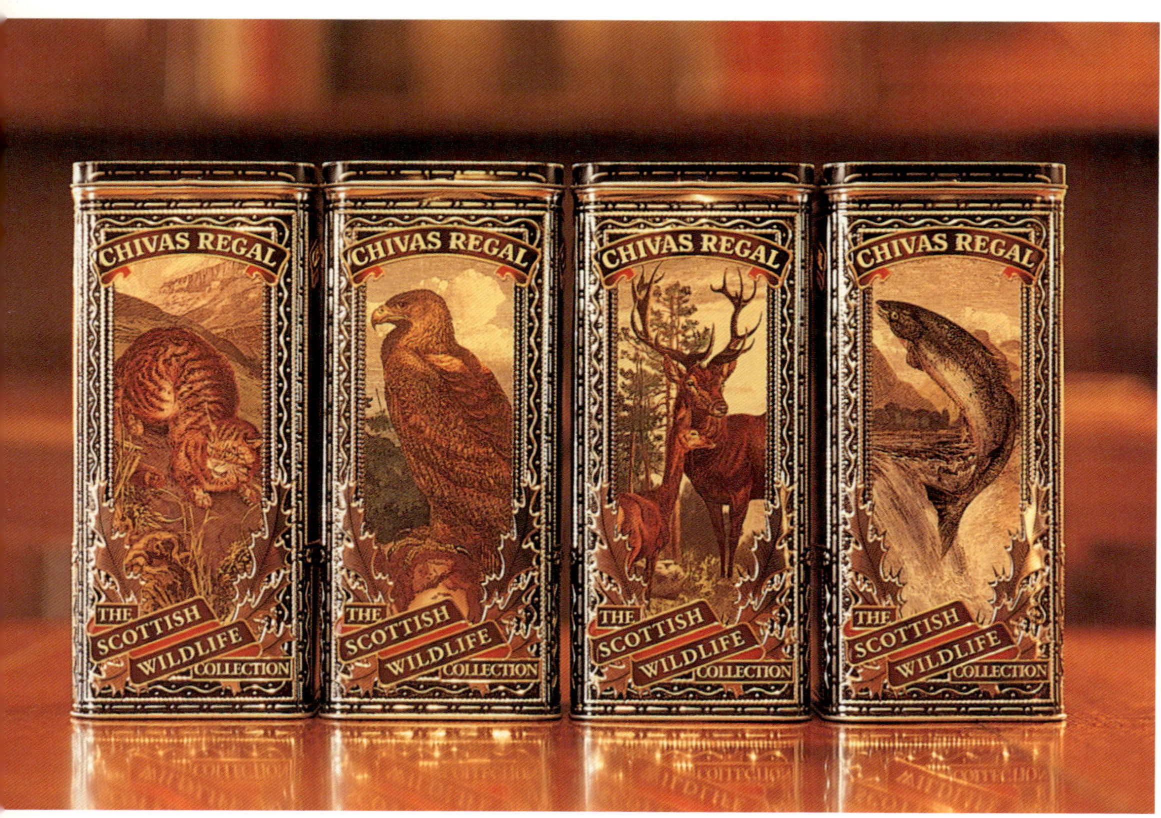

These classic canisters showing Scottish wildlife once contained another of Scotland's famous flavours – malt whisky.

The Highland village of Plockton basks in real Scottish sunshine.

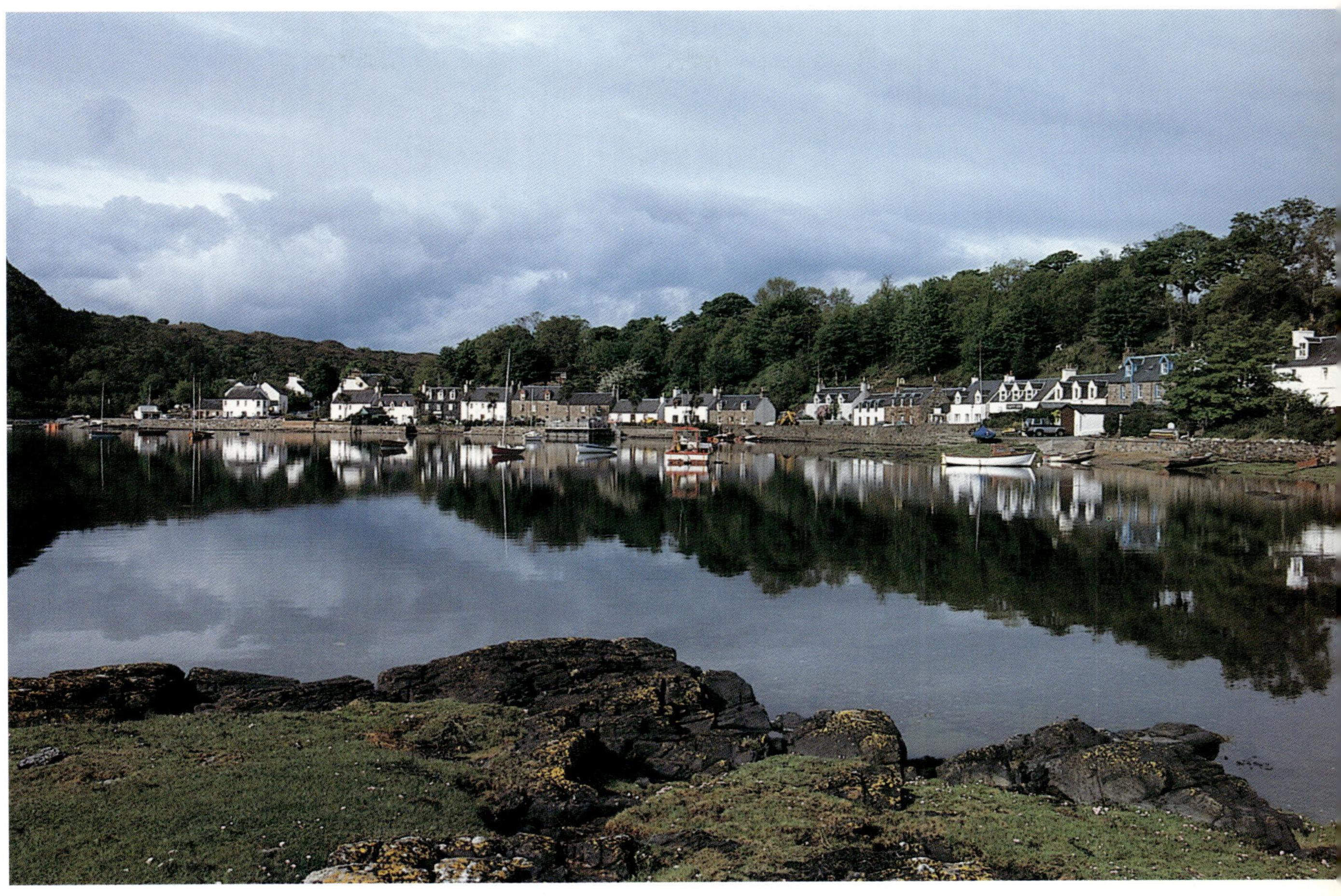

The tours are personalised and exclusive, so it feels as though the castle, country house or distillery has opened just to welcome you and your fellow passengers. There are options on each visit, such as to walk in the gardens, sit in some magnificent castle rooms, amble around the towns and villages – or stay behind on the train. Those who do venture forth are welcomed back after every trip with trays of drinks judged suitable to the weather and mood – from mulled wine to Bloody Marys, or hot chocolate with a Cointreau spicing if so desired.

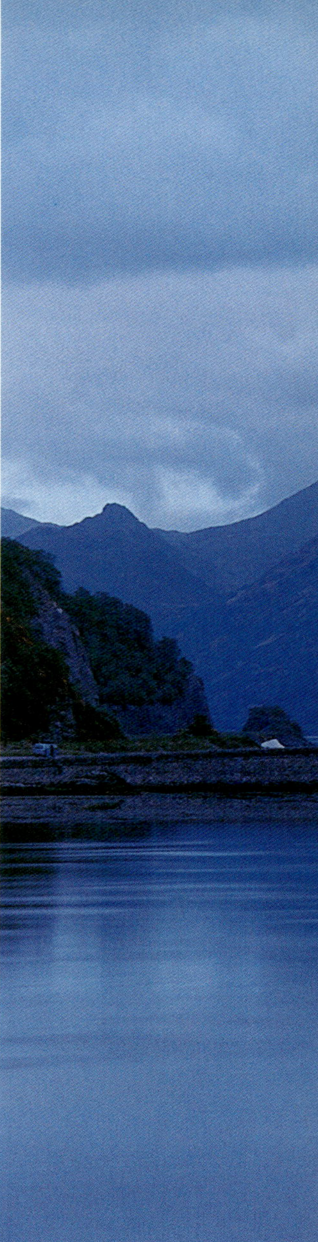

Who were the travellers on this unique train? Mainly North Americans, English, and Europeans were on board, and these made for an interesting mix of personalities. The young crew and the train manager provided constant cheerful attention and service, and the tour guide a depth of information on the sights to be seen both from and off the train.

The cost of the tour is inclusive of meals, wine and other beverages and all of the sightseeing excursions. There are also two-day train trips, and special golf tours that embrace some of the courses with which Scotland is more than well endowed.

The next day we travel west along one of Scotland's most scenic routes, heading to the Kyle of Lochalsh. Nearby is the Eilean Donan Castle, a spectacular ruin that is dramatically silhouetted against mountains and at the meeting point of three lochs. And in the distance is the Isle of Skye, once the home of Bonnie Prince Charlie, to where we journey the following morning to attend a cooking demonstration, with defiant lashings of butter and cream, by local cook Claire Macdonald at Kinloch Lodge. Afterwards we could read newspapers by the fire, or stroll on the loch's shores before returning to lunch on the train.

On the fifth day, the train returns to Edinburgh, early enough for a full day seeing the sights of this engaging city. Or for some passengers who are loath to leave the comforts and privacy of their luxurious home on wheels, there is just time to make a short visit to the Royal Mile's shops before re-boarding the train for another journey in another direction.

We too would have happily remained on board, to enjoy more of this revival of the romantic age of railway travel, on what is often described as the world's most exclusive train. It is a journey and experience that truly gives great value for money. And a lasting memory of Scotland, gained from a most favourable perspective.

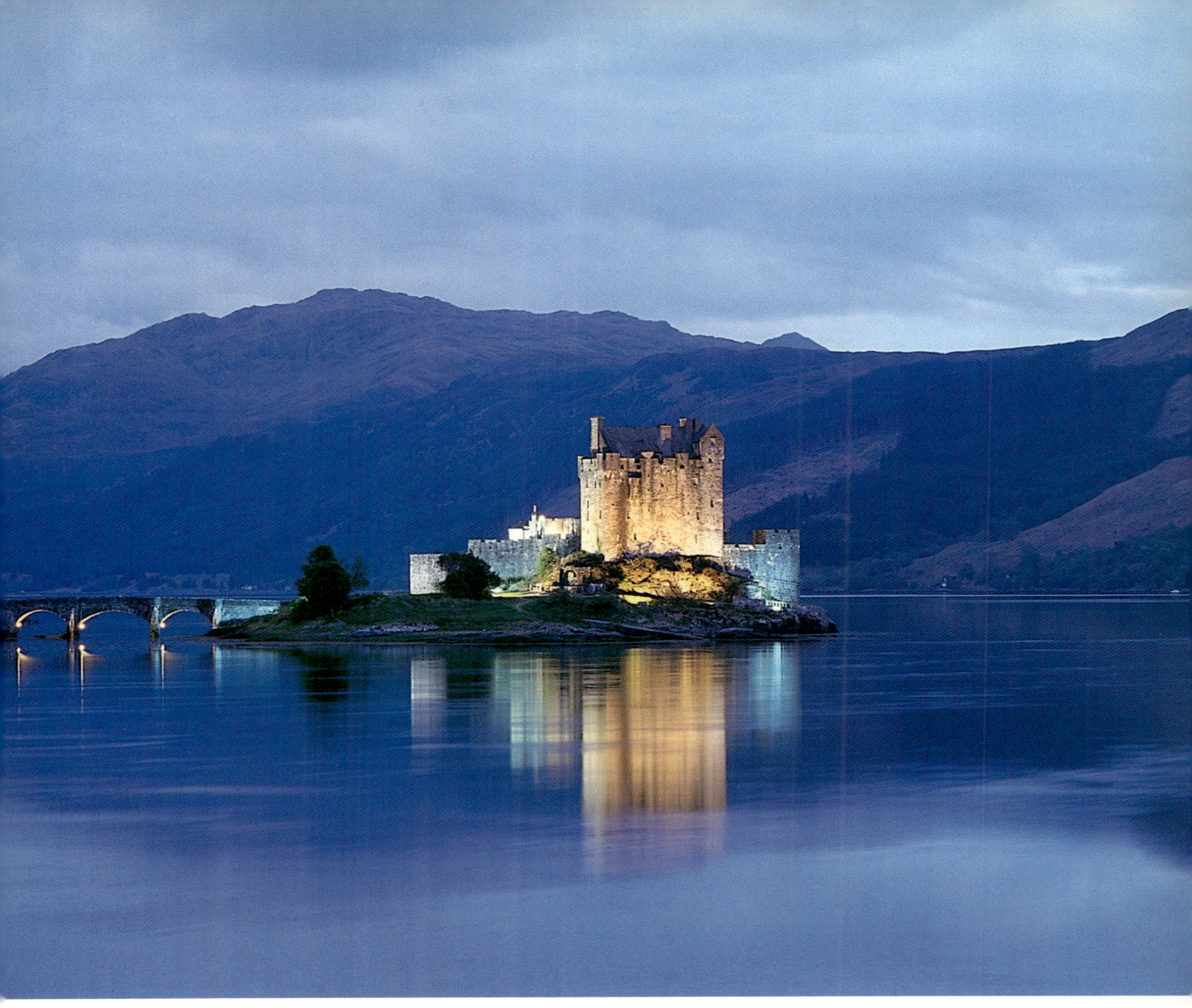

The ruin of Eilean Donan Castle.

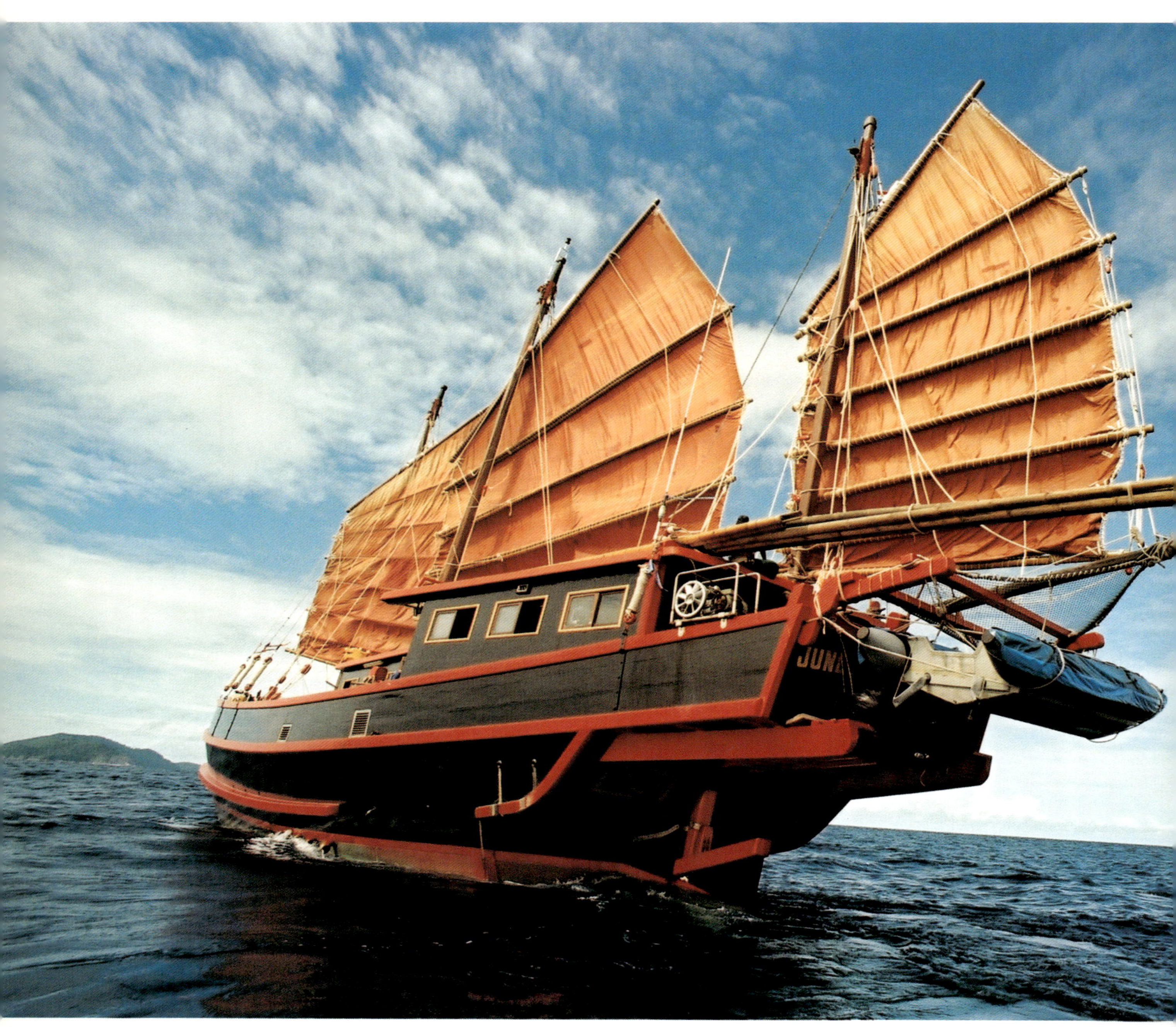

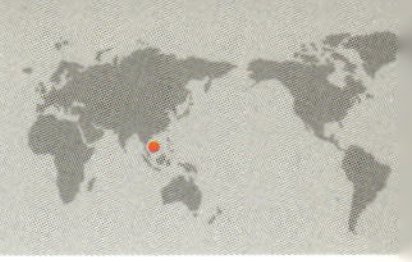

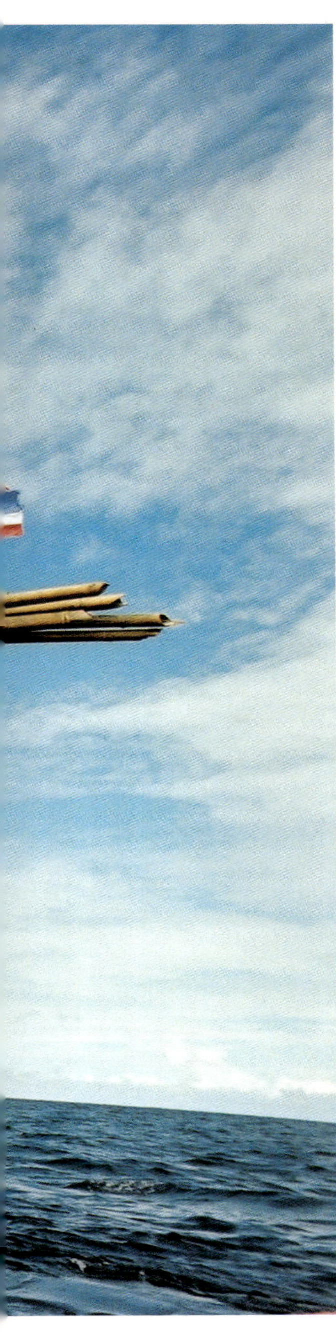

Dive, Dive...

The Junk, Similan Islands, Thailand

It's 7.00am, and the ship's rooster crows his raucous wake-up call to the sleeping passengers below deck on the sailing junk 'June Hong Chian Lee'. In just over an hour's time, they will all be overboard and under water.

The Junk is sailing in the Andaman Sea, part of the Indian Ocean, which spans the western coastline of Thailand. We have come to spend five days diving northwest of Phuket in the Similan Islands, a marine national park considered to be one of the top ten dive sites in the world. Its nine granite islands with their spectacular landscapes above water and breathtaking scenery below stretch some 128 square kilometres (331 sq miles). It's here that the richest variety and abundance of reef fish in Thai waters live, in multi-coloured coral gardens.

The classic sailboat was built in Malaysia in 1962 and originally used to transport charcoal, part of a small merchant fleet that traded up and down the coastline from Burma to Malaysia. Her name means 'Respect Wind Travel Forever', an old sailing adage that has obviously been adhered to. Now fully restored, the Junk is an exotic live-aboard dive boat based in Phuket, equipped with all that is needed for divers and offering a standard of comfort and cuisine not often associated with diving boats.

If you are not already a diver, you can either learn to be one during the trip and become a certified diver, or just enjoy the sailing experience and scenery. You can go snorkelling and swim in the clear warm waters and just lie on the white sand beaches. The dinghy driver will happily transport you to shore, he obviously relished his role and was prepared to race across the water given any chance.

There are up to four dives scheduled every day, including a night descent to view sea creatures that glow in the dark. As half of marine life is asleep during the day there is plenty to see after hours. Well-prepared briefings were given before each dive, illustrated with beautifully drawn maps. The depths of sites such as Fantasea Reef, Christmas Point, Beacon Beach, Sharkfin Reef, Elephants Head and East of Eden are plumbed. Rocky Point, a deep dive site with a dramatic underwater architecture of caves and gorges, provides swim-through passages in boulder towers. Its rock formations are underwater playgrounds for grownups.

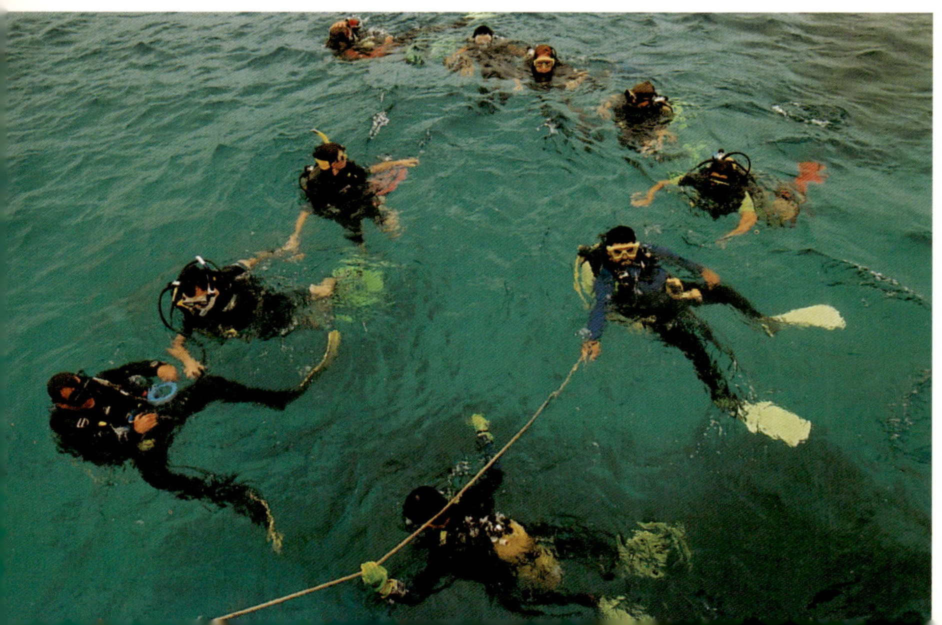

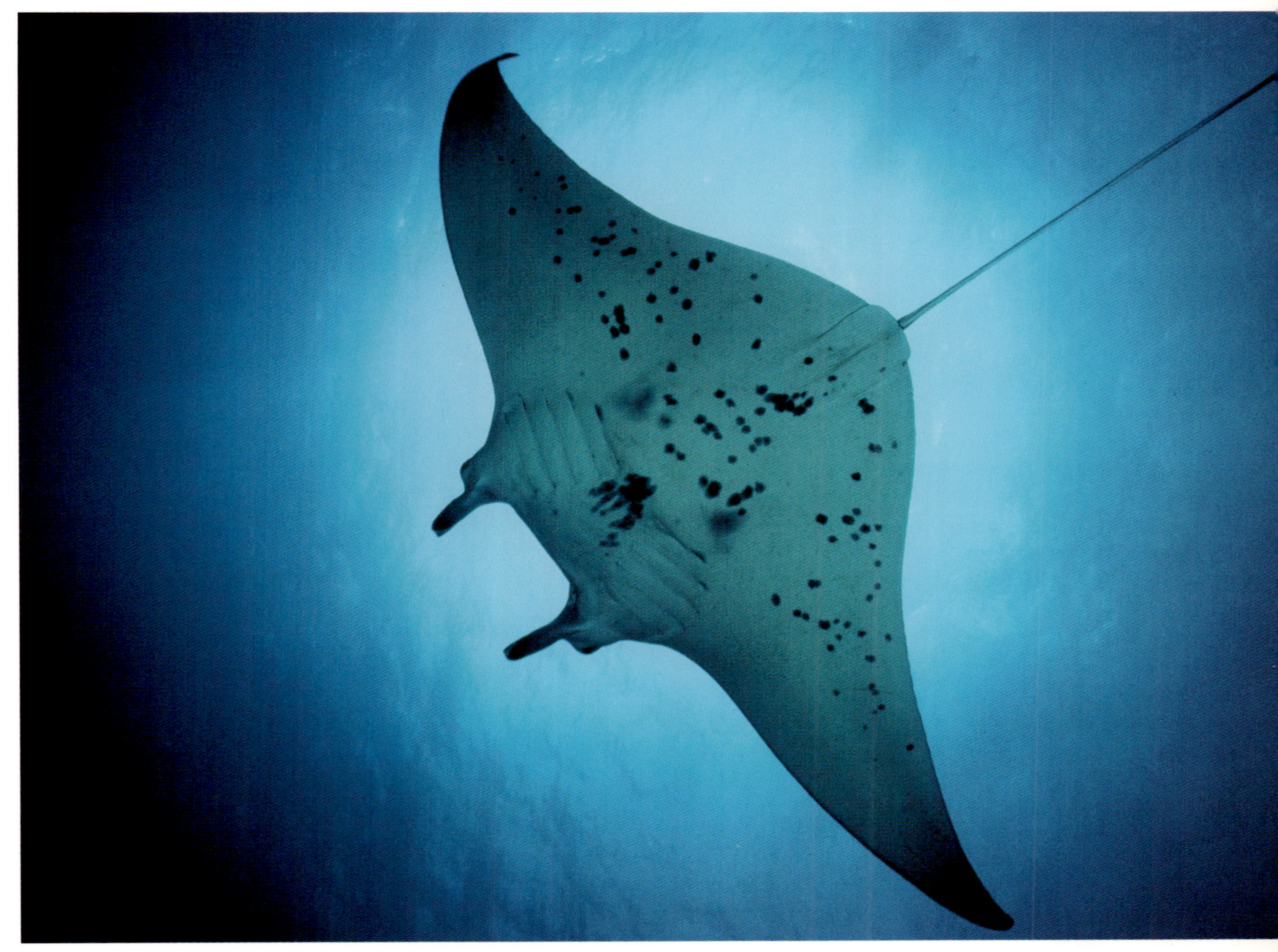

With the often spectacular coral gardens and myriad of marine life, the divers come back on board excited and round eyed reporting what they saw. All experience the adrenaline high of a sudden close encounter with a large fish, maybe a shark or a manta ray. To many, diving feels like flying, especially over the deep dive sites, when you can swoop over huge rocks enjoying the exhilarating sensation of weightlessness.

The submerged scenery is given high praise. It is an underwater heaven says Ali, a diver from Dubai, wondering aloud why God made the underwater world so beautiful when so few people can see it.

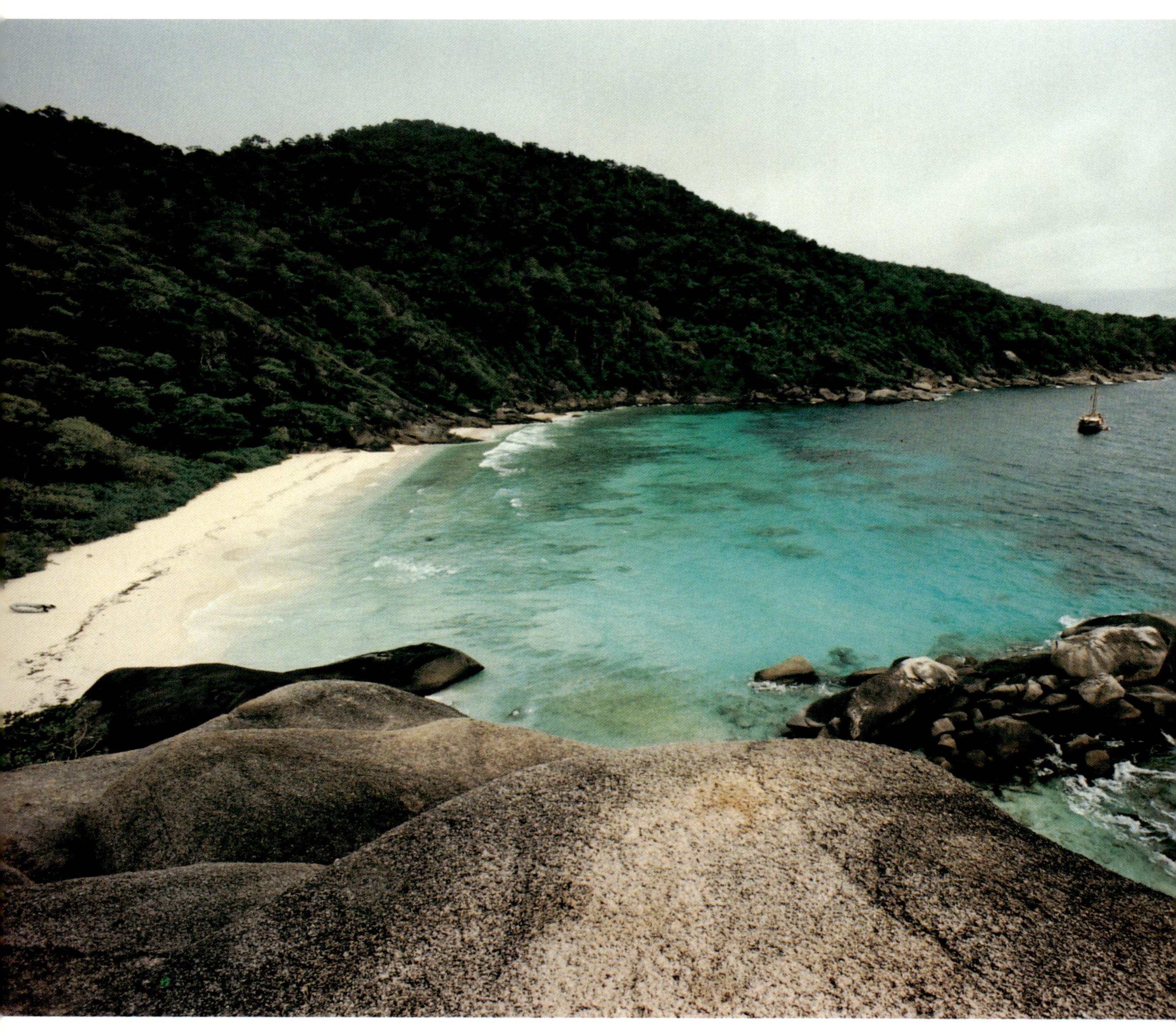

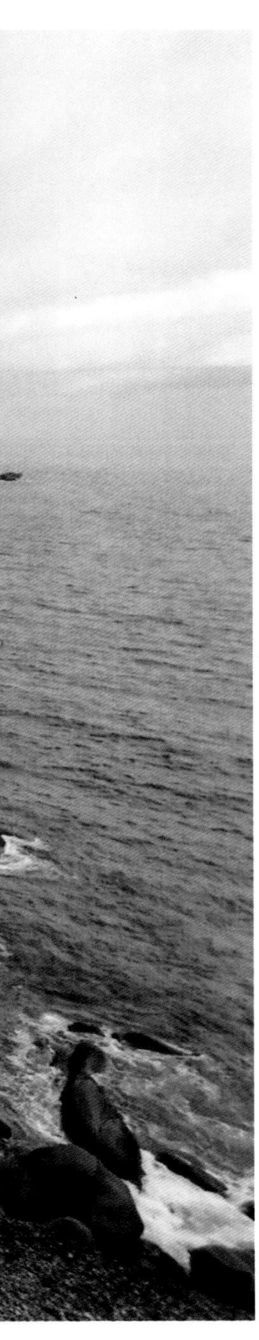

From the massive boulder on Similan Island number eight, with the Junk anchored in the bay.

Circled with coral reefs, the Similan Islands are either crowned with lush greenery or a collection of rocks, stacked in amazing piles and sculpted by nature into fantastic shapes. Many have pristine white beaches. Most are uninhabited, and although they each have names, they are referred to numerically, from one to nine, which seems rather prosaic in such a poetic landscape.

Rangers from the Royal Thai Forestry Department patrol the waters to enforce the marine park's protected status. Mooring lines are banned and no fishing is permitted, aiming at the protection and regeneration of coral. Thailand has fringing reefs of coral, coral that extends outward from land, whether a submerged rock or an island. Here in the Andaman Sea there are also patch reefs, coral formations around totally submerged structures away from the shores. There are over 200 known species of hard corals, and a vast amount of soft coral, in a colourful palette of pinks, purples, oranges and reds. The coral is flourishing, and the reefs are congregating places for crowds of tropical fish.

Large specimens of marine life are attracted to the deep waters here, such as the graceful aerodynamic manta and eagle rays, gentle whale sharks, oriental bonitos, and dogtooth tunas. Great barracuda, leopard sharks, rainbow runners and queenfish are also frequent visitors. Sea turtles sometimes swim into view but keep their distance from divers; ferocious-looking moray eels disguise their gentle nature. Smaller fish shimmer, flit and zigzag in the blue waters – grouper, trout snapper, triggerfish, and angel, clown, lion and batfish. And while the area is becoming more and more popular for fish and people, it is still reasonably free of cruise boats.

No shoes are allowed on board the Junk's teak decks. On arrival, you are politely directed to put your shoes in a crate and pick them up when you leave. This sudden release of city feet from their wrappings defines the start of our time-out.

Eighteen passengers can be accommodated in six shipshape cabins, some double, others three or four bedded. All have hot water shower bathrooms and air-conditioning. Traditional Thai cushions serve as headrests. These radiantly coloured pillows are especially comfortable and covetable souvenirs.

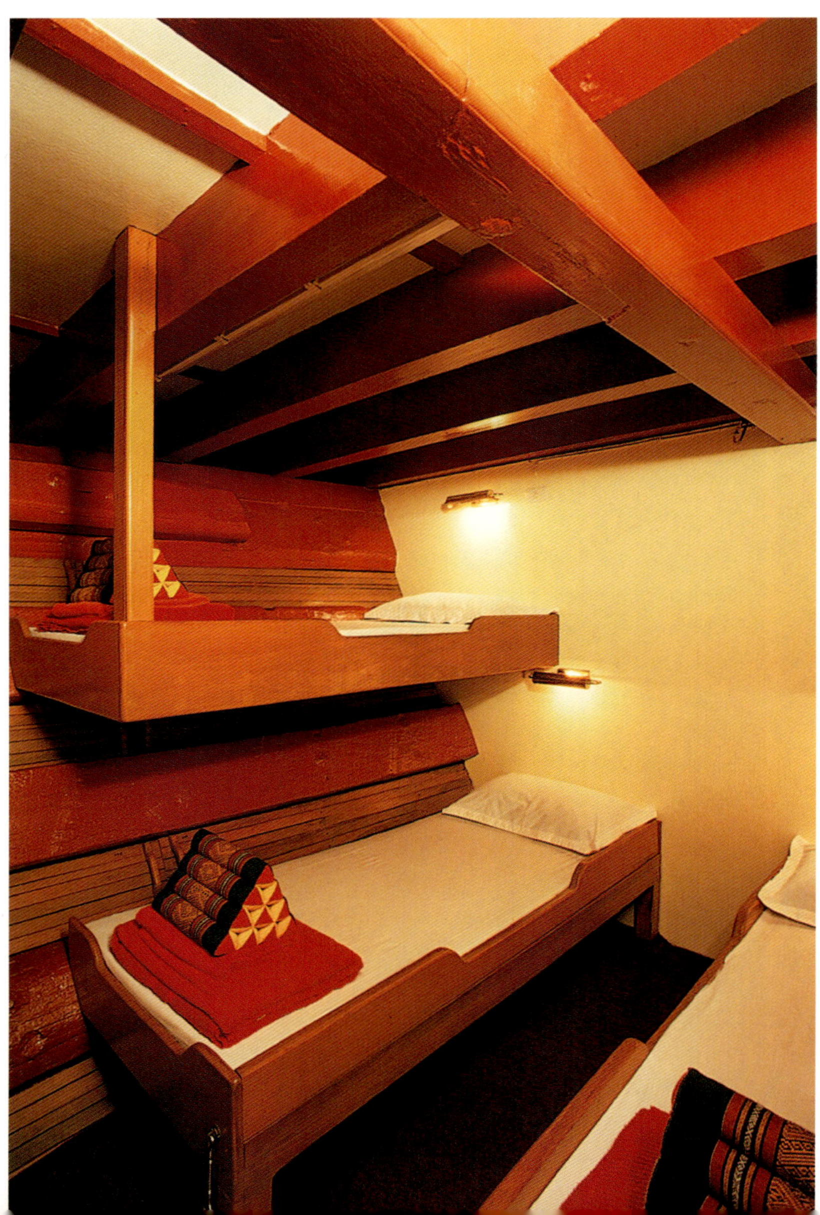

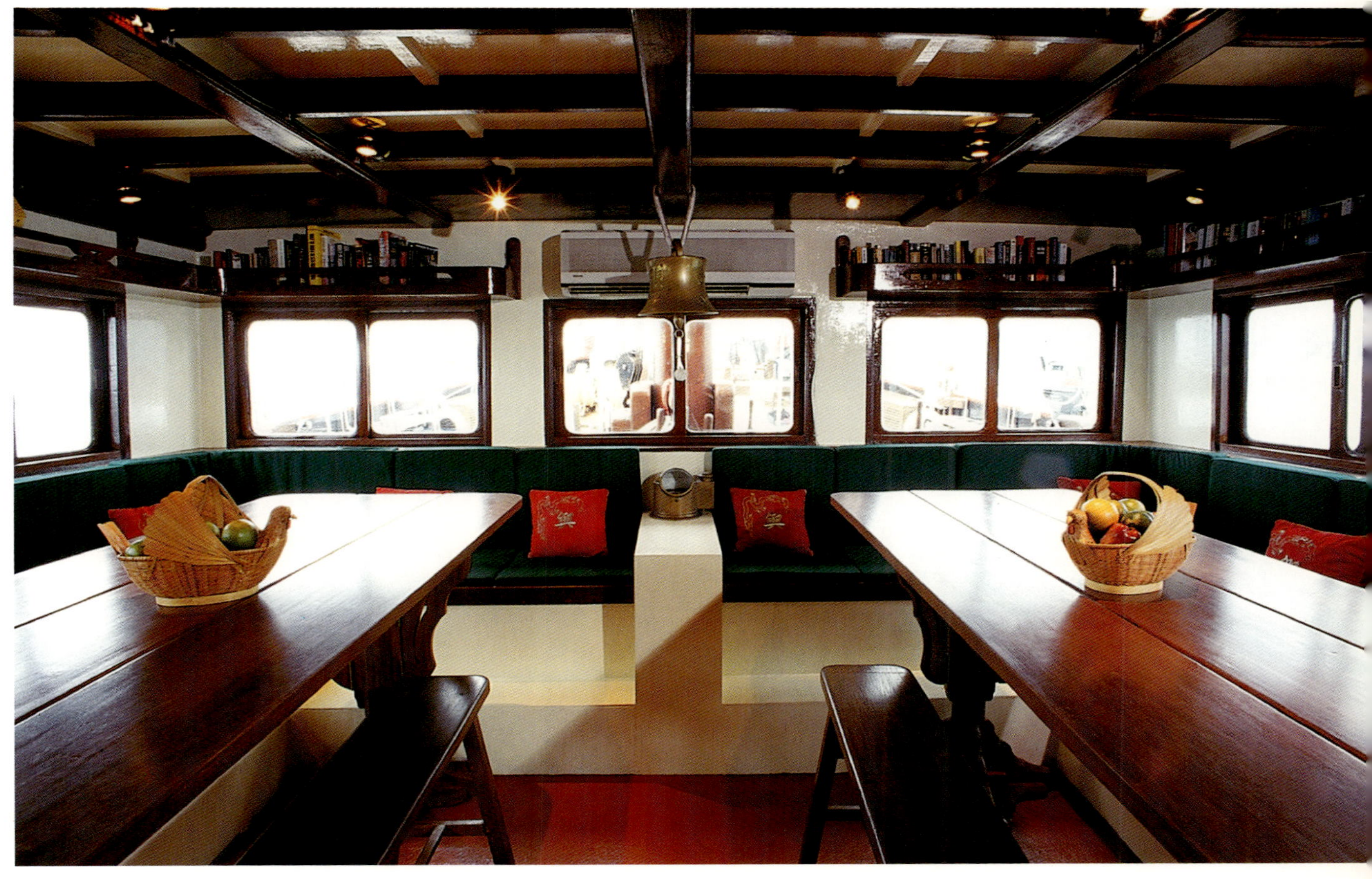

The large comfortable lounge doubles as the dining area, where the Thai cook delivers delicious food, and plenty of it, to expectant and mostly appreciative guests. Primarily Thai food is served, together with an abundance of tropical fruits. Some of the hot-spiced dishes were rather strong for more tender taste buds, but crew were always there to explain what each dish was, so nobody was uninformed, even if then surprised. Most of the spicy fragrant food was very much to our taste.

There is a good library on board, with books in many languages, so readers will be happy. And the Junk's immense deck is ideal to relax on between dives, nurture a suntan and watch the prolific stars in the clear night sky above.

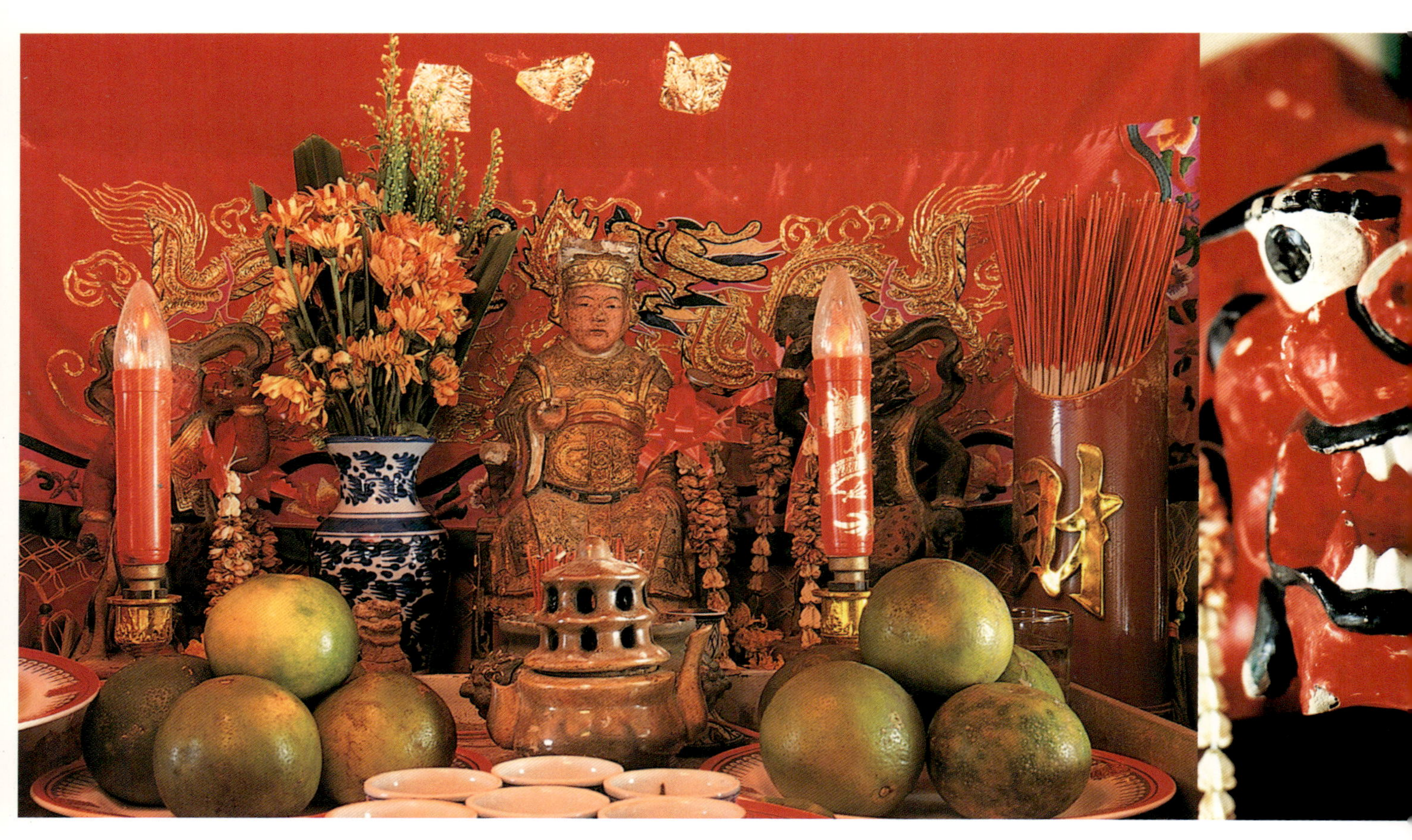

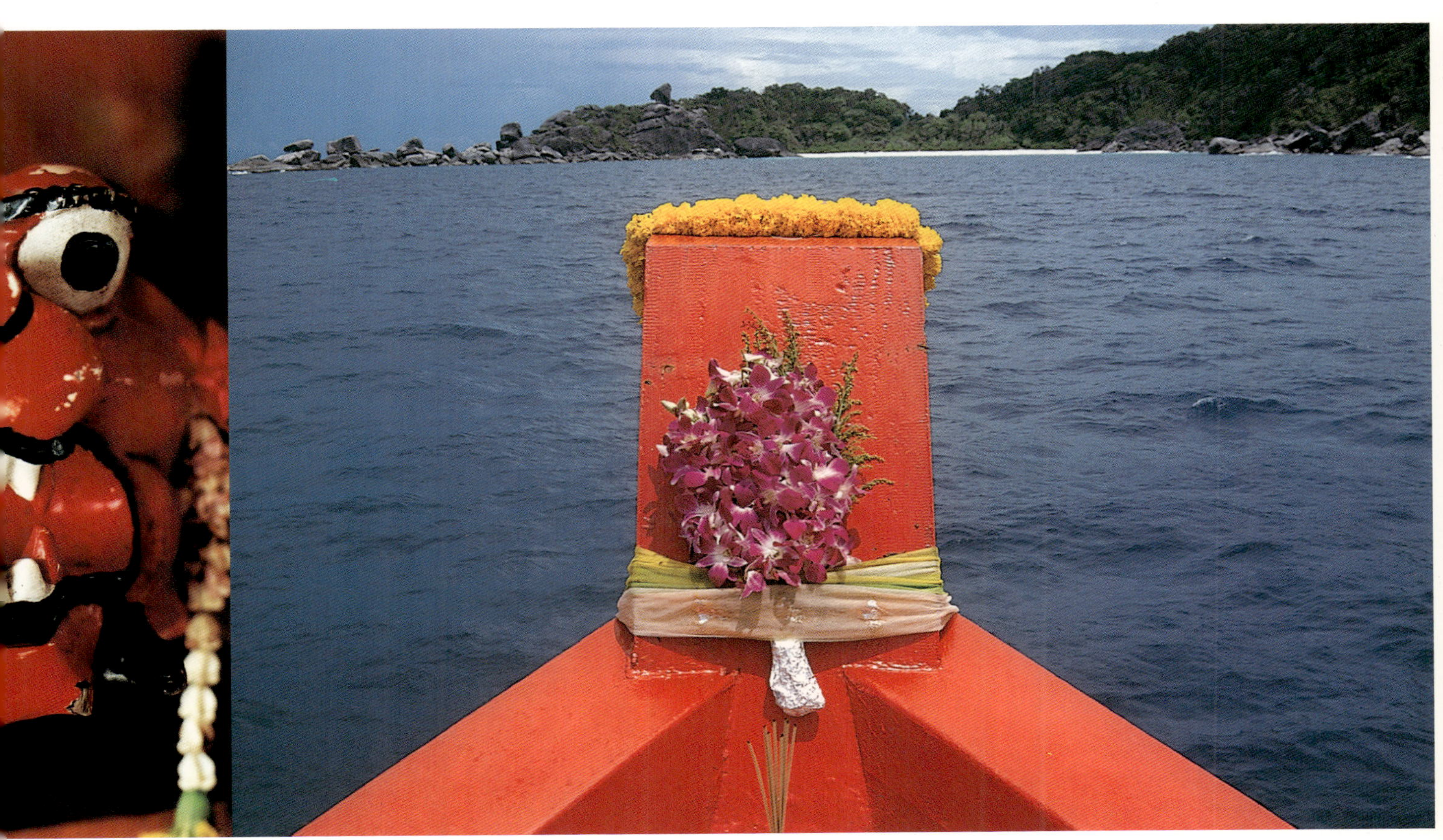

No doubt Macha Poh, the Chinese goddess of the sea, has seen many sights from her shrine on board. Fruit, sweets and incense are put at her feet to keep her in a good mood, and ensure she protects the ship. Two fierce-faced dragon soldiers, Chian and Lee, representing the Yin and Yang – the passive female and active male of the universe in Chinese philosophy – guard the entrance to the shrine.

A fresh garland of orchids is placed every week at the bow, considered by the crew to be a sacred part of the Junk, as it is where the spirit of the boat lives.

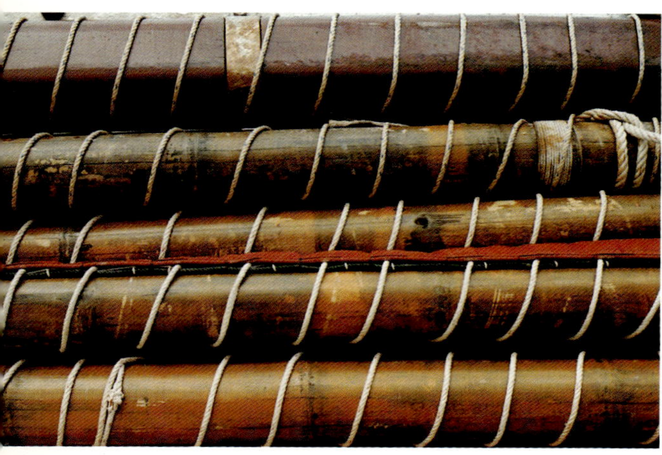

Bamboo and rope rigging supports the canvas sails.

Thailand offers very comfortable and safe diving conditions. Water visibility is often more than 30 metres, and the average ocean temperature is 25 degrees. The calm sea conditions, together with the clear blue waters, spectacular corals and myriad marine creatures in the ocean depths attract divers from all over the world.

Diving around and under the huge boulders of the aptly named Elephant Head Rock, voted one of the best dive sites in the region, reveals even more unusual rock formations. Caves and crevices, swim-throughs and holes all offer places for humans and fish to explore.

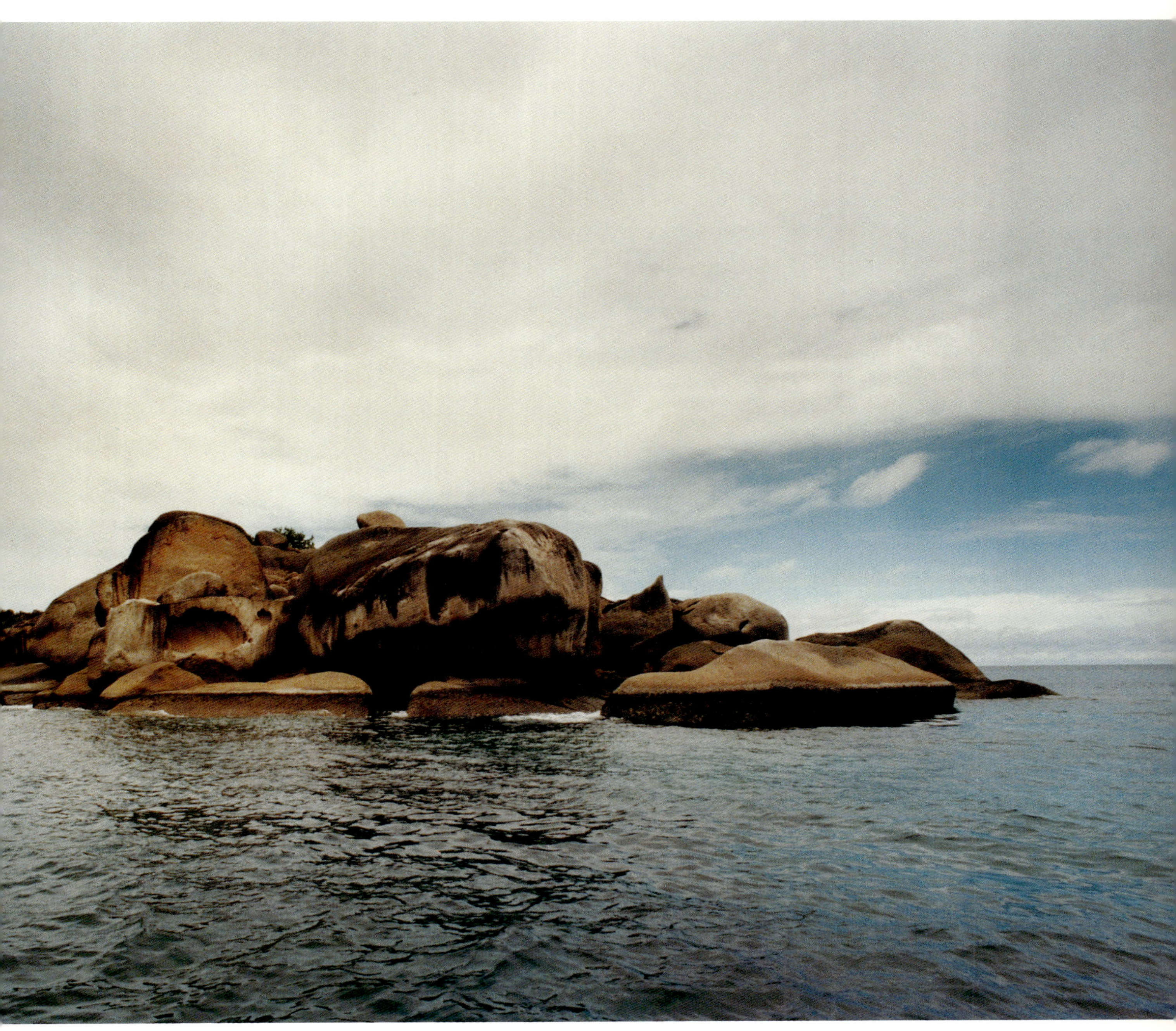

Elephant Head Rock.

We arrived on board late at night, so it is not until the morning that we see the magnificence of the Junk. As the dinghy races away with its load of rubber-suited, tank-wearing divers, the view of the boat looking back is truly exotic. With the sun shining on its gold and black paintwork and the red sails unfurled, it seems a fairytale boat, like a decorative prop from a Hollywood film.

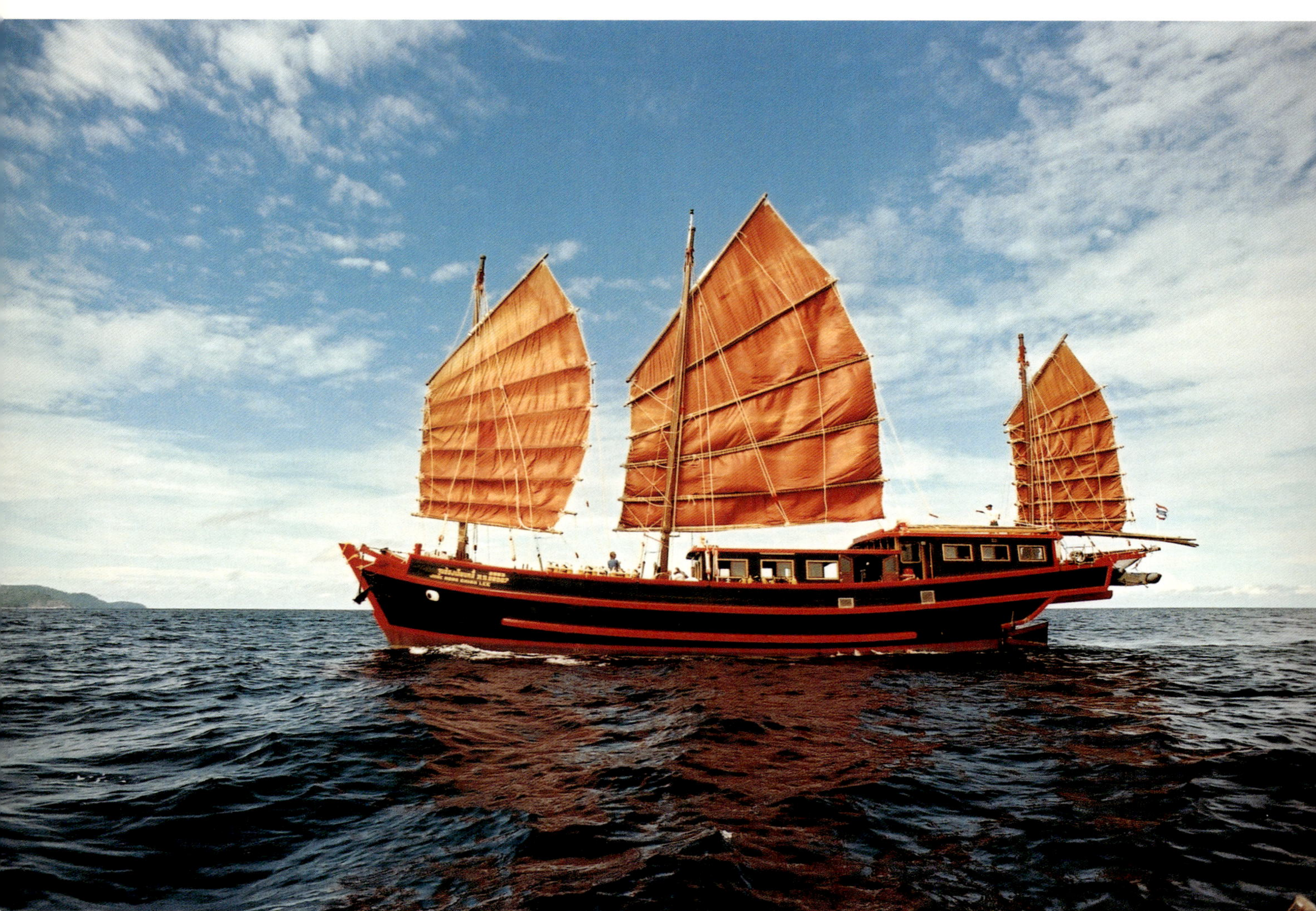

Gold dragons gleam in the sun, standing sentry at each side of the boat as added protection from bad spirits.

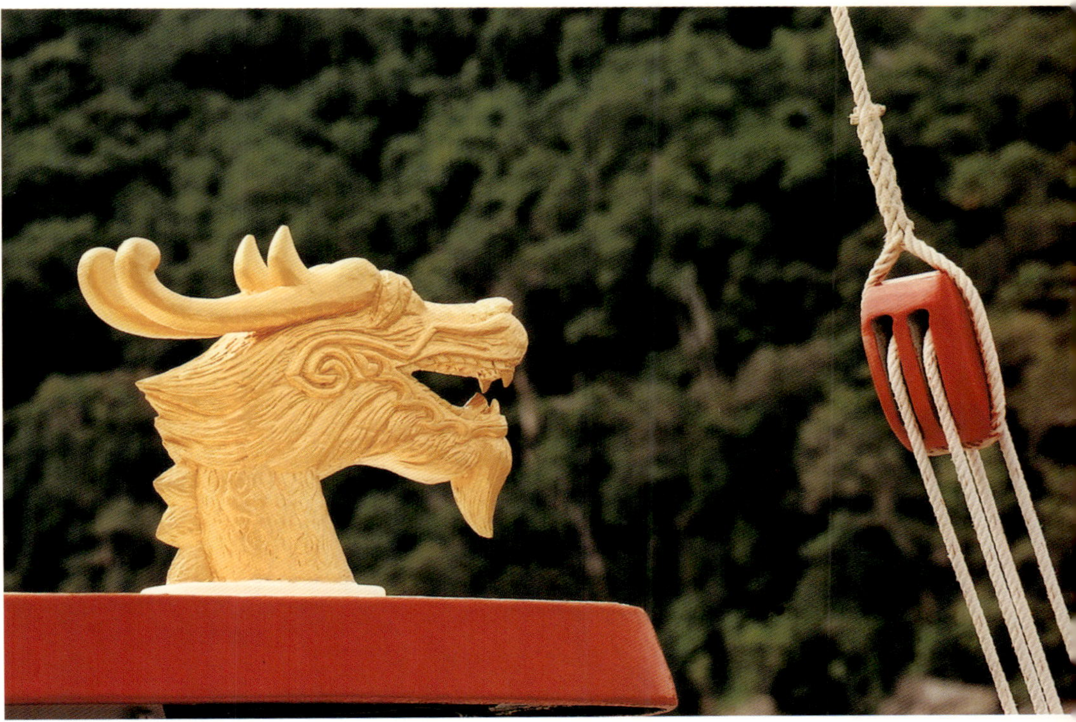

Reassuringly large – 30m (75ft) long – and stable, the junk is constructed mainly from a hard teakwood. The masts that rise 23m (57½ft) above the deck are made from trees that date back over 300 years. Although it dates from the past the Junk is now fitted with modern equipment, including satellite navigation. Powered by a diesel engine, it cruises at a speed of eight knots motor sailing, and has a crew of nine, including the boatmen, the chef and his assistant.

Once described as a 'luxury junket', it definitely is in comparison to many other live aboard dive boats with its stunning looks, facilities and food.

This is a holiday where you are under pressure, but by deliberate choice and only when you are underwater. The pleasure of learning or practicing a skill, and the scenery, sun and sea air combine to give a relaxing and purposeful holiday. Meeting a diverse group of passengers from many different countries united in a common pursuit, and swapping stories of great, good and bad dives was an added bonus.

The Junk 'June Hong Chian Lee' | 235 Ratuthit 200 Pee Road | Patong Beach | Phuket | Thailand | t: +66 76 342186 | f: +66 76 342453 | e: info@thejunk.com | www.thejunk.com

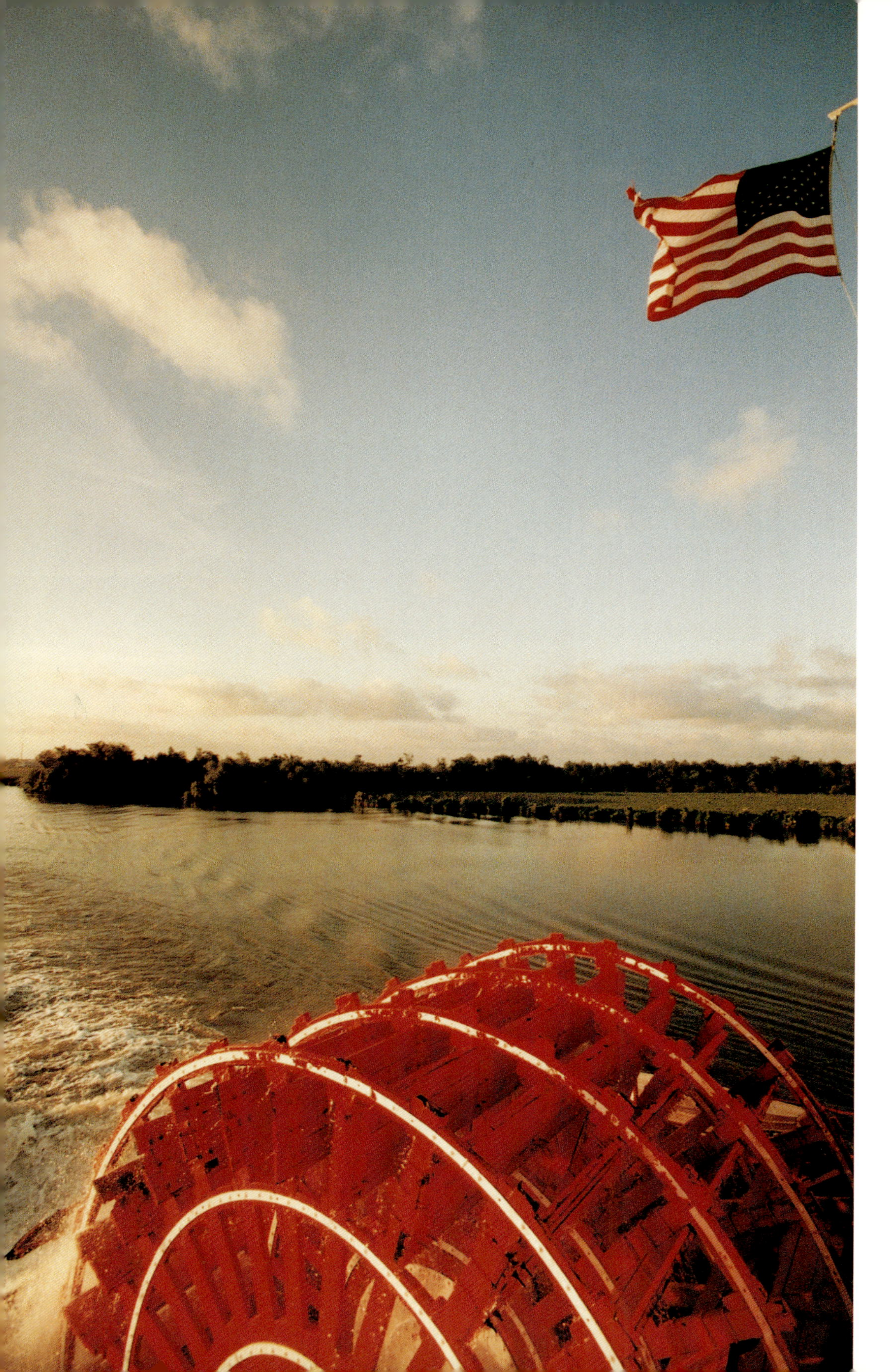

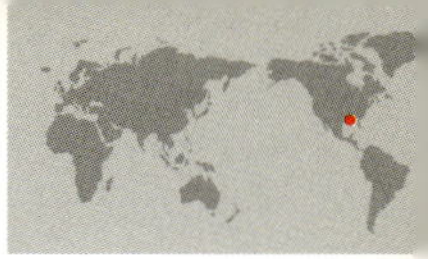

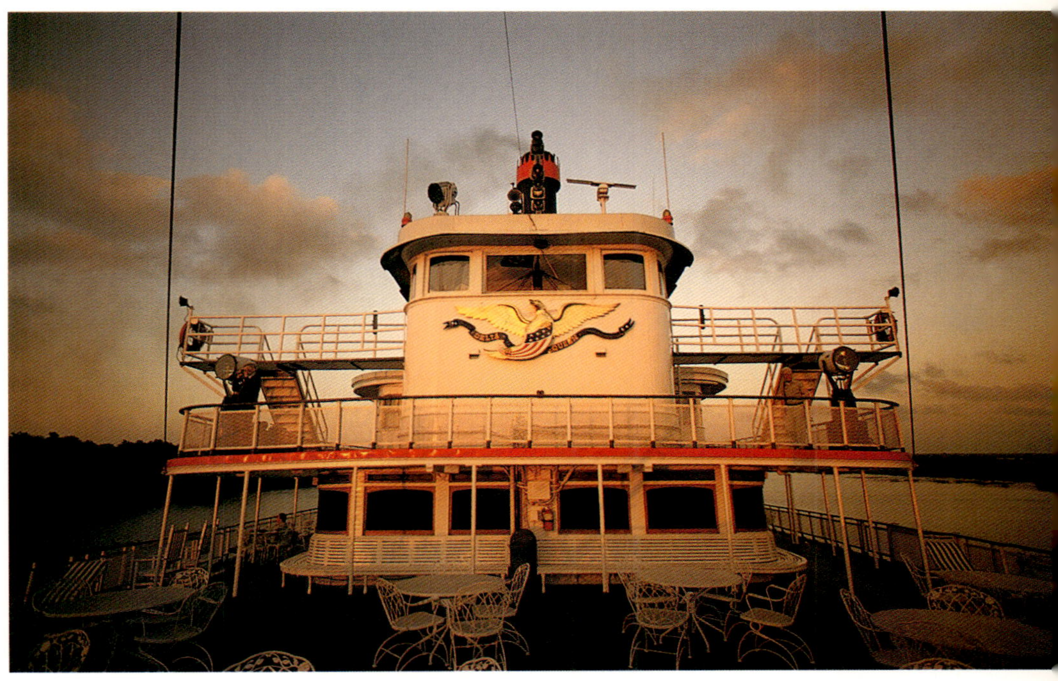

Laissez les bon temps rouler!

Delta Queen paddlewheel steamboat, Louisiana

The enthusiasm and bounciness of a buoyant America was nowhere more evident than on board the Delta Queen paddlewheel steamboat as it moved out from Robin Street Wharf in New Orleans. The whistle sounded several husky blasts as we left the shore and swung out into the Mississippi River for eight days on a cruise billed as the Cajun Culture Tour. Our departure was accompanied by the shrill salute of the calliope, the traditional steam-powered piano at the stern, where the paddlewheel propelling us steadily churned the water.

We are 'steamboating' on the waterways of South Louisiana, headed first for the Gulf Intracoastal waterway and down to the Atchafalaya Basin, where hardwood forest, cypress swamps, marshes and bayous make up one of the few great wetland semi-wilderness areas left in America. It's here that the curious story of the Cajun people is chiefly centred.

**Let the Good Times Roll*

The paddlewheel steamboat is a true 'as seen in the movies' classic, once described as a floating wedding cake by writer – and steamboat pilot – Mark Twain. Samuel Clemens' pen name was taken from the frequent call of the leadsman, 'Mark Twain' being a measure signifying that the river water was 2 fathoms or 12 feet deep.

Riverboats are enshrined in much of American literary history and music, from the story of Huckleberry Finn to the musical 'Showboat'. Where there were once thousands of steamboats moving goods like cotton and grain up and down the mile-wide Mississippi river, there are now only a few.

The smallest and most authentic of the fleet that remains is the Delta Queen. Built in 1927, with a working paddlewheel powered by steam, she is a listed national historic 'landmark', conveying passengers to view other historic landmarks during her journeys in the Old South, connecting the past with the present.

On board we were served a series of lectures, from Cajun music history to Mississippi river control. The informative and lively lectures were far more than mere briefings desultorily delivered as a background to the shore tours. These were in depth dissertations from specialists. Ecologist Bill Fontenot; photographer and writer Greg Guirard, and artist and photographer Elmore Leonard Jnr.'s presentations were complemented by comprehensive slideshows illustrating Cajun life, and local flora and fauna.

Louisiana is truly a place where the river rules; the history of this Southern state is as much the story of the Mississippi. The role of the Riverlorian – the person riding with the boat who talks about the river's history culture and characters – was supplemented by engineer Herbert Juneau's address on the navigation and flood control systems of the region.

And in this Land of Plenty there was plenty of food featured on the Steamboat Bill of Fare. A vast choice was presented for breakfast, lunch, dinner and supper, from traditional river fare and themed food, to interpretations of hot spicy Cajun cuisine and hearty southern cooking. Dishes such as shrimp and sausage jambalaya with crawfish étoufée, and catfish gumbo, were among the many culinary choices, reflecting the Cajun country and the flavour of our cruise.

Like the food, there was an ample spread of on and off board activities to choose from. Shore tours ranged from excursions to cypress swamps and egret sanctuaries, verdant gardens and sugar plantations, antebellum mansions and a World War II warship. And if it wasn't hot enough in this sultry climate, a visit can be made to the home of Tabasco sauce, the fiery pepper seasoning whose burning taste can brand your tongue.

In addition to the lectures, the on-board activity menu was an eclectic mix of entertainment exercise and romance. Listening to the trad band sounds, promenading, even jogging, around the deck, learning to play the calliope and renewing wedding vows were just some of the amusements presided over by aptly named Cruise Director Jazzou Jones.

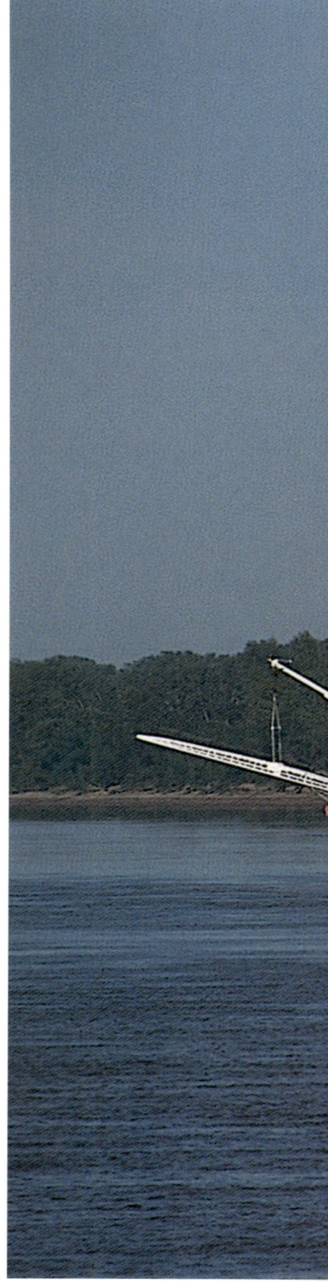

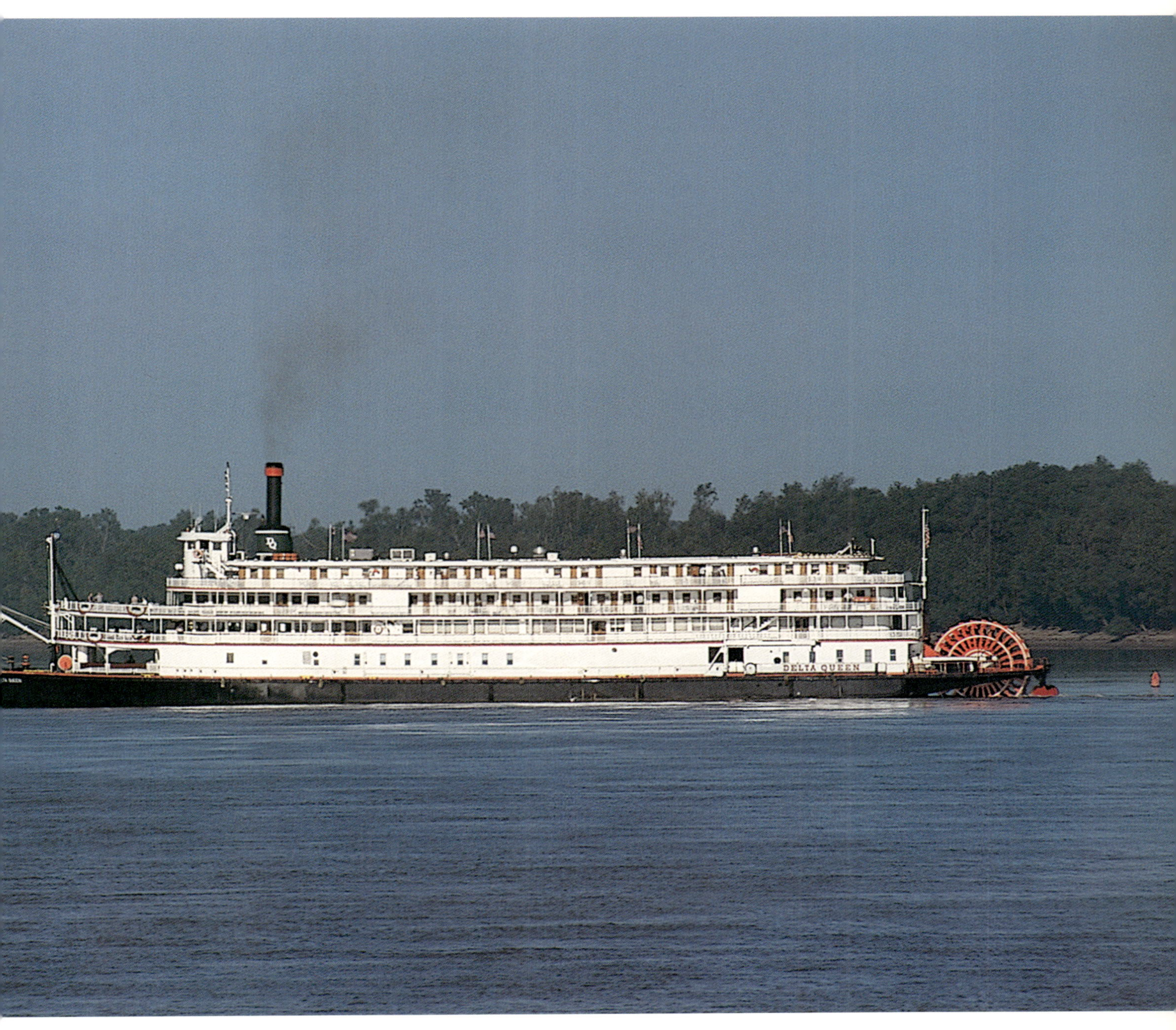
DELTA QUEEN

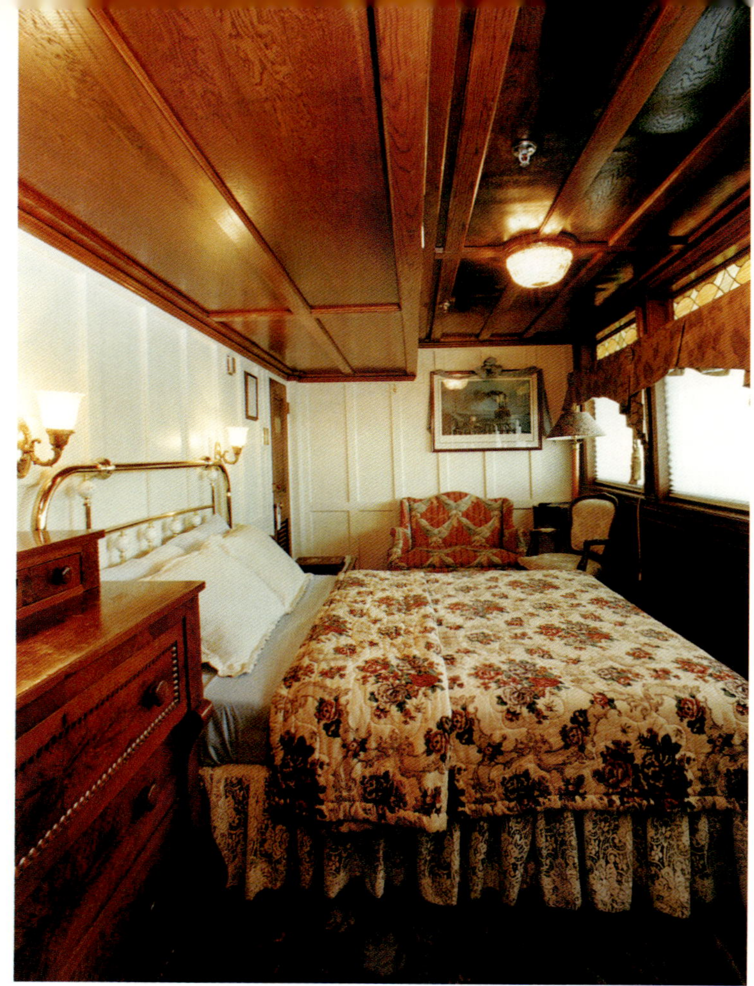

The Natchez Suite, Stateroom 120.

Byron, gentleman-waiter, is, like most of the crew, addicted to a life of rolling down the river back and forward from the steamer's New Orleans home port.

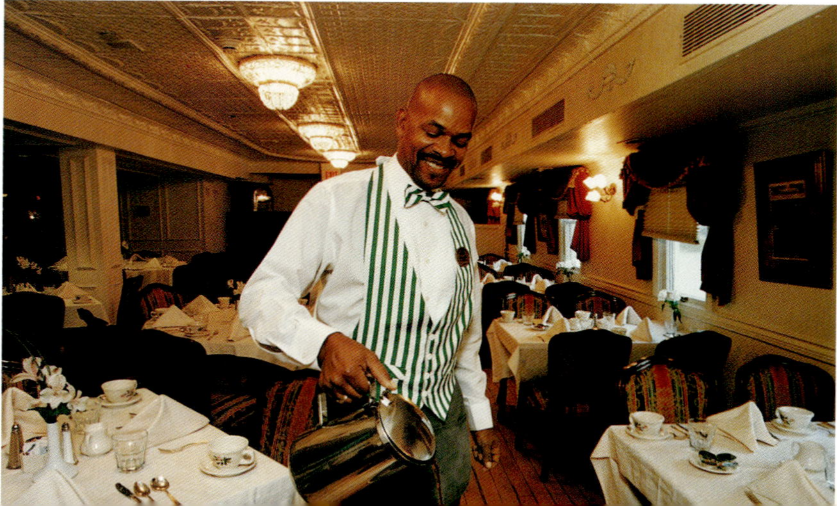

The Grand Staircase makes a stately entrance to the Delta Queen. Its sweeping curve would have suited the slow descent of a crinoline-skirted southern belle to an admiring beau below, in days gone by. The old fashioned elegance continues in the suites, staterooms and the various lounges. As was traditional, the dining room doubles as the venue for after dinner shows. This classic room, with its pressed tin ceiling and ironwood floor, also serves as a cinema and lecture theatre.

Southern comfort extends to every stateroom. Whether a suite or stateroom is chosen, each has a river view and a private bathroom. Some staterooms have upper and lower bunks and although not as roomy, they are nonetheless restful – once the upper bunk occupant has learnt to keep his or her head down.

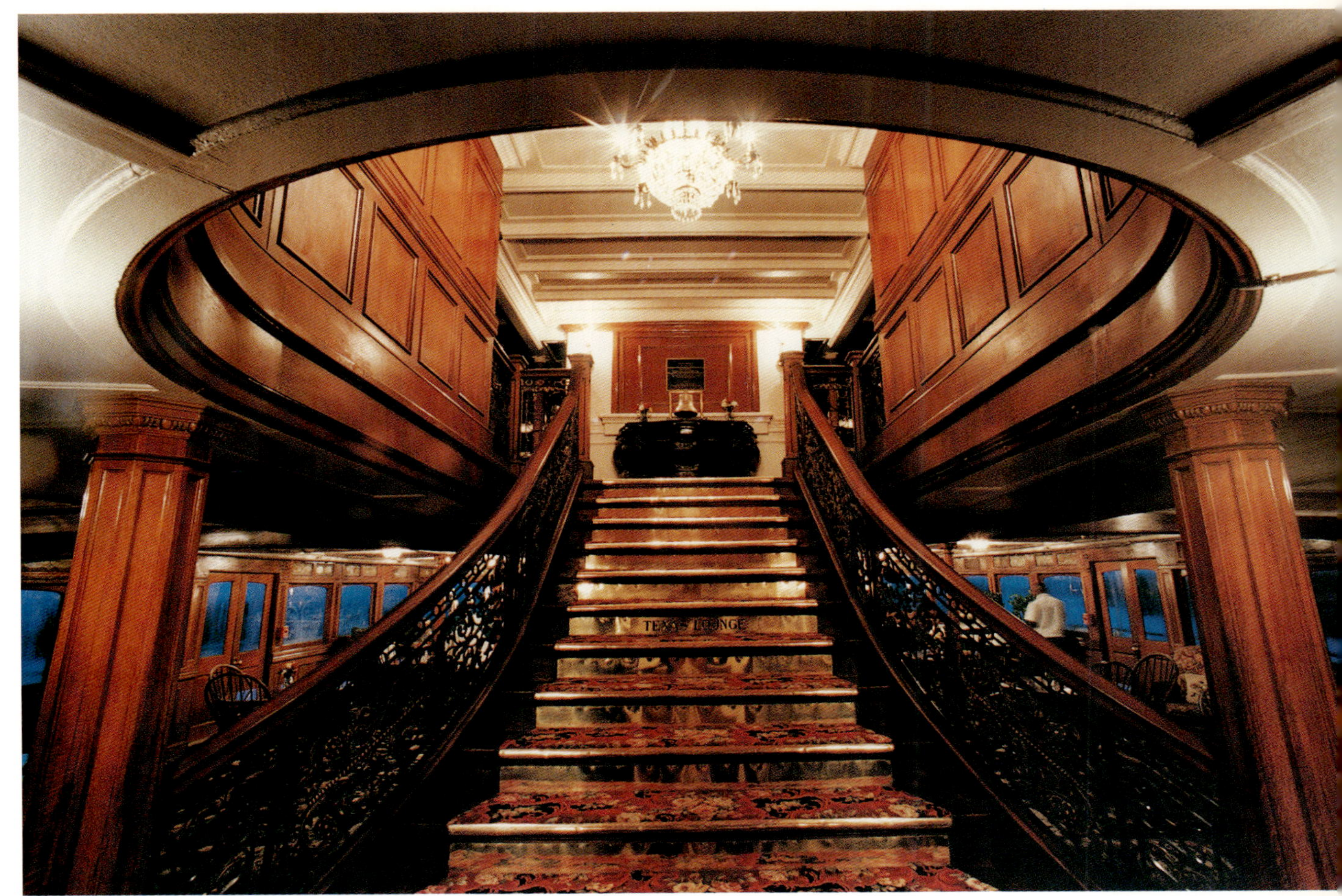

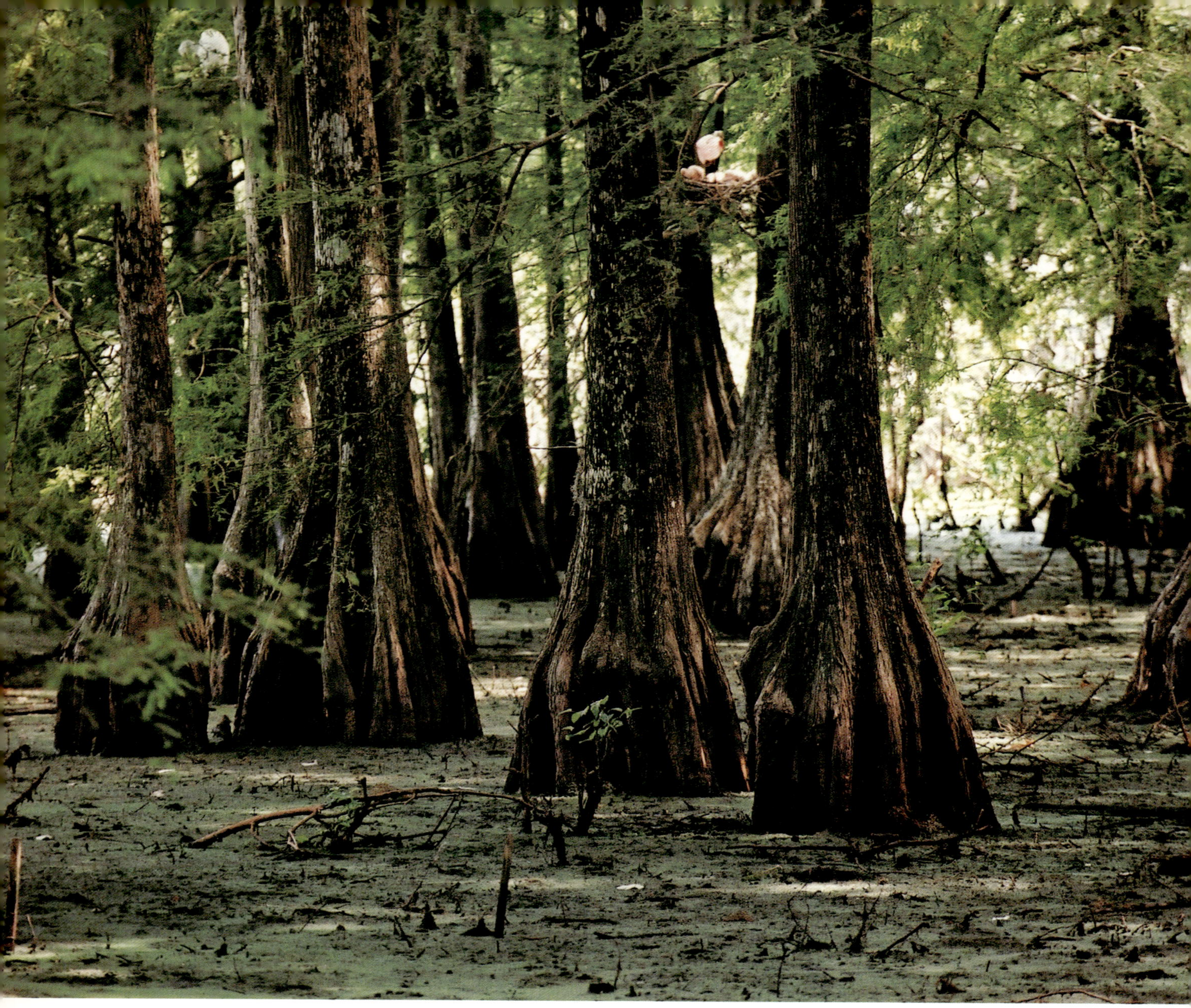

A roseate spoonbill, often called the Cajun flamingo, is nesting in the centre of these cypress trees.

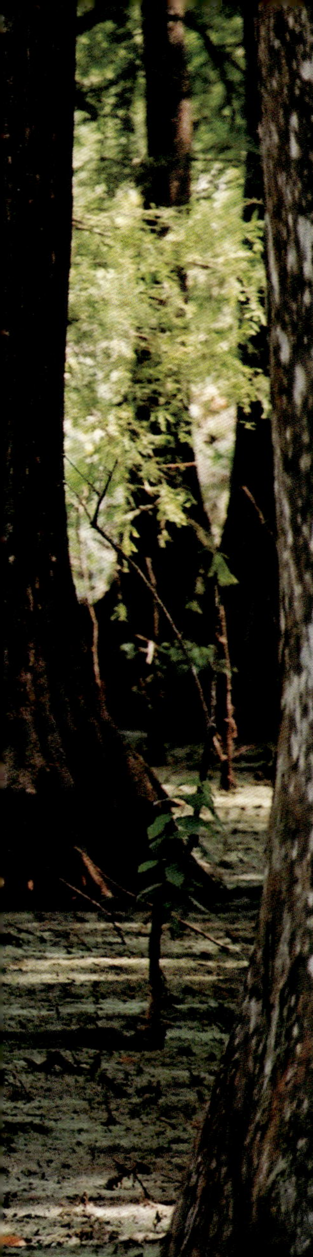

The swamps of the Atchafalaya Basin have a sad dignity and an eerie beauty. Aptly described by Greg Guirard as 'the land of dead giants', they are littered with the stump remnants of once magnificent cypress trees butchered before conservation was thought of. It is said that bald cypress trees built Louisiana, from the 1700's to the 1950's. Cypress wood does not rot, and was the most durable available in the New World.

There is a special Cajun connection and affinity with the swamp and bayous, it was here that many came for sanctuary.

The Cajun story is a sad account of displacement, first from their native France, which they fled as refugees from religious wars, and then from Nova Scotia as victims of the war between French Canada and Britain in 1755. They regrouped in Louisiana, where other French speakers were resident, and made a livelihood in the swamps and bayous, catching crawfish catfish and picking Spanish moss. Finding solace in a close-knit family life and music, the Cajuns developed into a very separate people, with traits of self-reliance tenacity and independence. These were survivors and adaptors, whose struggle continued over the years. Their dialect French was once banned, and their way of life and income affected by the silting of swampland and commercial farming of crawfish. Now there is somewhat of a Cajun renaissance, led by the popularity and influence of their captivating music. Known for their ability to take it easy and enjoy life despite its difficulties, their mantra could well be 'let the good times roll'.

Often called the 'red-eye swamp' because at night all that can be seen in its blackness are the red eyes of watchful alligators, there is plenty of wildlife to see here. White ibis and snowy egrets, roseate spoonbills, herons, pelicans, eagles, owls, warblers and woodpeckers live here in abundance, together with a multitude of underwater creatures, such as crawfish, shrimps, crabs and catfish.

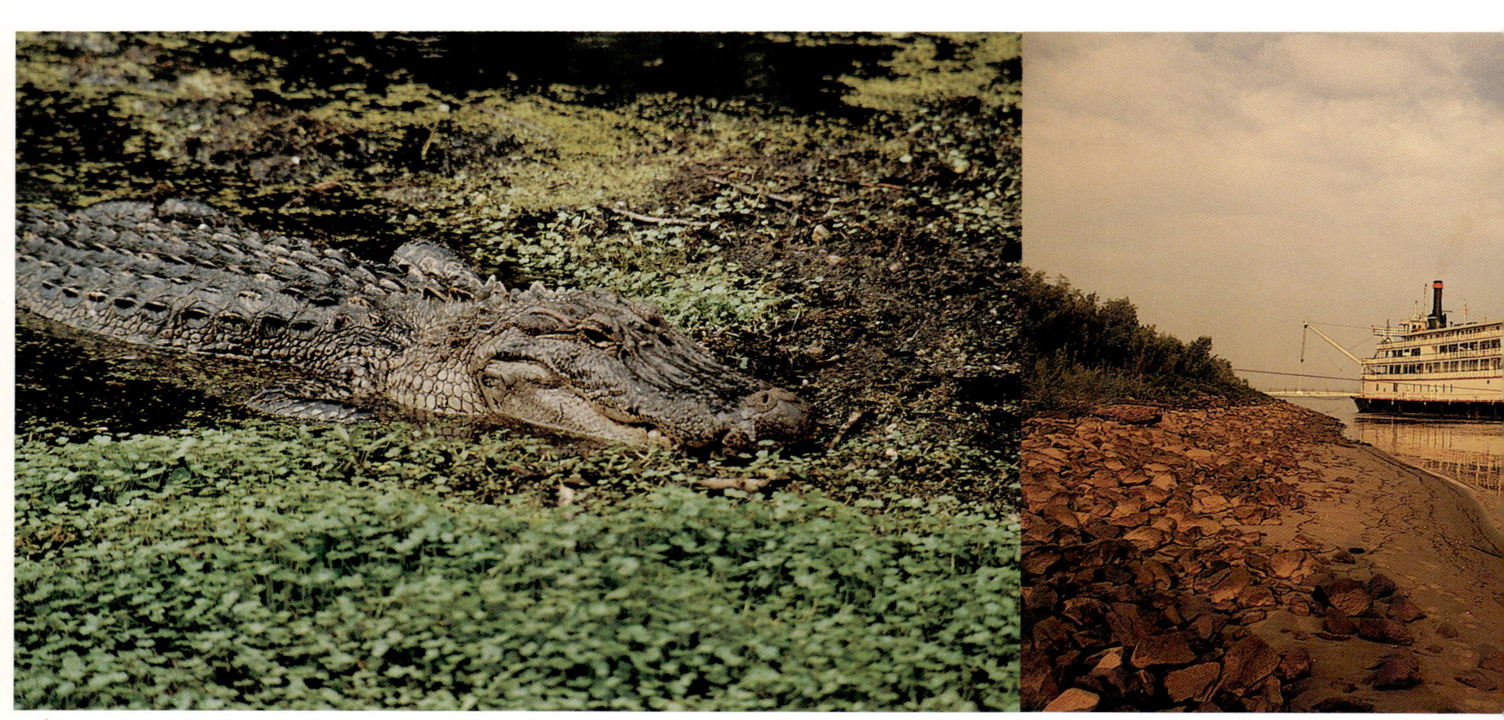

Partly camouflaged in the swamp, the American alligator, alligator mississipiensis, *keeps a keen hooded eye out for potential danger or dinner.*

The steamboat ties up on the levee, the protective river embankment of this wide and deep flowing river.

'THE BELL RINGS, THE WHEELS STOP; THEN THEY TURN BACK, CHURNING THE WATER TO FOAM, AND THE STEAMER IS AT REST.'

Mark Twain

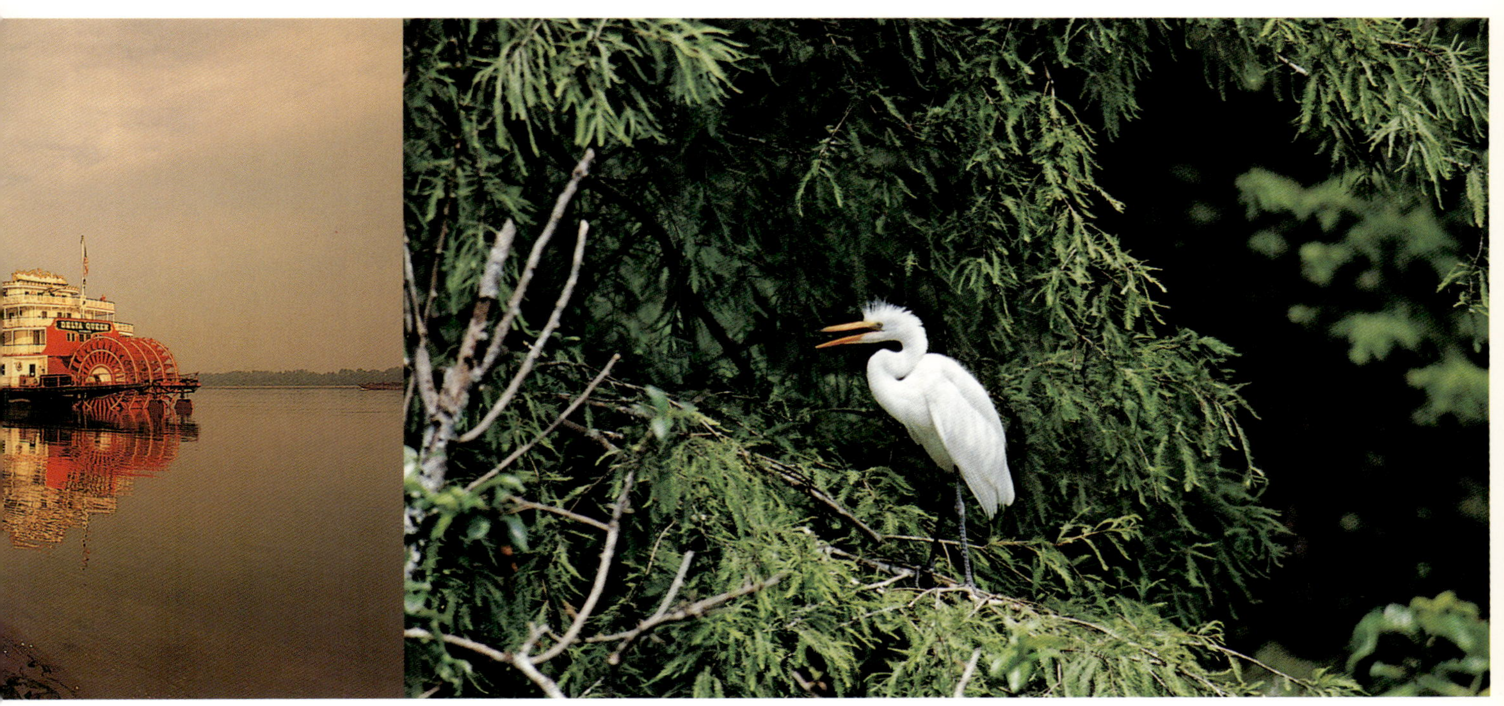

Each day's cruising on the majestic Mississippi presented new sights.

Sometimes, watching the passing river from the dining room window over a leisurely breakfast, the alert observer was rewarded with the sight of a lazily swimming alligator, moving slowly past the Delta Queen as though it too had a charted course to keep in the shipping lanes of this constantly busy waterway.

No alligator dishes feature on the steamboat's extensive menu. The protected animal can be seen in the rivers and swamps of Louisiana, but not artfully arranged on a plate.

Live oak trees form a canopied approach to Oak Alley mansion.

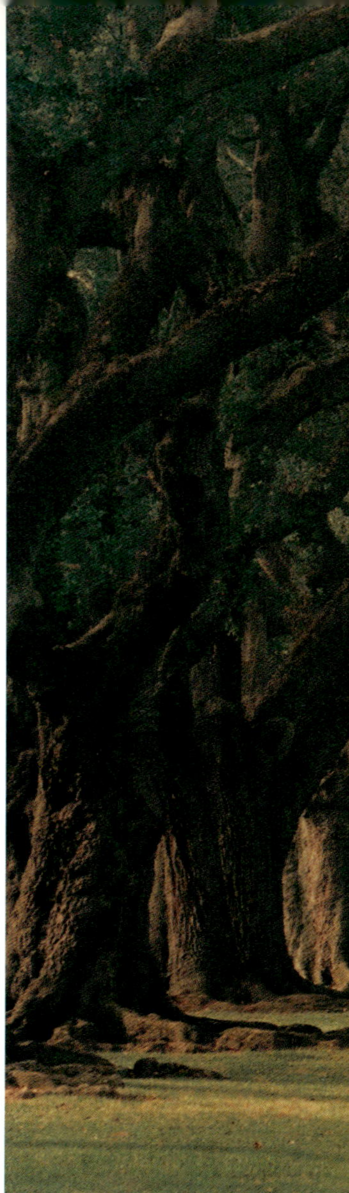

Another trademark tree of South Louisiana is the live oak, desired for both its shade and its durability. During the era of wooden ships live oak was used extensively by ship builders because of its hardness and strength Twenty-eight live oak trees planted over 300 years ago march from the Mississippi up to the antebellum (pre-American Civil War) mansion of Oak Alley plantation. The historic house was featured in the movie 'Interview with the Vampire', but of course was not really burned down – it was all done with Hollywood smoke and mirrors.

Spanish moss festoons many of the trees like old Christmas garlands. Many species of orchids and irises bloom in this temperate zone, as do magnolias. Redolent of hot nights and white shoulders of southern belles, the magnolia is the state flower of Louisiana. Dogwood and pecan trees are at home here too.

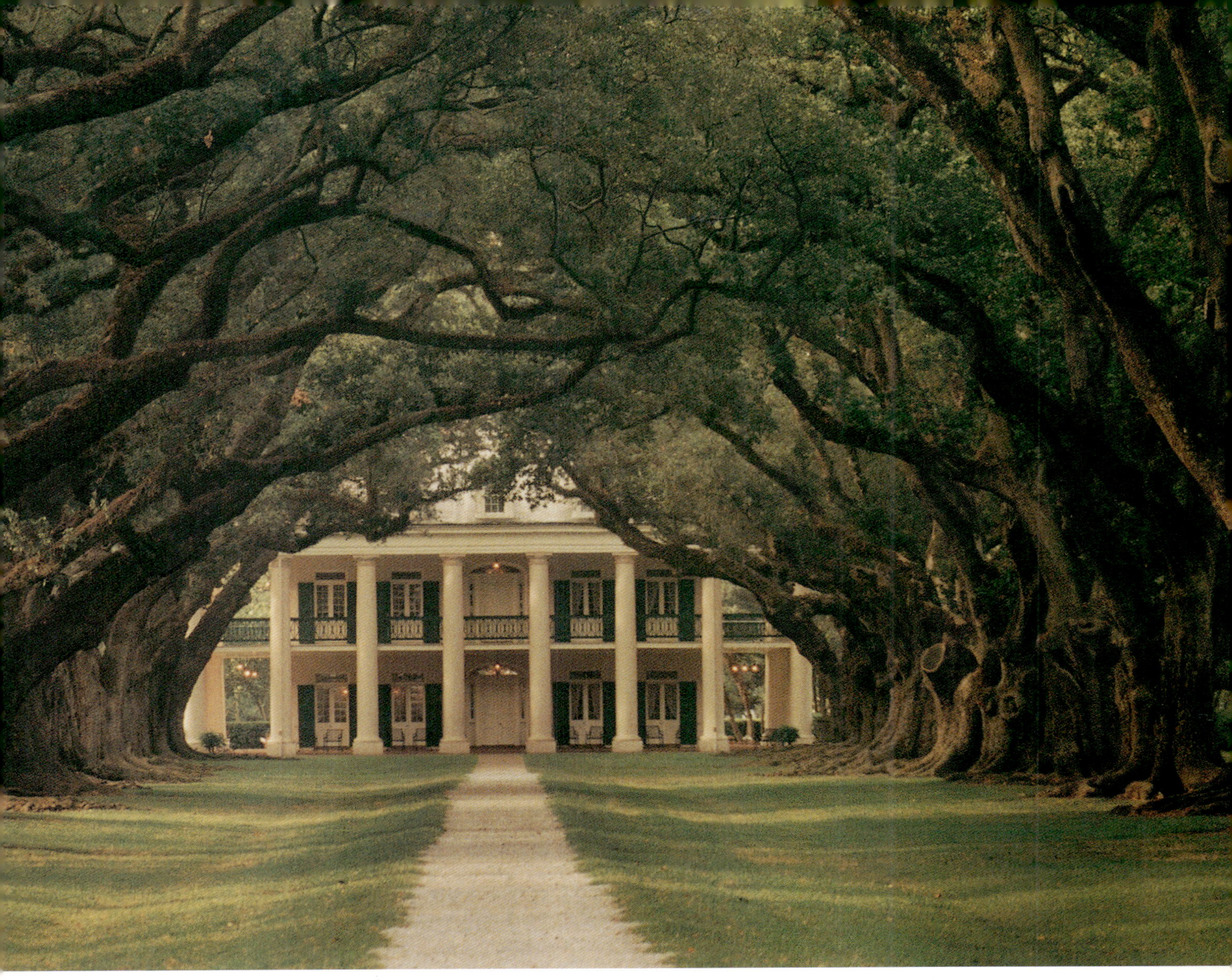

'FROM BATON ROUGE TO NEW ORLEANS, THE GREAT SUGAR PLANTATIONS BORDER BOTH SIDES OF THE RIVER ALL THE WAY... AND NOW AND THEN YOU SEE A PILLARED AND PORTICOED GREAT-MANOR HOUSE, EMBOWERED IN TREES.'

Mark Twain, 'Life on the Mississippi' 1883

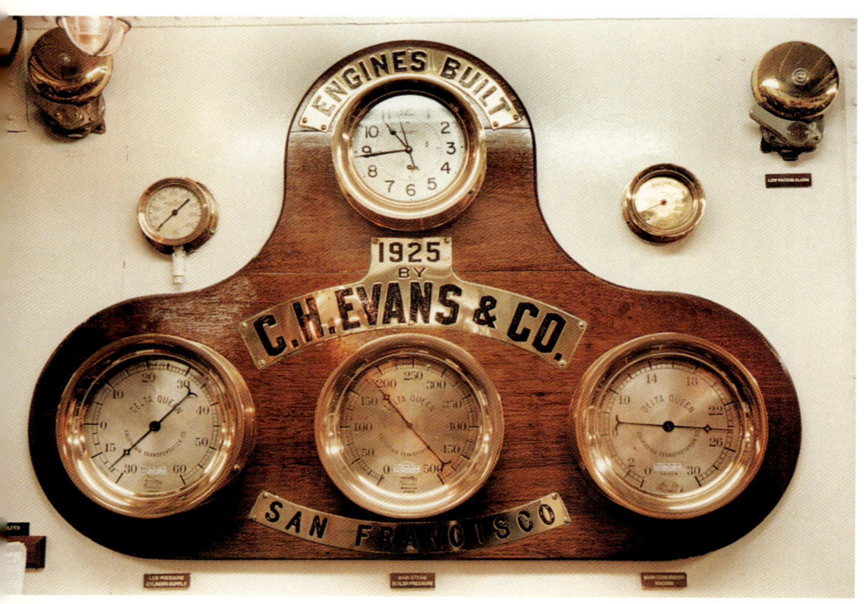

The fierce heat of an early and already record hot dry summer was felt even more down in the engine room. Open at all hours to visitors who would like a closer view of the 44-ton wooden paddlewheel, the sweltering climate in the engine room made one grateful for the air-conditioning above.

From the ebullient banjo and rollicking ragtime to Dixieland jazz, the music menu was a plentiful one. At the centre of attention was the guest Cajun band. The fiddler, accordionist and guitarist of the lively Mark de Basile Band played their spirited music to an enthusiastic audience who demanded encore after encore. The fiddle and accordion were the two main instruments that produced the irresistible toe-tapping music that grew from its original 'house music' to larger audiences in dance halls and on records. The guitar was added in to the mix, and Zydeco evolved as black musicians brought a blues element to Cajun music.

The silence of old-fashioned steam power rather than the din of diesel, and just cruising on a slow boat on a smooth river both contribute to a soothing experience. Although the Delta Queen's average speed is 6mph (9.6kmh), time seemed to speed by from New Orleans to Baton Rouge and back.

'WE HAD A DELIGHTFUL TRIP IN THAT THOROUGHLY WELL-ORDERED STEAMER, AND REGRETTED THAT IT WAS ACCOMPLISHED SO SPEEDILY.'

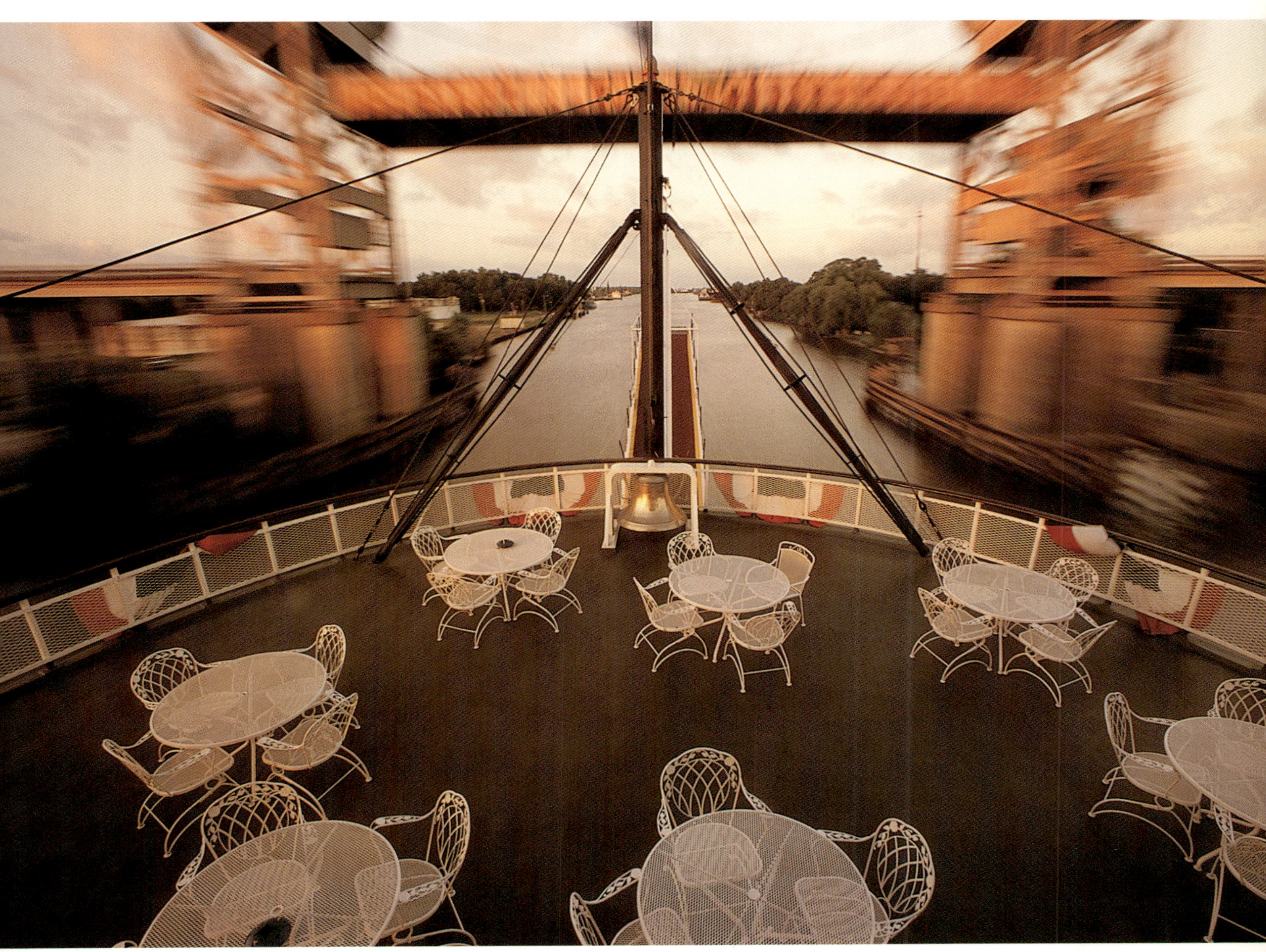

The Delta Queen Steamboat Company | Robin Street Wharf | 1380 Port of New Orleans Place | New Orleans | Louisiana | United States of America

t: + 1 504 586 0631 or 0800 543 1949 | www.deltaqueen.com

The Experience Music Project
and the Space Needle.

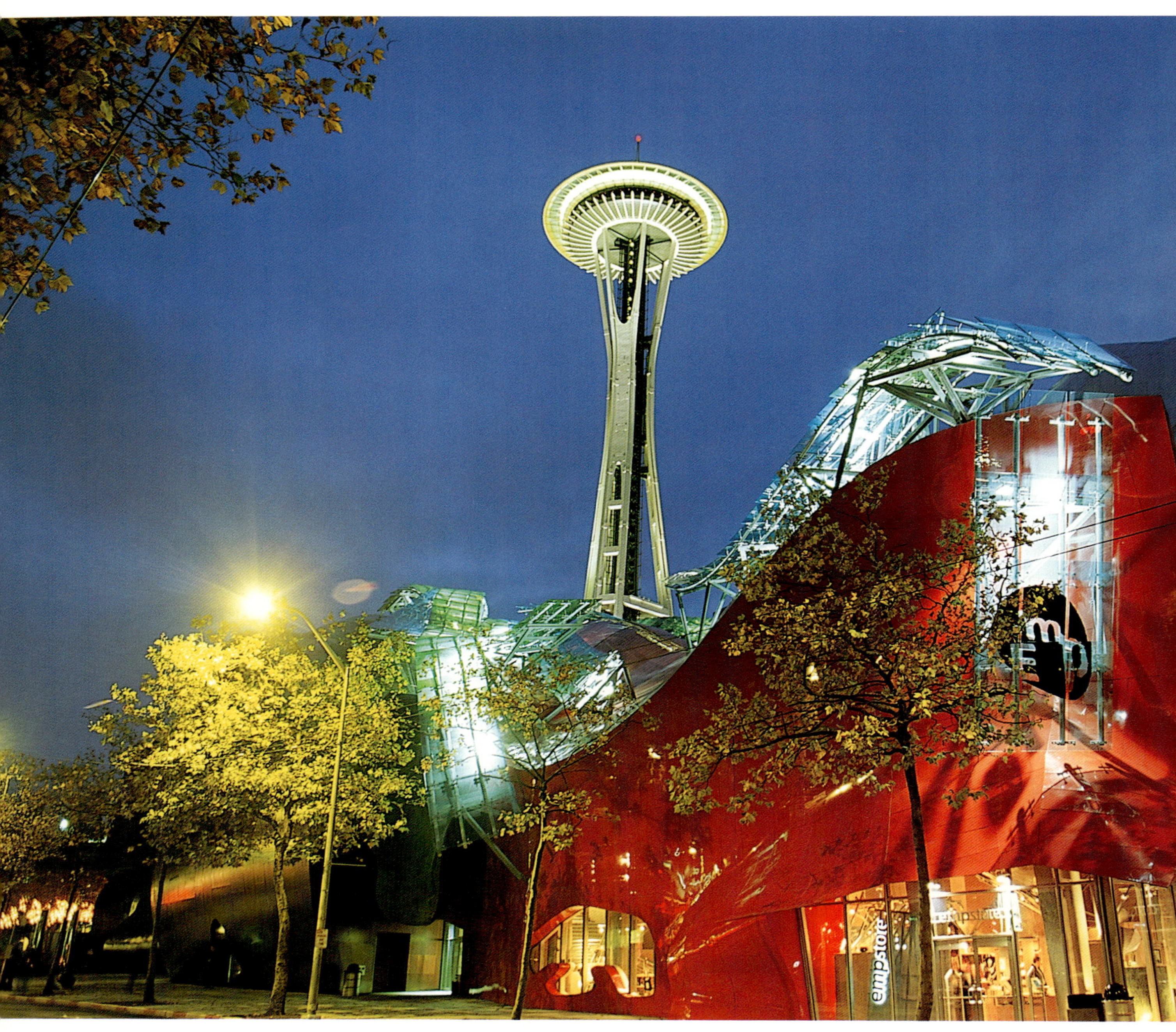

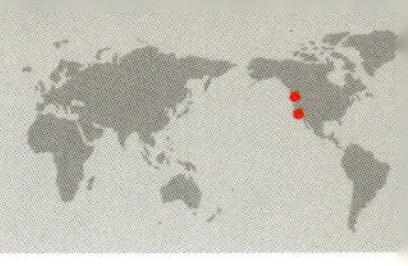

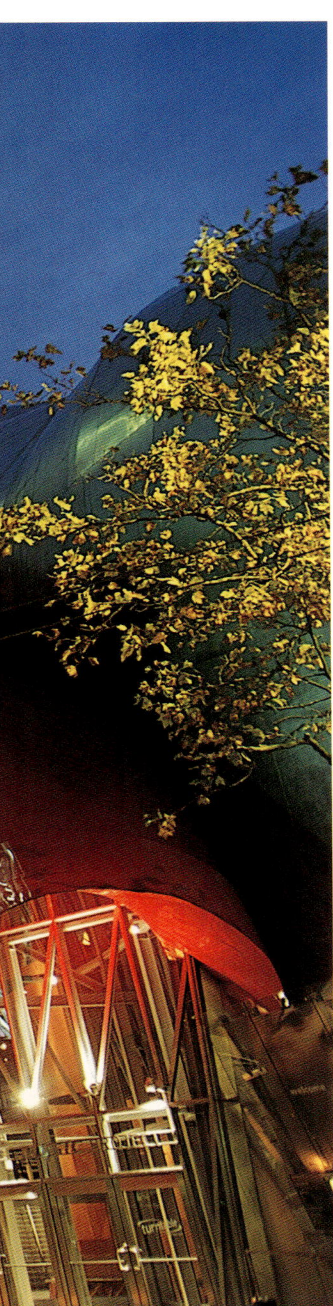

Making Tracks...

The Coast Starlight train, Seattle to Los Angeles, United States of America

The air is invigorating in Seattle, delivered fresh off the sea. It's from this energetic city that we will leave to head south, on the Coast Starlight, bound for Los Angeles.

Before our departure we got high, riding to the top of the Space Needle, built for the 1962 Seattle World Fair and suitably painted in cosmic colours of astronaut white, orbital olive, re-entry red and galaxy gold. From the observation deck, 184 metres above the ground, we looked way down on the city buildings and the bay, basking in another clear day.

Reclining at the foot of the sleek silver tower is the curvaceous multi-coloured bulk of the Experience Music Project. Designed by star architect Frank Gehry – his brief to achieve a 'swoopy' look, loosely based on smashed guitars – the sculpted building houses an interactive rock 'n' roll museum, where you can view rock artefacts as well as mix music and perform on virtual stages. Here you can experience the ecstasy of being a pop music star, without the agony of tedious pre-fame effort. To the screams of adoring fans on a video, you can play guitar, drums and keyboards pre-programmed to make you sound good. You have to deal with how you look. You can jam along with other visitors, and listen to solos by music legends before strapping on a guitar and being instrumental yourself. This is a very cool, more hip version of karaoke.

After you have been almost famous, you can pay homage to the '56 Fender Stratocaster used by Eric Clapton to play his guitar anthem 'Layla', see the biggest collection of Jimi Hendrix memorabilia, and more. In this hallowed hall, the significance of Bob Dylan, Janis Joplin, Jimi Hendrix and many others in the American rock fraternity is explained visually and aurally. Old and young rockers can and do hang out here, permanently in the groove.

After our air guitar gig, it was time to move from soundtracks to railway tracks and join the express down to Los Angeles.

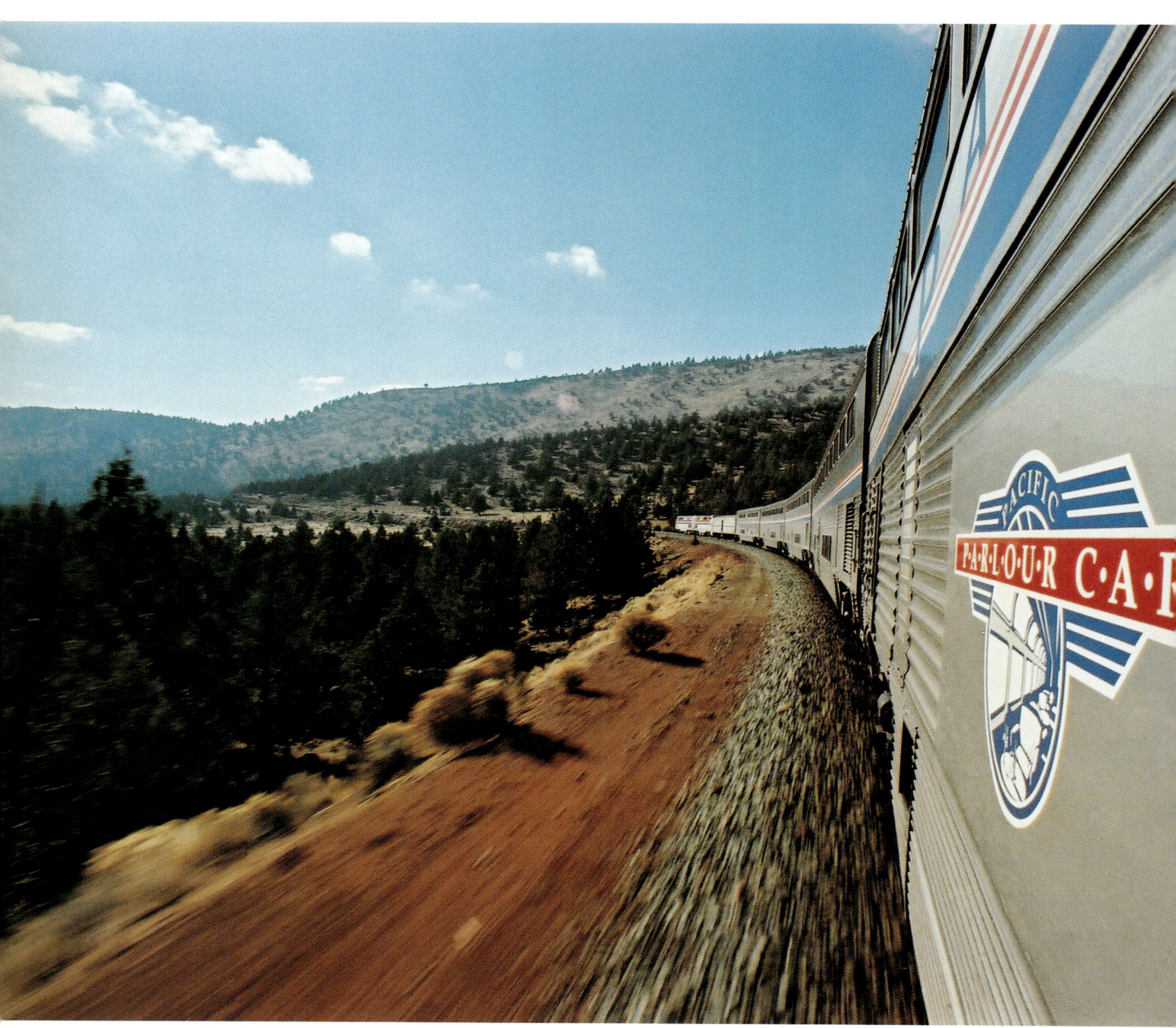
PACIFIC
P·A·R·L·O·U·R

The dual level cars of the Coast Starlight's Superliner coaches give passengers a heightened view of the terrain and a smooth ride – there's no rock 'n' roll on this trip.

The journey is two full days with one night on board, travelling 1389 miles through three states on one of the most scenic train routes in the United States. While you can choose to travel coach class and sleep in your comfortable seat, the sleeping cars offer a more luxurious experience. Here you have a choice of cabins, all with comfortable seats that turn into comfortable beds. The selection of sleeping accommodation of course varies in space and price, from the Standard bedroom, for one or two people – and if two, then at least one should be quite small – to the Deluxe with sofa, armchair and private bathroom included, or the Family Bedroom. Attendants make up the beds at night and remake them in the morning, which is just as well, as this seems to require folding skills similar to those needed for origami.

Travelling on the Coast Starlight sets me to wondering why an aeroplane can't be more like a train, with spaces to stretch out in when you're not in your seat. For example, a sitting room like the Pacific Parlour Car, a lounge for sleeping car passengers. This is a pleasant place to read, join a wine tasting, or perhaps listen discreetly to others' conversation. You can even observe the passing landscape. That there is much talking, playing cards, and pastimes other than watching from the window, means that this is as much a social experience for many travellers as a journey from one point to another.

Passengers can watch movies in the cinema if they are more interested in virtual scenery, or to pass the time after it's too dark to see the real sights. Another place to visit is the Sightseer Lounge with its wrap-around domed windows and swivel armchairs. The choice of several alternative locations on board is very appealing. Knowing that it is possible to move around and sit elsewhere makes travelling on this train most agreeable.

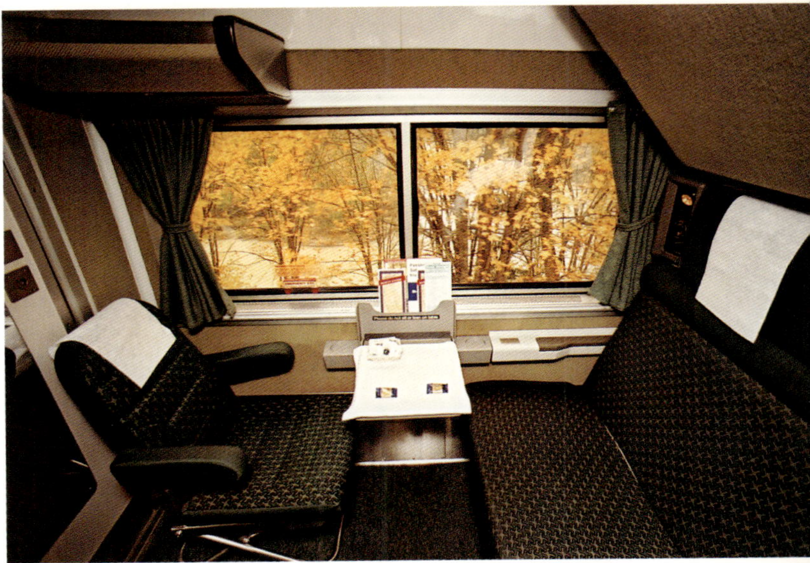

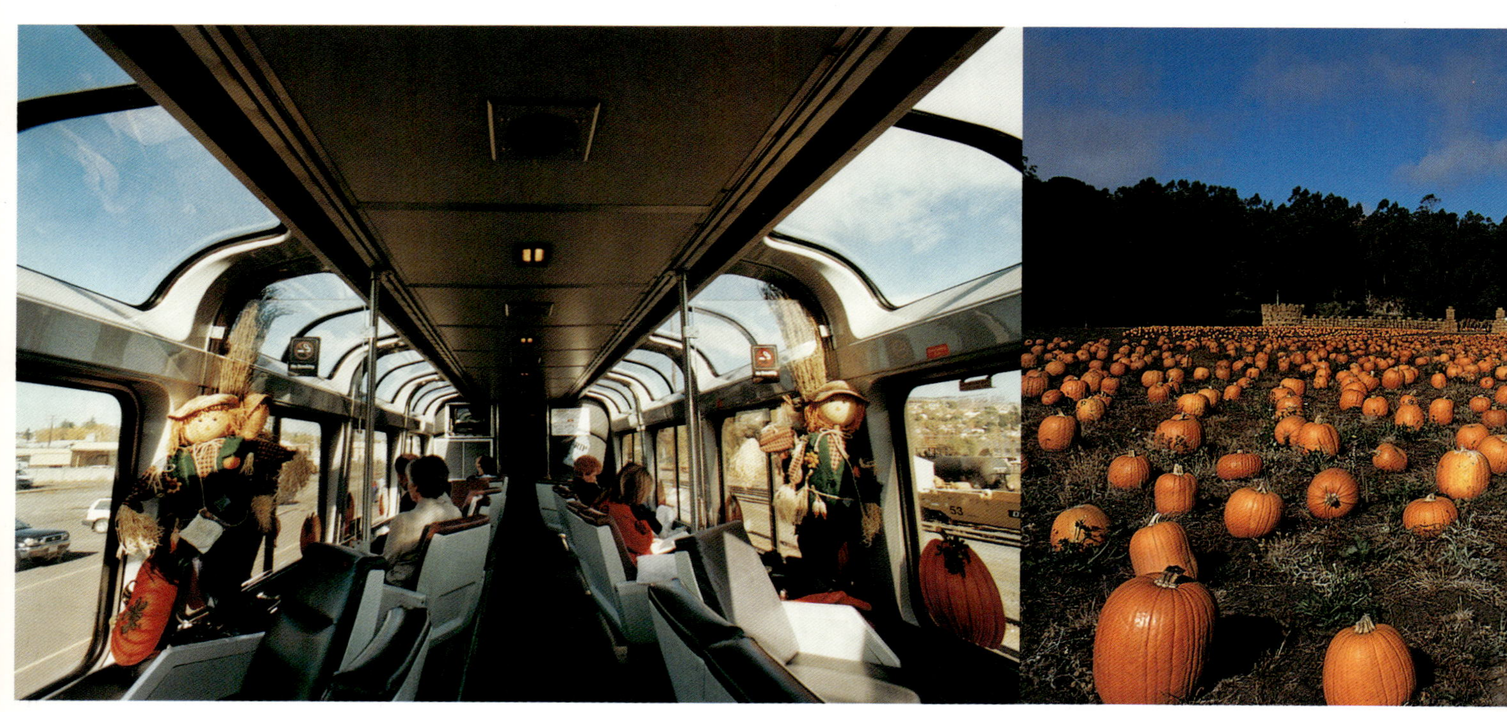

At first we wondered about the standard of housekeeping on this train. Spiders and cobwebs were woven over the table flowers; indeed a tangled web seemed to be the standard ornamentation all over the train. Then we realised we were on the Hallowe'en 'cruise'. Ghoulish faces at the windows were not ghosts, but gruesome decorations celebrating the scare festival of Hallowe'en, enthusiastically embraced in America and elsewhere. The frightful festivities culminate on the night of October 31st. Pumpkins are in hunting season.

Retail sales of Hallowe'en products in North America alone are frightening; billions of dollars are spent buying costumes and candy. The trick or treat time is not only for children, many adults don costumes for the night, rated one of the year's top three party occasions. Arriving in Seattle on Hallowe'en, we were confronted with streets full of costumed grown-ups, playing on the streets in weird disguises. This would have been a shock to a visitor ignorant of Hallowe'en, who might think that the city was populated by gruesome beings, outcast from normal society and forced to roam about, scary and sleepless in Seattle.

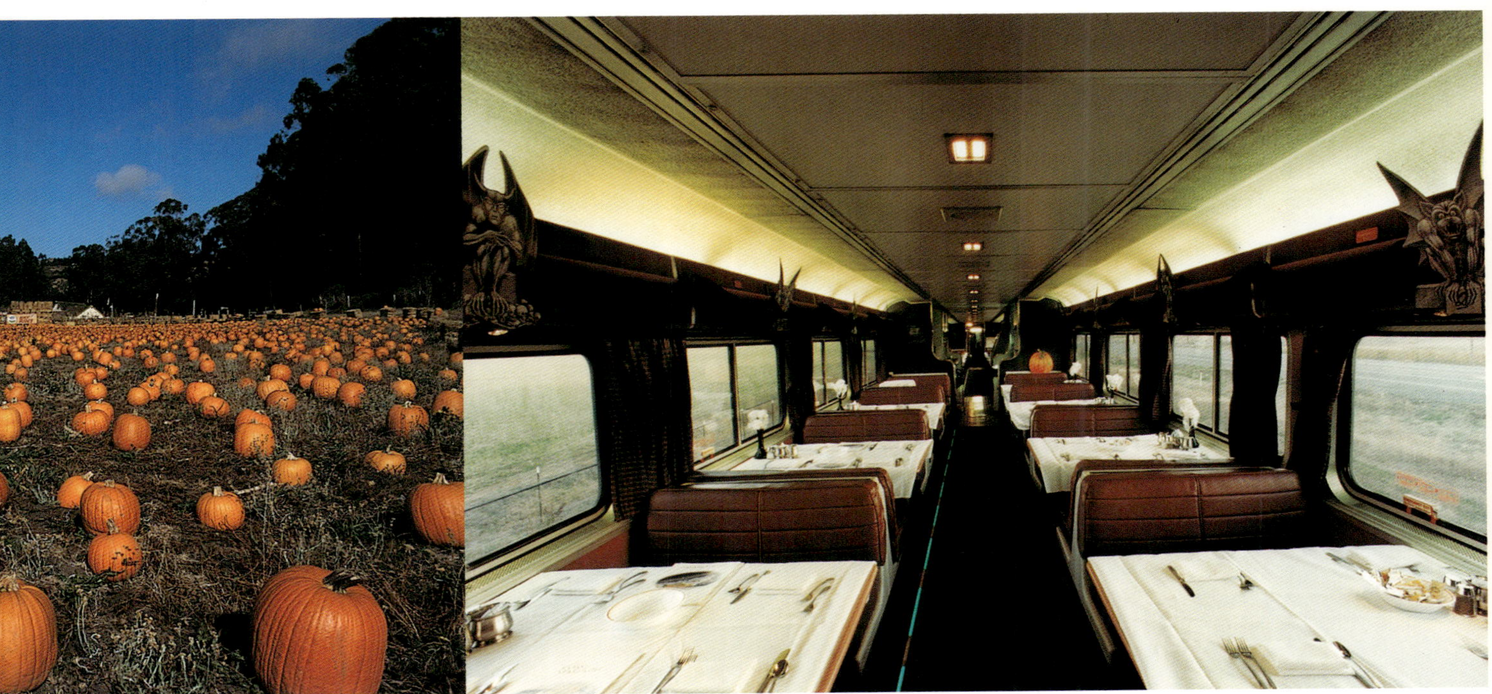

Despite the dread-ful decorations in the dining car, the food was reassuringly sensible. A simple grilled salmon sandwich, salad and a glass of local wine made a satisfyingly tasty lunch. You can have your meals delivered to your seat or sleeper. However, eating in the dining car is a sure way to meet your fellow voyagers. Our dining companions were mostly retired Americans seeing their country at a leisurely pace, and their easy mannered sociability made each mealtime an enjoyable experience.

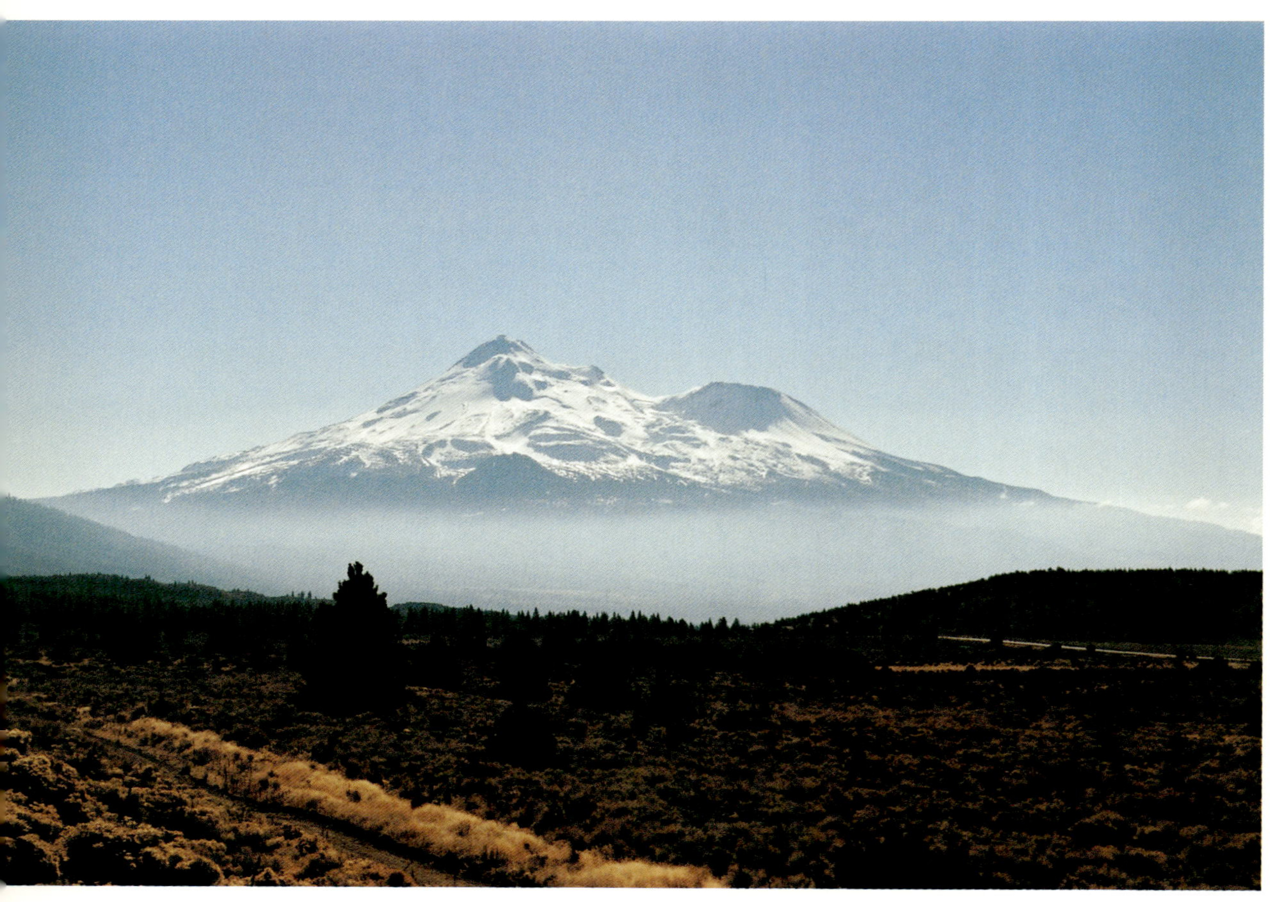

Mount Shasta.

In the foothills of the Cascades mountain range, our journey became a non-moving experience for some twelve hours. Our lack of locomotion was caused by a freight train breakdown on the steep hillside ahead. The stricken train had 182 cars, of which only two could be moved at one time, requiring the rescue locomotive to make 91 trips to move it out of the way. This meant a temporary sidelining of the Coast Starlight, and an extra night spent stationary, sleeping on the train. However, the upside was that we saw views normally hidden in the darkness of overnight travel. The downside was for the crew, dealing with the complicated logistics of working out new onward connections for many passengers.

For many miles, once we are on the move again, the chief view in the windowframe is of Mount Shasta, one of the most spectacular mountains in the United States. Covered in snow most of the year, its recent volcanic past is evidenced by the lava flows visible from the train. Its demeanour now is a demure one, picture perfect in the brilliant sunshine.

Forests, mountains, plains and shoreline flash by, revealing vignettes of American landscape and life, much like a flick-book telling its rapid visual story. From the window it's very much a 'now you see it, now you don't' experience, with sights often passed too quickly to be pointed out to others. From baseball players running on a field, people cruising in houseboats on rivers, to rows of campervans lined up to the view on a coastal cliff road and long lines of automobiles and mammoth trucks hauling goods on the freeways, the curious spectator's gaze is always rewarded.

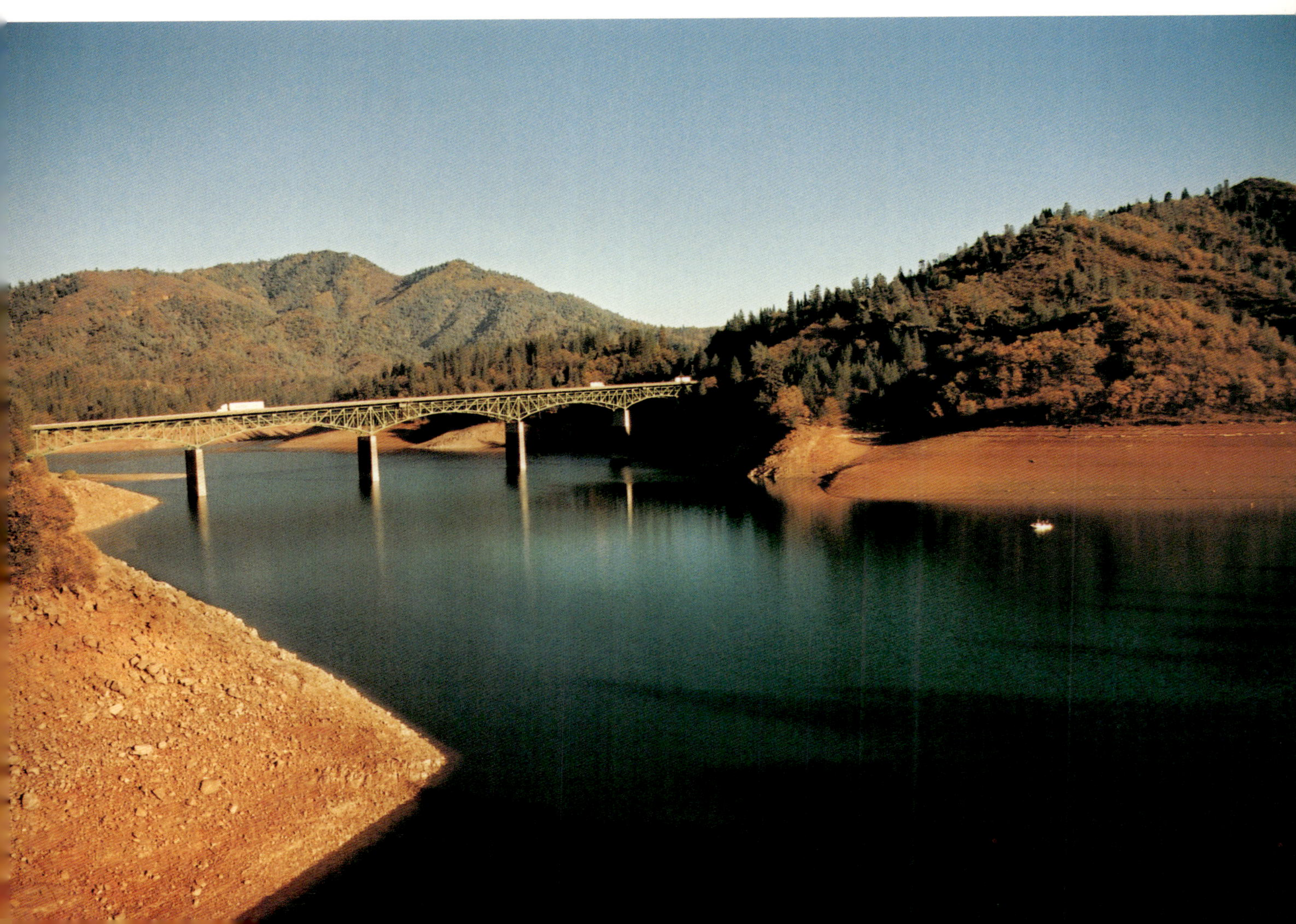

For the train passenger, there is no need to hurry. As if there were, there is 'coffee to go,' available from the Parlour Car and café, but here you can sit down with your cup and watch the world rush by as you drink and don't drive. Train travel means you can do nothing with license.

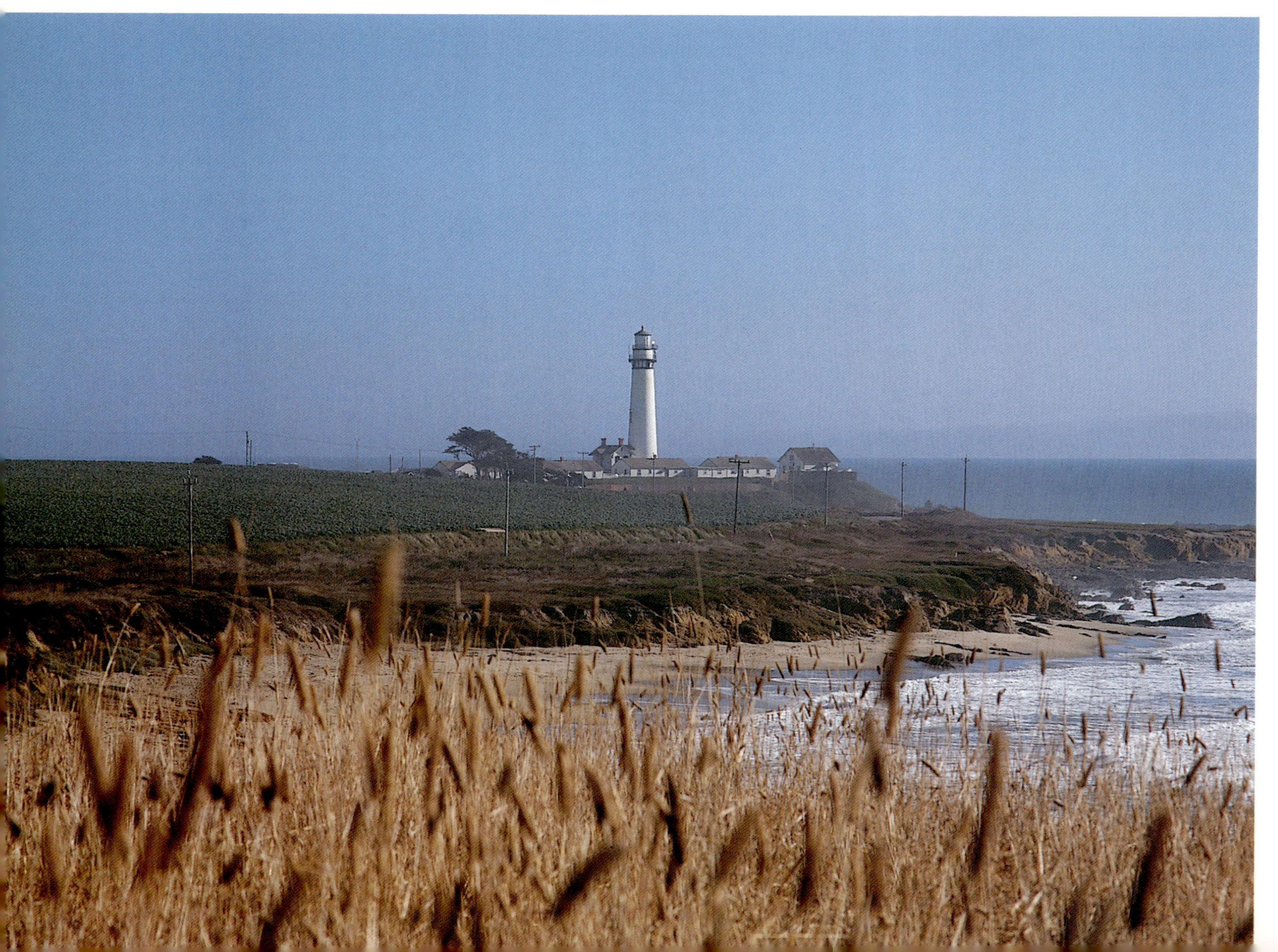

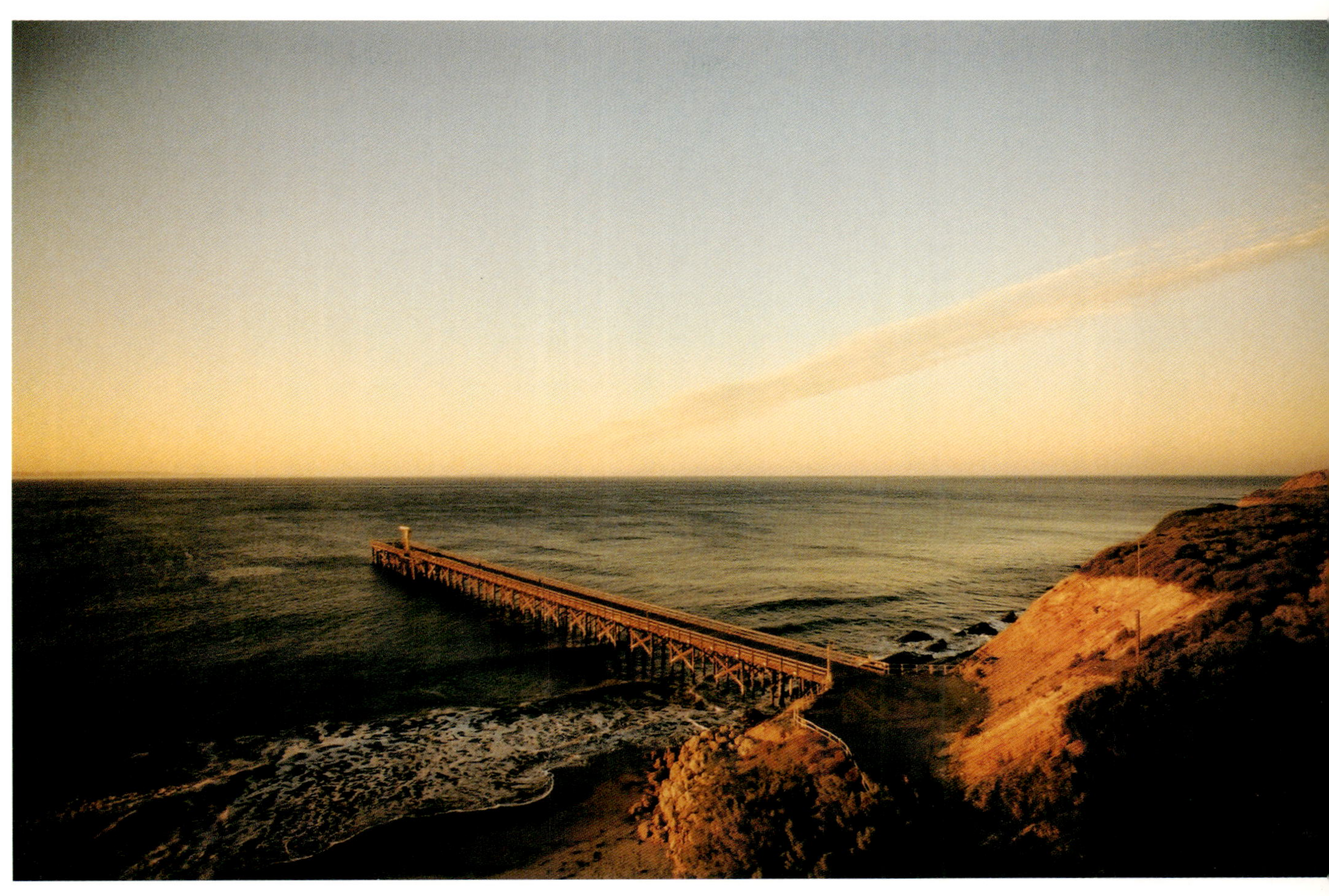

After an early morning arrival in San Luis Obispo, we head towards the California Coast. The train is often tracking parallel to Highway 101, one of the best drives in America, from San Francisco to Los Angeles. This is a far less stressful way to travel it. 'Go by train', the old advertising line, could truthfully be extended by the phrase 'and get there calm'. We didn't see or hear anyone on mobile phones, or hunched over laptop computers. This is a trip for the leisurely classes, not those in a hurry, who are no doubt flying overhead.

On a dazzlingly clear day, we have our first sight of the Pacific Ocean, like an enormous swimming pool, edged with golden beaches and palm trees. The Californian landscape and climate of dreams and films becomes real.

Point Conception lighthouse, bathed in the golden light of California.

Arrival is at the ageing, but still elegant, Los Angeles Union Railway station.

The impressive entrance hall, with its soaring ceiling and arched windows, and rows of roomy leather seats, is a favoured movie location. Opened in 1939, the station was where most people first arrived in this city, stepping down from a train, until air travel and airports took precedence. For a time the railway station declined, but now, according to a notice in the foyer, it is being 'rehabilitated'. A blend of Spanish and Art Deco style, its forthcoming facelift will, with any luck, restore rather than remove its best features.

A sense of anticipation must have risen, and no doubt still does rise, in the hearts of the newly arrived hopefuls attracted here to what has become a city of dreams. Directly across the road from the station is part of the original village, El Pueblo de Nuestra Senora de Los Angeles, founded in 1781.

Somehow it seems less stressful arriving at train stations than at airport terminals. Perhaps it is because stations are smaller than airports, in most cases, and as train stations are usually in or near the centre of a town, one's arrival seems to be somehow more accomplished.

Our leisurely trip on the Coast Starlight makes us to contemplate taking other train journeys, to see more states. Another time we may board the Empire Builder, or the California Zephyr, Heartland Flyer or the Texas Eagle; all good evocative names that the Amtrak Company has chosen for the trains it runs around America.

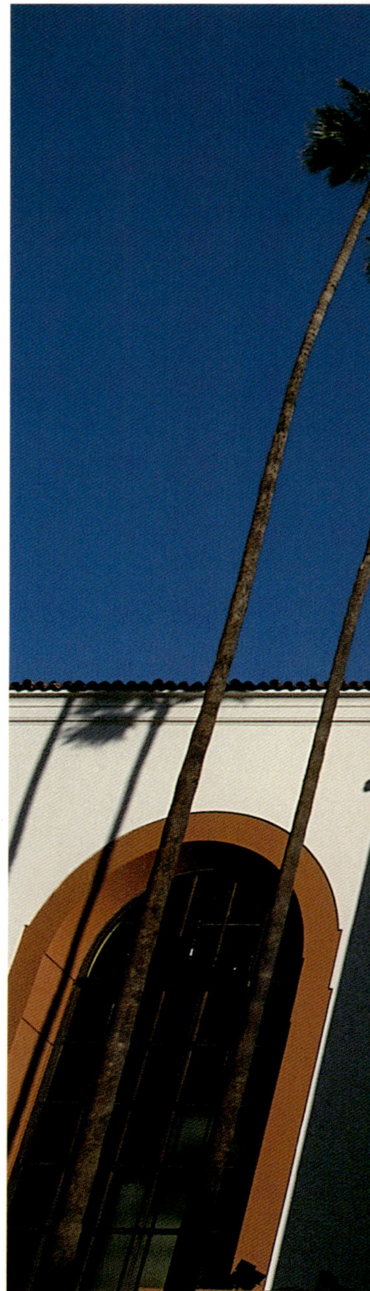

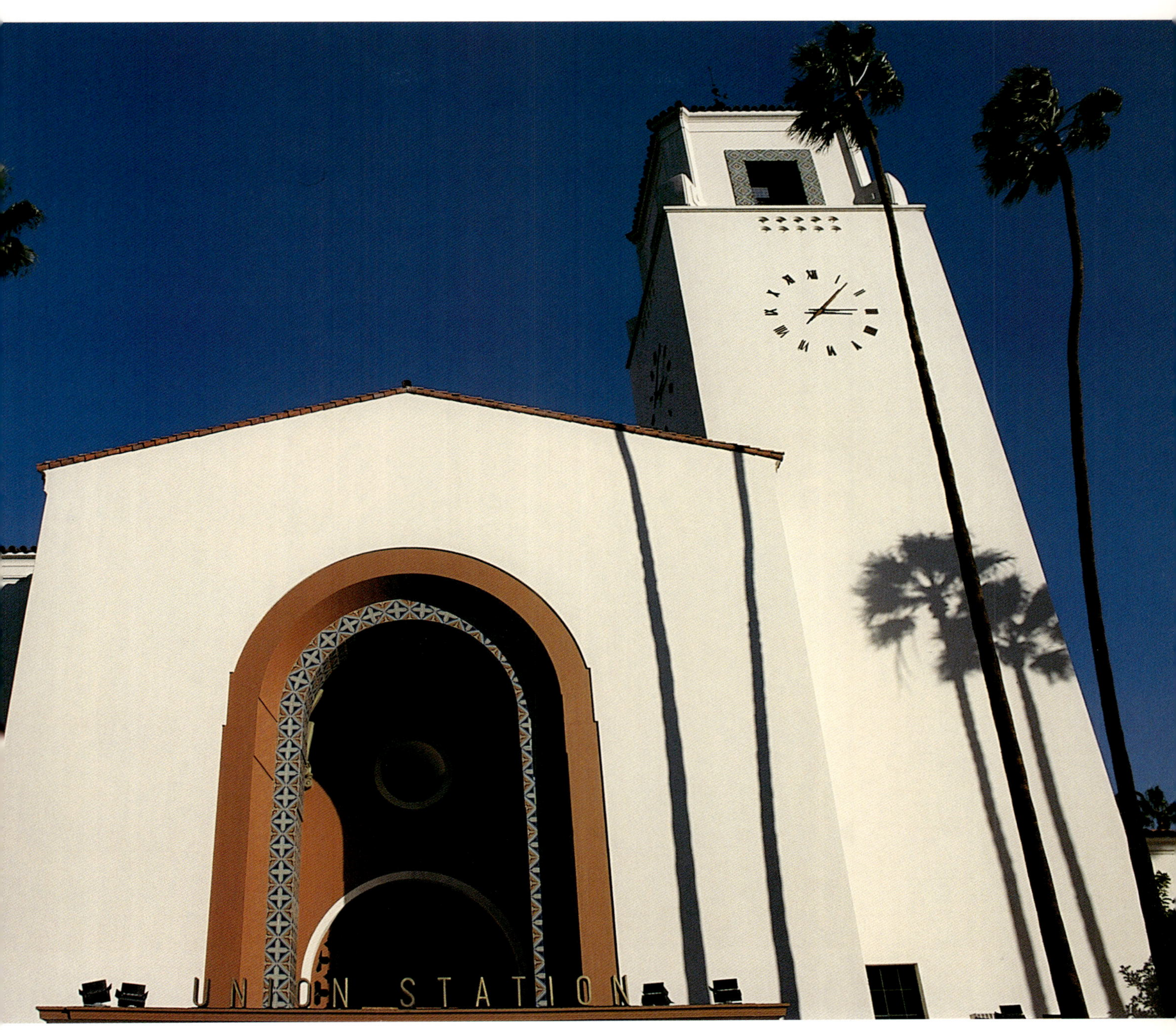

The Coast Starlight	*Travels daily from Seattle to Los Angeles, and vice-versa*	*www.amtrak.com*

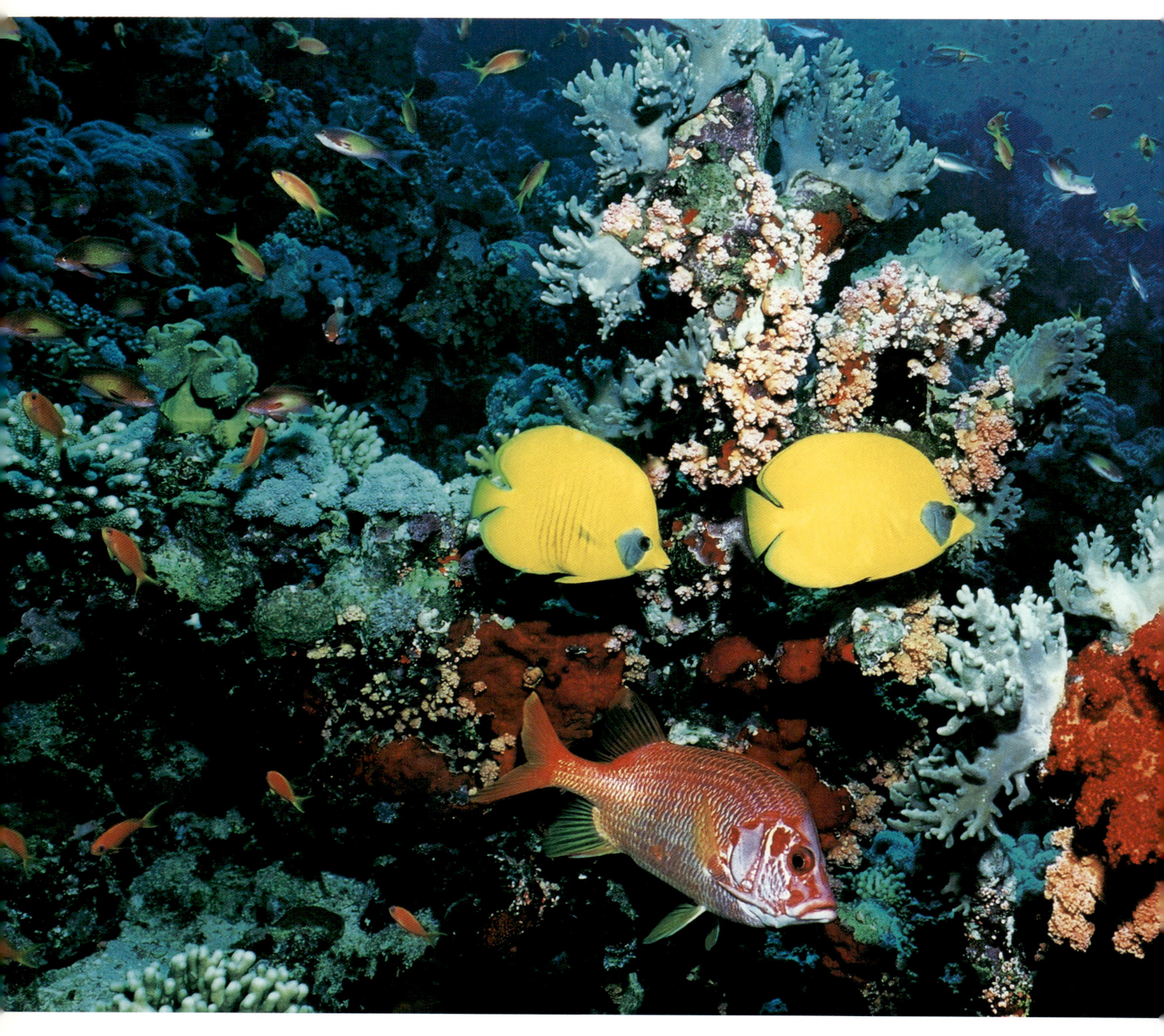

IS THIS AN AQUARIUM IN REVERSE,
WHERE HUMANS ARE THE SPECIES ON DISPLAY FOR THE FISH?

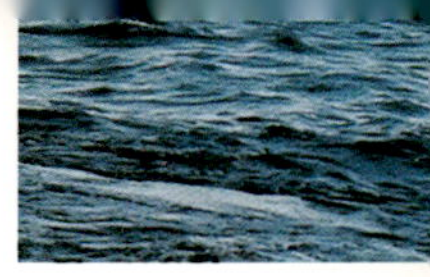

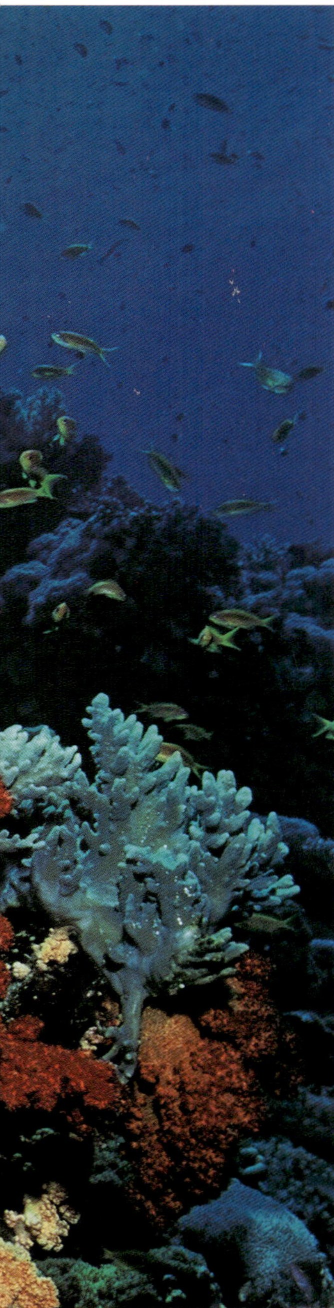

Going Down, Under...

The Poseidon tourist submarine, coming soon to an ocean near you

The silent underwater world beneath us is mapped and charted; yet few aquanauts and fewer tourists plumb its depths.

Although deep underwater is still a zone relatively free of leisure travellers, there are already over 40 tourist submarines that dive beneath the world's oceans. In the past decade, a fleet of contemporary submersibles has carried over 3.5 million people in comfort and safety, operating at locations in most of the world's major oceans and seas. Other than scuba diving, a ride aboard one of these vessels is the only way most people will ever directly experience the natural environment of the myriad inhabitants of the living coral reef.

Soon the mysterious marine universe will become new territory for travellers on underwater cruise ships.

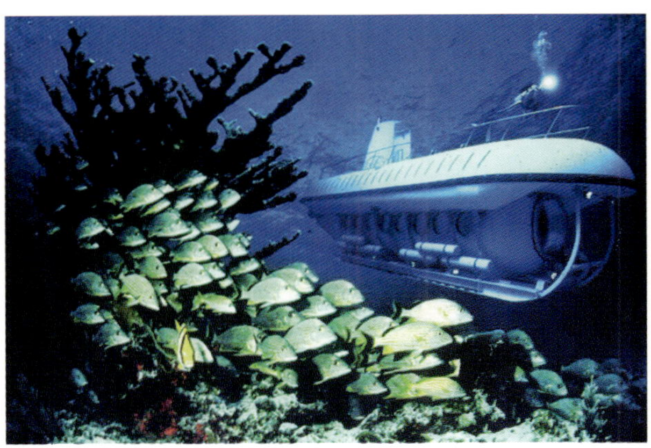

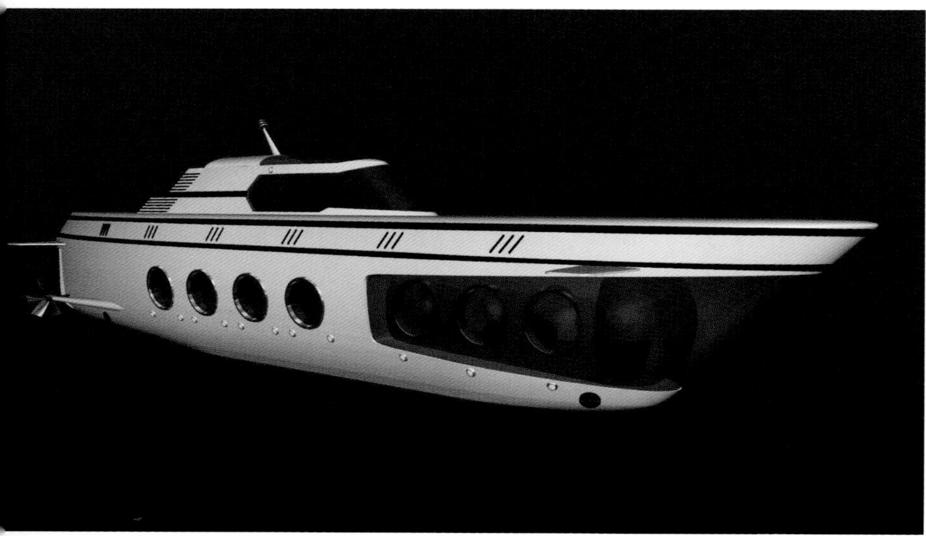

The Seattle 1000, described by designers US Submarines Inc as their 'megayacht of the deep'. With a length of 36 metres, and beam of 6.5 metres, the Seattle has a cruising range of 3000 plus nautical miles, extensive enough for a transatlantic crossing. It can remain submerged for several days, and has an operating depth of 305 metres.

Interiors of some of the luxury submarines on the drawing boards now will rival those of the finest super yachts, providing private staterooms with ensuite bathrooms, and spacious living and dining rooms. Passengers will voyage in air-conditioned comfort in interiors maintained at surface pressure, regardless of diving depth. And unlike surface yachts, when the surface going gets rough, the submarine can descend into the smooth quiet undersea environment, continuing on to its destination. Extended cruising capability will give passengers the opportunity to explore a multitude of sub sea environments, and marvel at the abundance and diversity of life underwater.

When the luxury 86m (286ft) submarine Poseidon is launched in the Caribbean Sea sometime soon, some 72 passengers will embark on a two-day cruise, staying overnight on the ocean floor in spacious staterooms, dining on meals prepared by top chefs, and relaxing in a large lounge viewing the seascape through observation portholes 3m (8ft) in diameter. Crewed by a staff of 40, with a support ship on the surface, and surrounded by luxury, the submarine's fortunate occupants will be able to eat, drink and sleep underwater, while having an unsurpassed view of the undersea world from panoramic viewports. "Suddenly, brilliant underwater lights illuminate the darkness. Within moments the sea life, attracted by the brightness, pirouettes in front of the viewport. Squid, shrimp and large pelagic fish dance from light to shadow."

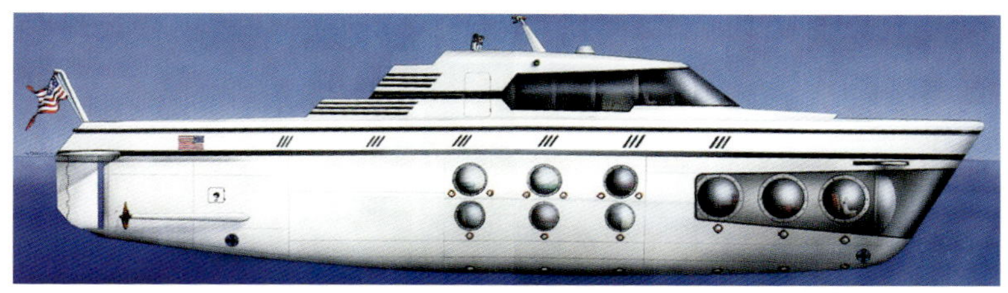

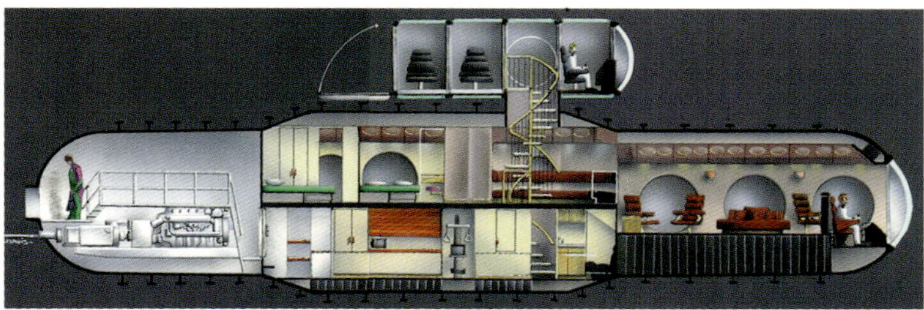

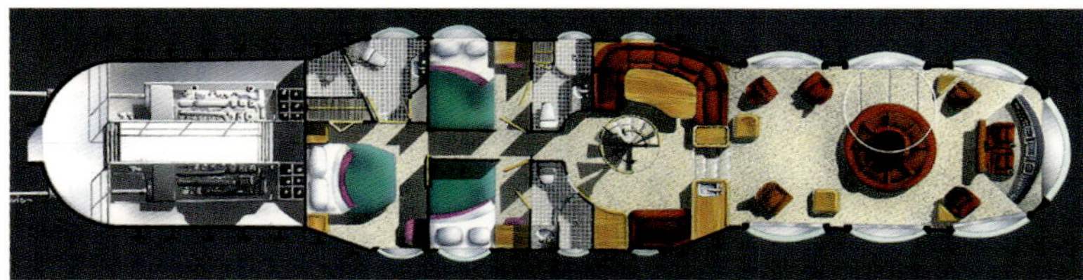

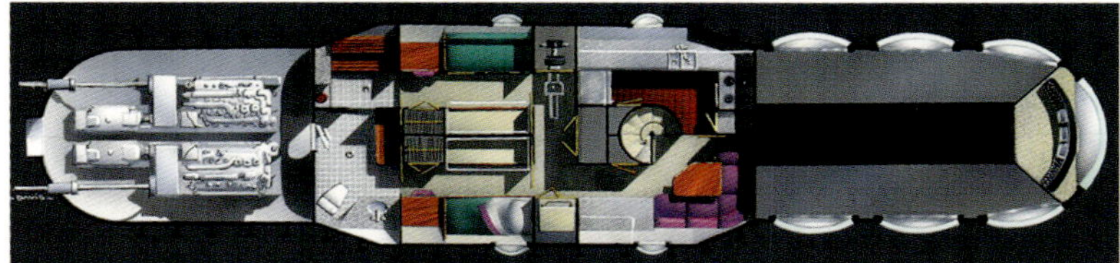

In these graphics, the private staterooms with ensuite baths, spacious living and dining rooms as well as crew quarters and galley can be seen. Virtually every room has a viewport, and the main lounge is surrounded by viewports 2.3m (6ft) in diameter, for an optimum ocean outlook.

Poseidon's premium accommodations and service will provide the ultimate five-star undersea vacation opportunity for many. The luxury submarine will spend a year based in each of the world's oceans and offer two-day cruises for an average ticket price of US$4600. Most of the trip will be spent submerged, diving to depths as great as 305 metres.

The wonders of the underwater world will be revealed – from the stunning soft corals in the South China Sea, the crystal clear waters and ancient shipwrecks of the Caribbean, to the profusion of Pacific Ocean reef fish and marine marvels of the Galapagos Islands.

US Submarines, Inc. | *Florida* | *United States of America* | *info@ussubs.com* | *www.ussubs.com*

Flying, Dreaming...

Sleeping on a skybed

A good night's sleep may well be one of the essential ingredients of a long and healthy life, together with a sensible diet and regular exercise. Many sleep researchers believe that the busy day-to-night life we lead in our increasingly non-stop society is having a negative impact on the quality of our sleep, affecting our health and inhibiting many functions when we are awake.

And that's just on the ground. Up in the sky, at an altitude of 35,000 feet, millions of people cruise across the globe every year. For most of us, a long distance flight is not something to be enjoyed, rather an experience to be endured. The journey usually alters our sleep patterns, putting our circadian rhythms out of kilter, sometimes for days. We don't feel properly rested, and blame it on jetlag, an unwelcome by-product of jet travel.

How much of the fatigue we feel after a long flight is due to crossing time zones, and how much is sleep deprivation, is difficult to decide. Before you go on a long trip, you usually stay up late packing, organising and tidying the house and then you probably leave early for the airport. Not many of us sleep well on planes, we are lucky if our eyes close for a few hours. The atmosphere in the cabin can be dehydrating, food, alcohol and caffeine is constantly served, and you get little, if any, exercise. So, when you feel tired as you tour around Sydney or Paris, who can say it is all because your clock is out of sync?

A jet aircraft is rarely regarded as a kind of flying hotel, although you may spend a night or more on board. There are usually hours of sitting in a seat with limited room or opportunity to move around. Lying down on a comfortable bed, what a weary traveller looks forward to at the end of the day, is only a flight of fantasy for most passengers. It is hard to believe that air travel was once considered glamorous.

In 1938, the Boeing 314 Clipper, the largest of the flying boats that spanned the oceans before World War II, epitomised elegance in air travel. Its 40 passengers were provided with sleeper berths, dressing rooms, a lounge, dining salon, and other luxurious facilities. And in the days before jet speed, the Boeing 377 Stratocruiser's passengers settled down in comfortable bunks for intercontinental flights. The Stratocruiser set a new standard for luxurious flying with its stylishly decorated extra-wide passenger cabin and gold-appointed dressing rooms. A circular staircase led to a lower-deck drinks lounge, and flight attendants prepared hot meals for 50–100 people in a state-of-the-art galley.

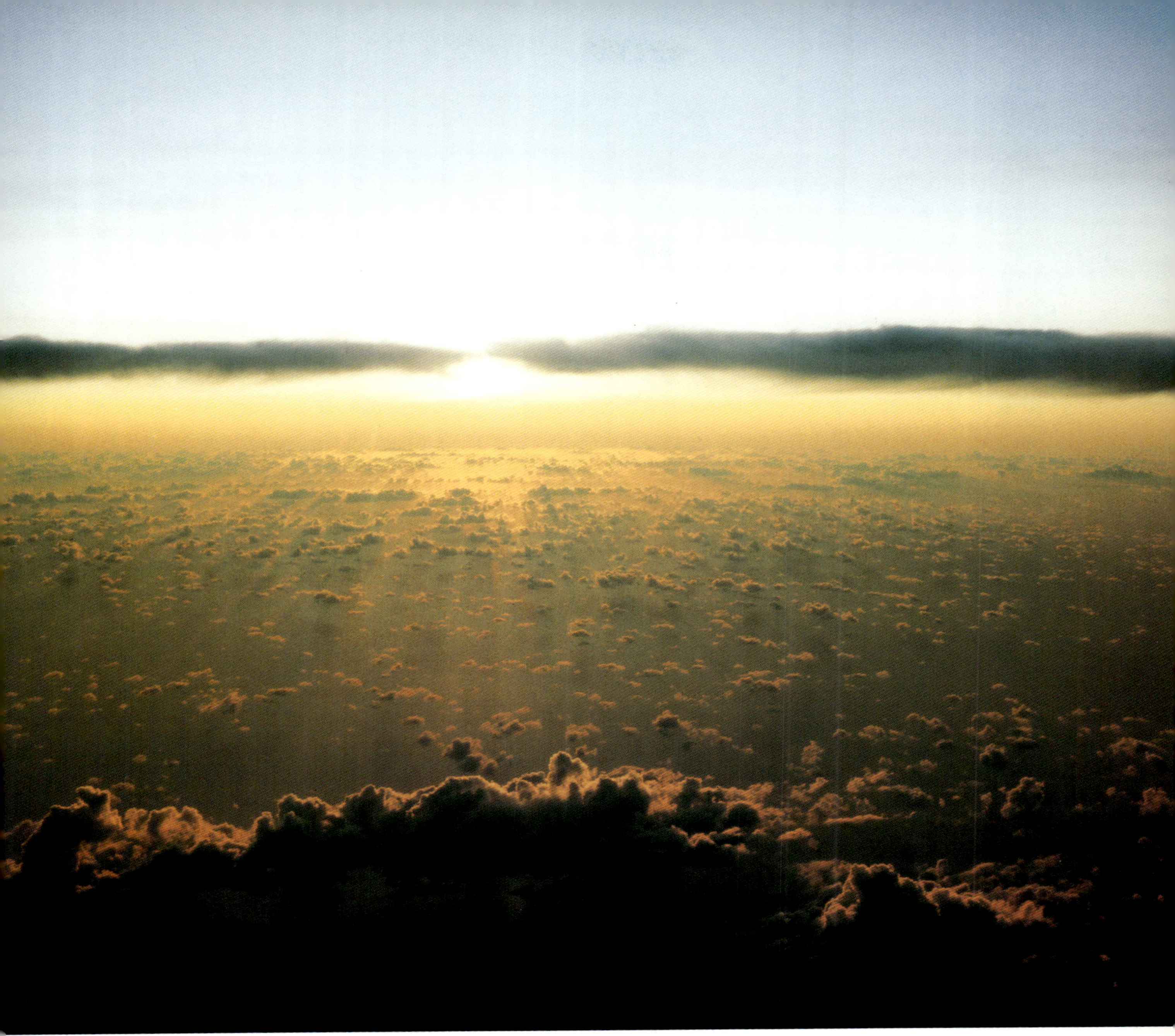

'WE ARE SUCH STUFF AS DREAMS ARE MADE ON,
AND OUR LITTLE LIFE IS ROUNDED BY SLEEP...'

William Shakespeare,
'The Tempest'

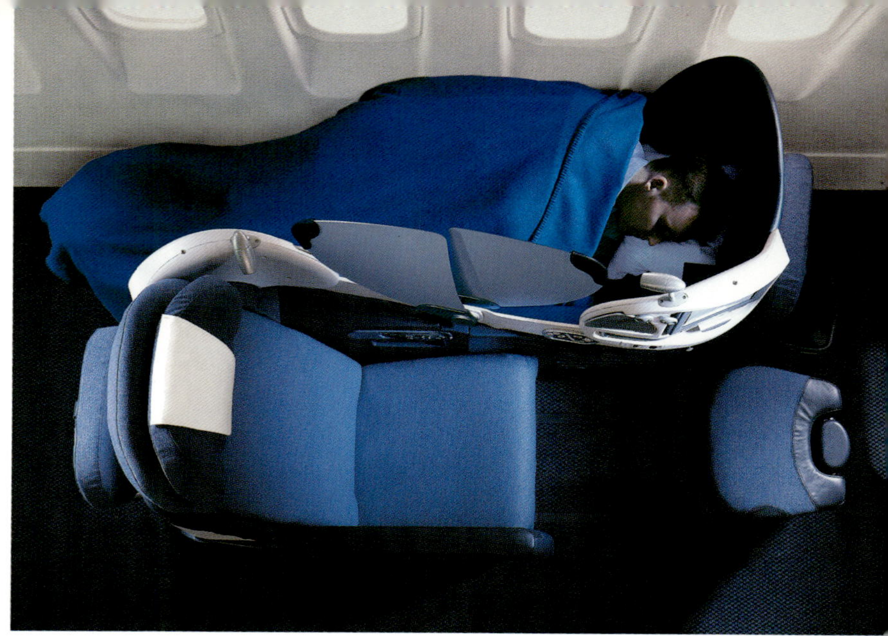

'TIRED NATURE'S SWEET RESTORER, BALMY SLEEP!'

First class sleep on British Airways.

That glamorous era ended. As more people could afford to fly, air travel and aircraft size grew at a fast pace. The main focus was on carrying as many passengers as possible. Comfort issues became less critical, especially in economy class. Although business class cabins had fewer people and seats had more room, sleeping was still in the chair.

However, for some time now, a truly flat bed in the sky has been a first class way to fly for the fortunate few. For example, British Airways has individual cabins with seats that convert to six foot six inch long beds. Passengers can choose whether to sleep, work, or relax in complete privacy at anytime during their journey. They can eat when it suits them; a snack or a five-course meal can be ordered at any time during the flight. Each cabin has a 'buddy' seat, so travellers can talk business with a colleague or dine with another passenger, in privacy. Seat doubles are available for passengers travelling together. Breakfast can be enjoyed in bed.

Beds aren't a novelty in first class, and now business class is catching up. British Airways plans to redefine business travel, and set new standards of comfort. In response to consumer research, the airline is delivering the potential for real sleep. A unique lounge-style layout in the Club World cabin aims to provide the best possible personal space and privacy. Seats are placed in pairs, one forward facing, the other rearward, and arranged to create more of a living-room arrangement than the standard serried rows. Each armchair converts to a fully flat bed, at the touch of a button. Individual privacy screens can be opened or closed, depending on whether the passenger is travelling alone, or wants to converse with the other passenger.

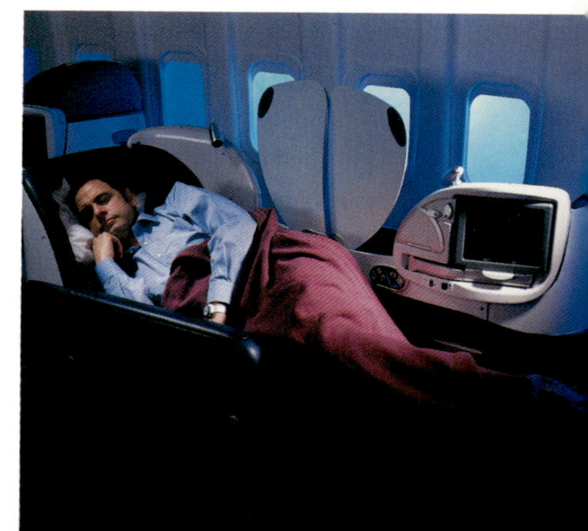

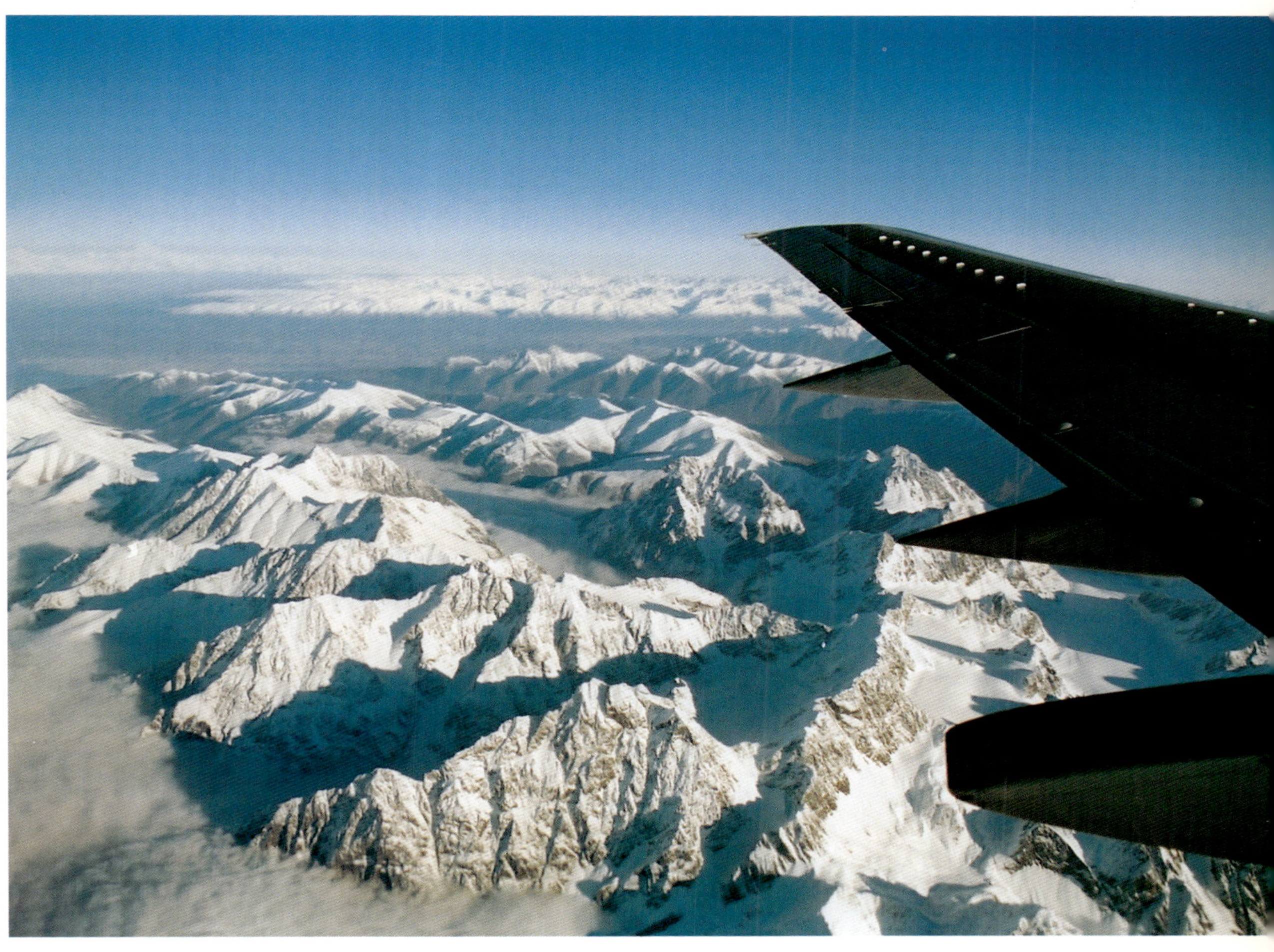

More cost-conscious air travellers can anticipate a major re-definition of economy travel, as pressure grows to provide better space and comfort for all.

If air traffic continues to grow at the current rate of five to six per cent a year, the jumbo jets of the future may be bigger slower planes. Much greater passenger comfort could be the compensation for less speed. Already there are plans for giant airliners, like aeronautic cruise ships, complete with day care rooms, libraries and elaborate sleeping facilities. The new double-decker, super-Jumbo Airbus due in service soon will have a passenger capacity of 500 to 600, with enough room beneath the passenger deck for cafés, gyms and sleeping cabins. If such plans transpire, you will be able to go downstairs for a coffee, eat at tables with real legs – not ones that fold down from the back of your seat or lever out of the armrest – and then go to bed in your hotel on wings.

British Airways www.britishairways.com

the Boeing Company www.boeing.com

Airbus Industrie www.airbus.com

'MOUNTAINS ARE THE BEGINNING AND THE END OF ALL NATURAL SCENERY...'

John Ruskin, "Modern Painters"

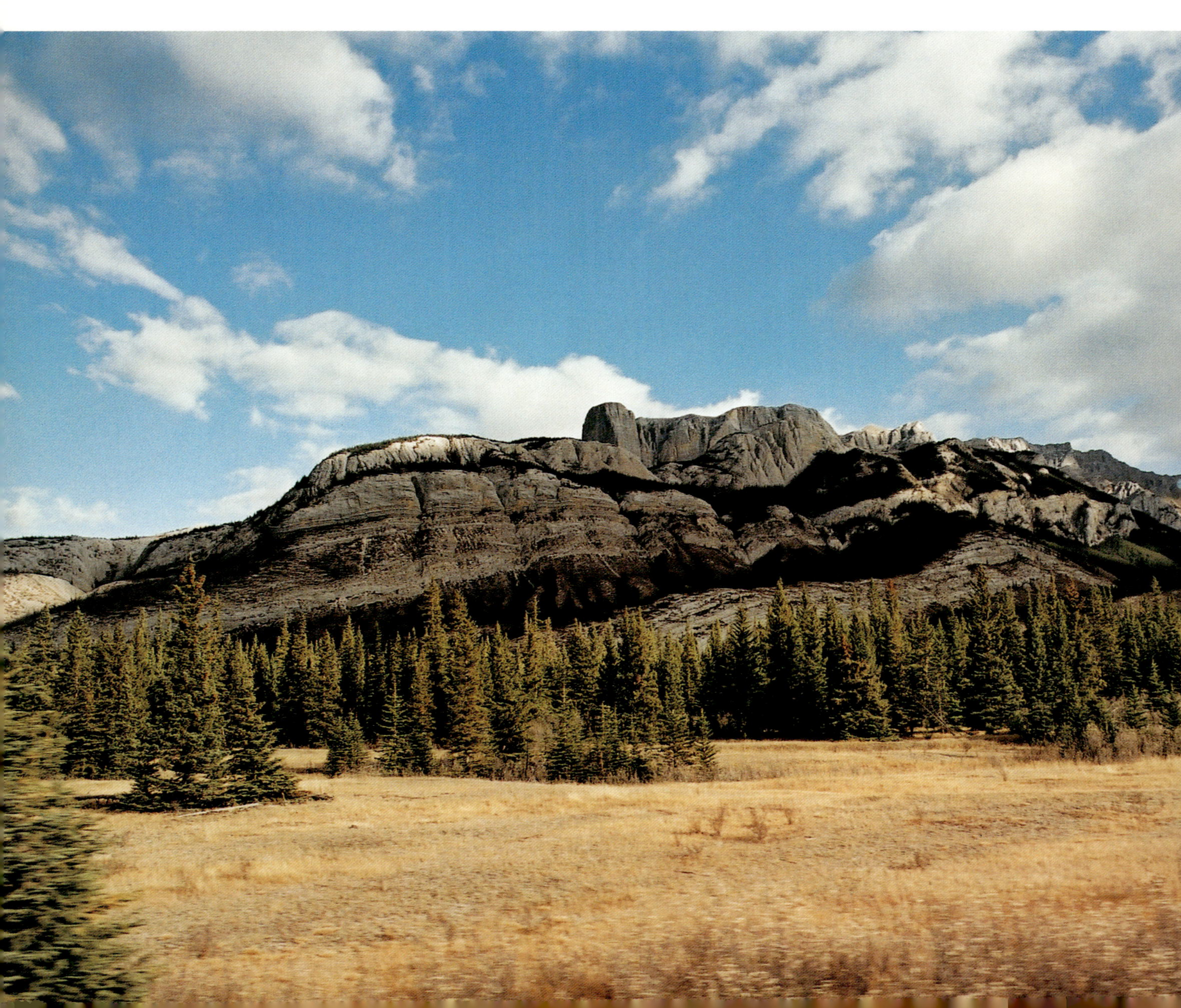

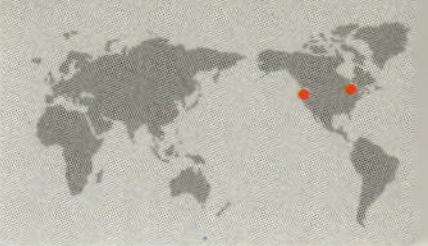

Continental Drift...

The Canadian train, Toronto to Vancouver, Canada

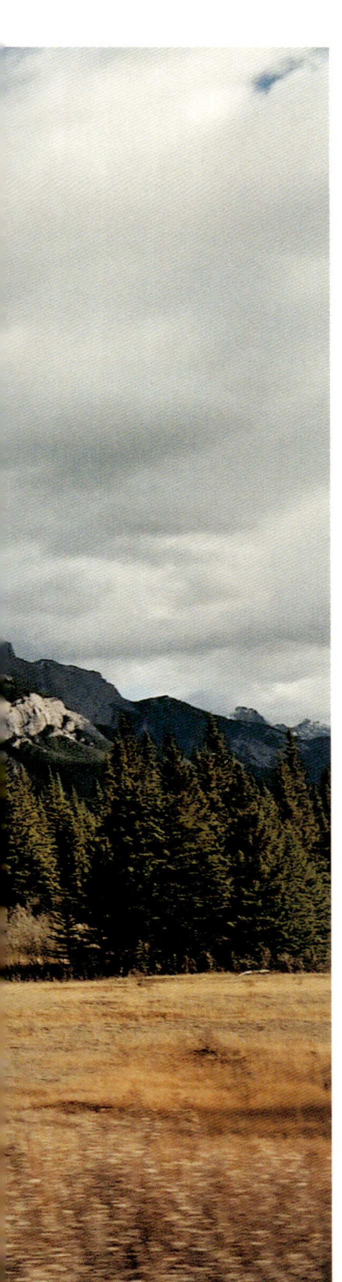

We boarded the Canadian trans-continental train in late autumn, leaving from Toronto to travel straight through to Vancouver. This will take three days and nights, one of the world's longest cross-country train trips, traversing five provinces – Ontario, Manitoba, Saskatchewan, Alberta, and British Columbia – and two time zones of the second largest country on earth. Thirty million people inhabit its ten million square kilometres (four million square miles) – approximately three-square kilometres of space for each person.

This is a vast land – vast seems too small a word to use as a descriptor for such an immense space – stretched out between the Atlantic and Pacific Oceans; divided by the dramatic Rocky Mountains, the sight of which is the principal purpose of the trip for most of the train's passengers.

On a crisp, clear autumn morning, we leave Toronto and head out along the northern shores of Lake Couchiching, whose bright blue waters are scattered with islands. The train is flanked by row upon row of elm trees, their slender silvered trunks dazzling in the sunlight as we flash by. We look out onto backyards, farmlands, and boat moorings on the 'shining waters' of Ontario, which contains one fourth of the world's fresh water. Perry Sound on Lake Huron, with its thousands of islands, sparkles mirror-like in the sun.

We will soon leave this genteel prettiness behind, and move into the wild and rugged terrain of Canada's predominant geographic feature, the Canadian Shield. Millions of years of glaciation have scoured the shield's surface, leaving a striking terrain of bare rock and countless lakes, rivers and streams. Forests – spruce, larch and pine trees, plus poplar and aspen – cover much of it. The train winds a track between great outcrops of granite with views of watery slivers extending out beyond. The colour palette from the window is a triumvirate of gold, red and silver – gold grasses, reeds and leaves, red berries and foliage, silver trees and rocks.

The creation of Canada's first national railway line in 1885 was a feat described as 'an act of insane recklessness', by an opposing politician. Laying tracks across this leviathan land seemed a Herculean task. However, although dogged by difficulties and steeped in scandal, it was achieved and proved itself a worthy connector device, eventually a dominant factor in the uniting of then separate provinces into one country.

The stainless steel rail cars of the Canadian first went on the rails in 1955. Since then they have been restored, and although modernised, wisely kept in the spirit of their original art-deco styling.

The sleek silver train can be seen snaking ahead from the Park Car, whose observation dome is shaped rather like the cockpit of a fighter plane. From here, you can see in front, up above and out to both sides at once. This panorama made the dome the most popular place to sit, and seats were often staked out for hours by the territorially inclined.

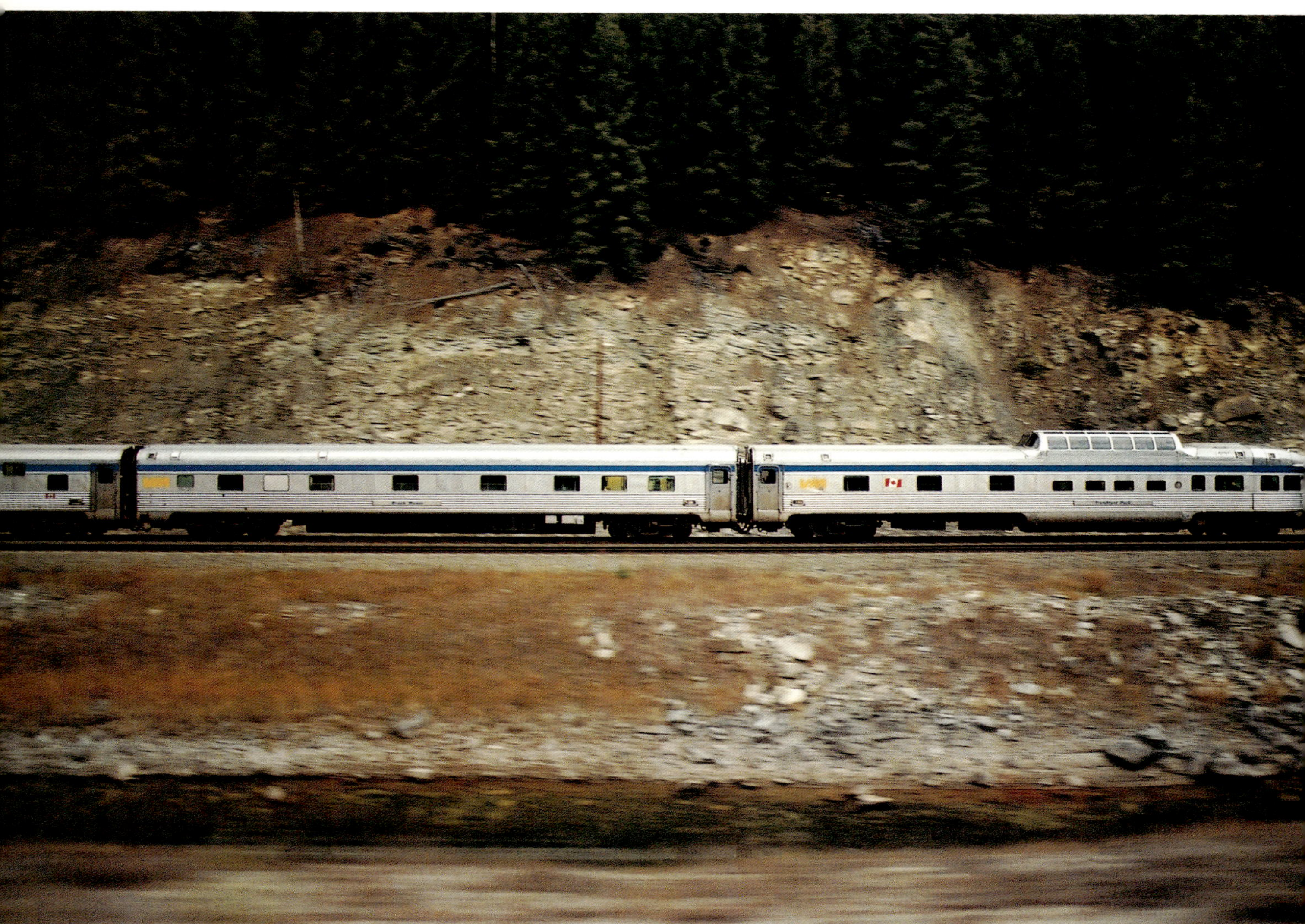

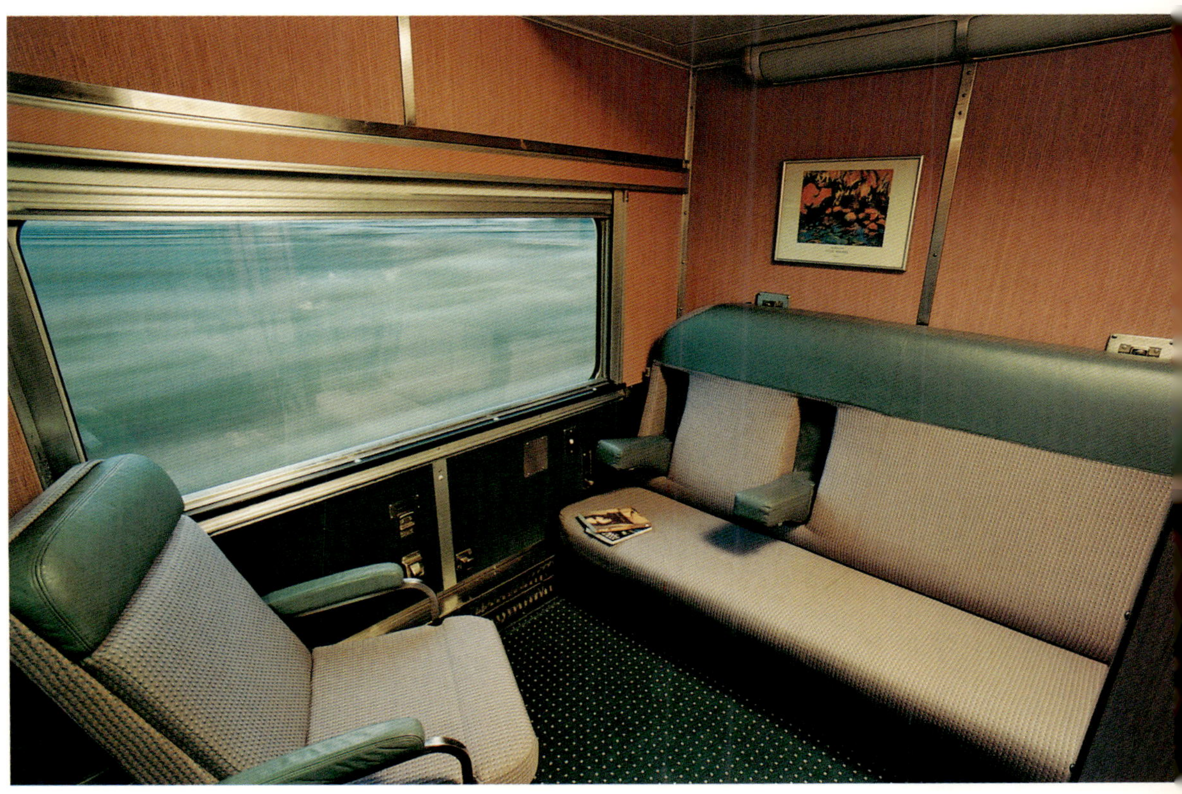

We travelled Silver and Blue class, which has sleeping and dining car status. The choice of cabins ranges from the compact berths and clever capsule-like single bedrooms, to double bedrooms and the positively spacious triple bedroom. A private basin and lavatory are in all accommodations except the berths. A large shower room with changing space is nearby, down the hall in each sleeping car, and generously stocked shower packs are given to each passenger so the lack of a complete en-suite is quite bearable.

During the winter months 'Romance by Rail' is on offer, an accommodation option where a spacious suite is made from two adjoining bedrooms, with one very large bed and a matching pair of washrooms. In this private cocoon you and your partner can sip champagne, order room service meals and stay sequestered from the crowd.

After waking in the morning, there is an immediate impulse to sit up and look out of the window to see where you are, and what can be seen. Sometimes who, or what, happens to be looking back at you is equally surprised by the sight of you. Lying back in bed and watching panoramas roll by, as though nature movies are being shown on the window, seems a luxurious pastime. Perhaps this is how royalty felt watching the passing parade from their ancient palanquins, borne aloft by bearers.

The views would be better appreciated if the train's windows could be washed every day. Our train departed Toronto with less than pristine panes. Determined to have clear vision, some enterprising passengers leapt out at the first stop, fossicked up sawhorses from the side of the tracks and brought water and towels from their cabins to clean their windows. However, this was the most energetic passenger activity we saw. Three days of being carried along for 4467 kilometres, gazing out of the window, reading, relaxing, not being expected to do anything, other than be seated, is quite soporific.

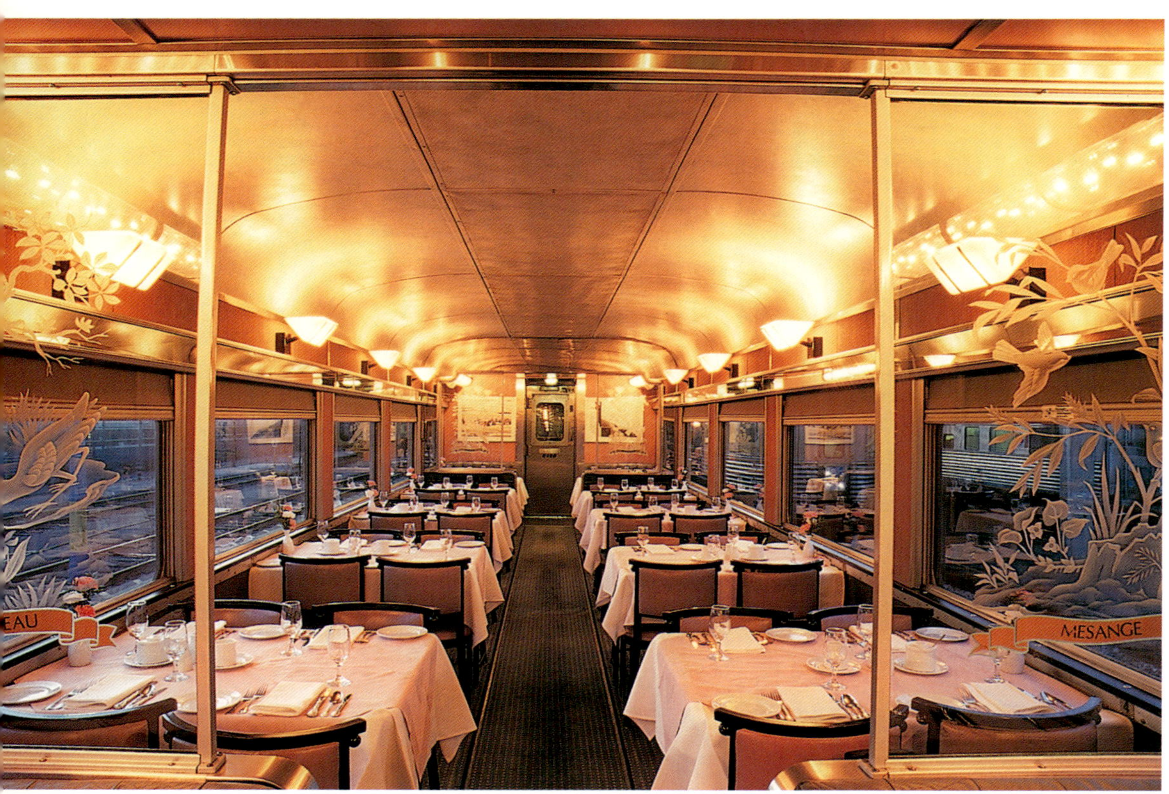

The Canadian dining room, good food and changing views.

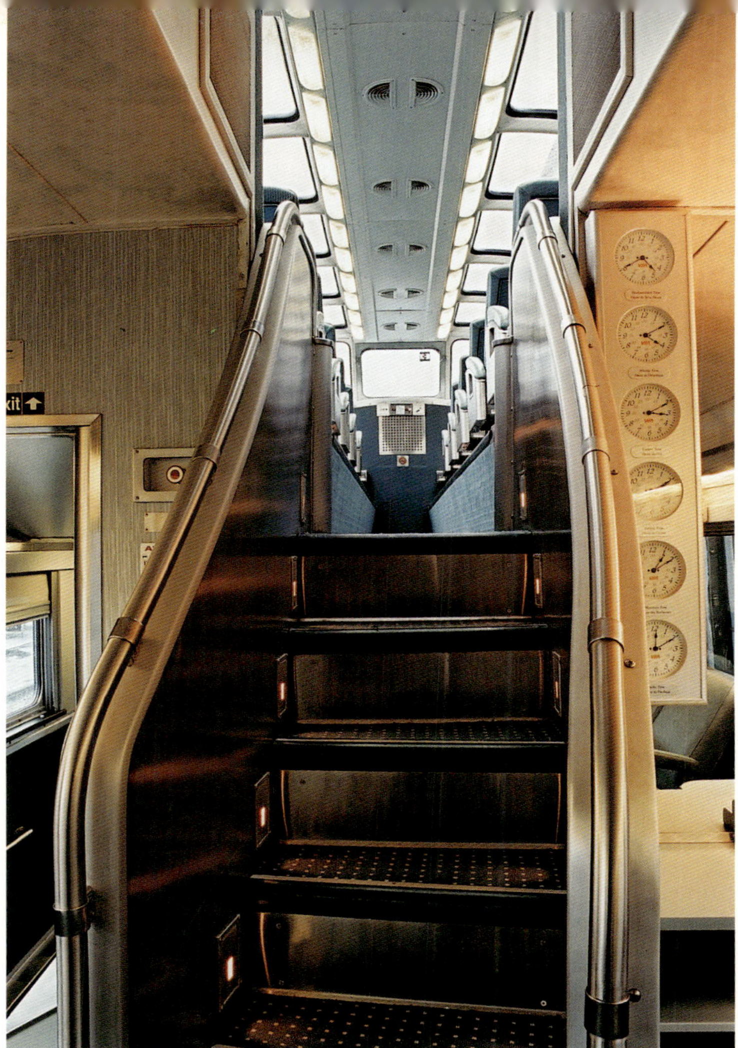

However, the call to lunch and dinner always got a very active response. Everyone is lying in wait for the central focus of the journey – the Rocky Mountains – to loom large into view, timed for mid afternoon on the second day. At the first stop that morning, in preparation for the sighting, every window on the train is thoroughly washed by huge hoses and the glass gleams as though it is new.

One activity you can choose is to pace the length of the train. Moving around on a swaying train, holding on to window bars to steady one's locomotion is a chance to observe the interesting manners that come into play when it is necessary to pass others in the aisles. In the narrow space, most people try to flatten themselves against the walls to let you by.

After we leave the small town of Caprecol, where we take the opportunity to leave the cloistered warmth of the carriages and walk along the platform in the crisp autumnal air, the train enters the increasingly remote interior of Northern Ontario. The landscape changes from the Canadian Shield to the Prairies, and its most famous part, the fertile southern belt where billions of tons of wheat are grown every year. Once this was home to vast numbers of bison. Two hundred years ago herds of 50–60 million animals lived here. By 1885 hunters had made them almost extinct. Now crops and grain elevators are the primary inhabitants of the immense space.

After hours of plainness, a change to a more rugged landscape heralds the start of our entry into the western mountains. These are part of the Western Cordillera, the massive 14,000 kilometre long mountain chain that spans the length of the both American continents – from Tierra del Fuego in the far south up to the far north of Alaska.

Canada's Western Mountains are made up of several ranges. The most famous is the Rockies, described by writer Samuel Butler as 'a mighty barrier rising midst an immense land, standing sentinel over the plains and prairies of America.' Conversation at breakfast centres on the imminent sighting of these fabled mountains, and where the best vantage points will be. This is also meant to be the paramount place for seeing wildlife, elusive so far on the journey.

I found myself becoming fixed on locating people in the landscape. While now and again there was evidence of habitation – houses, barns, and grain elevators – there was rarely a sighting of humans, except in the towns we passed through and at the railway stations. Whether you are watching for animals or people in this vast mostly empty tract of land, neither is often seen. Houseboats and seaplanes on isolated lakes were tangible evidence of humans, yet they remained concealed from view. After miles of nothing, I suddenly spotted some fishermen settled in boats under a bridge. Their startled faces looked up as the train raced over their heads, and I felt strangely triumphant at achieving my first sighting of locals in their natural habitat.

For each traveller, the journey will be unique, seeing different sights in varied light, weather and moods. Yet many of our fellow passengers seemed indifferent to the passing tableaux, either lost in books – often about foreign locations – asleep, or talking as though their lives depended on it, just being carried across the continent to their final stop. Perhaps some were frequent travellers of this route so were now totally familiar with the views to be had, like salesmen covering the same territory for years.

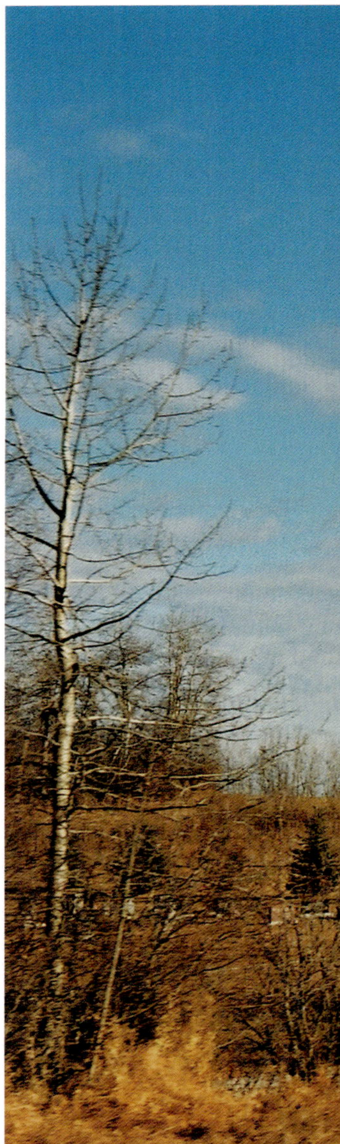

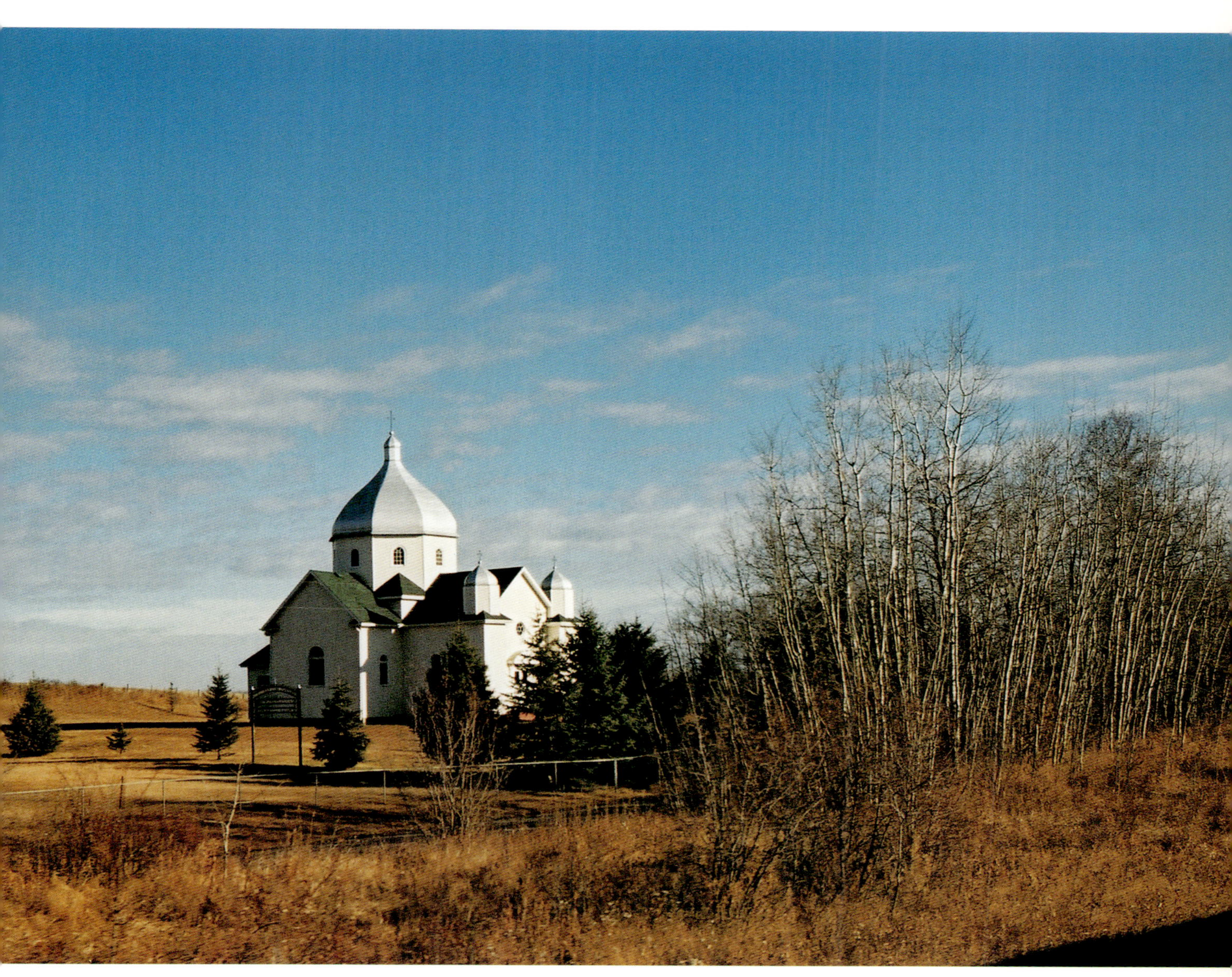

A Russian Church on the Canadian plains, a testament to settlers from other lands.

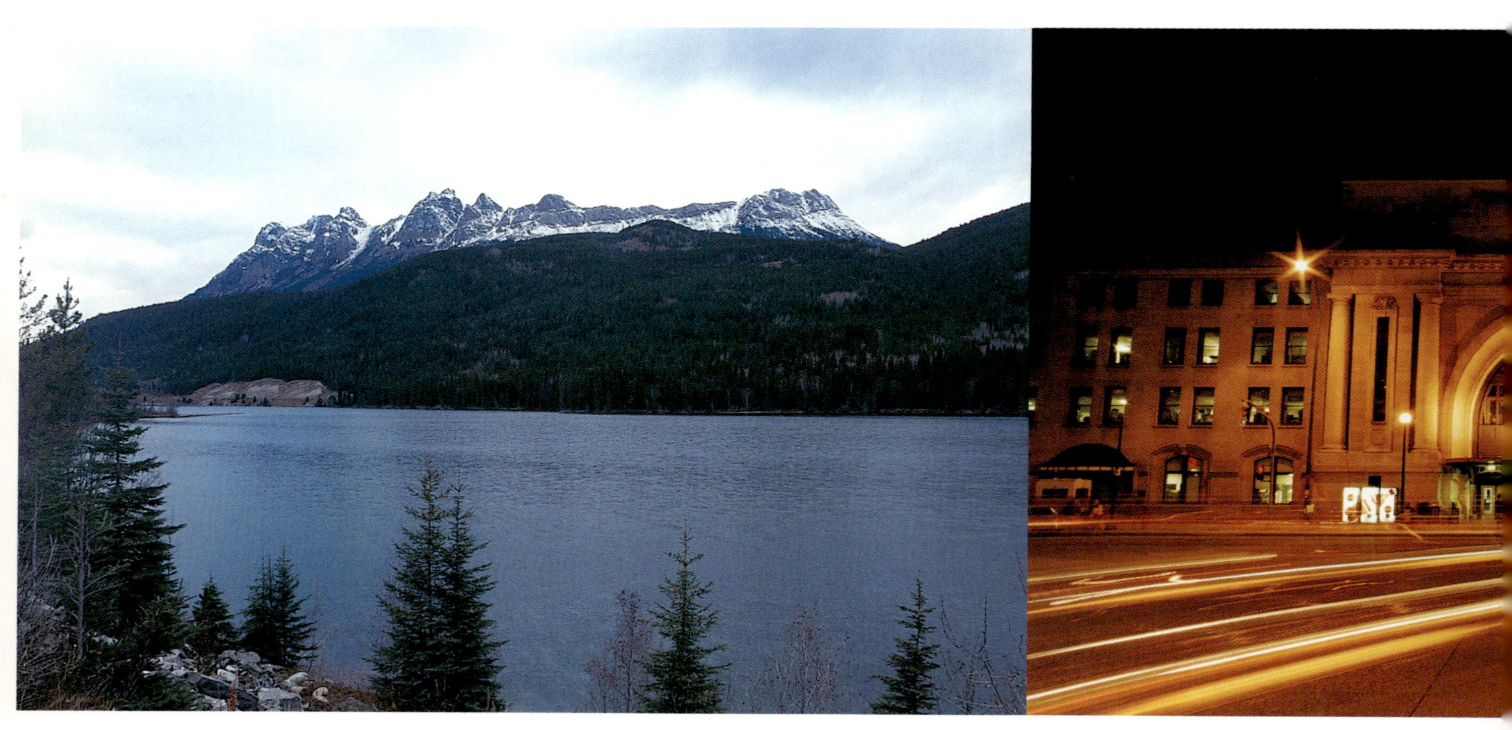

The peaks of the Rockies are reflected in the waters of Moose Lake.

Winnipeg is the geographic centre-point of the journey. The same architects responsible for New York's Grand Central Station designed the city's Union Station.

All at once the Rockies come into view. Everyone cranes to look; this is what most people have come to see up close. However, we arrived later than scheduled, so it was drawing close to dusk. And the weather is unhelpful, the mountains shrouded in mist, hidden from all the binocular and camera lenses focussed on them. There is disappointment, not with the scale and grandeur, which is impressive, but with the fact that the highest peaks are hidden from view by bad weather.

For many passengers the town of Jasper is a stopping off point. They will be able to see more of the magnificent Rocky Mountains when the weather improves, and rejoin the Canadian days later.

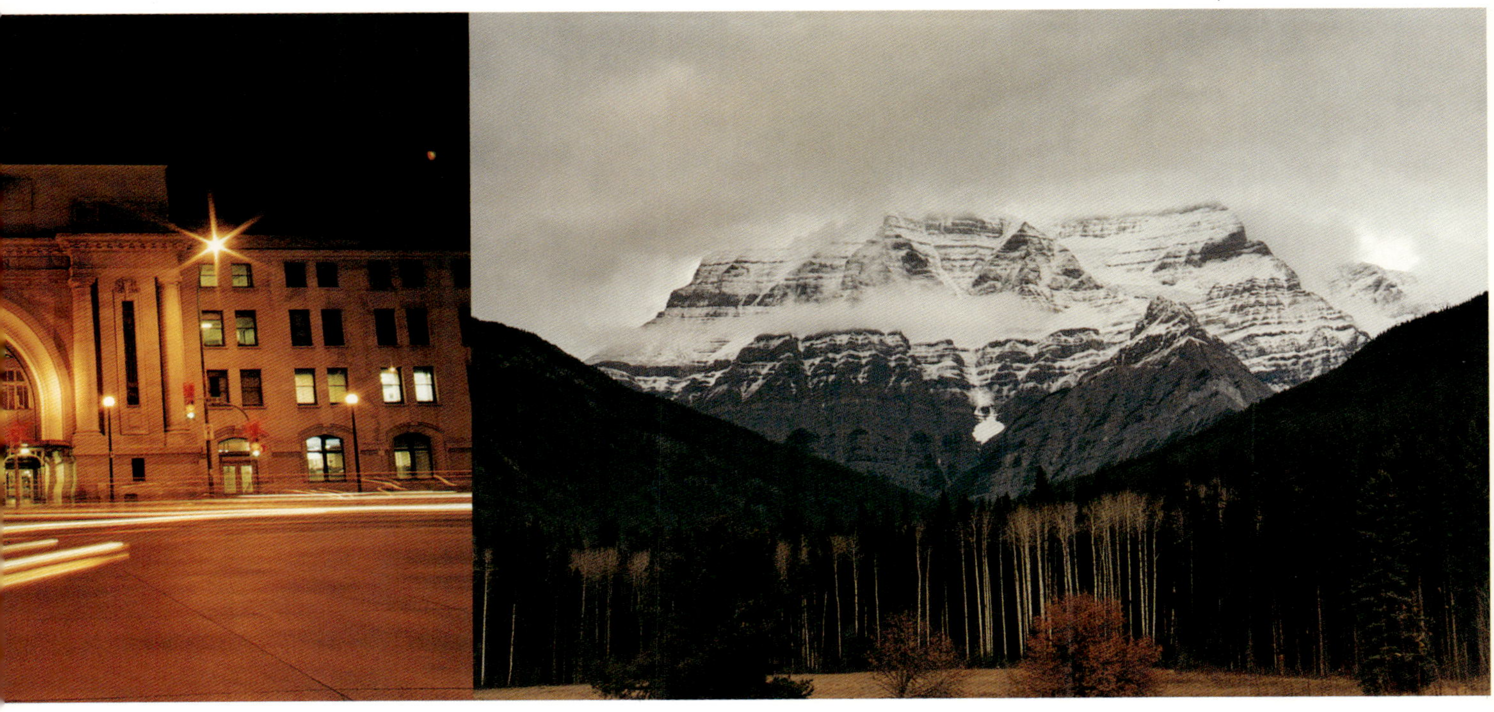

The bulk of Mount Robson, the so-called Monarch of the Rockies, is partly obscured. Little comfort is afforded by the fact that it is only fully visible on around 19 days each year.

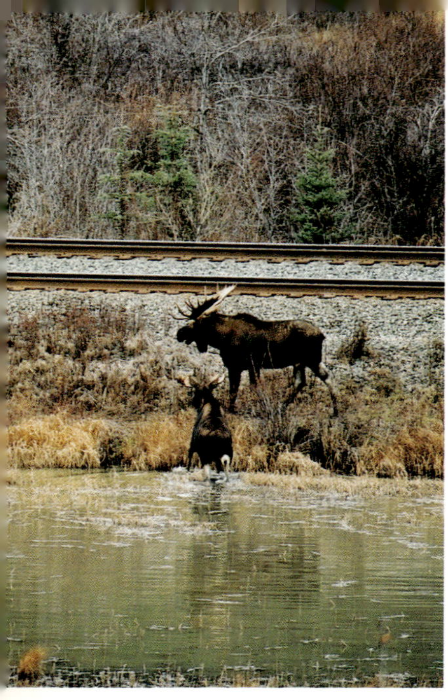

After we leave Jasper, we spot an elk. It watches the train go by, indifferent to the excitement of the wildlife hunters on board, and undamaged by the barrage of shots fired from the train – from cameras, not guns.

Often we felt as though we were being transported into nowhere, and that the train itself was rushing through the giant spaces looking for some company.

On the other hand, our sense of isolation was felt observing the country from the comfort of a populated train. Massive empty spaces are unfamiliar to largely urbanised people, used to the frequent markers of habitation – although all along the track are telephone wires running in concert with the train, companions in communication across this mammoth continent.

The journey ends in Vancouver, at yet another Union Station, the often-used name another reminder of how the railroad first linked this enormous country, bringing settlers to the interior and reuniting family and friends. Now, for those who fly over it, the time and sense of distance is greatly foreshortened.

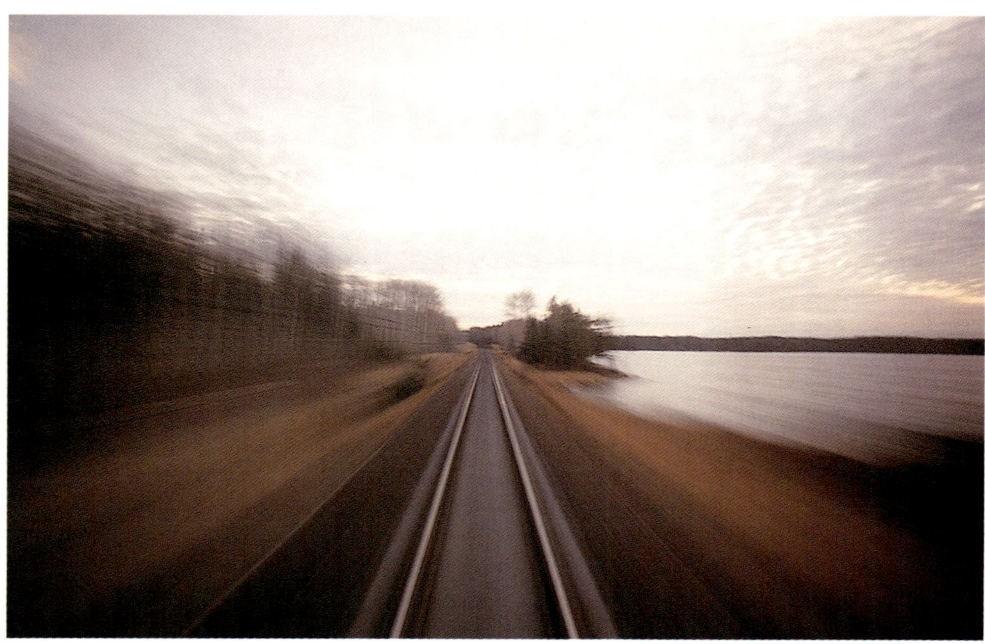

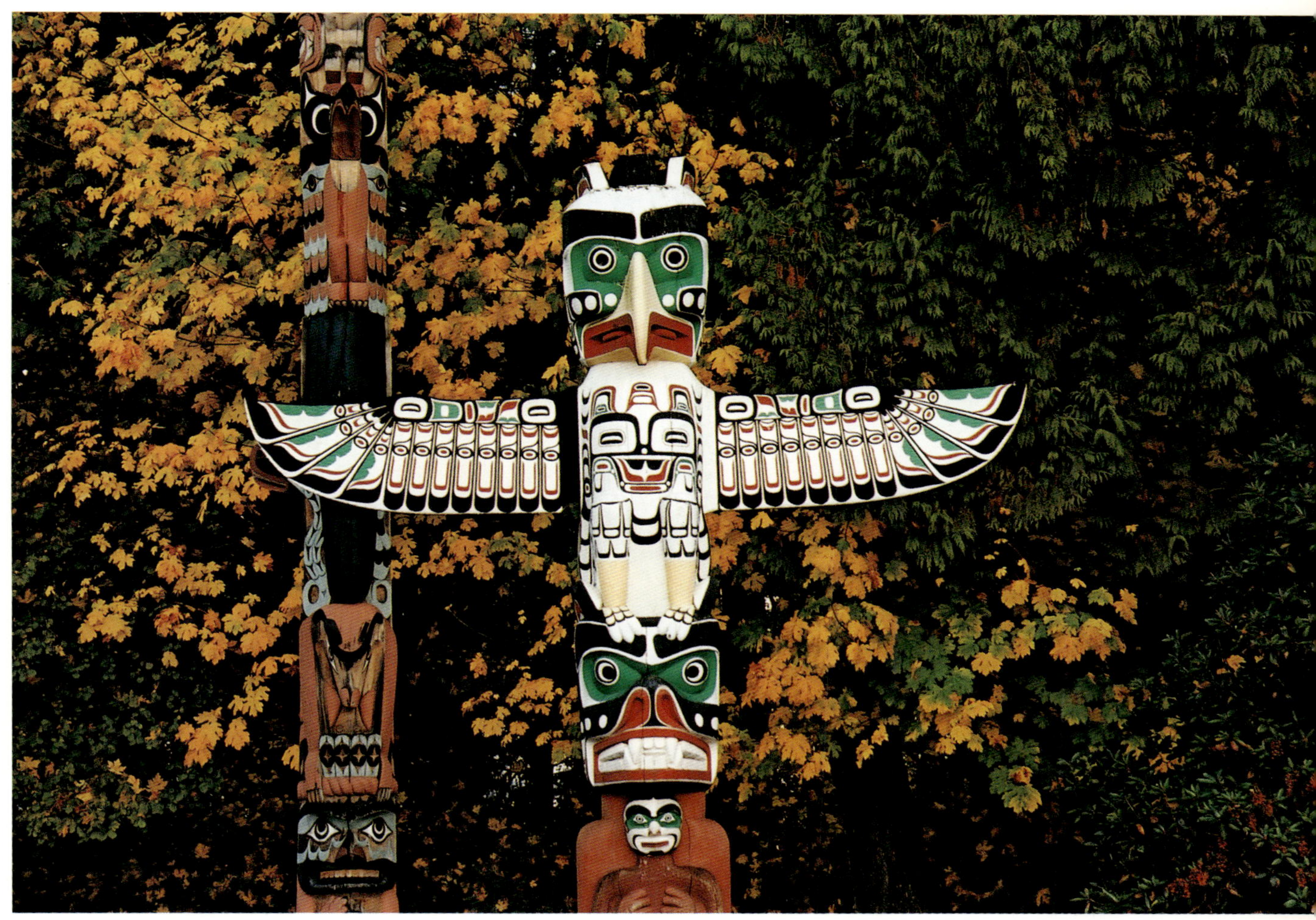

In Vancouver's Stanley Park is an impressive collection of totem poles, unique artefacts made almost exclusively by the Indian tribes in Canada's northwest. The colourful, elaborately carved cedar poles are a means of communicating stories, myths and legends. Spirits are often represented in the form of birds and animals such as eagles and beavers. Totem poles are meant to be read from the solid base to the top figure, as it points skyward to never-ending possibilities. These Indian art forms, telling stories of the land and its people, are a potent symbol of the indigenous culture of Canada.

The Canadian | VIA Rail Canada Inc | www.viarail.ca

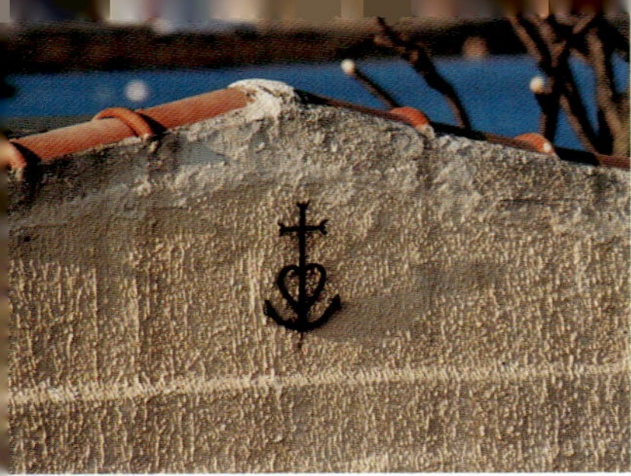

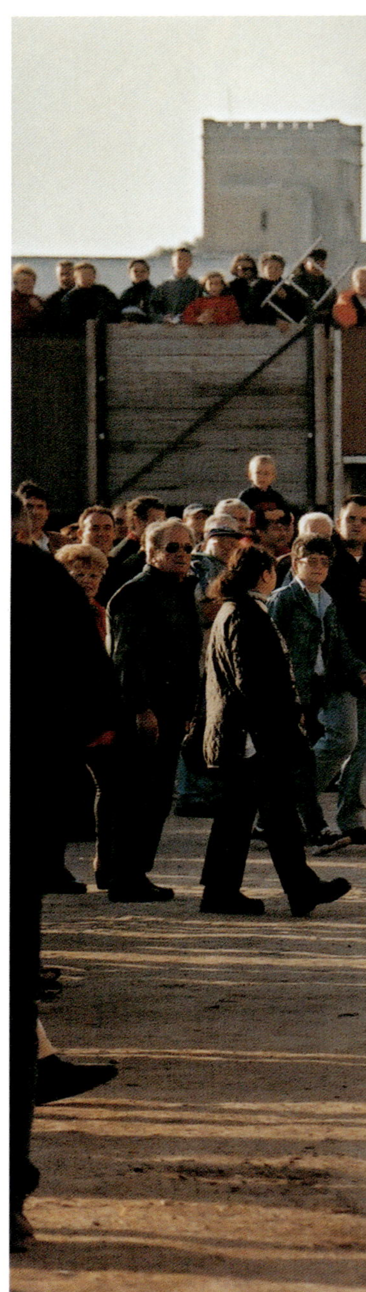

Bon Voyage...

the Saroche barge, the Camargue, France

We are in the heart of cowboy country – French style. This is the unique and unusual land of the Camargue, part of Languedoc-Roussillon, neighbour to Provence, in the South of France. We have arrived on the last day of the Fête Votive, a traditional fiesta celebrating one of the Camargue icons, the bull.

The landscape is one of curious contrasts, exemplified by black bulls, herds of white horses and on the water, flocks of pink flamingos. An immense plain formed by the Rhone Delta, the Camargue is made up of 140,000 hectares (346,000 acres) of wetlands, pastures, dunes and salt flats.

This exotic territory is home to the fighting bulls and to the white horses that the Camargue *gardiens*, herdsmen, ride. A distinctive breed, the Camargue horse is born dark brown or black, becoming white around its fourth year. It lives outdoors, well adapted to the humid heat of summer, and the blustery winter cold. The local cowboys are also resilient types. Tough characters outwardly, they play a major part in guarding *Camarguias* traditions. Their role has considerable prestige and during the summer months they are in constant demand, at the performances involving bulls and horses held in the many village arenas.

Here in the Camargue the special bullfighting events, *les courses*, have one vital difference to those of Spain – the bulls live to tell the tale. Among the most popular events are those in which agile bullfighters – *razeteurs* – dash into the arena to try to remove a cockade from the animal's horns, deftly avoiding attack. The drama of the show comes from the men racing to leap over the barrier and escape the charging bull. It is the *razeteurs* who occasionally get hurt, not the beast. After some of these events, the *gardiens*, mounted on their white steeds, run the bulls past the crowds of spectators, through the town streets, and out to transport taking them back to their farms.

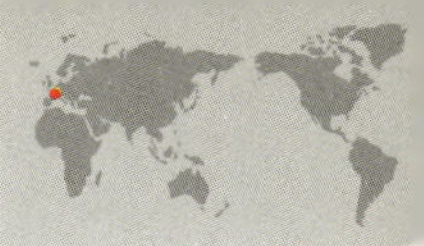

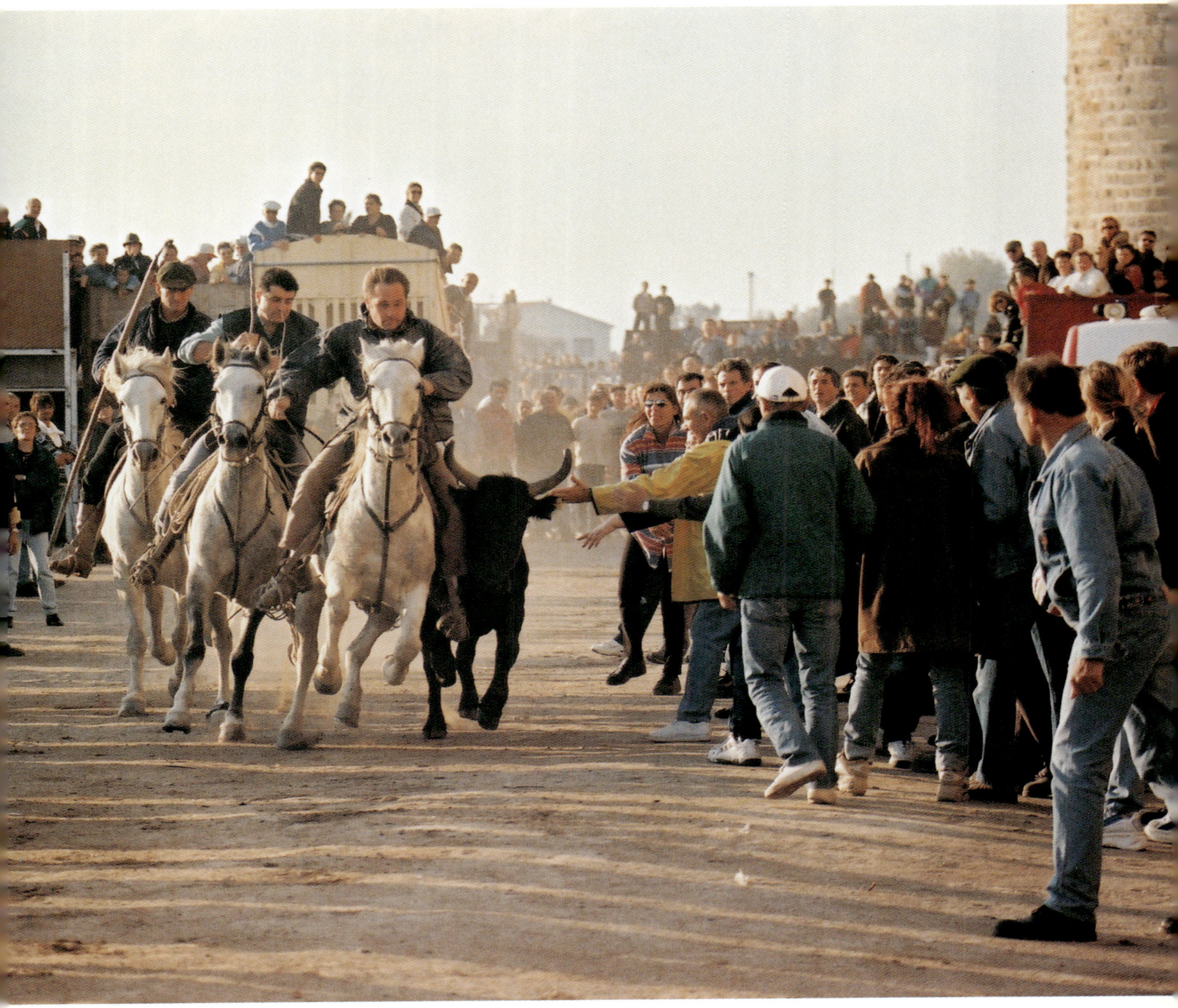

HOOVES THUNDERING, MANES FLYING, POWERFUL WHITE HORSES HERDING A PITCH-BLACK BULL RACE STRAIGHT TOWARD US, THEN A SPLIT SECOND BEFORE THEY WOULD BE ON TOP OF US, THEY SHARPLY TURN AND SWERVE, SO CLOSE WE CAN HEAR THEIR RAGGED BREATH AND FEEL THEIR BODY HEAT. THEY GALLOP PAST, THROUGH THE GATES OF THE WALLED TOWN AND DOWN THE CROWDED STREETS. OUR HEARTS RESUME BEATING. WE NEED A DRINK.

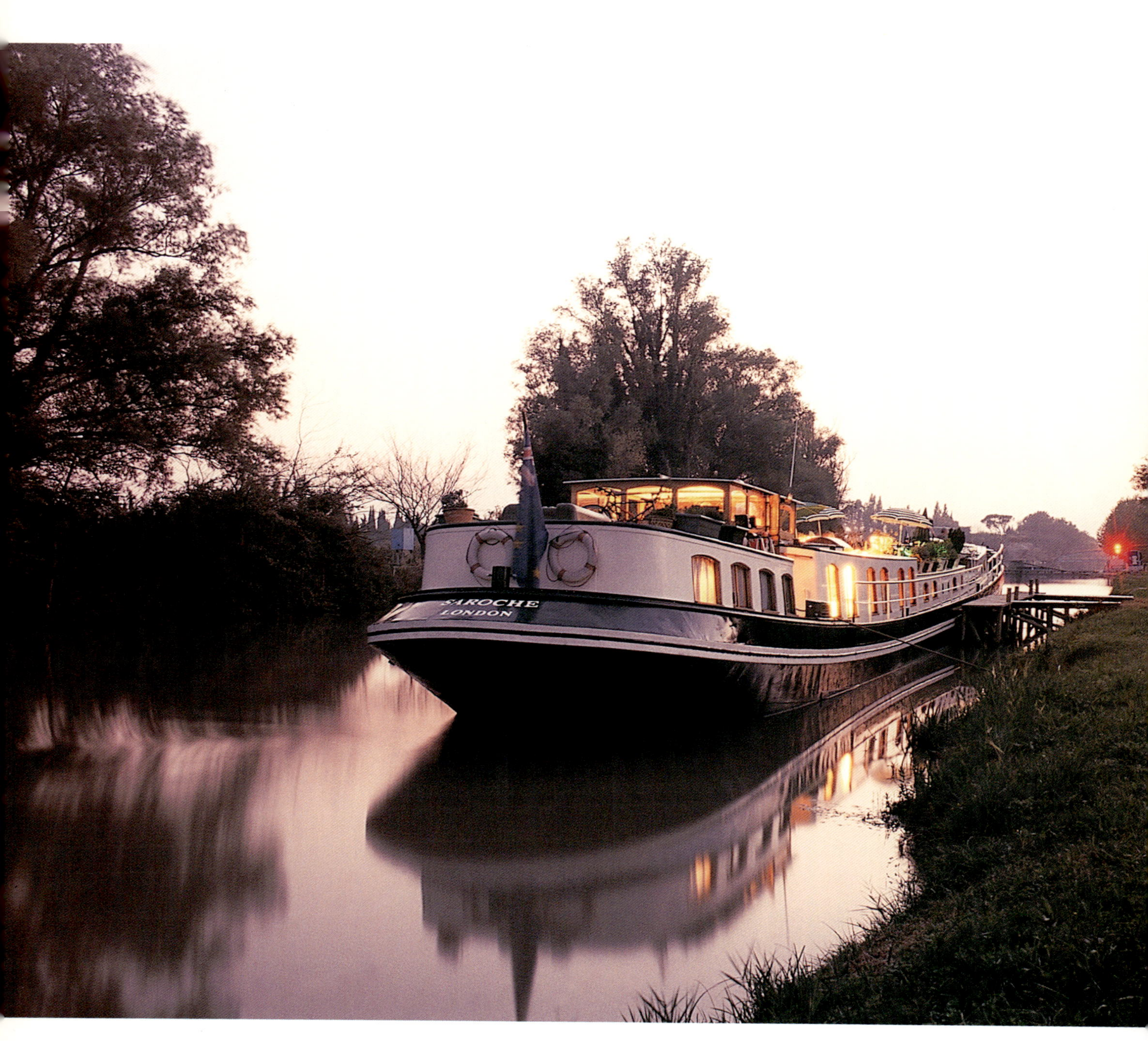

The Saroche's classic hull was built in Holland in 1926, and is a generous 39.25 metres (127½ ft) long, with a beam of 5.09 metres (16½ ft).

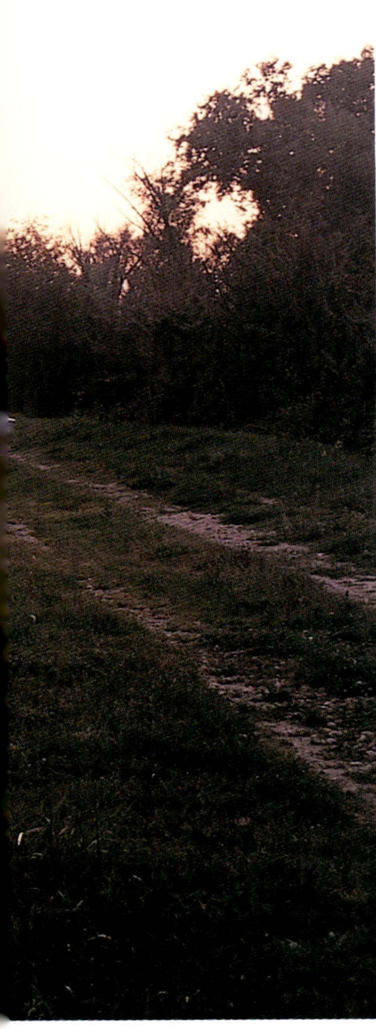

After the festival, we return to our waiting transport, moored on a nearby canal.

The French word for a barge is as may be expected a more elegant one – *une pêniche*. Our pêniche, our home for a week on the rivers and canals of southern France, is the stylish Saroche. We will cruise on this splendid water-carriage from the town of Beaucaire to the port of Sète, along the Canal du Midi linking the Mediterranean to the Atlantic, and on the Canal du Rhône à Sète to the coastal wetland of the Camargue.

There are some five thousand miles of 'floating highways' crisscrossing France. Once the main route for transporting goods, nowadays there is not the volume of cargo moved on the water by the classic barge. The working riverboat is now a less common sight than holiday and hotel barges.

We arrived in Montpellier, to be met at the airport by crewmember and guide Matt, and driven to the riverside at Beaucaire, the starting point of our buoyant week. Captain Kevin, an English mariner now resident in France and owner, with his wife Freddie, of this lovingly restored vessel, welcomed us aboard.

The first sight of the Saroche was a gratifying one. Its classic hull, gleaming paintwork, polished brass rails and arched windows attracted admiring glances from sailors and landlubbers alike. Totally refitted, the substantial yet sleek boat, powered by a quiet diesel engine, has an average speed of 6–8 kilometres on the inland waterways of the Camargue, and 10–12 kilometres on open water. This is not to be a stop-start cruise, as there is only one lock in the entire trip, in marked contrast to Burgundy, where the Saroche also cruises. There, 46 locks have to be negotiated in six days, and consequently travel is at a slower speed of 2–3 kilometres. The one and only lock of this expedition was the Écluse de Nourriguier.

After being unlocked, we moored nearby overnight. The lock closed at dusk, so there was no traffic passing until morning. In the dark and silent starlit night, the lights of the Saroche the only sign of civilization, it seemed as though we were in the middle of a most agreeable nowhere.

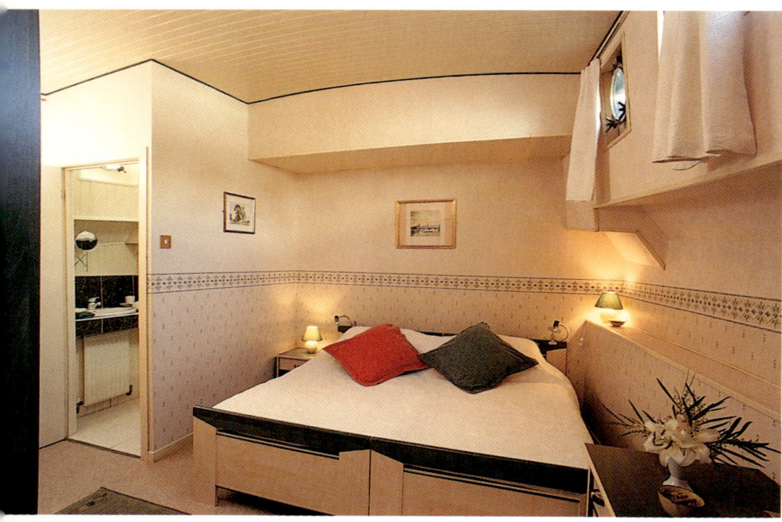

All of the three double staterooms on board the Saroche are large and well appointed.

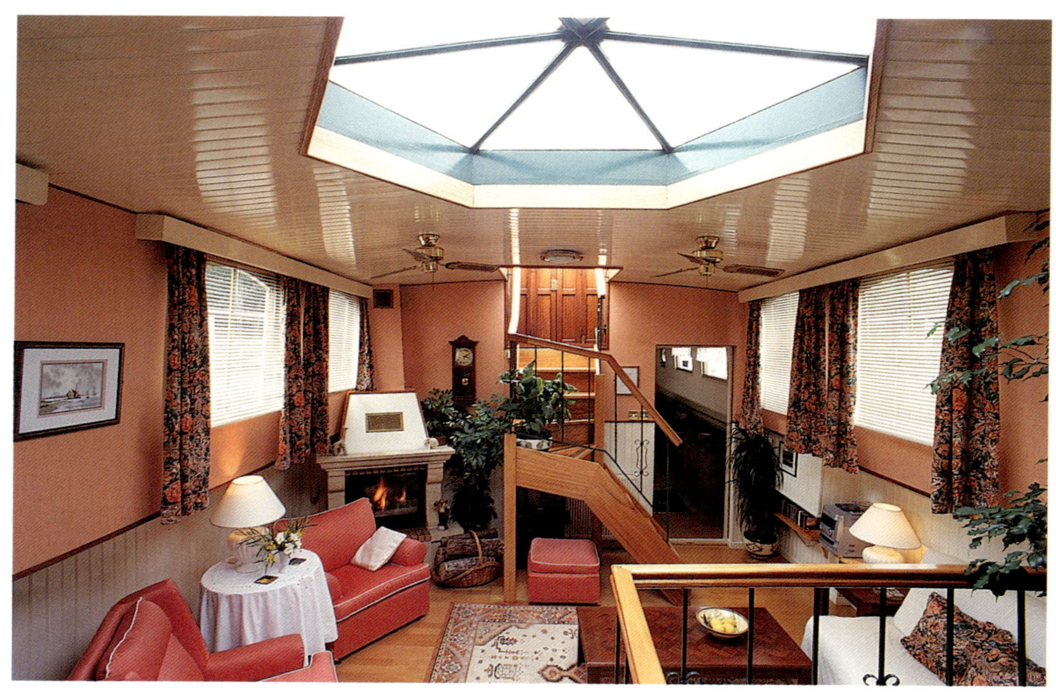

A wood-burning fire warms the comfortable sitting room on rare cool evenings.

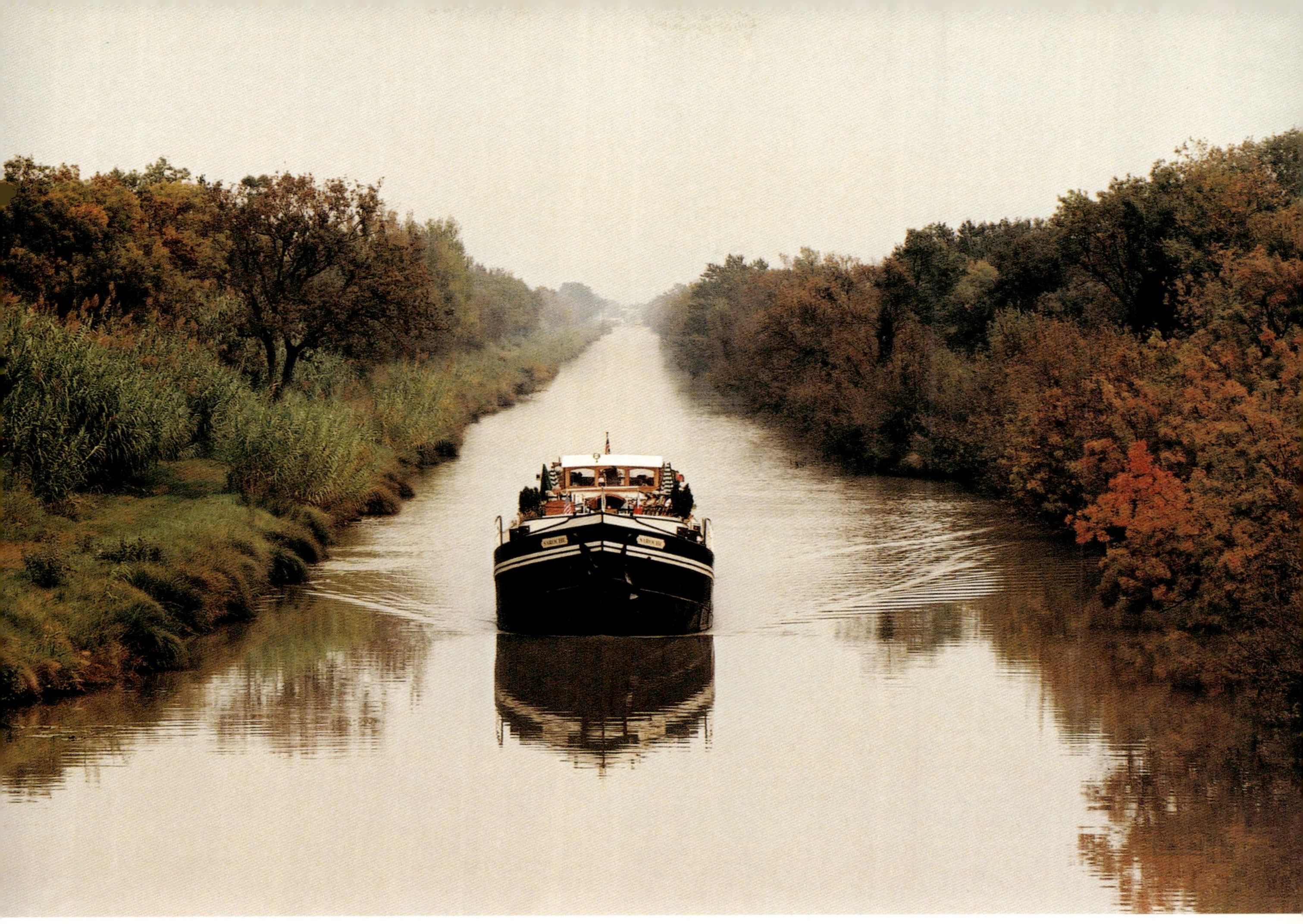

Six passengers, the full complement, board on a cloudless October afternoon.

Each of the Saroche's three en-suite staterooms is spacious and fitted out more like a hotel room than a ship's cabin. Luggage stowed, we met the four person crew, toured the airy, attractive lounge-dining room, took note of the well-stocked library and wine cellar, and then basked, glass in hand, in comfortable chairs on the boat's outdoor terrace. The warmth of the late autumn sun was more akin to that of midsummer. As the boat moved smoothly and purposefully out into the canal, it seemed that winter was a long way ahead.

The next relaxing eight days would be enhanced with excursions ashore to see local life and sights, and to shop and eat, a great combination of cruising, gazing and gastronomy. Most of our dining was on board, and as we discovered, this was a floating restaurant par excellence.

The first evidence of the famed French focus on food were the culinary herbs flourishing in pots on the Saroche's deck. Tarragon, thyme, rosemary and basil scented the air and flavoured the food. The chef de cuisine, Jodie, was a New Zealander, and as we soon decided, one of the country's best exports. She was delighting in the village food markets and eat-to-live philosophy in this gourmand's paradise.

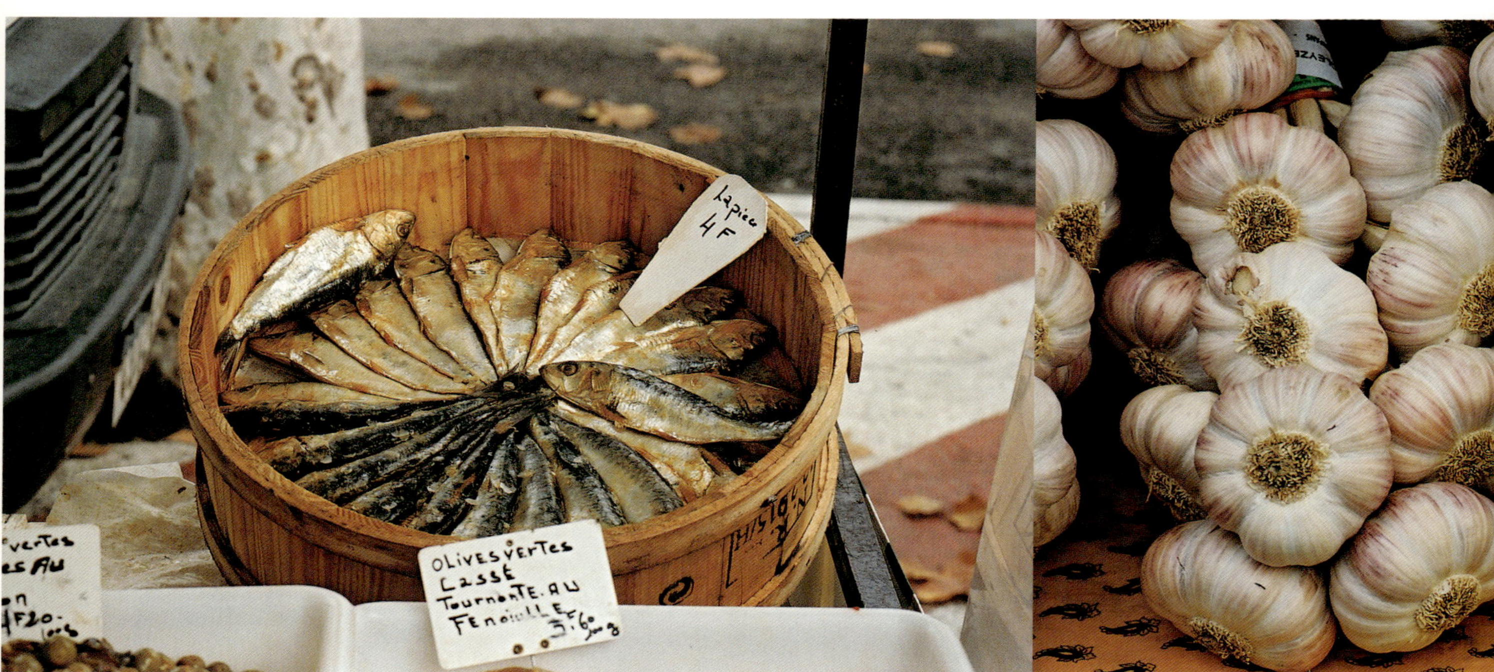

Scenes from the food market.

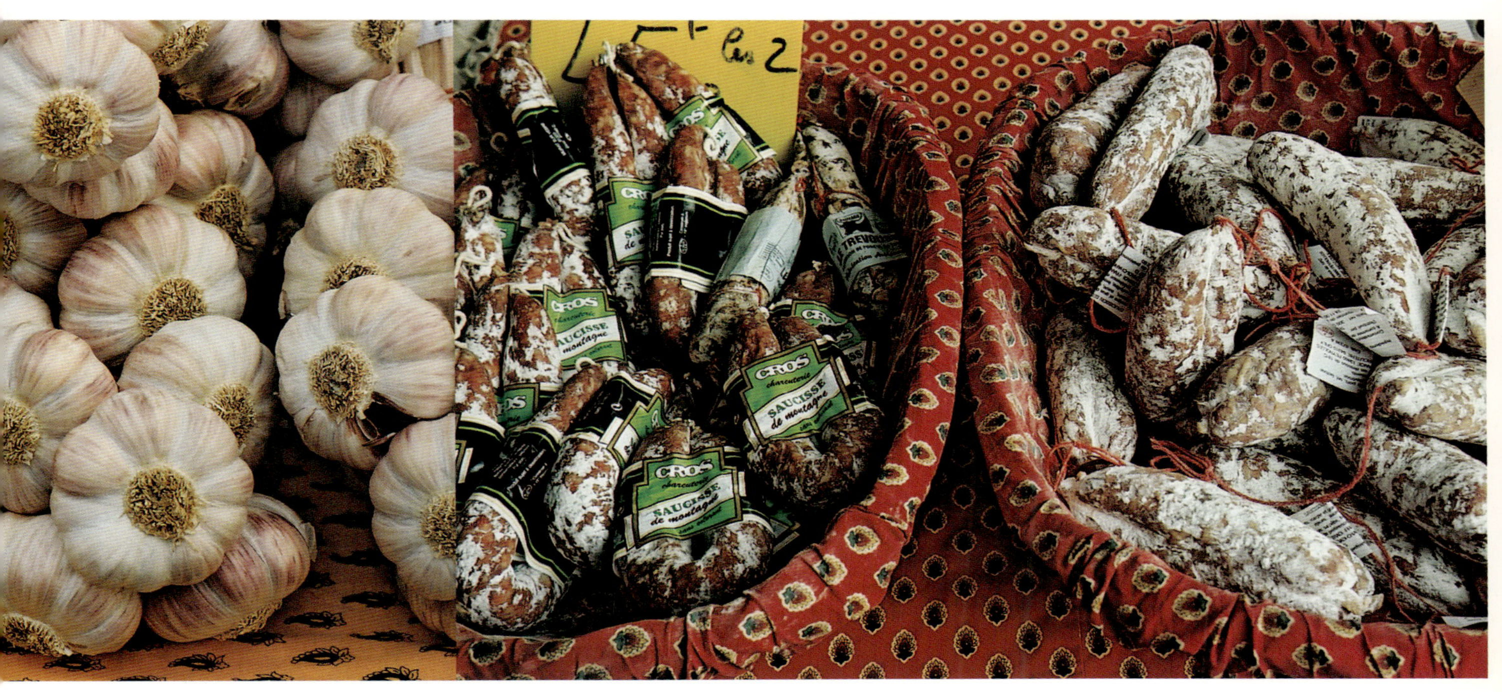

On the first evening, we are served a substantial Sunday dinner: goat's cheese salad, poached salmon, roast garlic studded lamb with a red wine and shallot sauce, local cheese, nougat ice cream with apricot and ginger sauce. The wines flowed, matched to each course and then some. After that set menu, the guests must make the decisions as to what they would like to eat. Each morning over breakfast, they are presented with a selection of eight entrées and eight main courses to choose from for the evening meal.

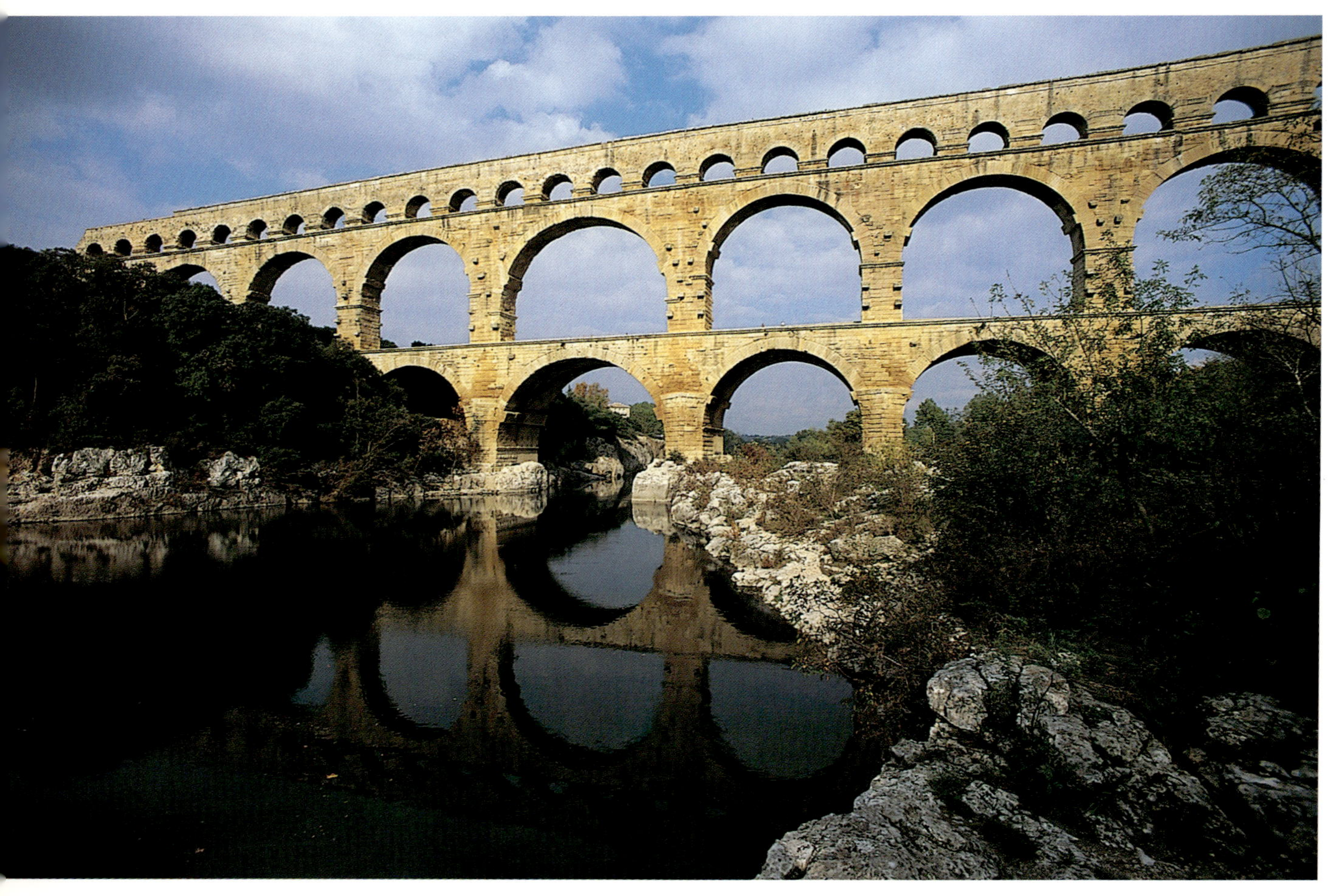

The Pont du Gare, the elegant aqueduct built by the Romans in 1 A.D.

The Camargue region is rich in both natural and man-made sights. Two thousand years ago, during the rule of the Emperor Claudius, the Romans built the three-tiered Pont du Gare aqueduct. Made of limestone cut from local quarries, it is the highest of all of the aqueduct bridges constructed by the Romans. As tall as an eighteen-story building, it was once part of a 48km (30 mile) long conduit, an ambitious architectural endeavour, bringing fresh water to the city of Nîmes. Nearby is the source of another very important liquid – vineyards, where rosé wines were first made. The area is famous for its *vins du sable*, wines produced from grapevines grown in the sand.

The marshes and lakes of the Camargue are home to a teeming aquatic life, the waters 'bristling with feathers and sparkling with scales'. Along the banks, fishermen have placed rows upon rows of their traditional hooped fishing nets. Pointing skyward, their shapes silhouetted against the sun, the nets look almost medieval.

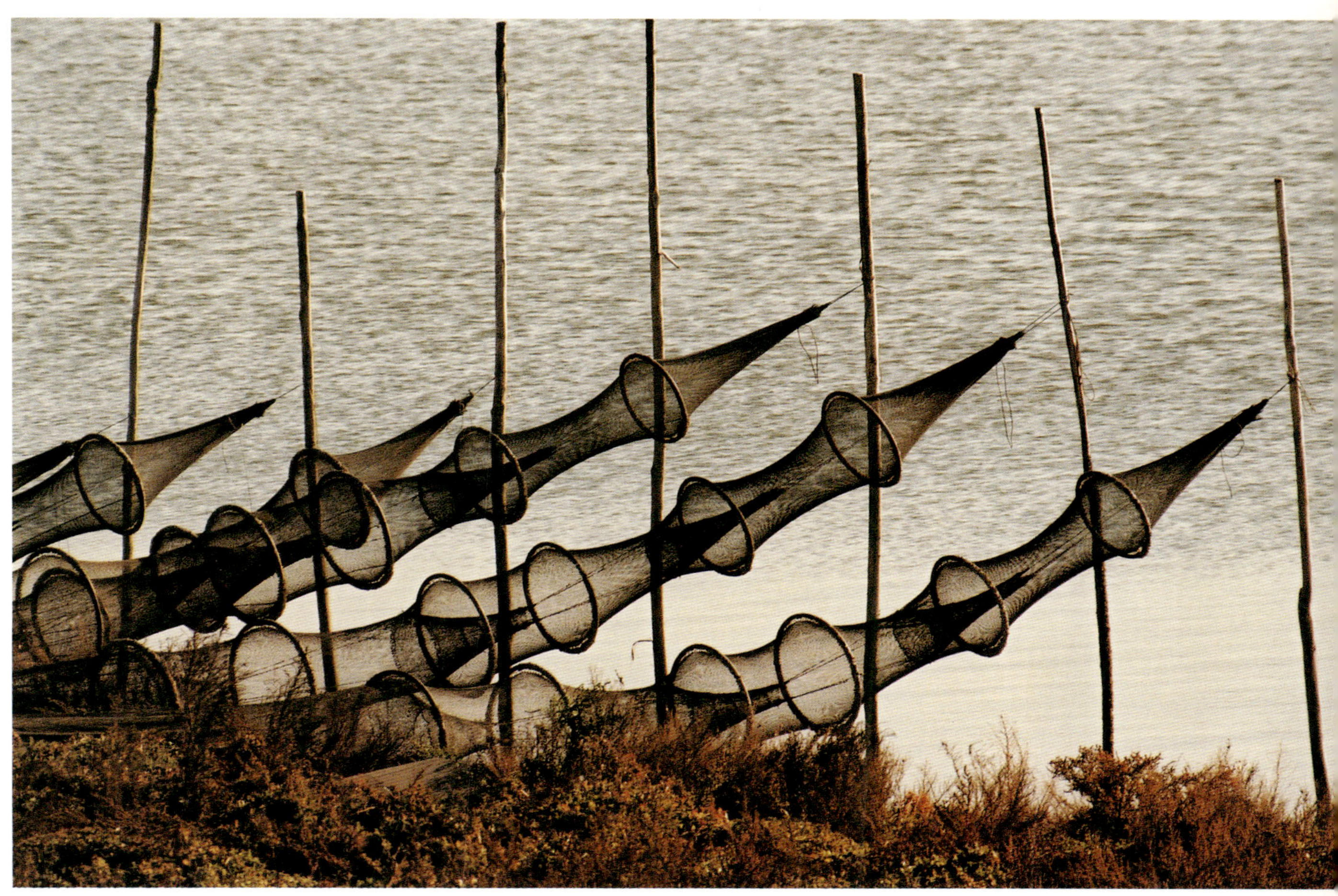

Traditional fishing nets drying in the sun.

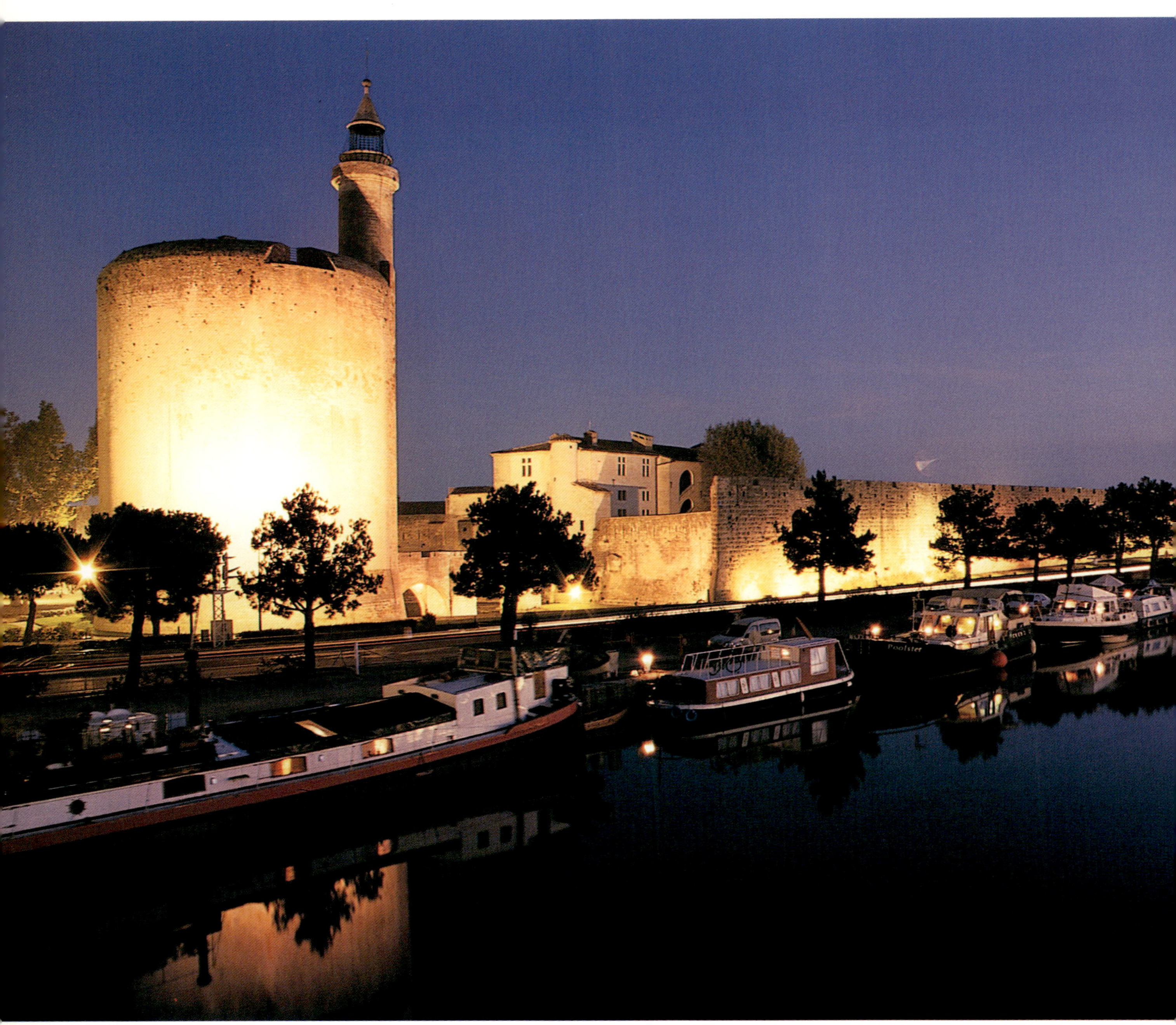

The walled city of Aigues-Mortes with the Tower of Constance to the left.

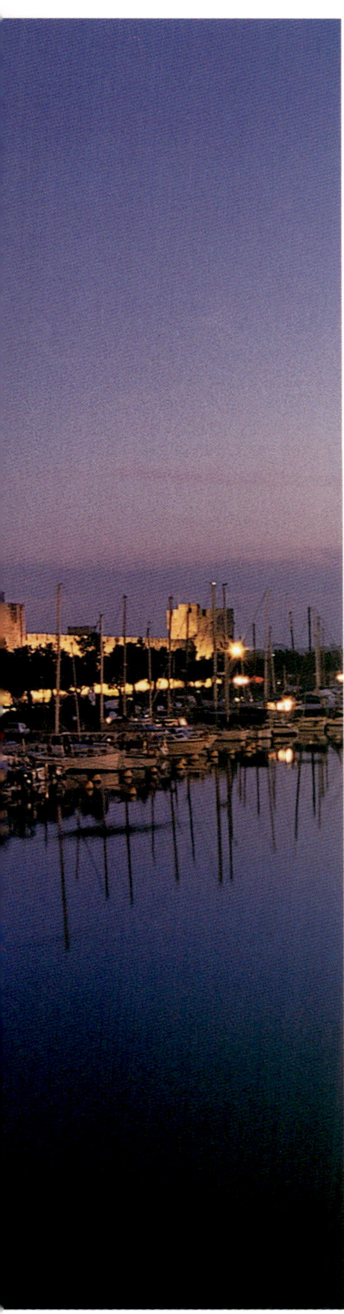

For two nights, we moor at the foot of the walled medieval city of Aigues-Mortes. It was from here in 1248 that King Louis IX left for the Crusades, military expeditions undertaken between the 11th and 14th centuries. The series of wars were organized by the Christians of the West to reconquer the Holy Land, then in Muslim hands.

The town, custom built by Louis as a gateway to the Crusades, is incredibly well-preserved, from the outside, looking very much as it would have done to approaching travellers long ago. Surrounded by a mile of ramparts, broken only by ten gates and five towers, Aigues-Mortes is an intriguing place, where outwardly little seems to have changed. Whilst there are no high-rise blocks, and hardly any modern buildings, inside the walls there is ample evidence of modern times, from television aerials to Internet kiosks. Shopping at the markets and in the stores is a pleasurable pastime, as is having coffee at a café in the central square.

Although the Camargue is the biggest rice-growing area in France, sea salt is by far the largest harvest. Near Aigues-Mortes is one of the biggest saltworks in the world. Throughout the summer, vast saltpans evaporate and the crystals are heaped into shimmering pyramids up to 8m (26ft) high that can be seen glistening from miles away. The delicious salt is a must-buy souvenir.

On the water, the flamingos look like weird unfolding plants, with long curved necks reminiscent of bean sprouts. Graceful in flight, their wings reveal a jet-black edging.

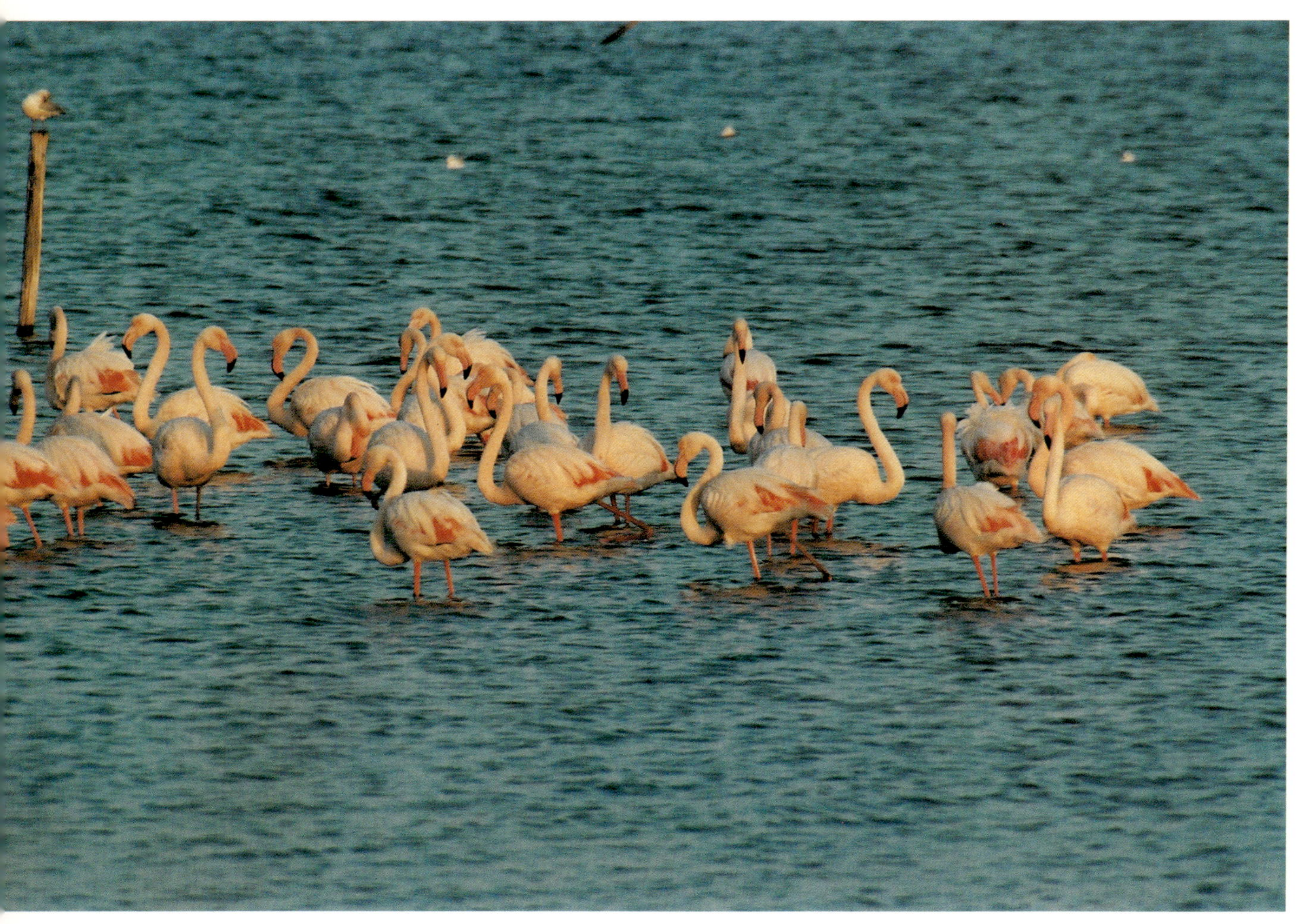

The flamingo is the official symbol of the Camargue.

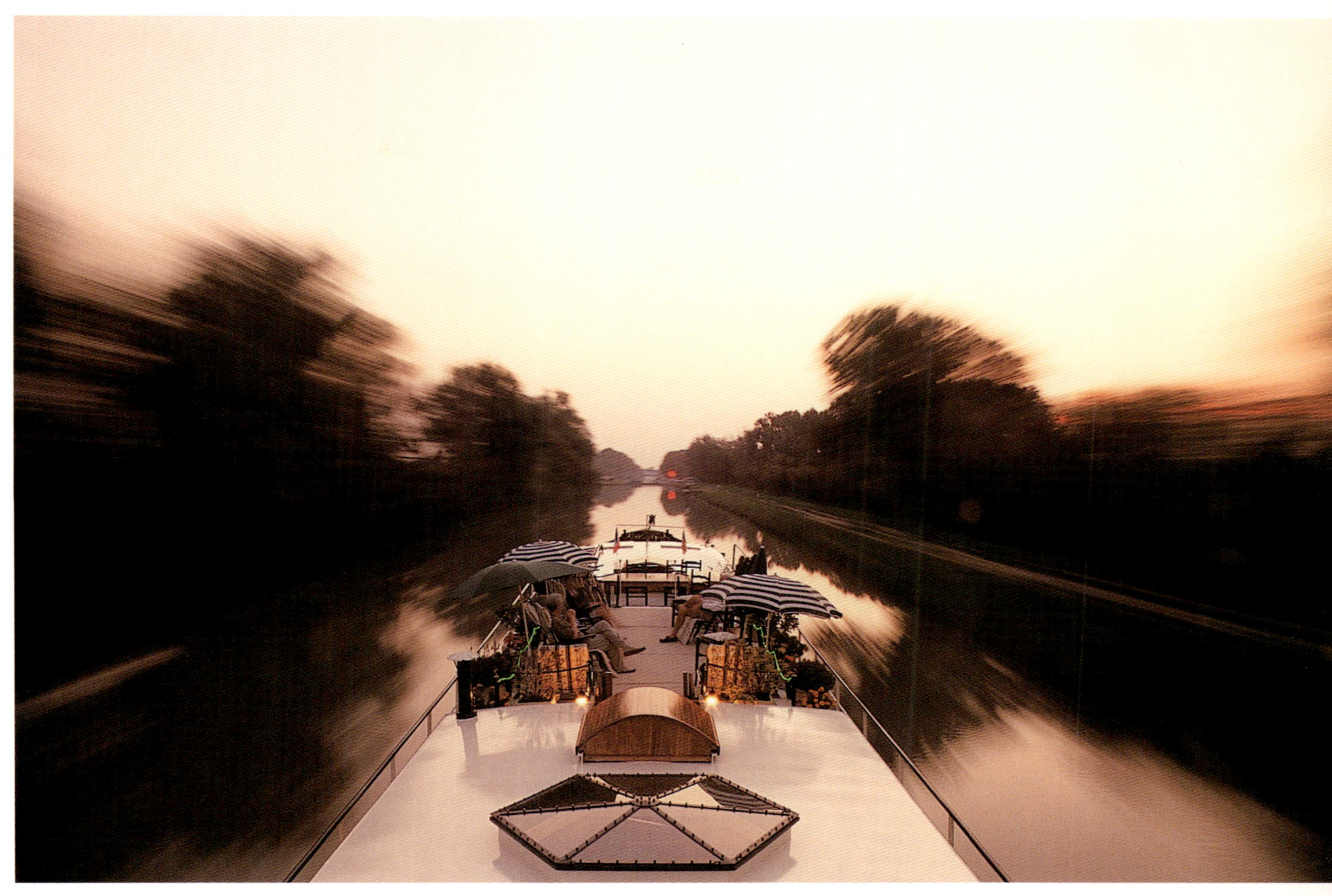

This is an ornithologist's paradise. We cruise through the narrow inland salt lakes, *étangs*, home to white egrets, kingfishers, and the curiously named bee-catcher birds. The Camargue is the only place in France, and one of the few around the Mediterranean, where the flamboyantly pink flamingos nest. The greatest number are present between April and September, when the flamingo population can reach 20,000 pairs clustered in flocks. They are protected birds, as the whole of the Camargue is a natural park. Effort is being made to keep a balance between the fragile indigenous ecosystems of the region and the effects of tourism, agriculture, industry and hunting.

Most days we cruised for three or four hours, stopping here and there to visit villages, vineyards, museums and monuments. After our shore excursions, we returned home, laden with history and shopping, to our welcoming and elegant water-carriage. Each time we saw her, we took satisfaction in the fact that our boat, while not the fastest on the floating highway, was unsurpassed in appearance.

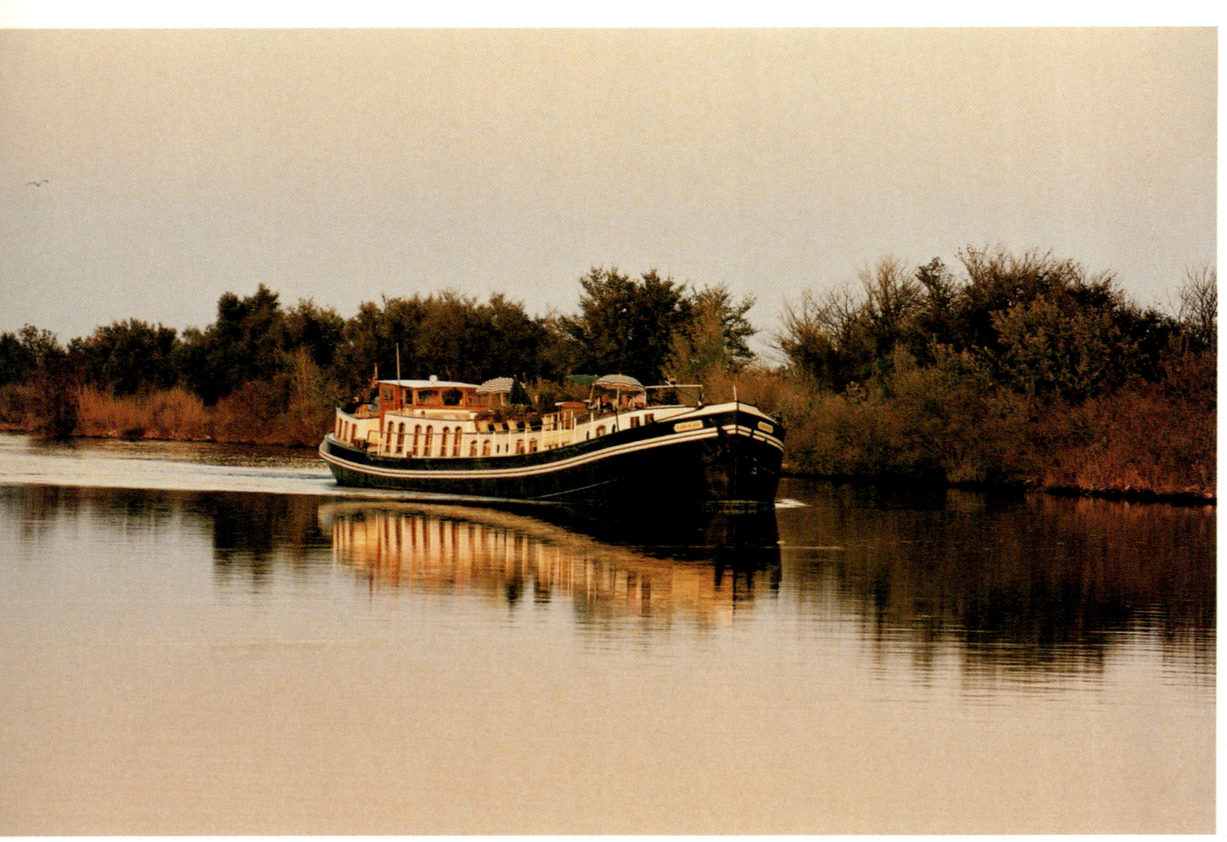

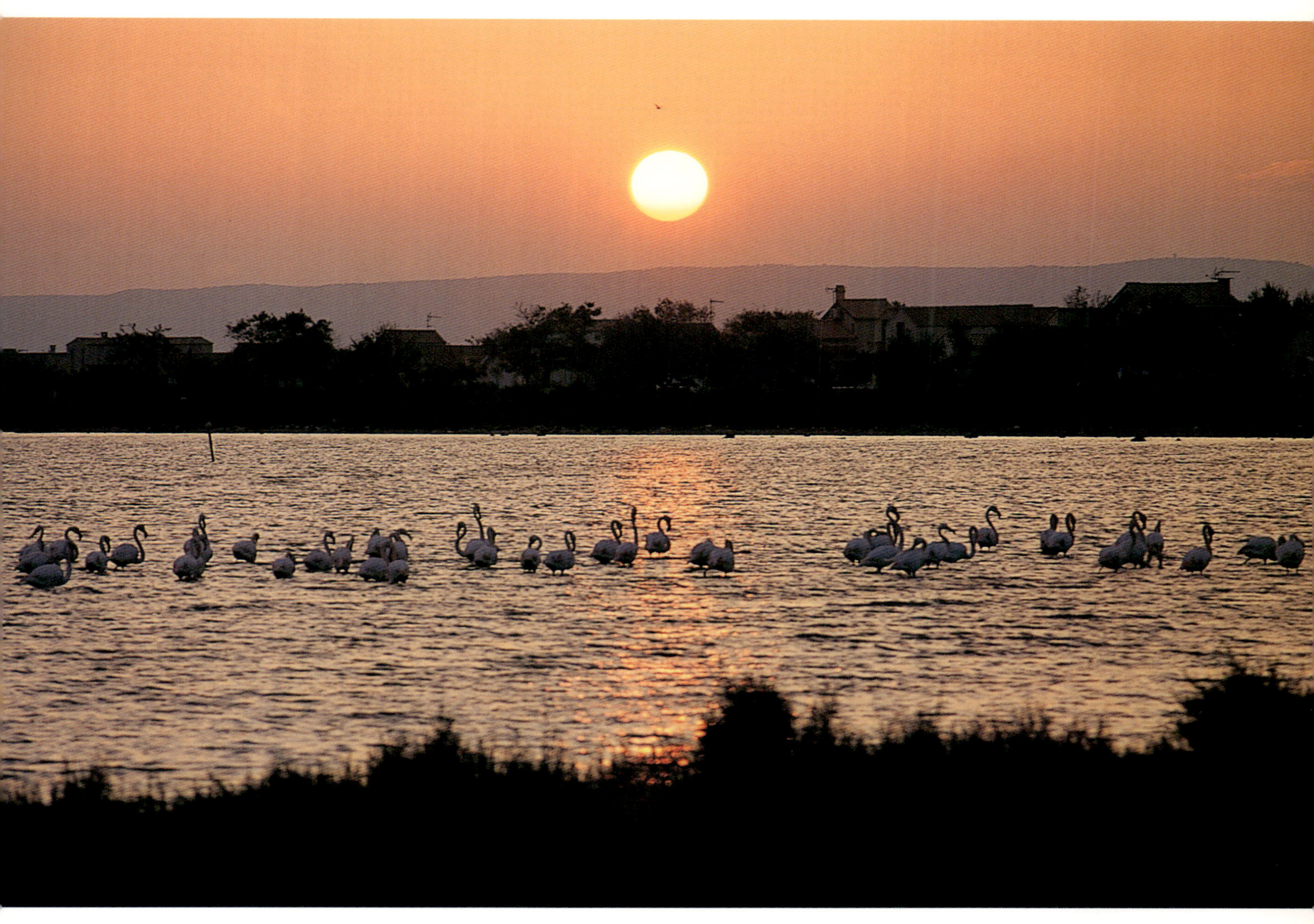

One of the most famous towns in the fascinating area of the Camargue is Saintes-Maries de la Mer. In May every year, gypsies from all over the world gather here to celebrate their patron saint Sara, a pilgrimage that dates from the 16th century. As we leave the Saroche, we plan a pilgrimage too, back to this beautiful *pêniche* and to the big sky country of the Camargue.

The Saroche | e: info@saroche.com | www.saroche.com

Space Odyssey Soon...

The unknown world is shrinking for the adventure seeker. Where next is there to travel in the quest for even greater adventure than that offered here on earth?

Out of this world will be the next frontier to cross, to 'boldly go' where few men and even fewer women have gone before – into the silence and stillness of space. Out there is a universe of travel possibilities. And as this will be as far away as you can go from 'the madding crowd', voyaging into space can truly be described as being 'out there'.

The space high above us has always been one to look up to, wonder and write about – from fantasy science fiction to factual scientific papers – and visualize in television programmes and movies. In 1969, one year after the launch of the seminal film '2001: A Space Odyssey', millions of people watched the Apollo 11 Moon Mission on television and saw the imagined become real. 'The Eagle has landed' were the words that heralded the arrival of humans on another sphere for the first time. Men stood and walked on the moon. From navigating by the stars as the early explorers did, mankind had progressed to navigating through the solar system. We had evolved from seafaring people to spacefaring pioneers.

Since the beginning of space exploration and the heroic exploits of the astronauts, millions of others have dreamed of going up there too. With the launch of the International Space Station in 2000, there are now humans living in space, for only the third time since Skylab and MIR provided astronauts with a home away from home.

Travel into space for tourists is not just a flight of fancy. Passenger voyages are already being planned. And once passage is booked, a place to stay will be required. Will there be a Hotel Galactica, a place in the universe for ordinary mortals to check into?

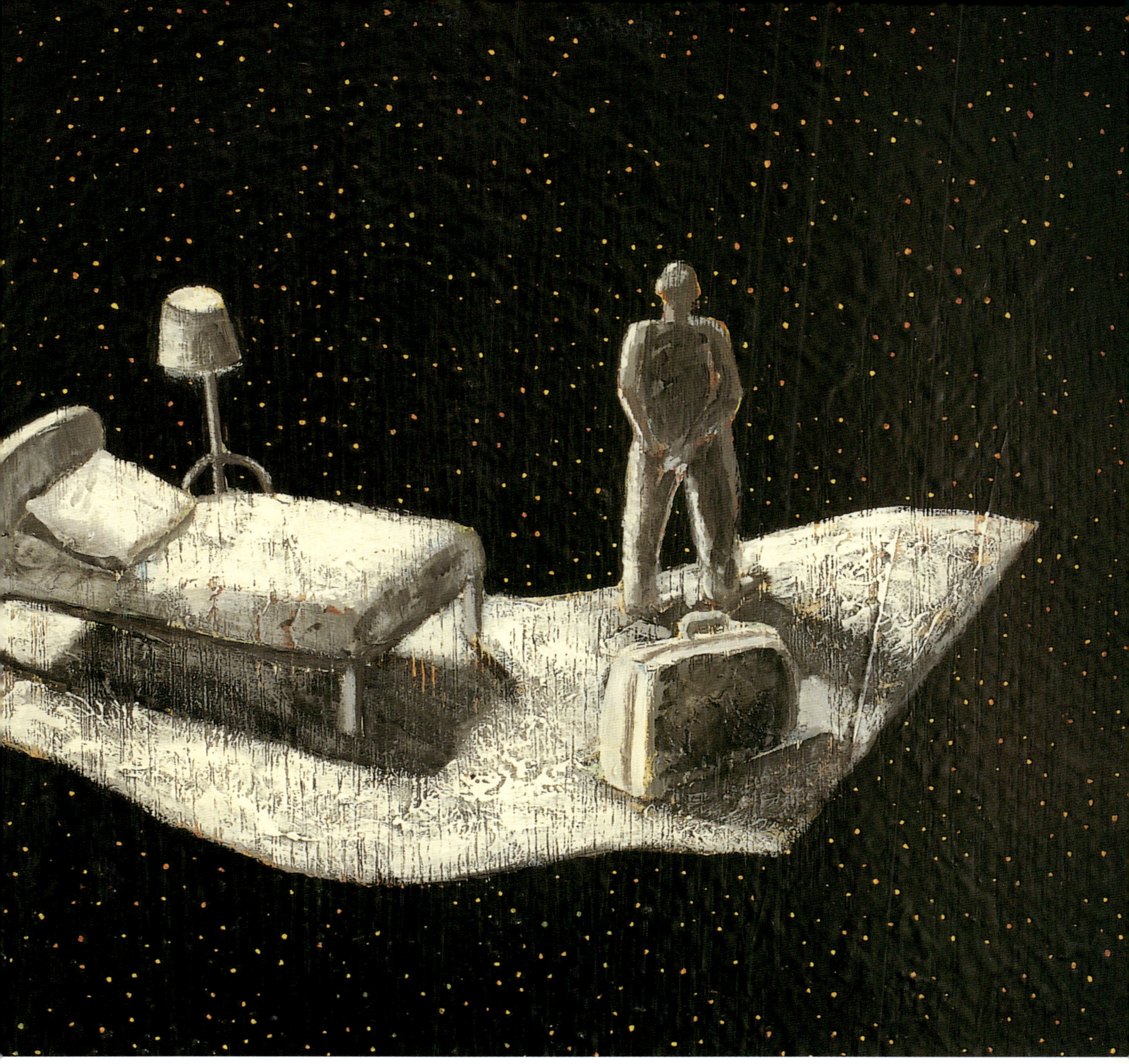

'TO CONFINE OUR ATTENTION TO TERRESTRIAL MATTERS WOULD BE TO LIMIT THE HUMAN SPIRIT.'

Stephen Hawking in his foreword to the book The Physics of Star Trek, *by Lawrence M. Krauss.*

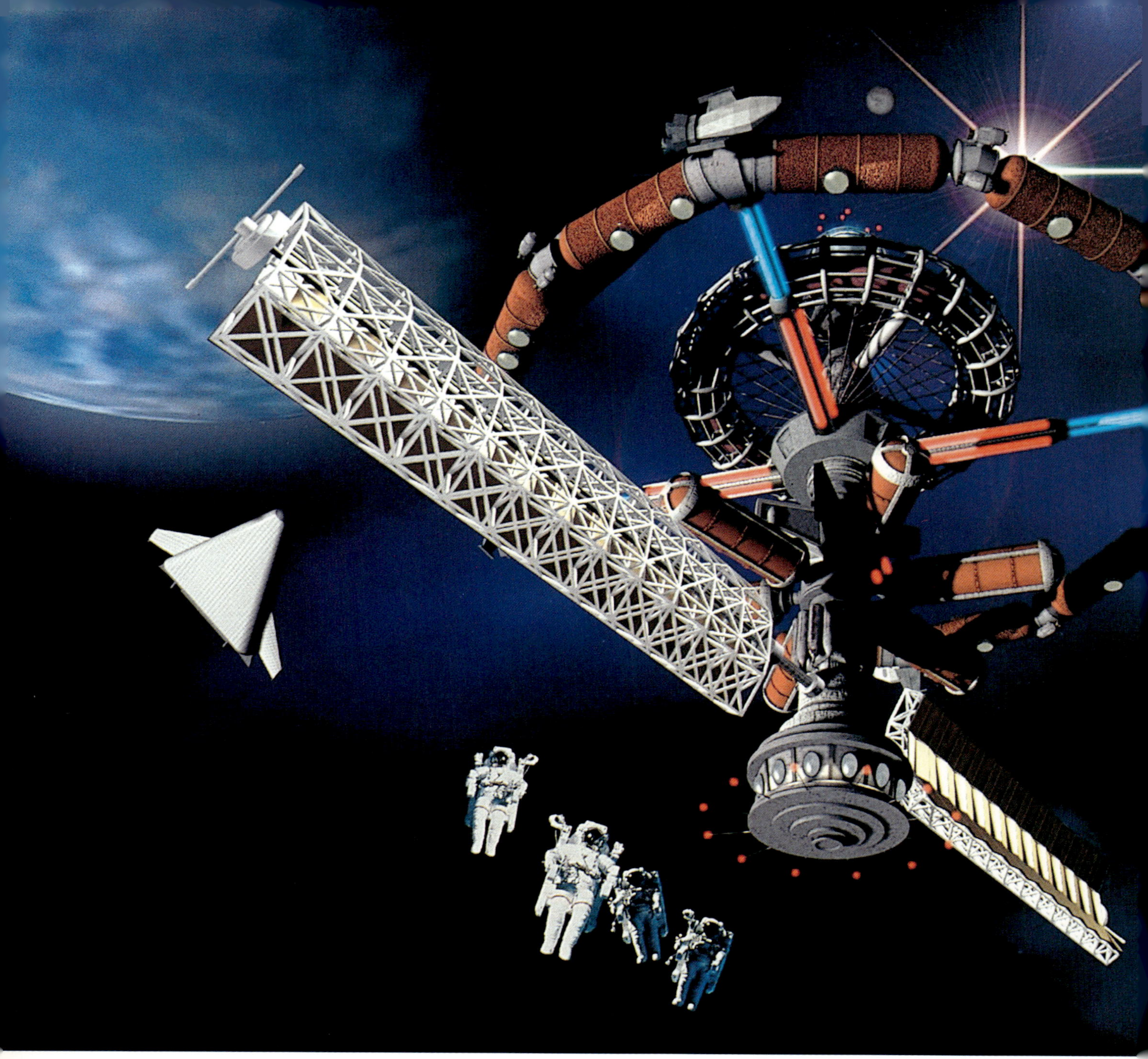

‘BEAM ME UP SCOTTY.’

Captain James Kirk, captain of the Starship U.S.S. ‘Enterprise’.

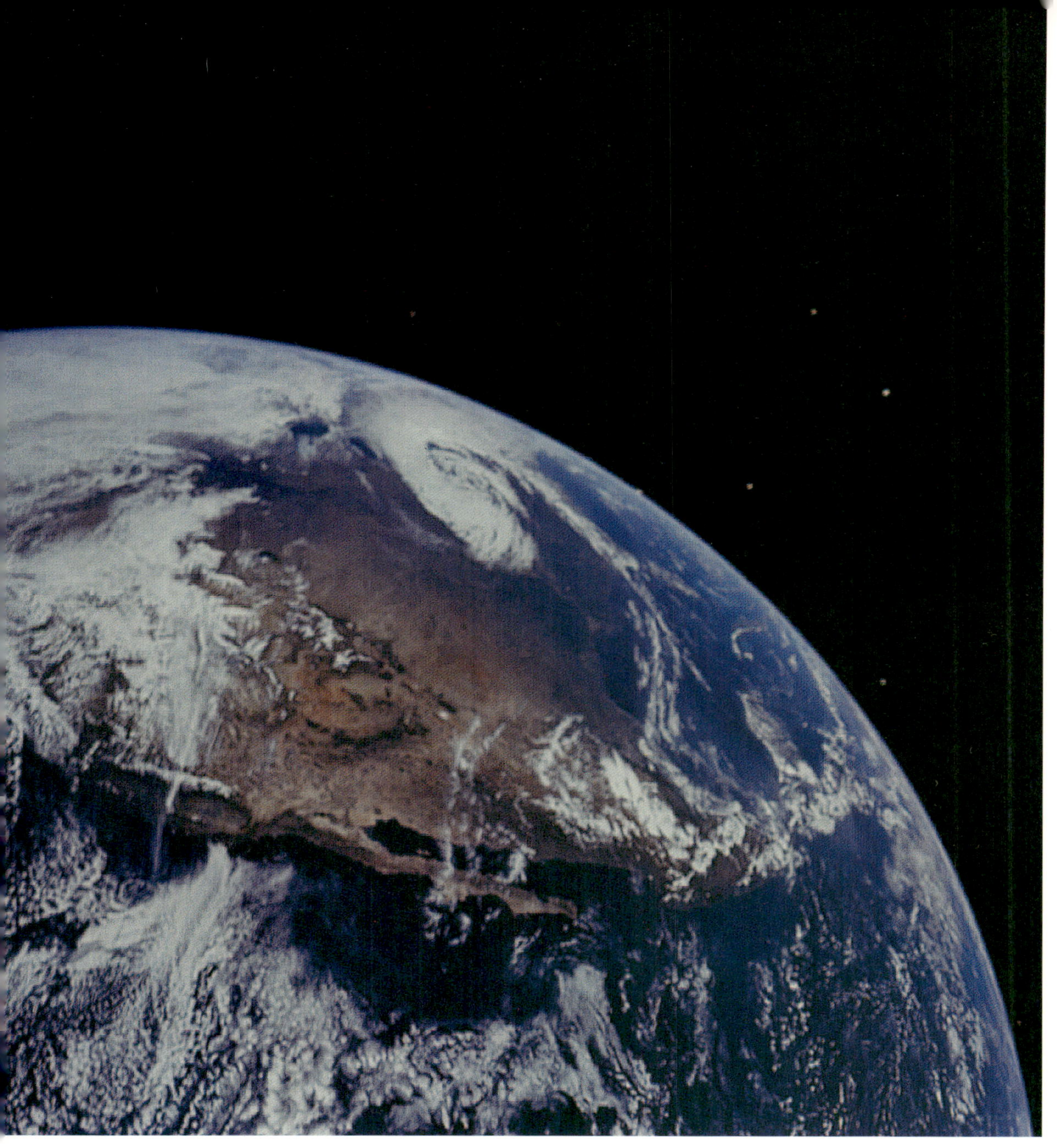

'THE VIEW FROM SPACE IS LIKE HAVING A GLOBE ON YOUR DESK. IT'S A BROADENING EXPERIENCE AFTER LOOKING AT PARTS OF THE EARTH ONLY ON MAPS TO THEN SEE THEM FOR REAL.'

Buzz Aldrin, former astronaut and the second man to walk on the moon.

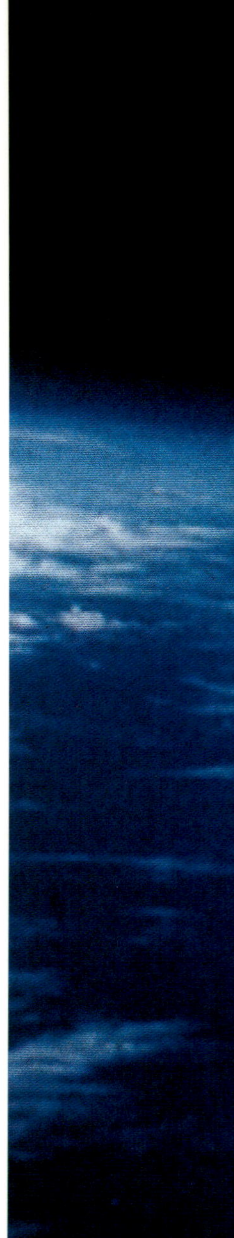

What else would there be to do in orbit? You might tire of stargazing and moonwatching, and hanker for other activities, all of which will have an added spatial dimension. Opportunities to play sports like tennis and squash, and go shopping, a favourite pastime of tourists elsewhere, will be provided. Getting married in orbit will at least cut down on the guest list, and make the honeymoon destination an easy choice. Space spas will pamper and soothe the stressed.

One of the great attractions of being in space is the state of weightlessness. The hotel will likely be divided between zones of micro and artificial gravity, to allow guests to experience floating in space, and provide a refuge for those suffering from space sickness. Most astronauts are affected with 'space adaptation syndrome'. However, it only lasts a few days, hopefully over before you come back down to earth.

To counter this syndrome, areas of the resort will rotate to provide some gravity, equal to about one-sixth of the earth's gravity. An area with artificial gravity will allow guests to lay in bed, take a shower, or sit down to a meal without having to be strapped down or stuck by Velcro to the wall.

And what of micro-gravity activities behind closed bedroom doors? The possibilities and challenges of weightless sex in space are what people are most curious about, but as yet there is no factual information that can be divulged here. This is positioning and performance detail still to be reported. However, it is guaranteed that the earth will move, or rather, orbit.

Those who are the first to journey to Destination Space will have the ultimate in travel stories to tell on their return. While they are there they can literally look back on where they have been. And who knows what other intelligent life they might meet?

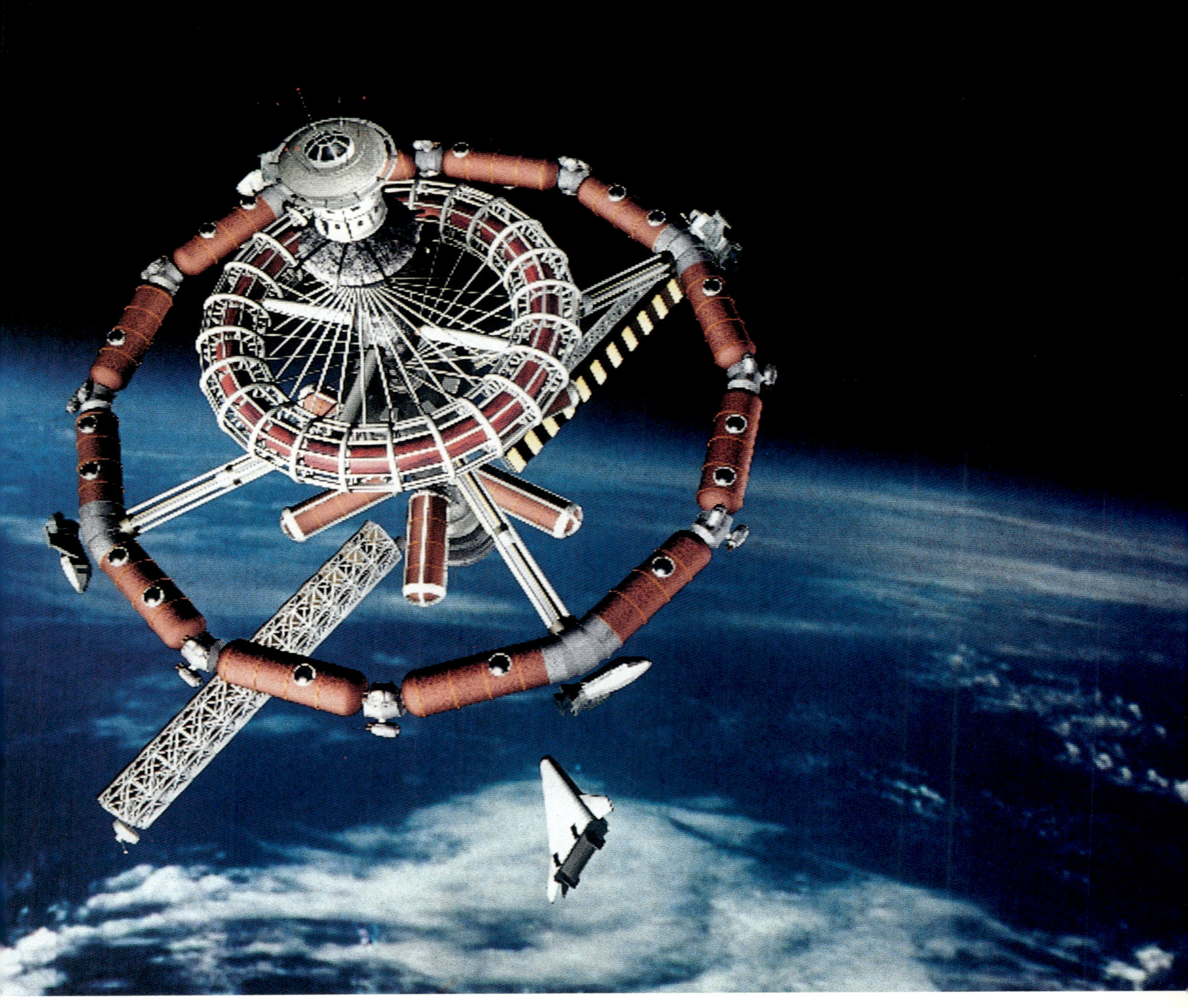

WAT&G is terrestrially-based, with offices in Honolulu, London, and Singapore | www.watg.com

Space Voyages, Seattle, USA | www.spacevoyages.com

National Aeronautics & Space Administration, (NASA), Washington, USA | www.nasa.gov

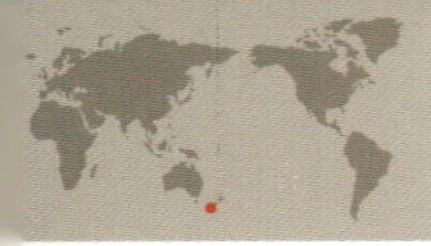

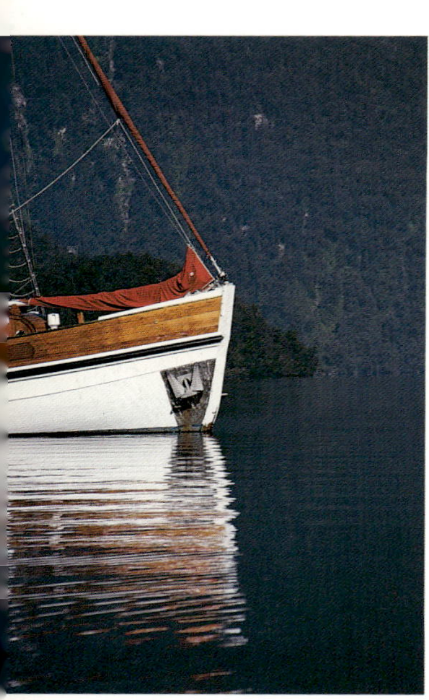

The Sound of Silence...

The Royal Yacht Galerna, Fiordland, New Zealand

To the pioneer explorers of the 17th and 18th centuries, navigating their frail boats around the globe was as much an adventurous journey as the voyage today's astronauts take into deep space, both leading the way into unfamiliar worlds beyond. And for those early seafarers there was an extra risk – perhaps, as some feared long ago, the Earth was not round but flat, and at any dangerous moment all hands would be lost, overboard, not from the ship but off the edge of the known world.

As they entered the calm waters of the fiords on New Zealand's rugged west coast, seeking shelter from boisterous seas and a well-earned rest from years of hard sailing to chart new lands, the mariners may have been met by a pod of dolphins. The self-appointed sentinels probably welcomed them into the harbour, weaving and diving around their ships, silvery flashes in the emerald green waters. Watching the dolphins' graceful water ballet, almost a show of greeting, the sailors would perhaps thought of their families far away, wondering whether they would ever see them again.

Curious and friendly creatures, bottlenose dolphins often ride the bow wave of boats here, and came out as if on schedule to escort our vessel as it sailed into Patea, the original Maori name for our destination, meaning the Sound of Silence. Doubtful Harbour was the more prosaic name was given later to this majestic place by English explorer Captain James Cook in 1770. On the day he sailed by the entrance, he decided the wind direction made it too great a risk to go in further. Its hidden beauty was discovered years later, yet no amendment was made to the rather unattractive name Cook bestowed on the lovely fiord, and the title remains on the charts.

Centuries later we journey here, seeking a few days of quiescence as respite from a noisier city life, sailing the truly silent Sound aboard the luxury charter yacht *Galerna*.

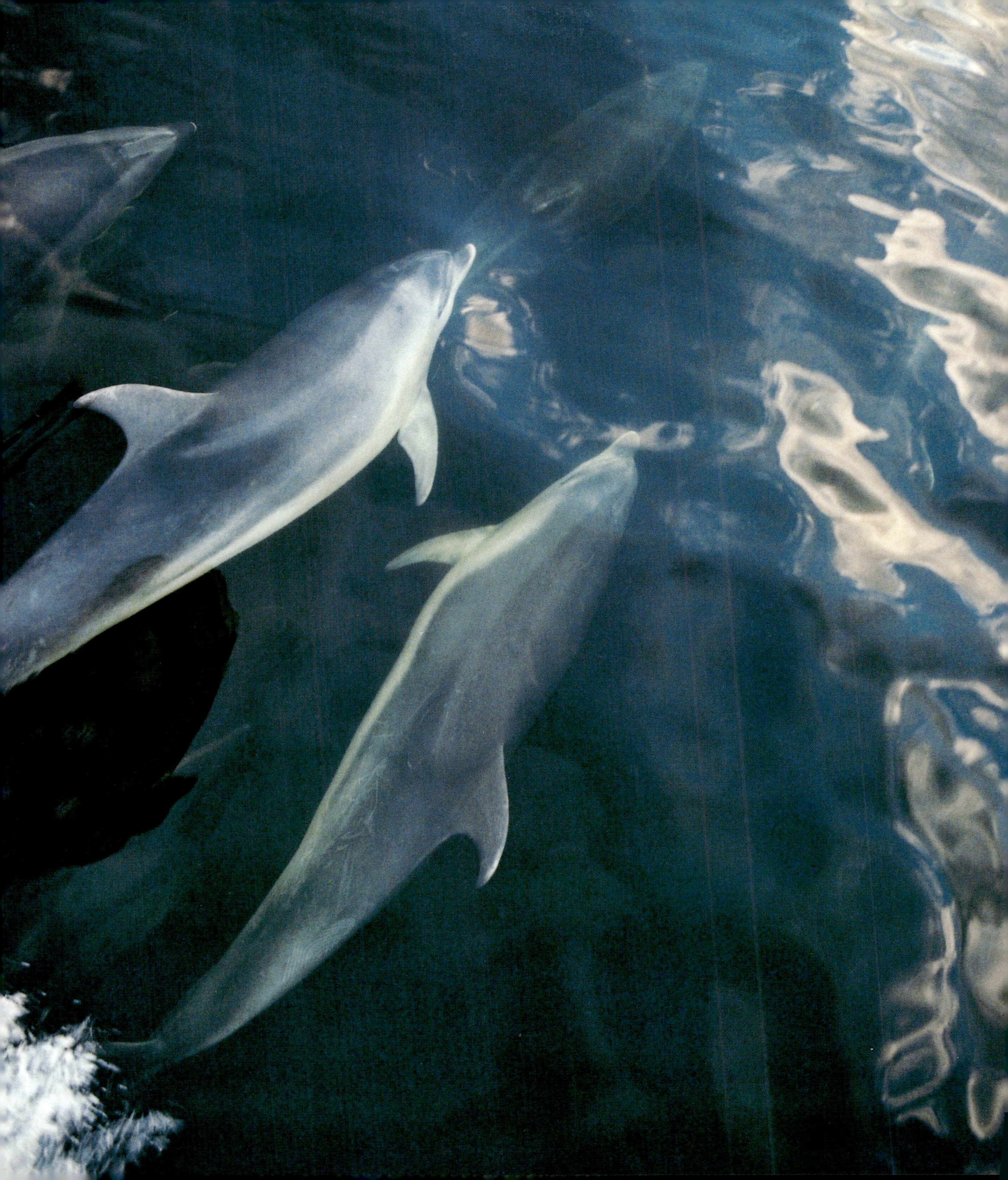

Doubtful Sound is far south in Fiordland, a remote part of New Zealand that is that country's largest and most stunning national park, a wilderness of towering mountains, deep valleys and long narrow fiords. Over millions of years, great glaciers have carved out a craggy terrain. Access here is deliberately kept limited, with just one public road and only a few tracks. Some of New Zealand's great walks are here, the renowned Milford Track, as well as the Routeburn and the Kepler. Why walk when you can sail, we decided, and opted for travelling by boat instead, of course intending to take regular strolls around the decks for exercise.

The perfectly clear day pictured belies the fact that this is an area of generous rainfall. Fiordland's annual average is measured in metres and its magnificent landscape is often hidden from view by veils of water and mist. So much rain falls that the top layer of the fiord is fresh water, with saltwater beneath. A bonus is that the rain keeps the dense greenery vivid, and the air so fresh and clean it seems to have a special fragrance.

The reward of fine weather is scenery on a spectacular scale. Vertiginous cliffs, with sheer rock-face walls, rise from the sea like great stone icebergs and soar up to the sky above, some looming more than 4000 feet above the water's surface. Beech and tropical rainforests cover much of the land, with lush ferns and moss cushions growing beneath the trees and bordering fiord banks. Its primeval wildness and mystery made Fiordland one of the evocative locations chosen for movie trilogy *The Lord of the Rings*.

Fiordland's most famous and accessible fiord is Milford Sound; consequently it is quite a busy place. As it is slightly more of an endeavour to reach Doubtful Sound, there is less water traffic, and more sailing space, as it is the deepest and biggest fiord, 22 miles long, with several arms and coves and water depths in excess of 420 metres. Scuba divers can visit gardens of rare black coral and join the teeming fish society hidden below the surface.

Nature is not always quiet; her noises are sometimes as grating as urban sounds – compare the rural rooster with city sirens. The chief and tolerable din here is the daily dawn chorus, led by the liquid songs of native tuis and bellbirds, choristers of the bush, and at times the thunder of myriad waterfalls.

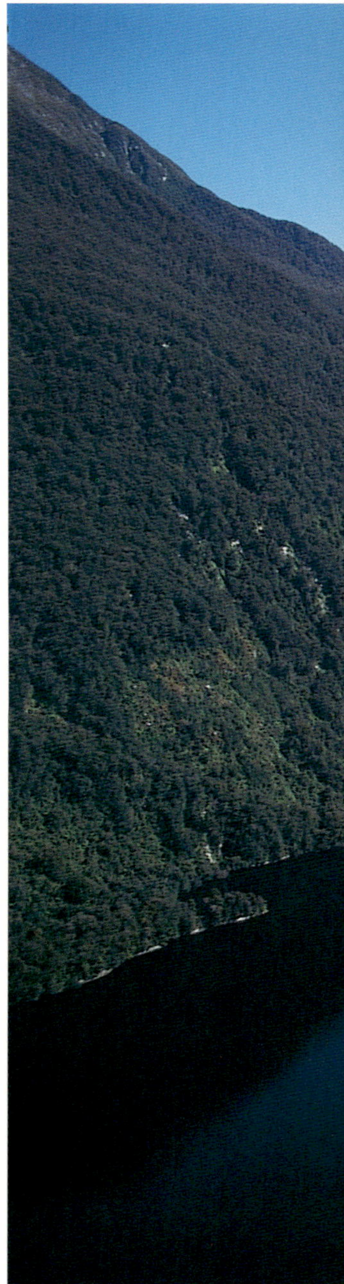

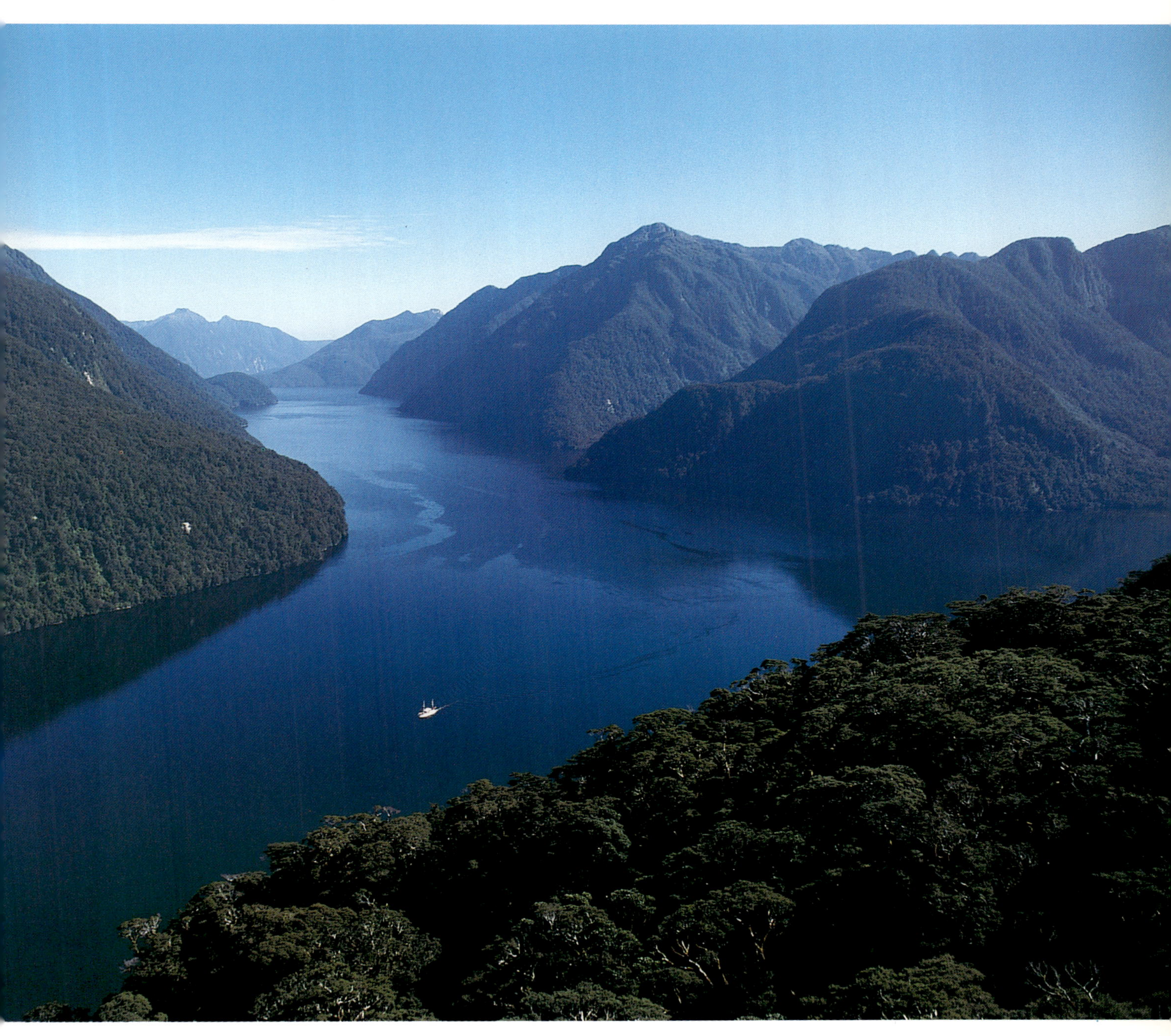

A bird's-eye view of Fiordland's Doubtful Sound, on a glorious South Pacific morning, with the Galerna sailing centre fiord.

After our helicopter flight over the Southern Alps, we were glad to have our feet on the solid teak decks of the stately Galerna. Once host to the Swedish Royal family, the Galerna was built in 1972 for their Highnesses' cruising pleasure in Scandinavian seas. Crafted in Norway and Sweden with solid timbers – oak, mahogany, ash and teak – the yacht is now at home in New Zealand, where she sails Auckland's harbour and Hauraki Gulf in the summer months of November to March. She travels south for the winter – April to July – to Fiordland, further down the coast to Stewart Island and sometimes as far as the sub-Antarctic Auckland Islands to observe the great Southern right whale migration.

The yacht is well equipped for game fishing and deer hunting expeditions, or gentler pursuits such as shooting scenery on a photography safari in this undeniably photogenic environment. It is an ideal escape vessel for a few days of comparative solitude, rest and recreation with good food and wine in deluxe surroundings. And in Doubtful Sound, there is often the satisfaction of being aboard the only boat sailing in a remarkable setting.

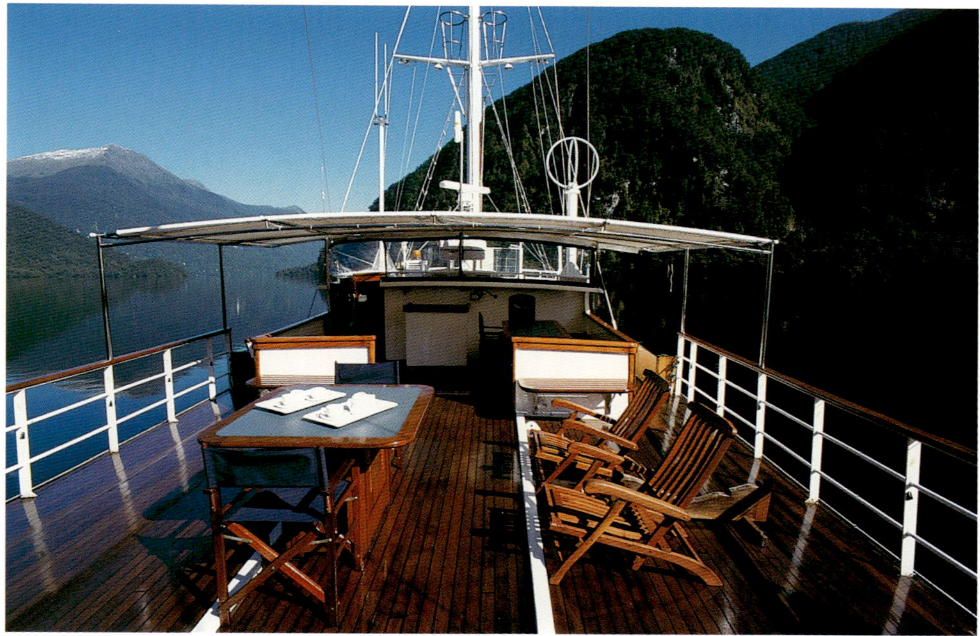

The upper deck of the Royal Yacht Galerna, a place to soak up the sun and silence;
Opposite, the classic yacht in profile.

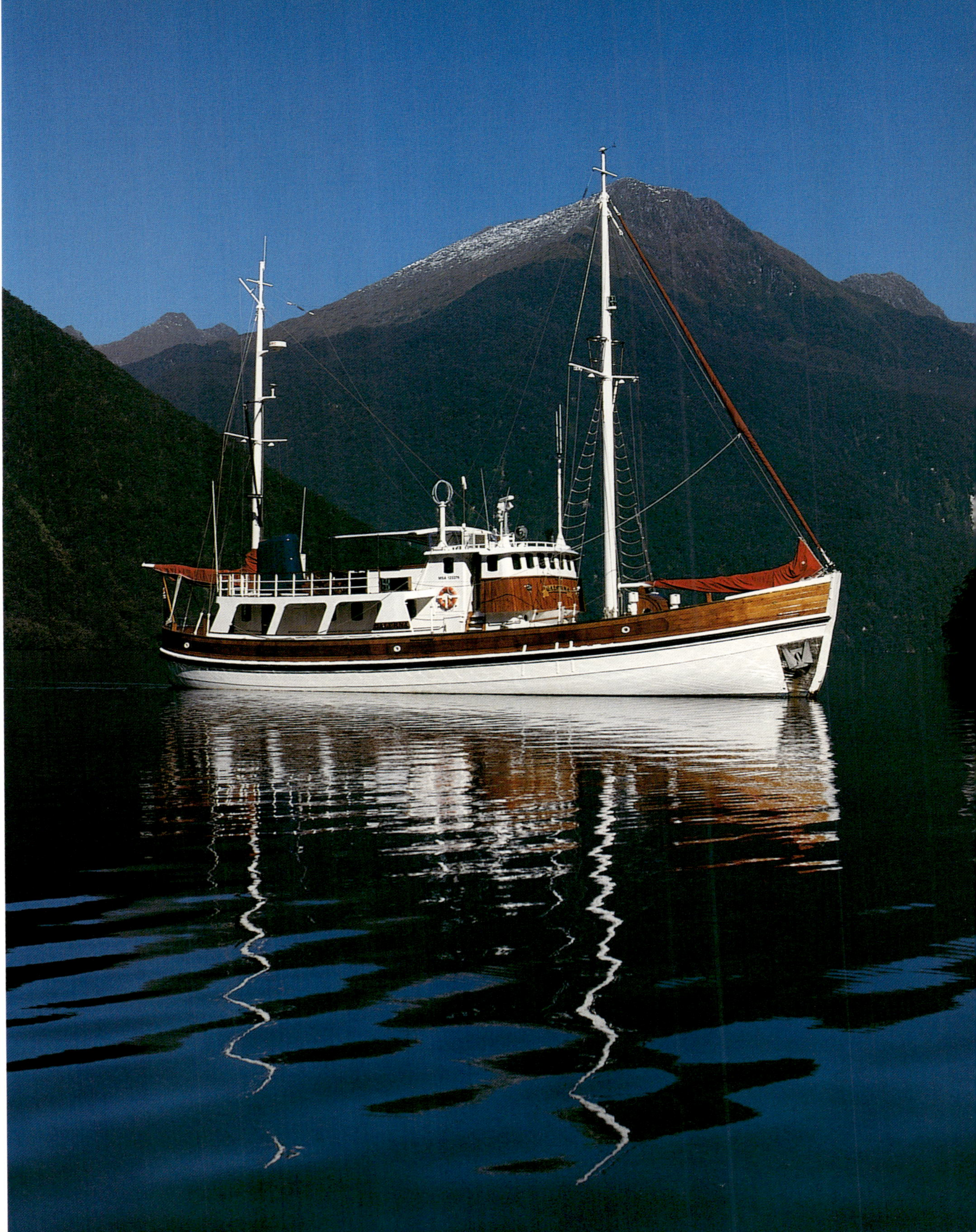

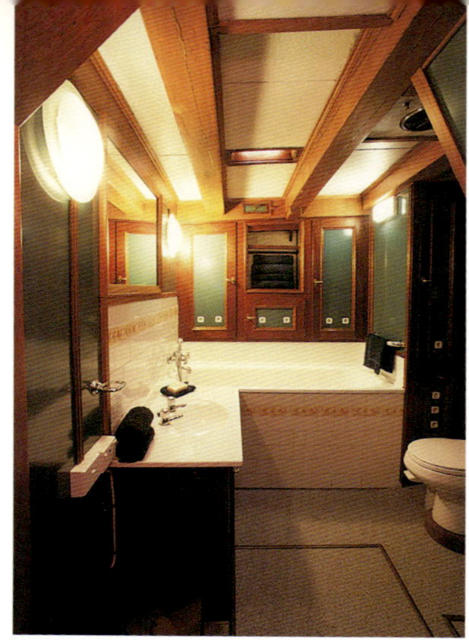

The Prince Henry Suite, with its appropriately royal queen size bed and en suite bathroom. It also has a sitting alcove and large Swedish sauna.
The Saloon, the yacht's comfortably appointed living and dining area, is on the opposite page.

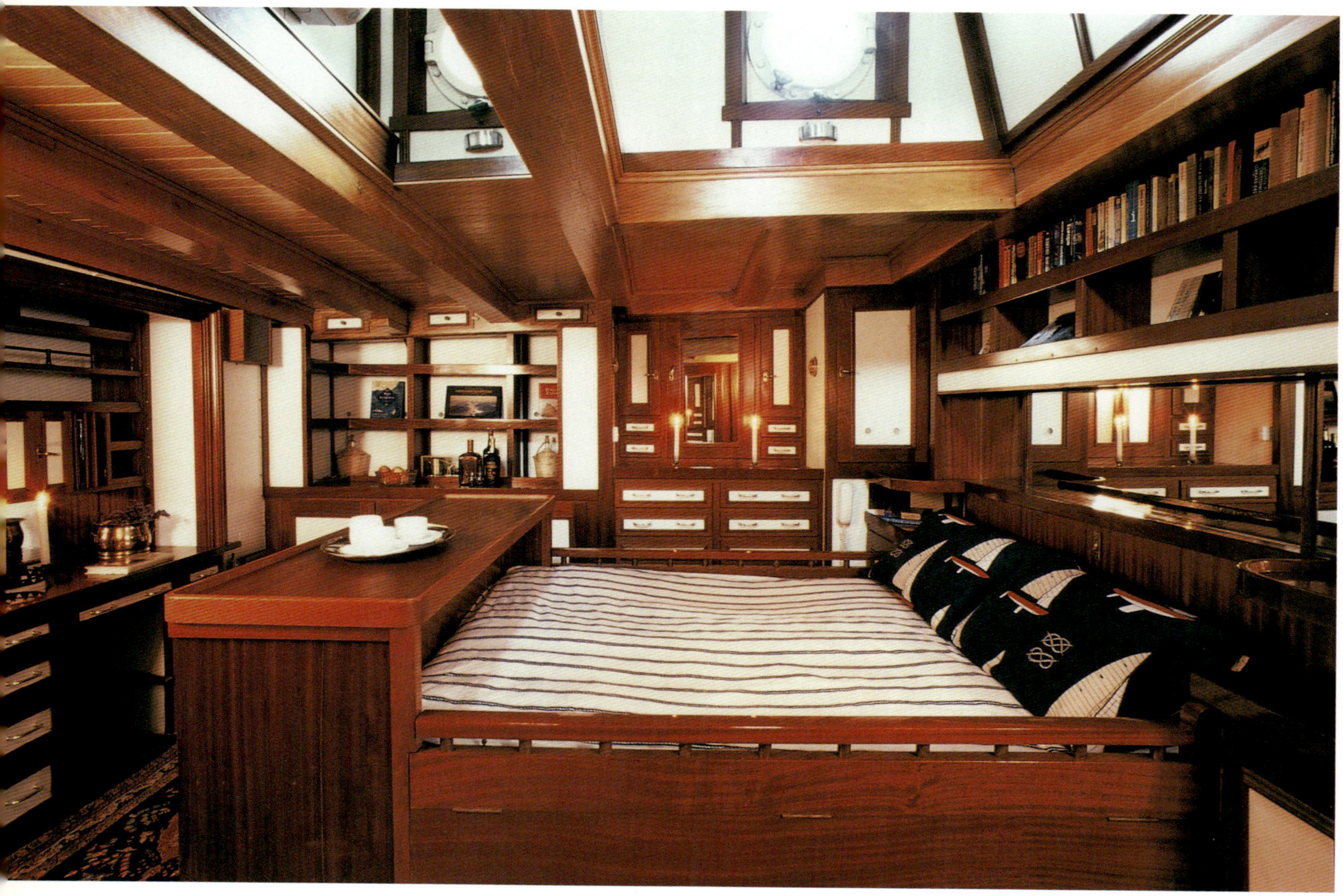

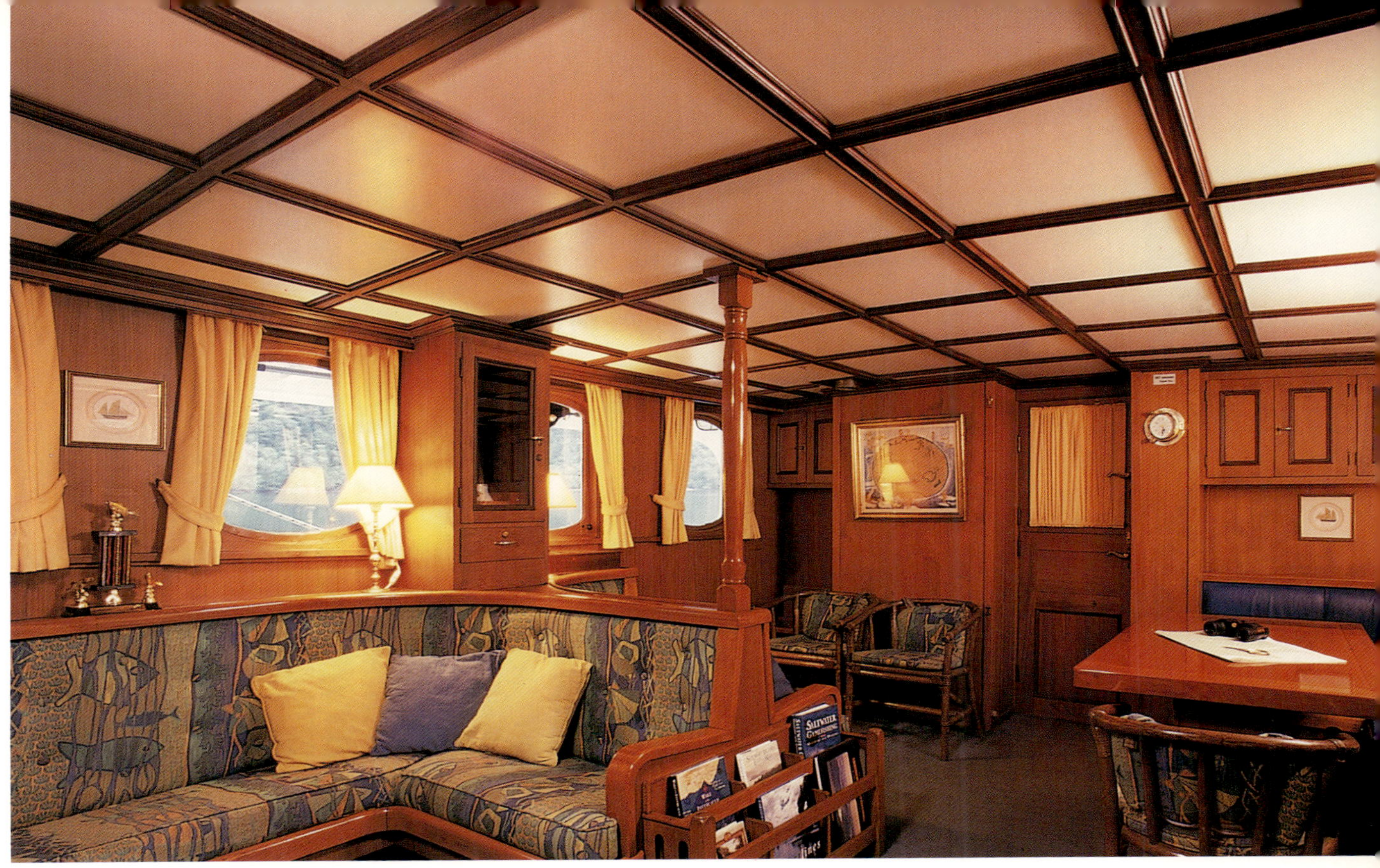

Spaciously laid out inside, the Galerna accomodates six passengers in three double cabins, and has a crew of four – engineer, boatmen, and chef – in addition to the captain. Although we had to settle for a short stay, we would have liked to keep this elegant yacht as an alternative floating home. It would be very agreeable to live aboard with its roomy attractive interiors, plenty of space for books and other essential comforts – as long as the crew came with the deal.

The on-board cuisine is centred on fish and shellfish – we could be sure of its freshness as we saw it harvested each day. Rock lobster, albacore and blue fin tuna, groper, cod, and paua (abalone) were on the menu, together with lamb and venison, matched with wines from the world's most southerly winegrowing region, Central Otago. Vineyards such as Chard Farm, Black Ridge, Rippon, Gibbston Valley and Mount Difficulty provided crisp chardonnays, aromatic rieslings and silky pinot noirs. The aroma of freshly baked bread wafted through the air each morning, acting as a silent yet persuasive wake-up call.

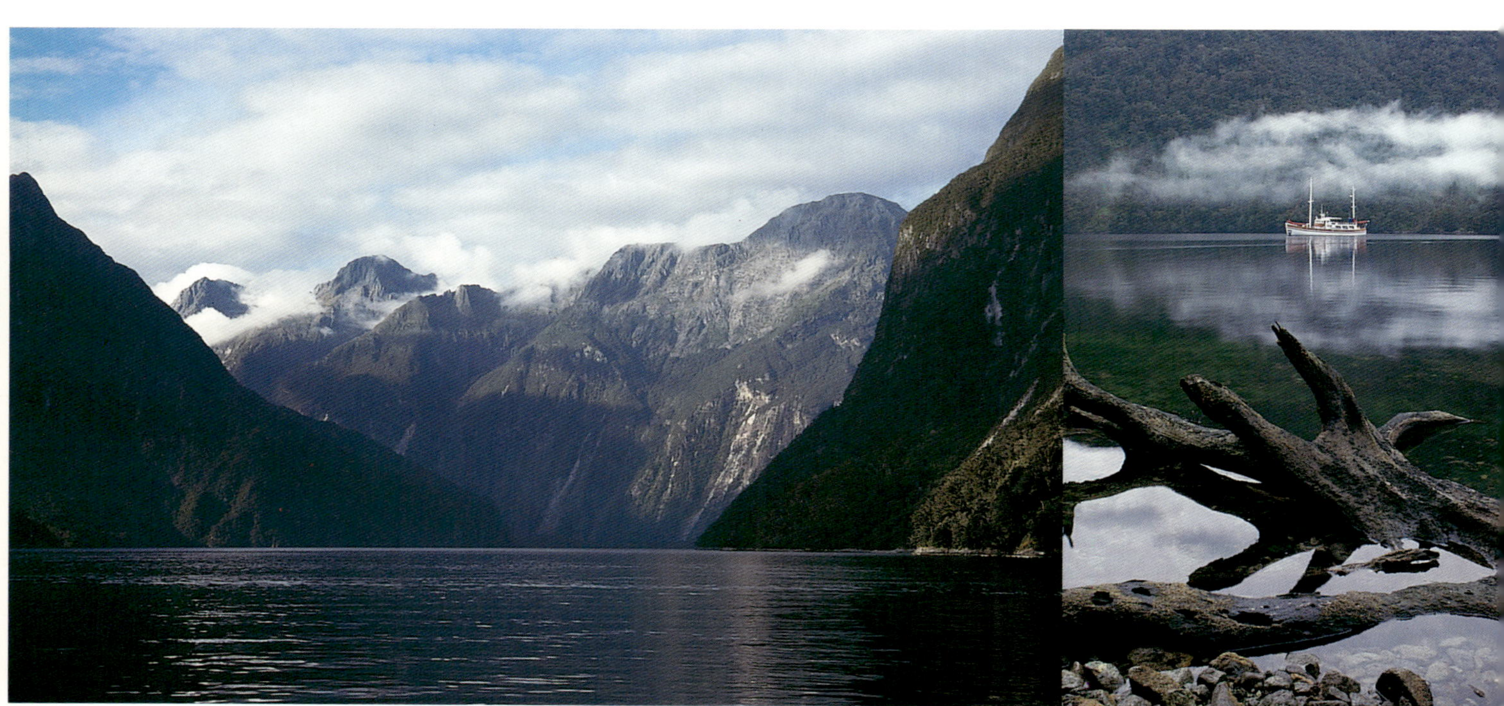

Few people live in this remote romantic region, its challenging often fortress-like terrain naturally preserves it from much settlement, but there is much wildlife at home here. Rare crested penguins, paradise ducks, kiwis, and herons are just some of the many resident birds. The native owl's plaintive call is often heard at night, sounding like a hungry guest in a restaurant crying out for 'more pork, more pork…'

Beautiful native pigeons and flashy parrots, from the mischievous kea to the kaka and rare kakapo live here, as do Southern fur seals, once hunted nearly to extinction, now protected. Sandflies, notoriously prolific, are the only savage creatures inhabiting the fiords. Although they usually stage a mass rally when alerted to my nearness, they must have been on holiday as only a few turned out, and my anti-attack lotion successfully repelled them.

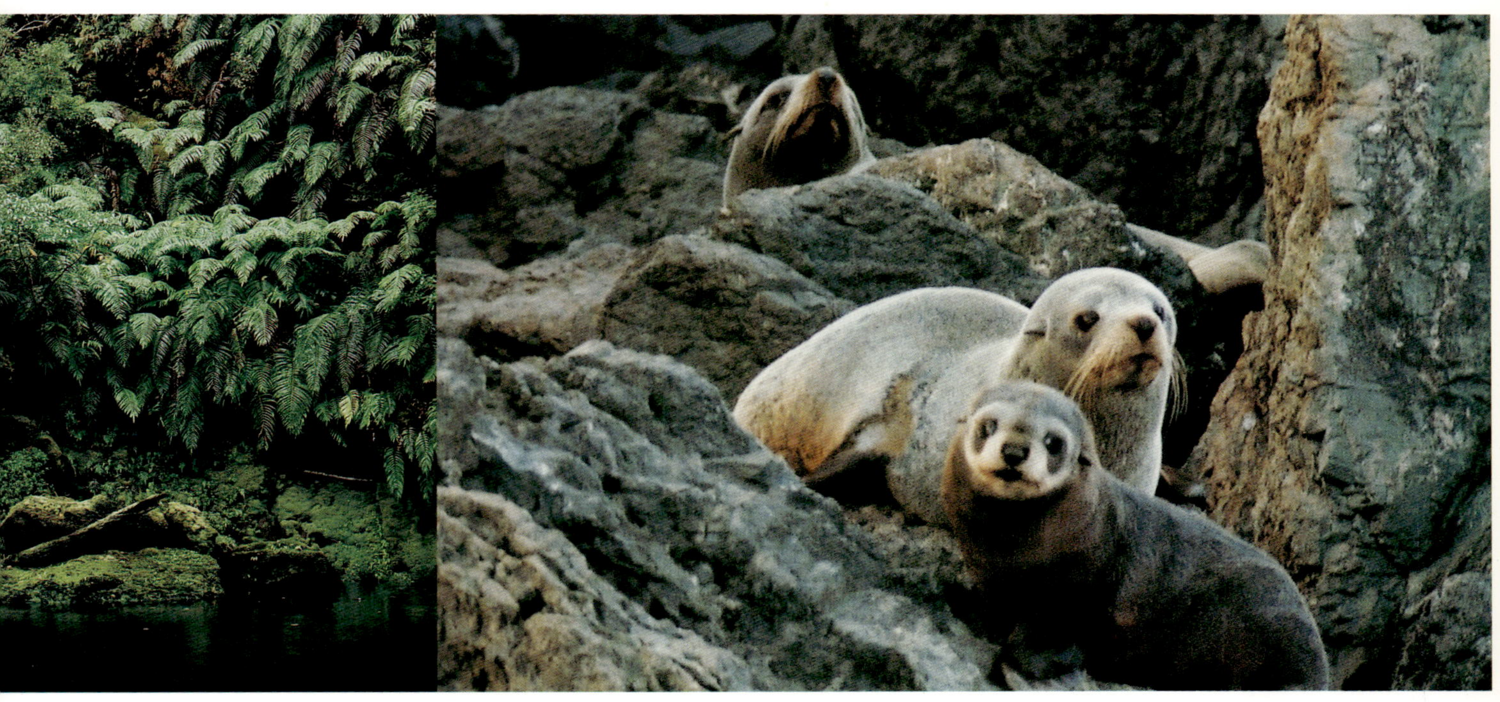

Following page: 'The remoteness and grandeur that is Fiordland, a boundless sea of mountains and valleys as far as the eye can see..'

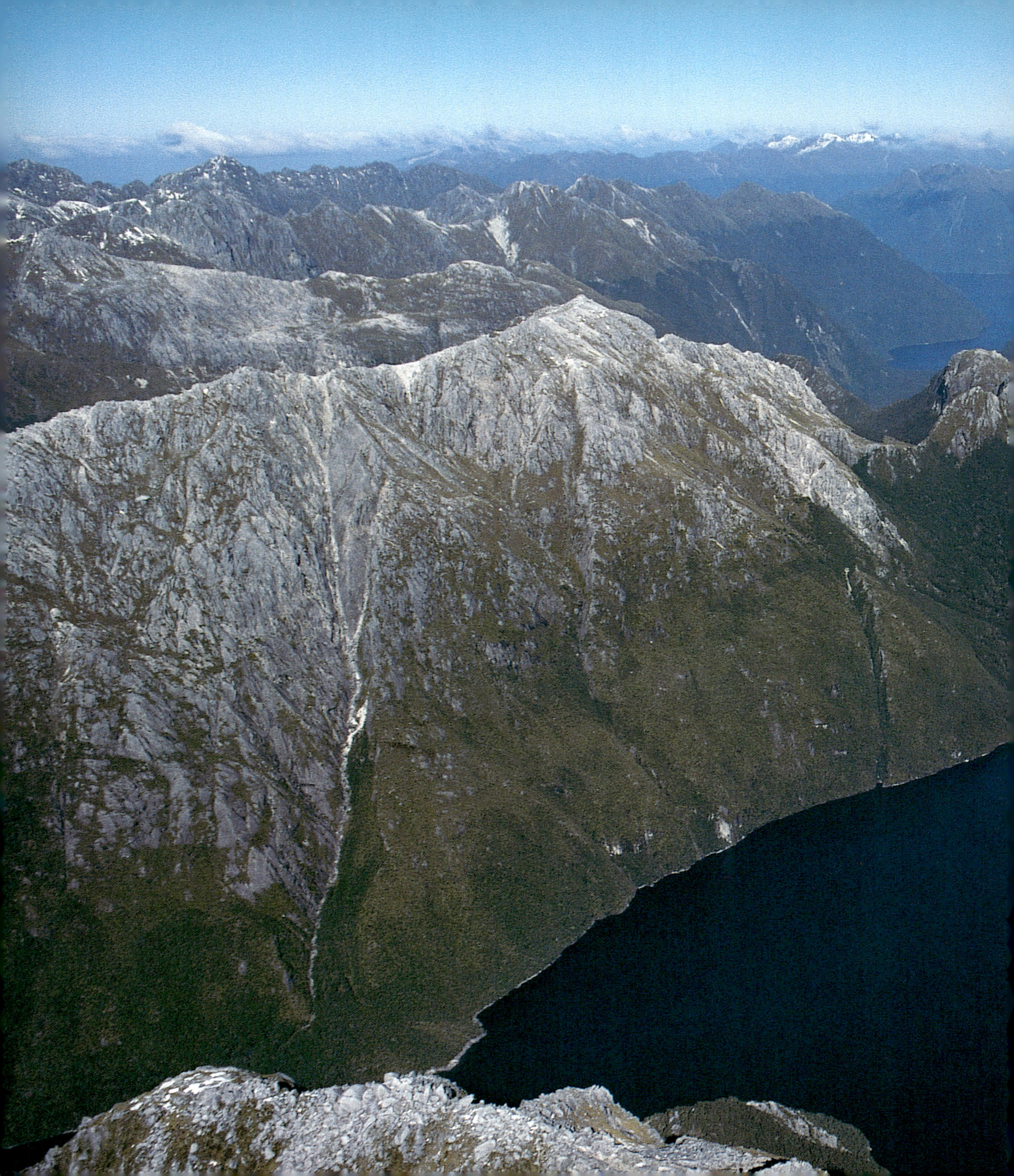

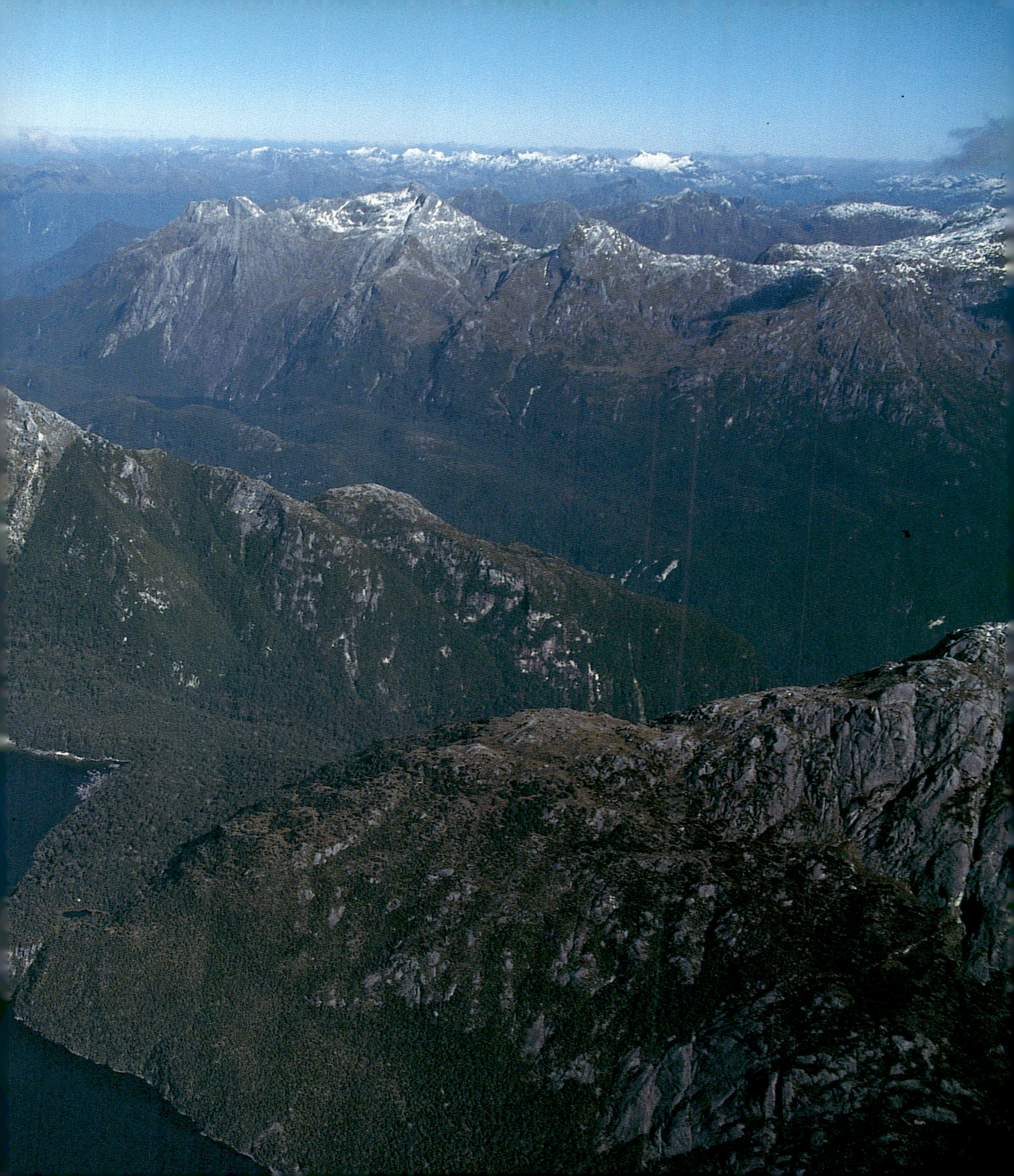

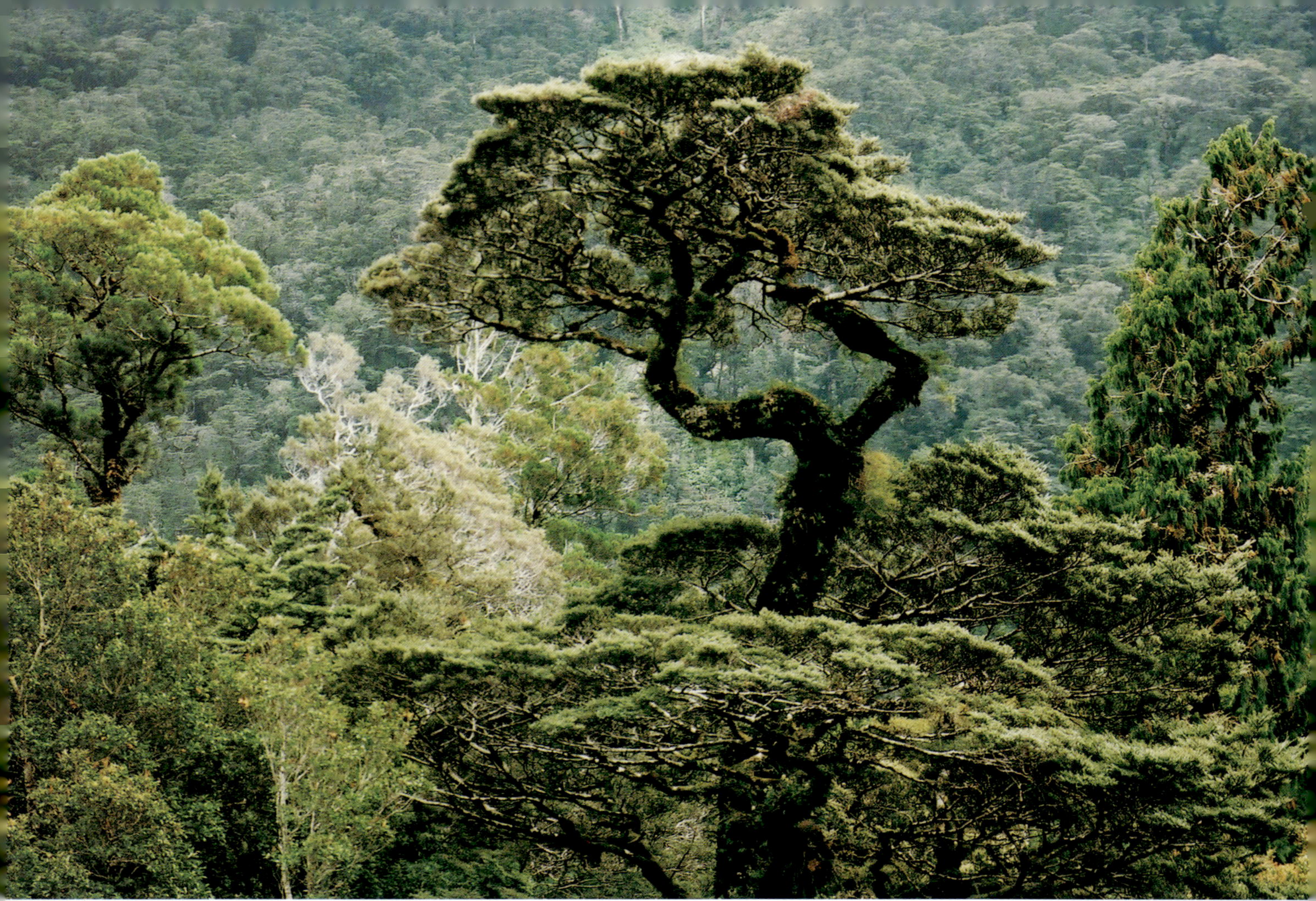

Forests of beech trees, some with bonsai-like shapes, line the valleys. In spring and summer, the green foliage is patterned with red splashes of the flowering rata vine, reminiscent of traditional Christmas colours.

Waterfalls are a constant yet changing feature, magnifying in size in response to the volume of rain. Like chain mail curtains made of water, the vertical streams cascade down the cliffs, white plaits often screening the dark granite rock face.

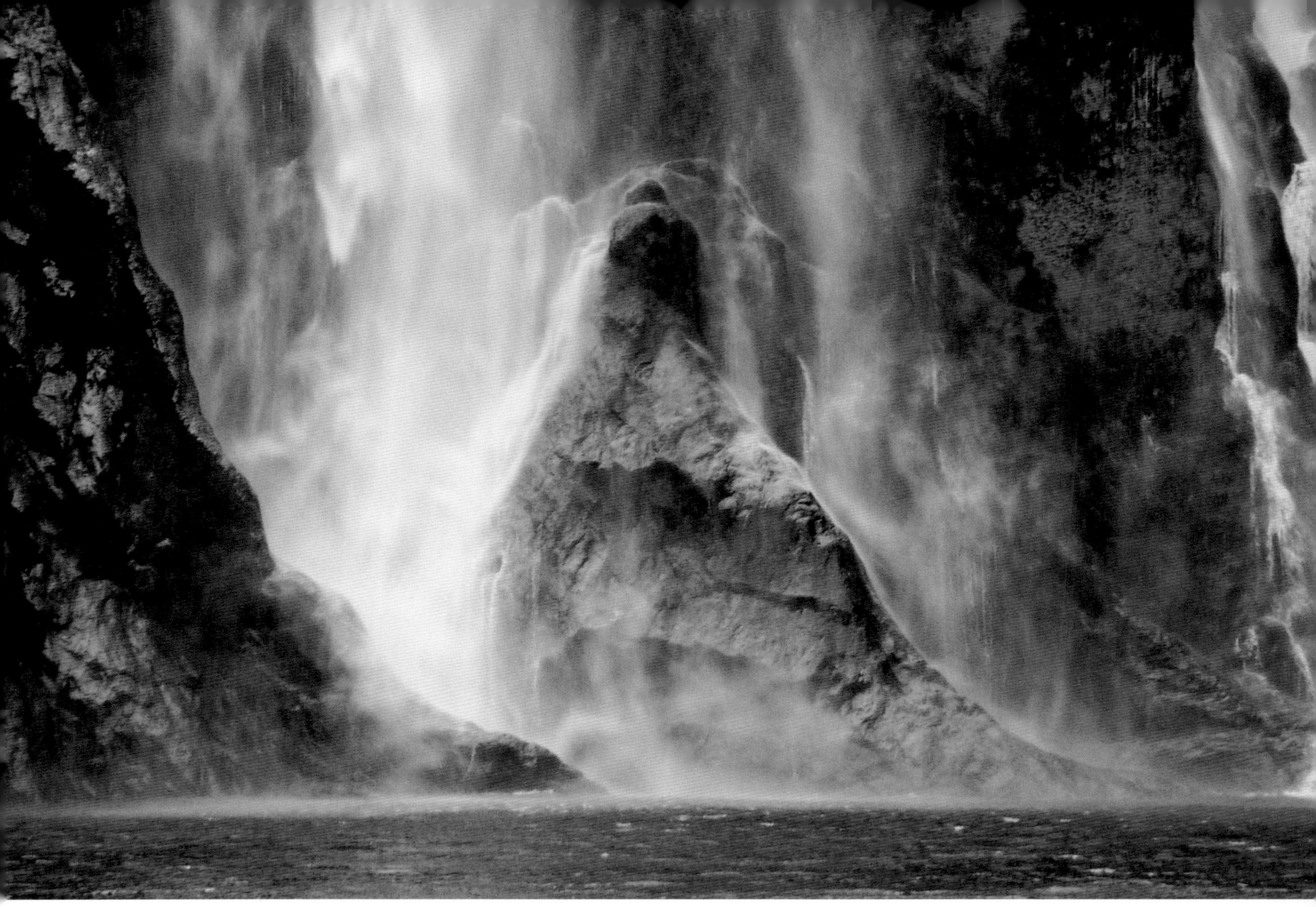

In our increasingly crowded world, where humans progressively encroach on wilderness areas, Fiordland is another special place to be protected so that future travellers may experience its stillness and restorative peace. As it was for the early explorers, the Sound of Silence and its sister fiords are a haven endowed with astounding scenery, a respite from modern day stress, noise and crowds.

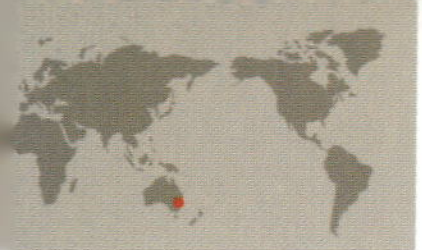

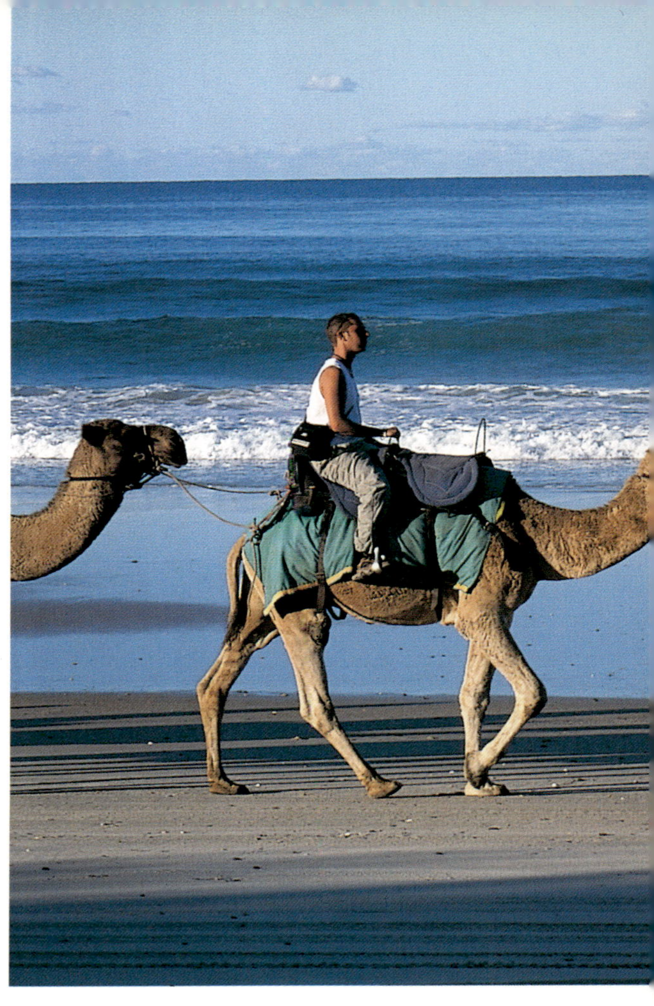

Camel Train...

The Camel Company Safari, Fraser Island, Australia

It's a long way from Afghanistan to Australia, but in the early 1880s, Afghan camelmen made the trip to help open up the vast Outback. With their camels, exotic-looking animals even in this land full of unusual creatures, the imported cameleers were guides for several major expeditions into the continent's immense dry interior, helped with the construction of the overland telegraph line and railways, and brought supplies and services to the inland mines and isolated farming stations. The cameleers and their hardy 'ships of the desert', so-called for their ability to carry heavy loads, made a vital contribution to the settlement of Australia's arid zones.

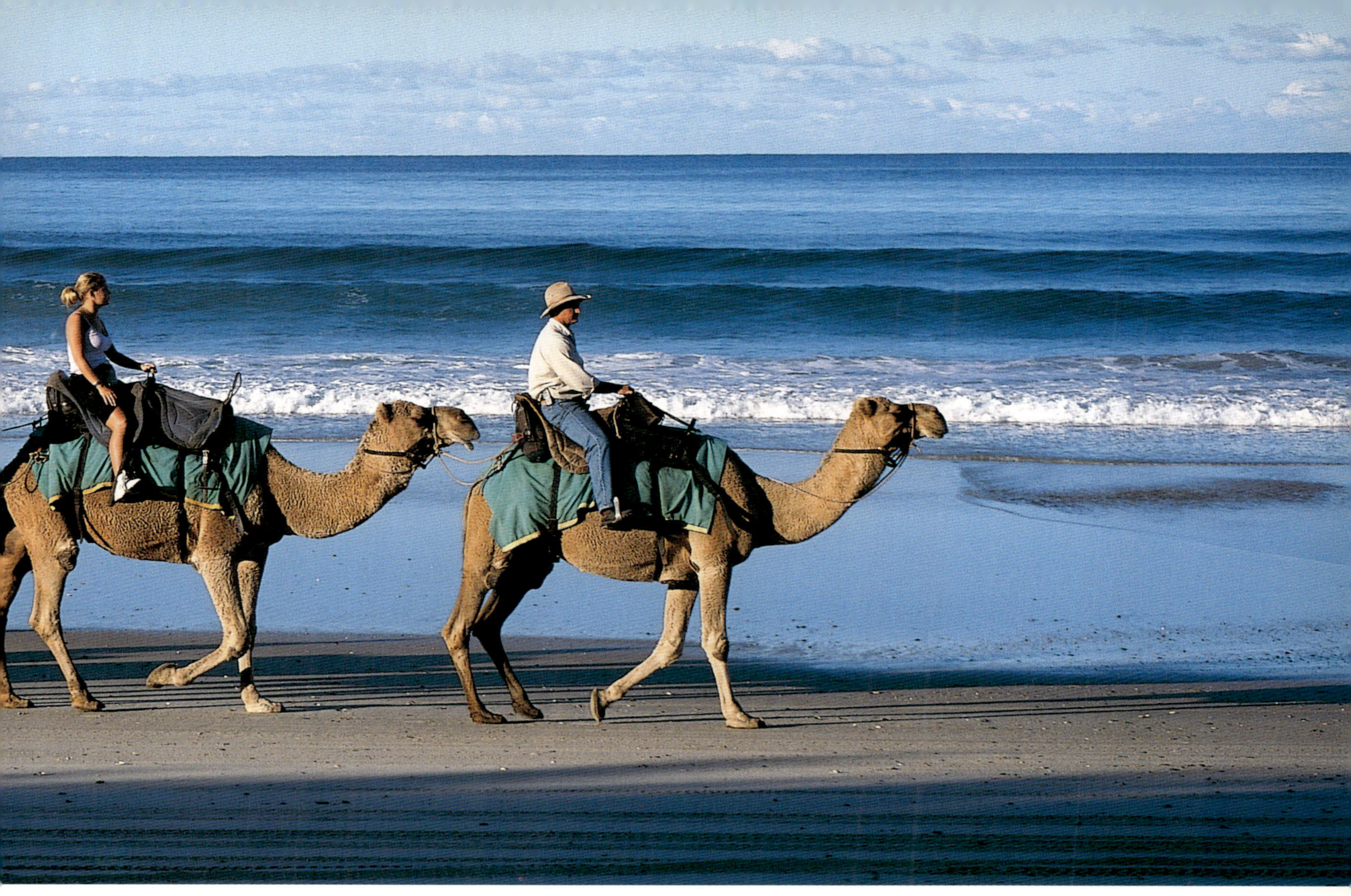

*THERE ARE THREE THINGS THAT CAN NEVER BE HIDDEN;
LOVE, A MOUNTAIN AND ONE RIDING A CAMEL...*

Arab proverb

Their pioneering work over, many descendants of those first camels range wild, or have been trained to provide a leisurely moving experience for the curious.

The lofty dromedaries afford their passengers with a grand view. Perched on a camel's back, whose average height is about 2.35m at the shoulder, the traveller is often above tree height, able to see far ahead. The animals walk at a steady pace, around five kilometres an hour, their looping gait generating a relaxing motion, for the rider similar to sitting in a rocking chair.

To try this ancient mode of transport we came to Australia's Sunshine Coast, a lush tropical region, to embark on the Camel Company's Wilderness Camping Safari on Fraser Island, a desert-like locality without the drawbacks, accessible yet still unspoilt.

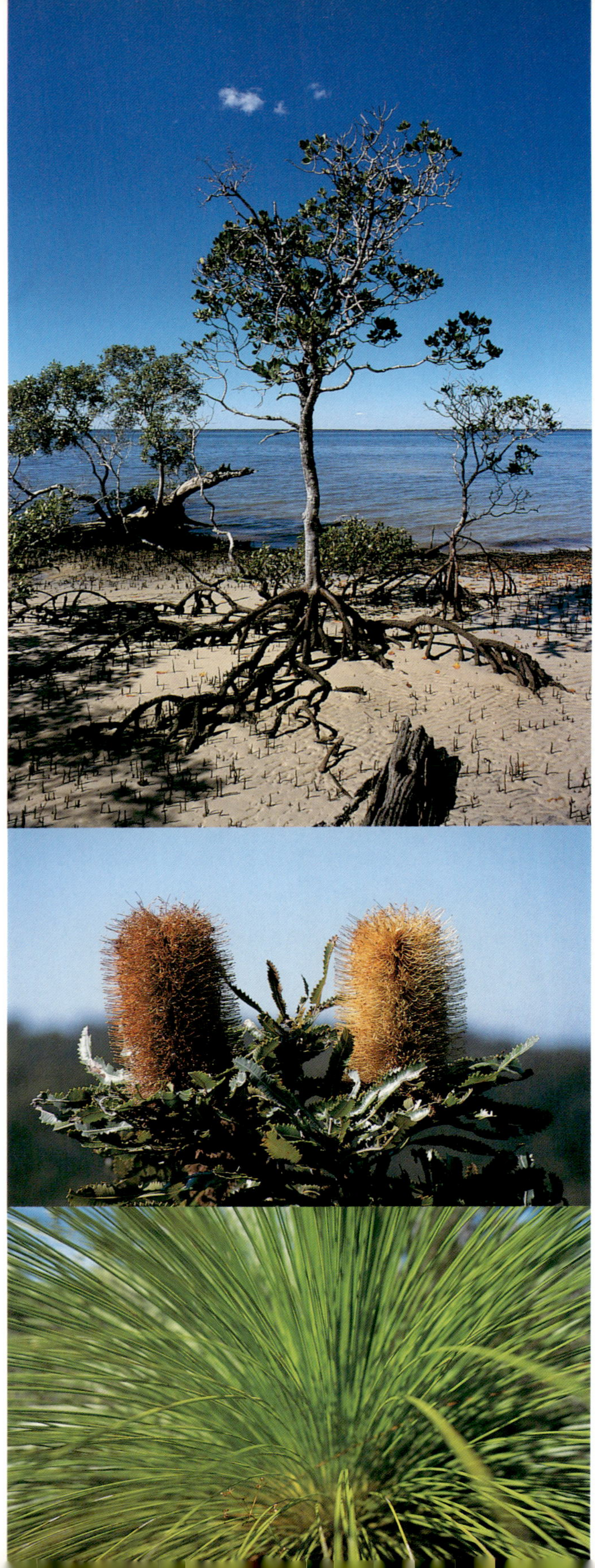

Just a ten-minute ferry ride across the water from the resort town of Noosa, Fraser Island is the world's largest sand island, its pleasant sub-tropical climate attracting visitors all year round. Formed by sands from Australia's east coast, deposited over millions of years by wind and sea in the Pacific Ocean, the island has an astonishing range of topography. Its dazzling white surf – pounded beaches, thriving rainforest, pristine freshwater lakes, vast desert-like sandblows, and high forest-clad dunes form a diverse surprising landscape. Fraser's mineral-rich sand was mined in the 1970s, leading to a successful conservation battle that brought the island international attention, resulting in its placement on the United Nations World Heritage list.

The camel train captain leads the procession through the bush

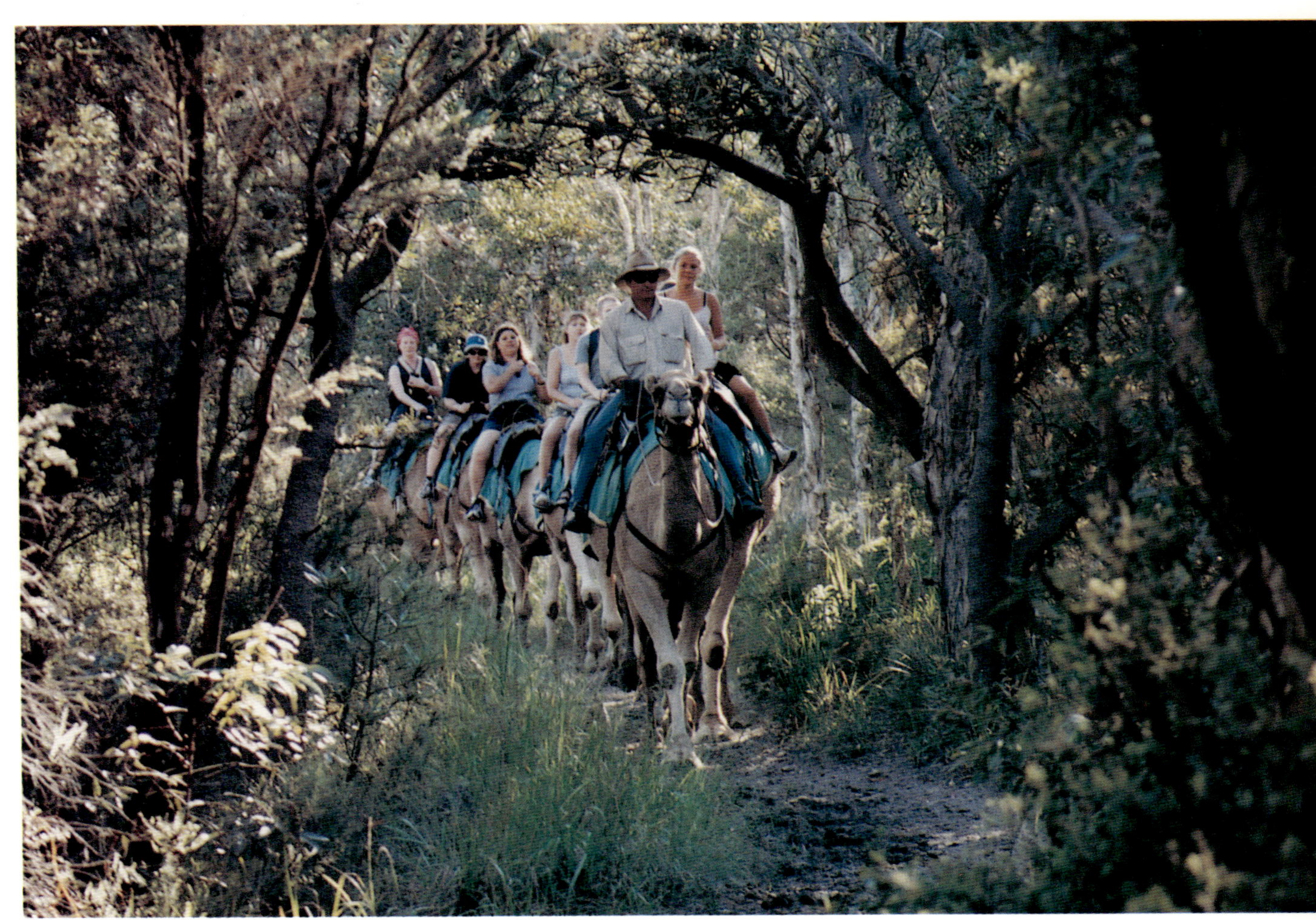

The camel train travels along the west coast of the island, accompanied by a four-wheel drive safari support vehicle that goes ahead to ensure the tracks are clear and to set up camp. We trek through forests of huge satinay trees – in the 1920s many were used to re-line the banks of the Suez Canal and repair war-ravaged London docks. Banksia trees, palms, foxtail ferns, and centuries old melaleuca trees form the thick green cover we thread our way through.

Bird life abounds, as does the animal population, including goanna lizards, dingoes and snakes. The last two are a reminder that despite its accessibility, this is still a wilderness area, not a wildlife park stocked with tame animals. The camel train captain and his crew are always on the lookout for birds and animals for you to see but not necessarily approach.

The safari takes a maximum of eight passengers, no experience of camel riding is required, and children are welcome. Most days we set off at around 9 to 9.30am, arriving at each camp before sunset. There are several pauses along the way, to 'boil the billy' for morning and afternoon tea, and to stop for fruit and sightseeing, so it is an unhurried and pleasant schedule. The safari overnights at three picturesque settings, the last for two nights, so that there is one day without 'cruising'. Time out can be spent just relaxing, swimming or bird watching. White-bellied sea eagles, braminy kites, galahs and brightly coloured parrots are some of the many birds we spot.

Our canvas village has 'rooms' in two-person tents with comfortable mattresses. Tables and chairs are set out amongst the trees. With a camp oven, bar and refrigerator, this is camping in comfort, a safari without hardship. Gourmet 'bush tucker' – colloquial for food – is served, home-baked provisions augmented with fresh fish caught along the way. A traditional Australian barbecue is part of the experience, with plenty of local beers, wines, and water to drink.

For first timers, the only startling aspect of camel riding is dismounting. When given the command, the camel drops to its knees, tilting the passenger forward, then lowering its hindquarters to rest on the ground. Buffer pads on the camel's knees support and protect the animal when it kneels. The inventor of gardeners' kneeling pads probably derived the idea from the camel.

For a while after being back on my own legs, I had the sensation of still moving, akin to what you feel when de-planing or after being at sea. However, there were no other effects, as these camels are fitted with specially designed saddles to ensure seating comfort.

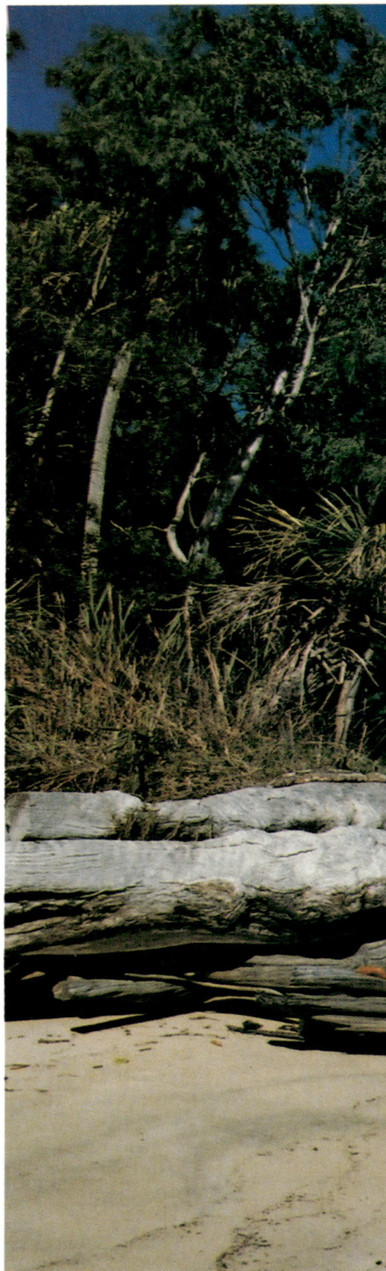

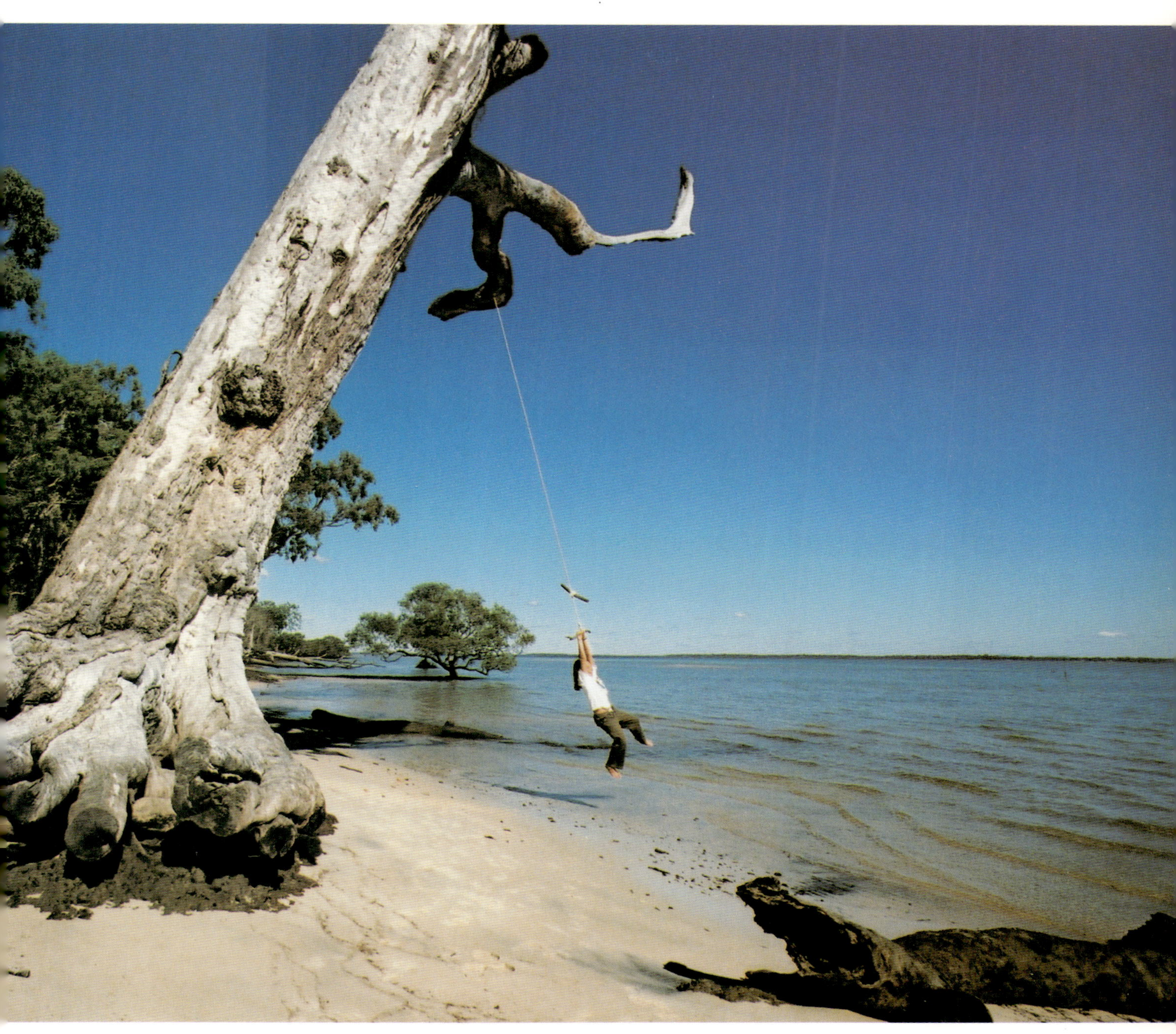

The beach at the safari's first campsite – spot the log pretending to be a crocodile...

At night, camels parked, the flames from the campfire reflect off a great variety of nocturnal creatures living in the bush. We saw luminescent green beetles covering a tree trunk like decorative lights, and a silent owl's wide open eyes acting like a mirror gave away his hiding place on a nearby branch.

Camels have a permanent look of disdain, as though it is fashionable in dromedary society to feign boredom. They hold their heads high, almost as if they are balancing an imaginary book on it to improve their posture. Despite their reputation for very accurate spitting, we didn't see any of them do so. Apparently they only spit in self-defence.

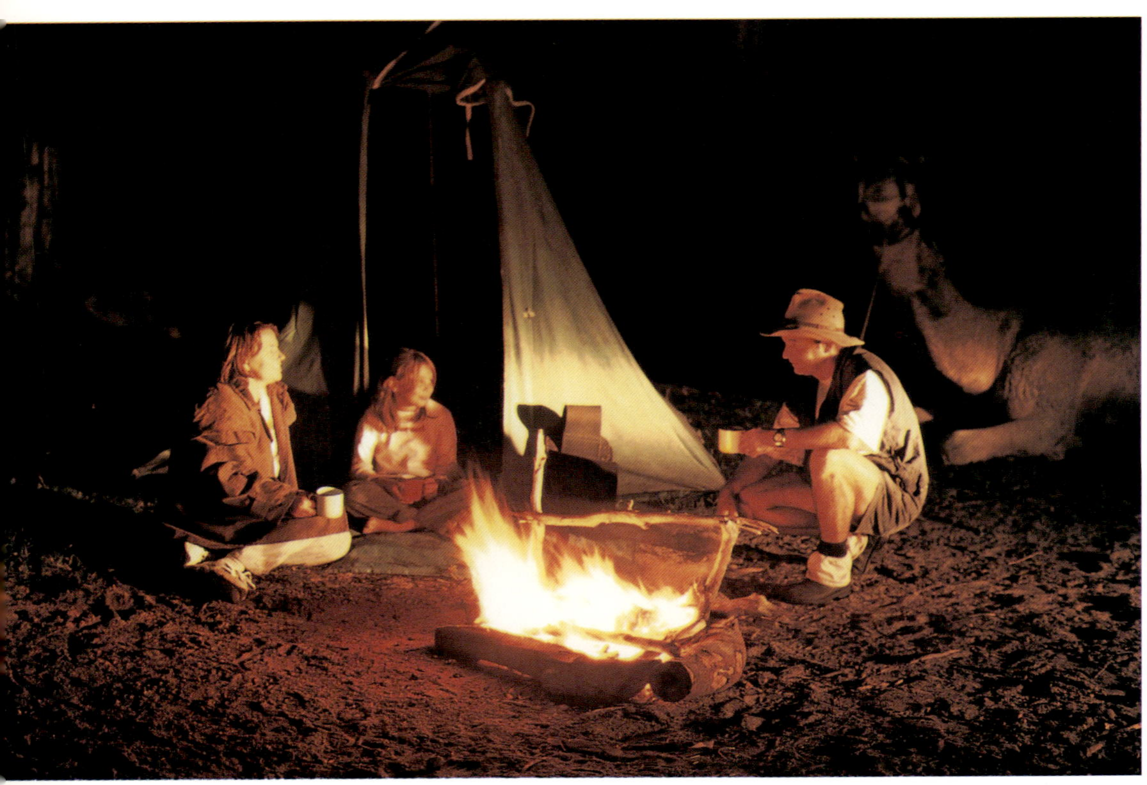

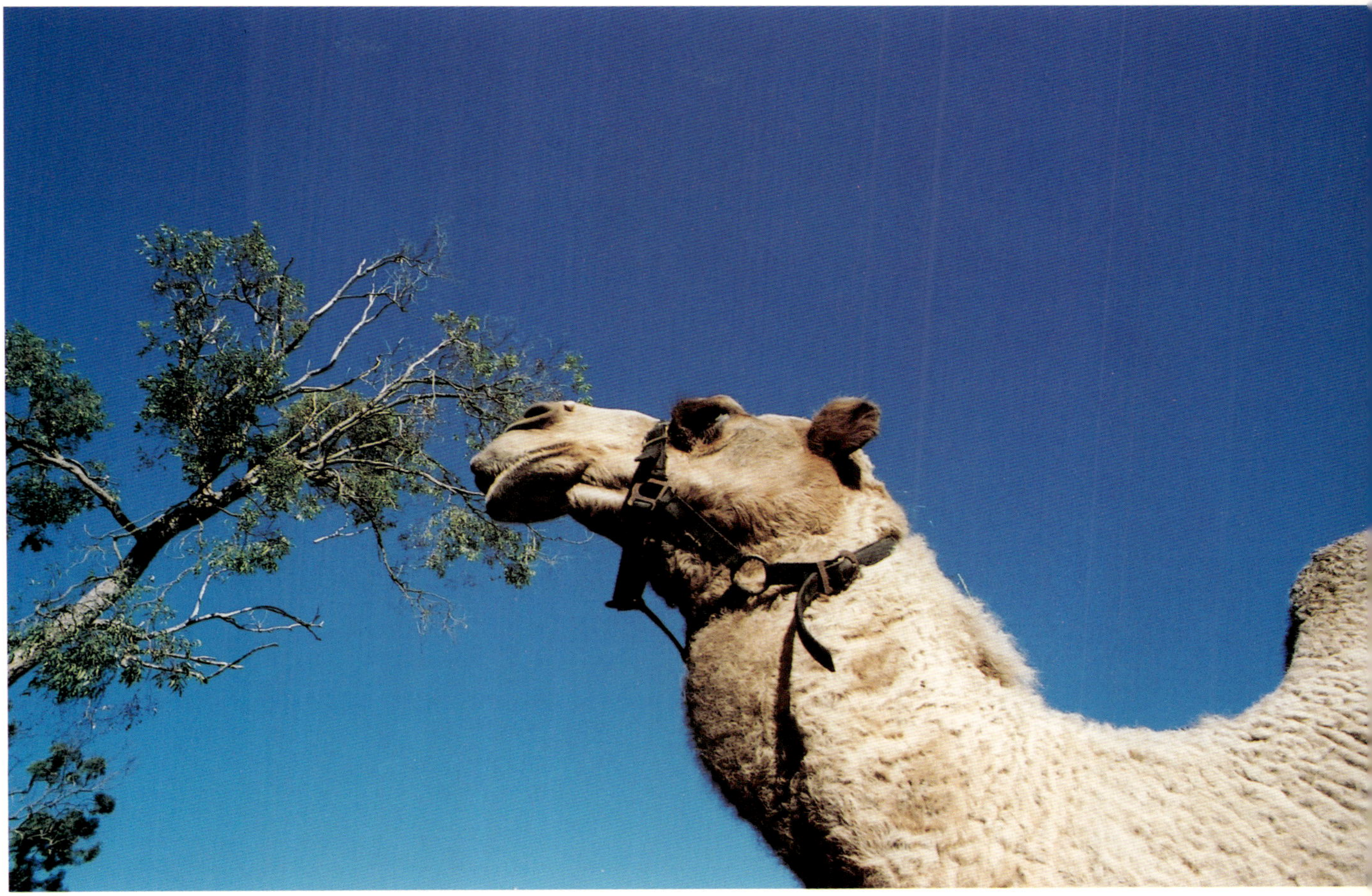

Camels reach great heights in search of vegetarian meals.

These camels all seemed perfectly good-humoured – even having what appear to be constant smiles on their faces, as if privy to some secret joke. I'll leave the last word on camel character to Dave, the camel train captain, who explained that 'camels are only as bad tempered as the people that work with them.'

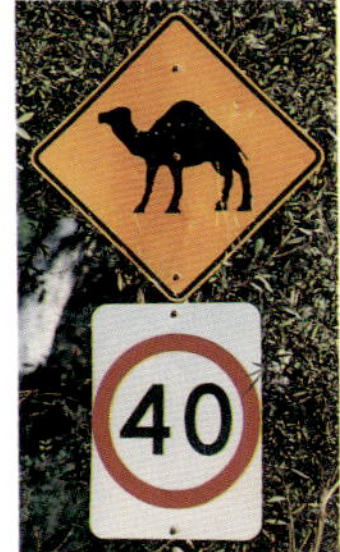

The Camel Company Australia | *Beach Road, North Shore* | *Tewantin* | *Queensland* | *Australia*

t: + 617 5442 4402 | *f: +617 5442 4397* | *camelco@bigpond.com* | *www.camelcompany.com.au*

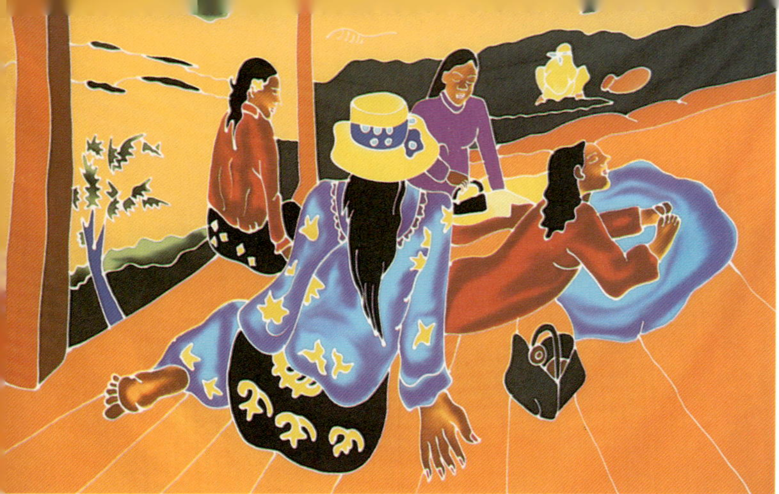

Painted Pacific...

Cruising in French Polynesia on the M/S Paul Gauguin

Tahiti, Bora Bora, Moorea... these are the evocative names of dream South Seas Islands, a tropical paradise that many have fantasized escaping to. Giving up his career as a stockbroker, leaving his family and 'everything that is artificial and conventional' behind, Paul Gauguin fled 'bourgeois France' in 1891 for Tahiti, making the decision to dedicate the rest of his life to art.

Gauguin lived here impoverished, ill and struggling for recognition, gaining fame and appreciation only after his death. One hundred years later, he has become a brand icon for Tahiti and the other Society Islands known as French Polynesia. Creative adaptations of his paintings adorn pareus, T-shirts, espresso cups, mouse pads and a host of other souvenirs for sale everywhere on these islands where he made his home.

The idyllic world portrayed in many of Gauguin's paintings was somewhat of an illusion even then, yet visually these islands hold much for the artist to commit to canvas, the photographer to film and the eye to admire. The land and seascape fulfil a fantasy vision of how tropical islands should look, with added character that makes them special. Islands with a backbone, the towering blue peaks of Moorea and Bora Bora look down on white sand beaches far below.

The ubiquitous Captain Cook arrived in Tahiti in June of 1769 to observe the celestial occurrence of the transit of the planet Venus across the sun. The other Venus observed was described in the mythical anecdotes taken back to England of what seemed a heaven on earth. Beautiful islands free of English-held conventions, warm balmy days and nights, an atmosphere redolent of desire with pliant voluptuous women – this looked like a simple satisfying life in a sultry climate. When they returned home, these first envoys from Paradise Found sowed the seeds of an enduring fable.

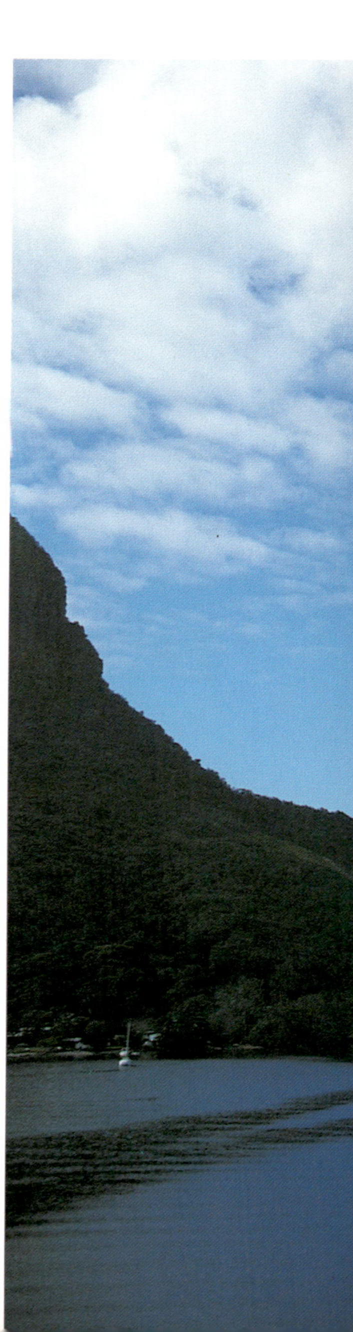

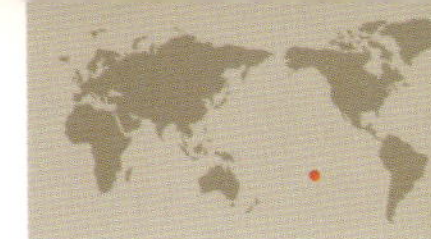

Opunohu Bay, Moorea has cliffs and peaks like ramparts, reminiscent of a looming castle drawn by Mervyn Peake or Edward Gorey - a tropical vista with some savagery in its visage.

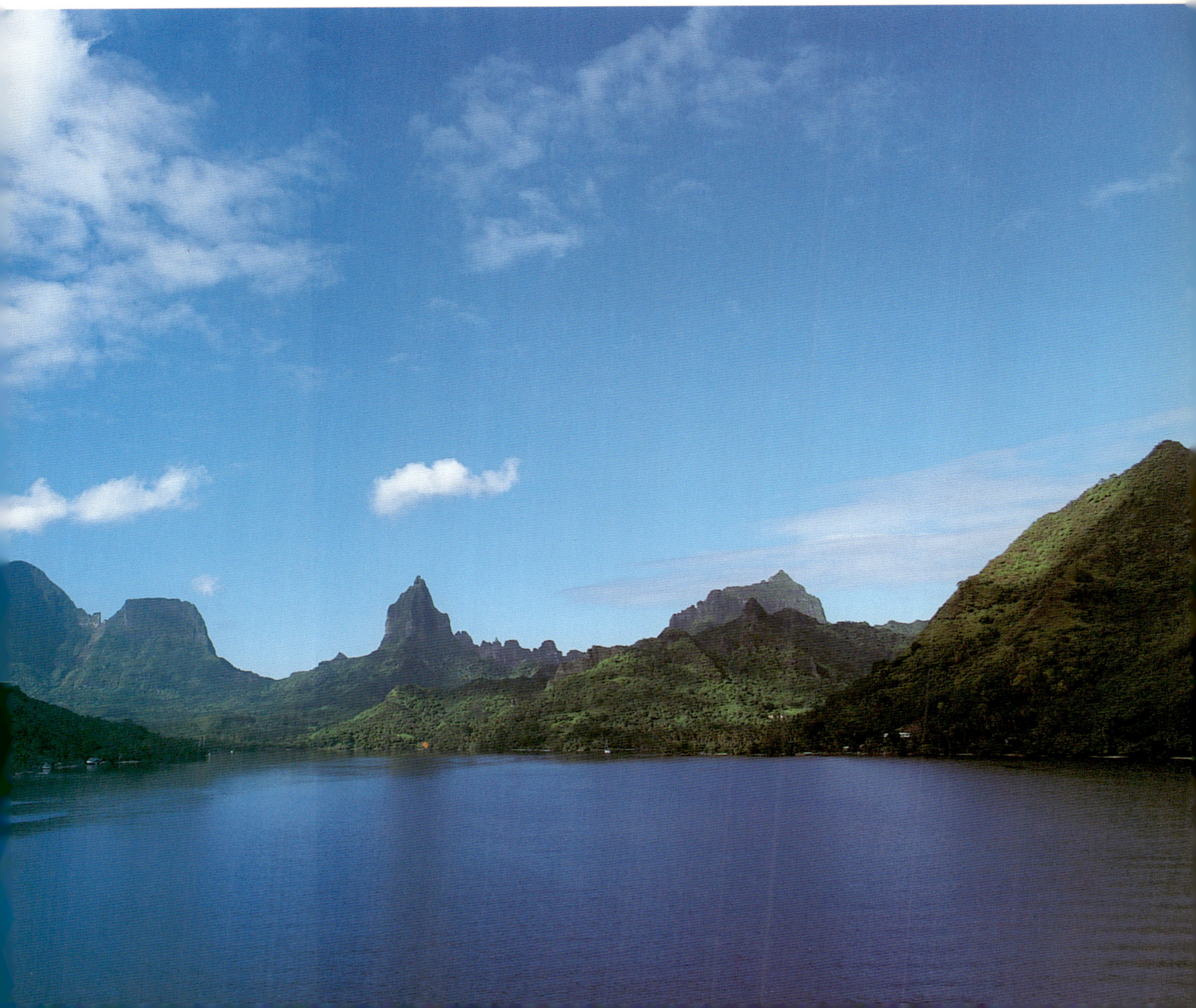

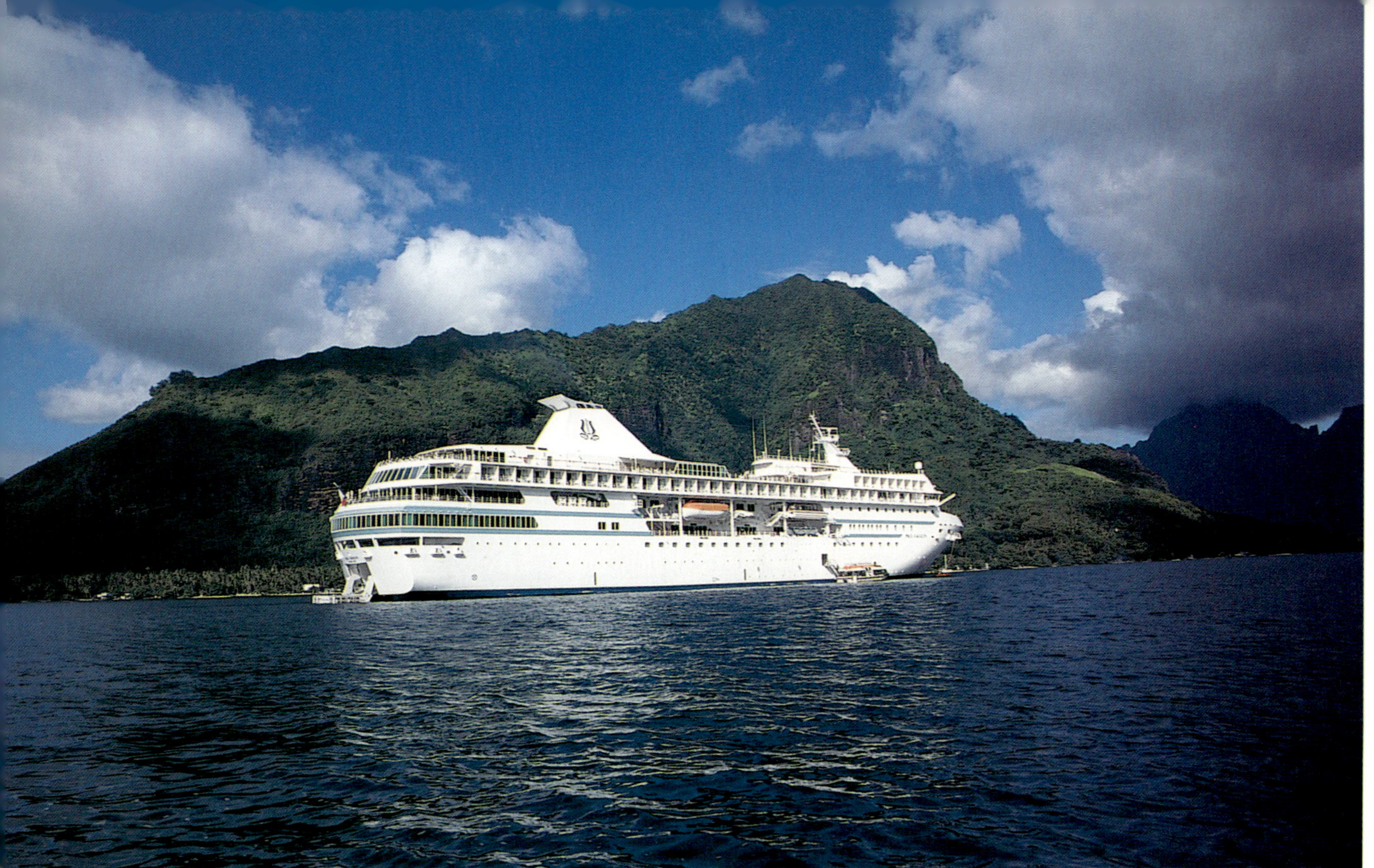

The Paul Gauguin at anchor in Moorea.

Lured by the still potent spell cast by French Polynesia, we fly to Tahiti to join the M/S Paul Gauguin, the artistically named cruise ship that sails on a weekly voyage around the Society Islands of French Polynesia. It leaves from Papeete, a boisterous port town with a colourful wharf area. At night, brightly painted caravans sell an exotic melange of crepes, pizza and Chinese food, to the accompaniment of music from local bands. Since our last visit, the town decorators have wound lights lavishly around every palm tree trunk on the waterfront, and added some fake trees that sparkle like firecrackers, so that after dark a veritable glitter-scape appears. We watch it fade into the distance as the ship sets sail for the island of Raiatea, once the centre of royalty, religion and history.

The Paul Gauguin is not one of the gargantuan cruise ships that increasingly loom on our horizons and in ports, often dominating the landscapes they sail by. This ship is a vessel of acceptably neat size and scale, and anchored at a respectful distance offshore. Other than in Papeete, it is not in port at any of the stops, so stands off from the view rather than being in it.

There are some 250 passengers on board, although the ship's capacity is 320, and there seems to be plenty of space for everyone, with some of the ample decks often free of other people. With four bars, three restaurants, a tastefully appointed small-scale casino, dipping pool, luxurious spa – from whose open door wonderful scents emanate – and a theatre, there is a wide choice of venues on this elegant floating hotel.

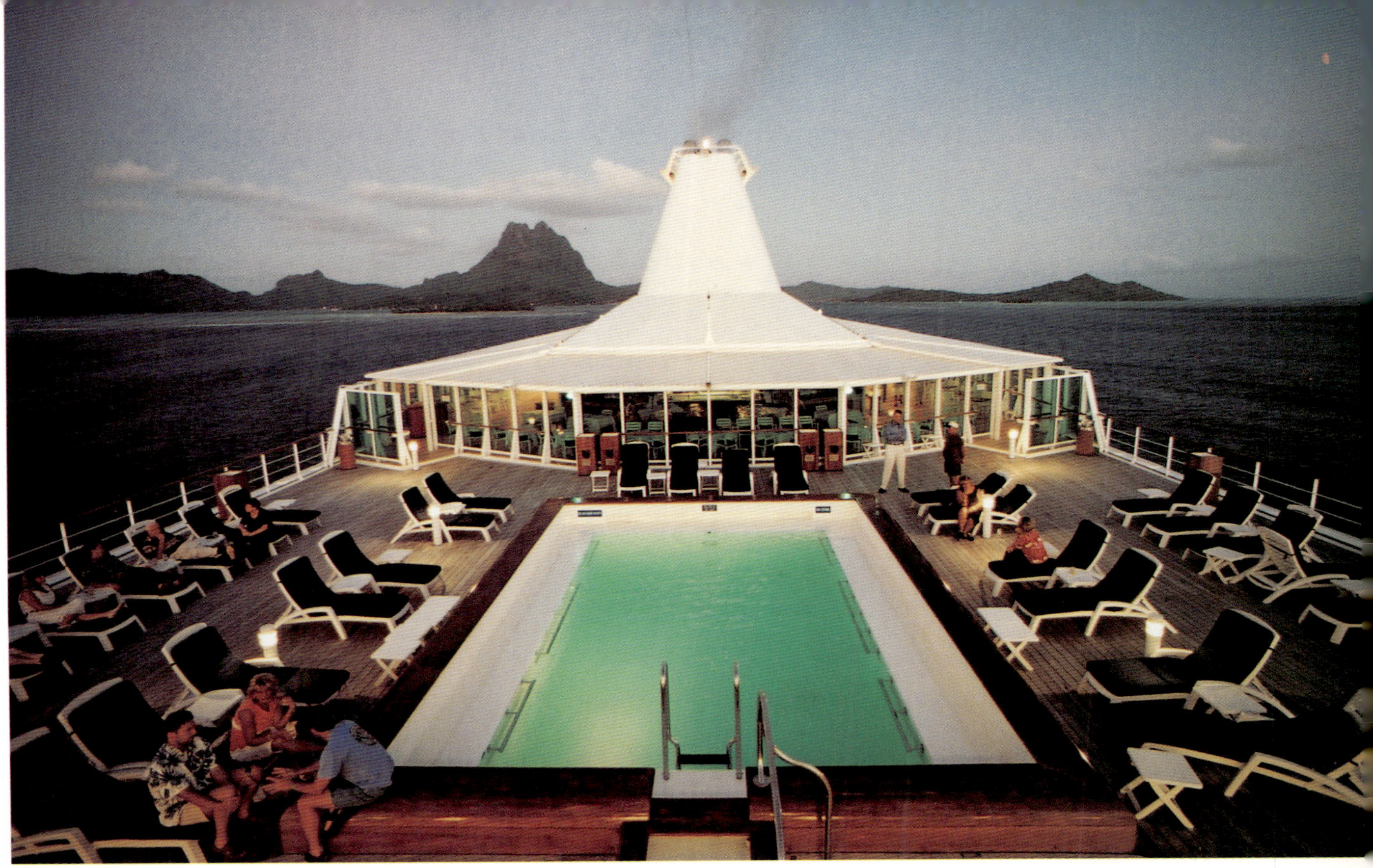

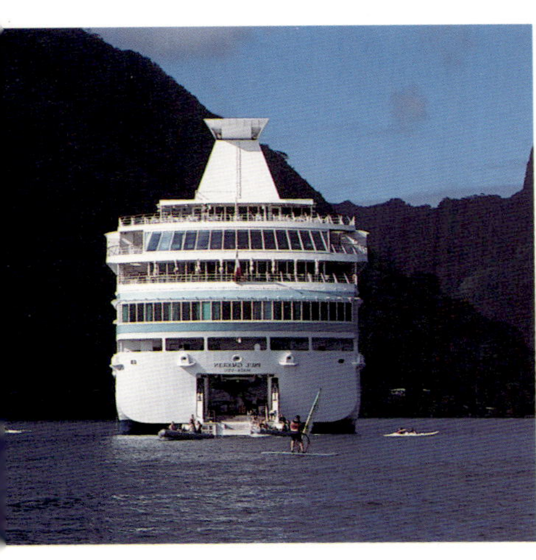

As well as on-boat activities, the ship has an in-built marina, as a platform for water sports, such as diving, windsurfing and kayaking. We could choose to be sporty, develop a tan, learn a language, become certified as a diver, and grow fit with the 'soft' exercise programme on offer. For those more languid than athletic, there is an excellent library – with books from fiction to biography to travel, all new hardbacks, and a mixture of popular and more cerebral titles in a wide variety of languages.

You can eat like a king, queen or just a common greedy person here. We rigorously tested the standard of cuisine in each of the restaurants, and agreed it would be hard to become jaded with the food on board. A two-star Michelin menu is one gourmet choice, devised by Parisian restaurant Apicius, and meticulously followed by the on-board chef. The 'house wines' – generously poured – deserve an appellation that better describes their quality.

Casual dress is de rigueur for dining at each venue, but the standard of fare served in La Veranda and L'Etoile restaurants warrants some sense of occasion. Some people were clothed as though they were going to a picnic.

A person could get seriously addicted to life aboard this ship, cruising the Society Islands and waited on by attentive staff. There are plenty of them – the ratio of 2 staff members to 3 passengers means that there is always someone nearby to attend to your needs.

The French-built ship is elegantly appointed; its restrained quality décor complemented by interesting – and covetable – artefacts, prints, photographs and ceramics that mostly have a direct connection to the area that the Paul Gauguin tours.

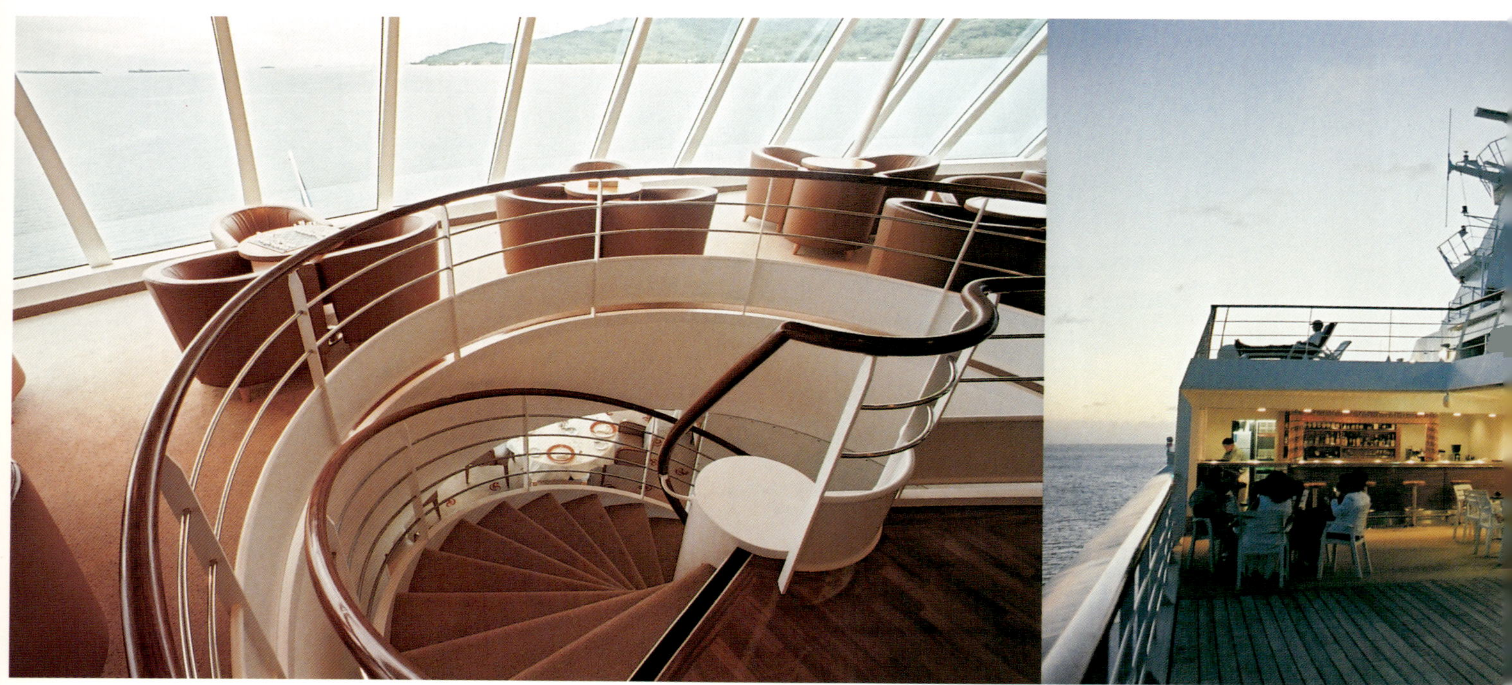

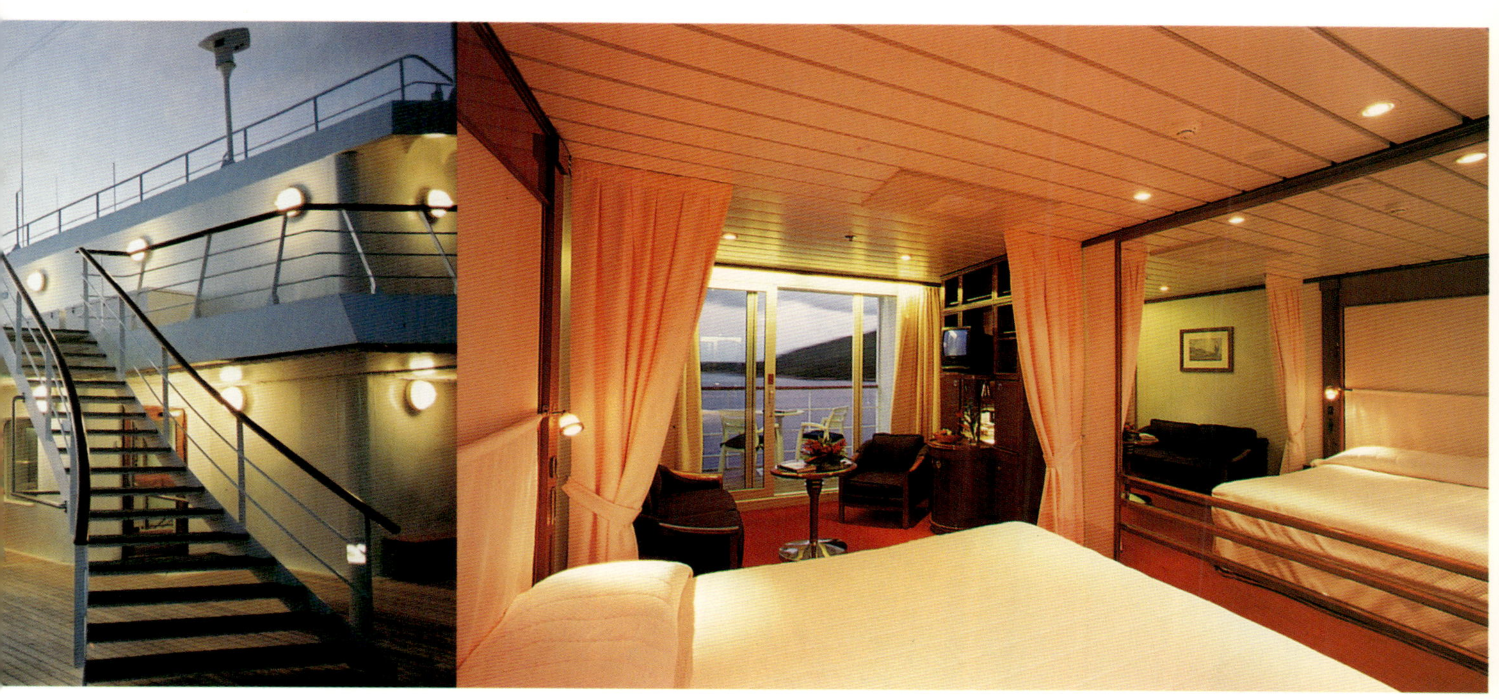

You could happily spend time in your very comfortable stateroom, enjoying room service, or watching newly released movies on the in-room video system. Many have a balcony for private outdoor moments. There is a mass of storage in each stateroom, their apparent size cleverly enhanced by the adept use of mirrors. The bathroom is a triumph of compactness, produced by designers who are obviously into miniaturisation already – not in scale but in managing to fit full-sized equipment into small spaces. Where do these people go after designing these essential spaces, are they available for residential work or kept locked away by corporate clients?

On two of the cruise days, we leave the ship's wooden decks for sandy shores at *motu* (islet) stops, where we can spend all day on the beach if we wish. Near the island of Taha'a is Motu Mahana, exclusive to the Paul Gauguin's passengers. The motu's sparkling white sand beaches, coconut palms and warm yet refreshing waters are a picture-perfect setting. The ship is far enough beyond to become distant, and able to be put out of sight completely. A gourmet barbecue – not a usual pairing of words – lunch is served and, with drinks at hand, shade umbrellas, and reclining chairs, it is a blissful environment.

Our next island stop is Bora Bora, famous for the fierceness of its warriors in the old days. The location for many movies, this island claims the title of Pearl of the Pacific, and Polynesian legend has that it was the first one to rise out of the sea. Circled by a crystalline lagoon, Bora Bora and its motus appear have a skirt of pale blue floating around them, with darker ruffles spreading beyond. Whipped cream clouds swathe themselves over and around the island's high peaks.

Missionaries hurried to the islands of French Polynesia to preach their gospel and left a legacy of churches that are outwardly more colourful than most. Whether brightly painted or pastel, the colour schemes reflect the vibrant surroundings of this earthly Eden.

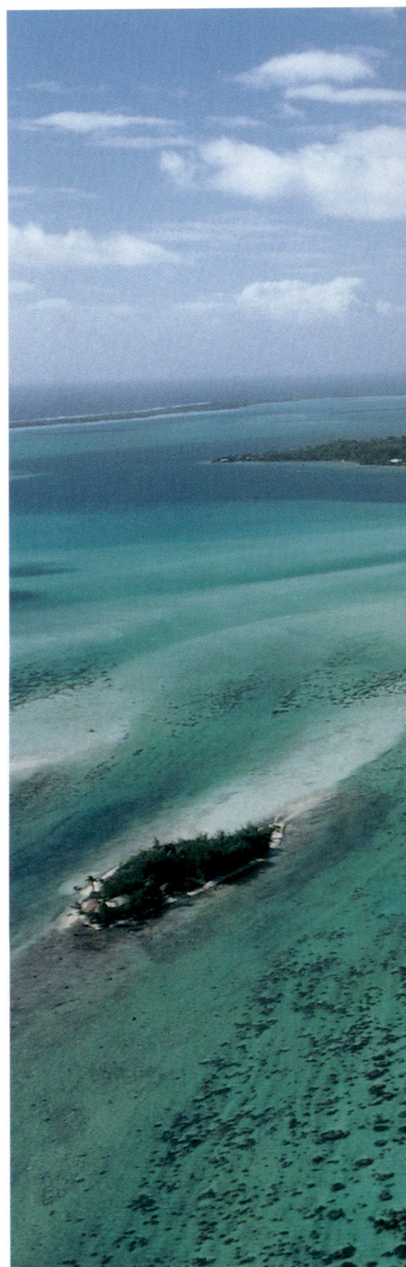

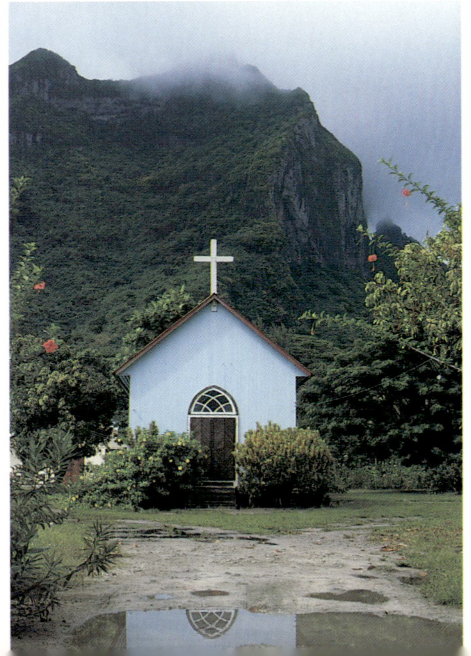

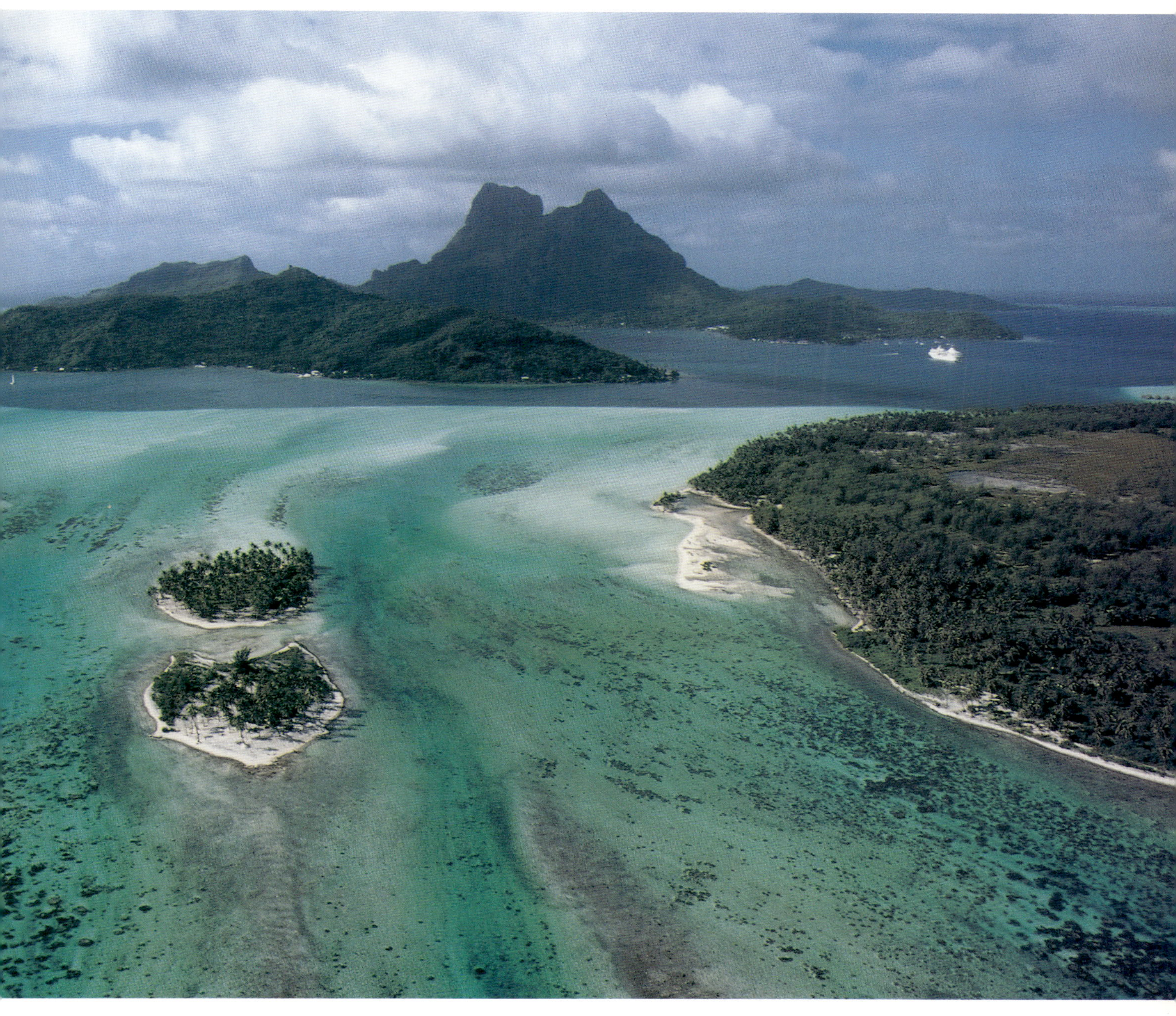

Flying towards Bora Bora, with the Paul Gauguin anchored at the top right.

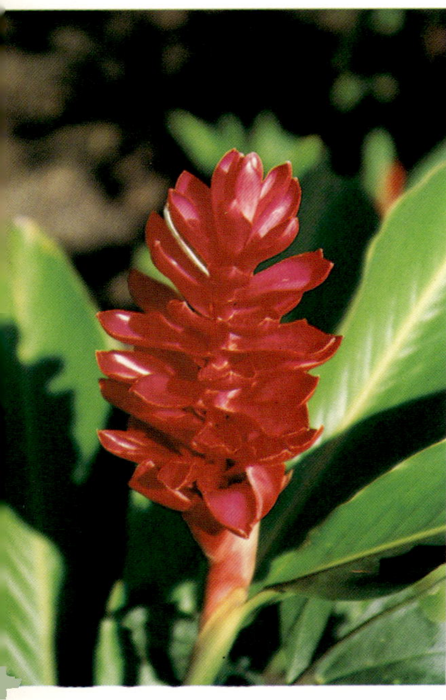

There is plenty to do if you choose to leave your deck chair, from joining shore excursions to attending on-board 'enrichment lectures'. A melange of educative and entertaining activities was presented; with no compulsion to join in or do anything other that what you pleased.

Visits to pineapple and vanilla plantations, ancient maraes, black pearl farms and waterfalls, feeding shark and manta rays – in an organised not spontaneous fashion – parasailing, riding wave runners, watching dolphins, travelling around the islands by 'le truck', the local transport, or off-road and up hill in four-wheel-drive vehicles, scuba diving and snorkelling – there is so much choice packed into one week that many of our fellow passengers were planning a return visit.

We listened to lectures on Tahitian history, enjoyed a dissertation on Captain Cook's peripatetic career as the world's most intrepid explorer, artful navigator and expert cartographer; heard the 'true' story of the mutiny on the Bounty, and learnt about French Polynesia's dolphin species and the singing abilities of humpback whales. A film showing the sleek acrobatic spinner dolphins – the only ones that can spin vertically or horizontally in the air like tops or ballerinas – dying, caught in the nets of yellow fin tuna fisheries in the waters between Hawaii, Mexico and Peru, converted me instantly to only eating albacore tuna. Unlike the yellow fin, albacore tuna apparently do not swim under dolphins; therefore they evade capture .

A troupe of young women from the islands are part of the crew, termed the Gaugines, entertaining as singers and dancers, and explaining Tahitian ways. This gentle local touch added a charming authentic flavour to the varied menu of evening shows.

The dynamic performance delivered by the dancers and musicians of the O Tahiti E group on our last night aboard could easily reinforce the commonly held image of islands full of strikingly handsome men and beautiful girls. Young and fit, dressed in striking costumes, the group presented a wonderfully coloured picture, giving a polished energetic demonstration of traditional Polynesian songs and dance. This was a grand finale indeed.

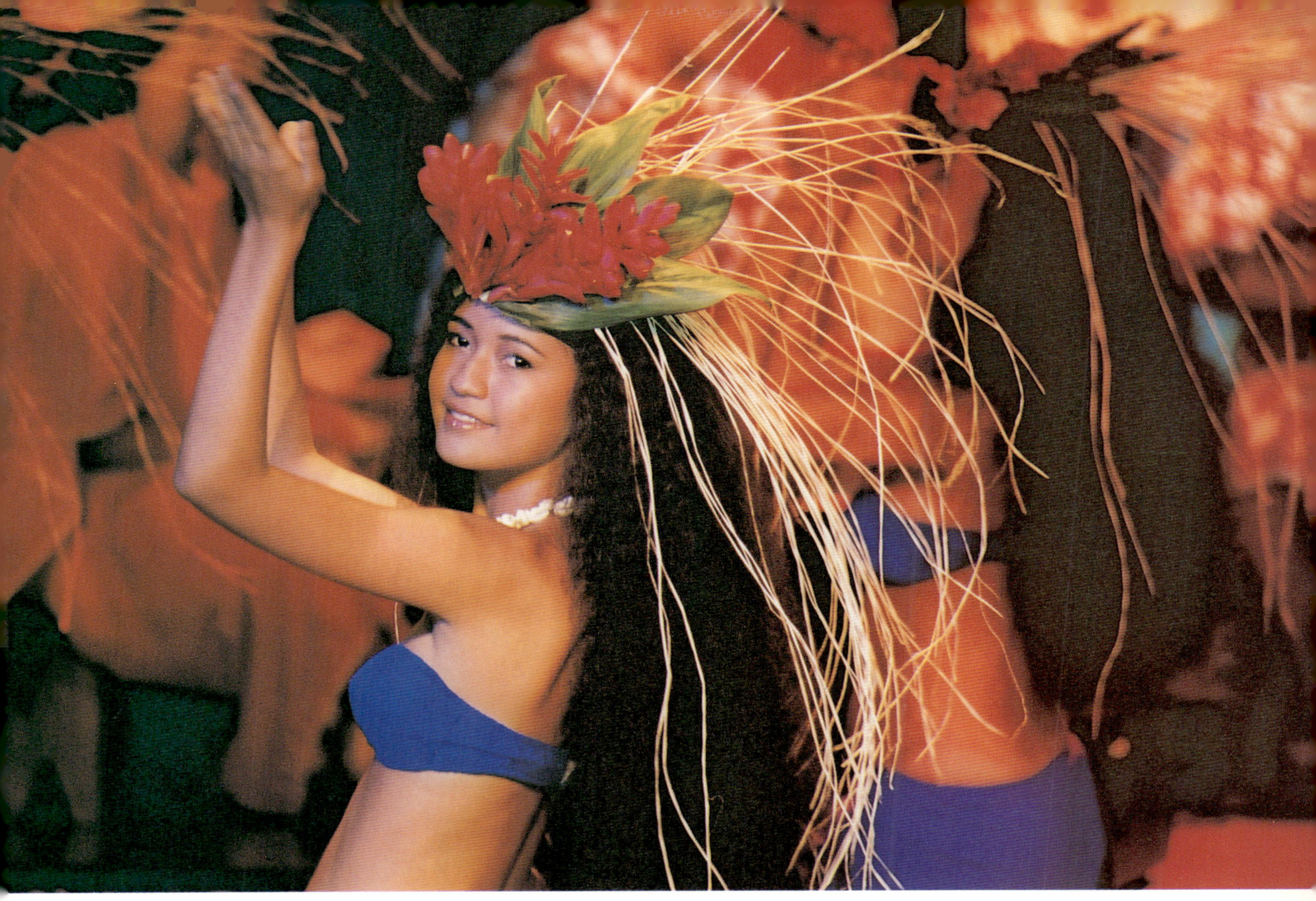

If this was similar to what the explorers saw when they first arrived in the Society Islands, no wonder the fables of paradise spread and became entrenched. Like the beautiful black pearls that are grown here, these islands are organic gems. Despite the growth and inevitable effects of tourism, French Polynesia is still quite fabulous, not yet a paradise lost, and journeying on the Paul Gauguin is one of the very best ways to see it.

M/S Paul Gauguin *Sails every Saturday from Papeete in Tahiti*

Radisson Seven Seas Cruises *www.rsc.com*

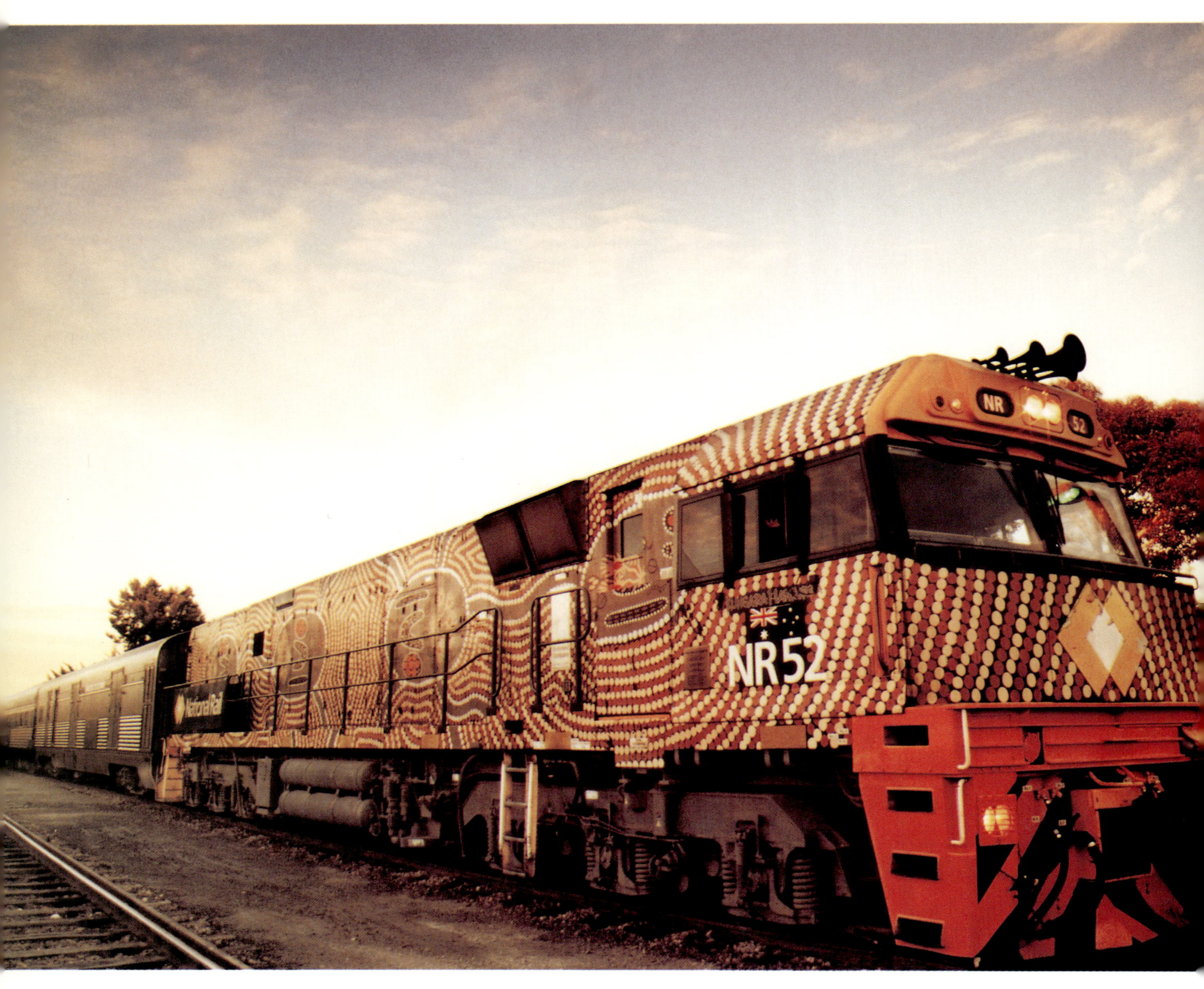
NR
52
NR52
National Rail

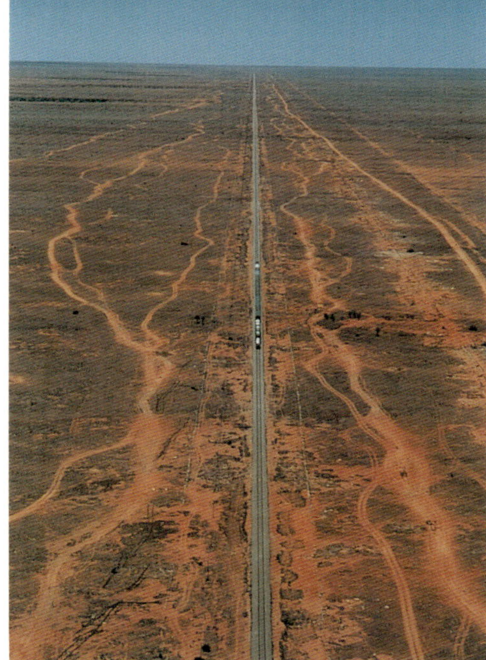

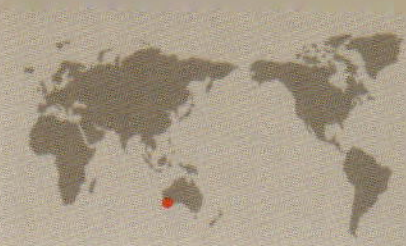

Cruising the Desert...

The Indian Pacific train, across the Nullarbor, Australia

Several people queried our plan to go to 'the dry heart' of Australia and travel across the Nullarbor Plain. A desert-like landscape twice the size of England, the vast limestone plateau is one of the driest places on earth. It seemed odd to them that we would chose to spend three days sitting on a train looking out at essentially the same scenery. We wanted to see it because it was there, and by train is the most comfortable way to do it.

The train spans Australia in almost a straight line, from the Indian Ocean to the Pacific, a distance of 4253 kilometres, but not all through desert country. At each end and centre of the epic journey are urban oases, the cities of Sydney, Adelaide and Perth. Cruising sea to sea by rail is a leisurely way to see part of the legendary Outback, together with sampling the upfront metropolitan life that Australia has to offer.

The colourful locomotive that heads our long train of 24 carriages certainly stands out from other engines we have seen. It is not covered in graffiti, but decorated with patterns copied from Aboriginal paintings, swirls of dots, circles and lines, seemingly abstract motifs that tell a story to the knowledgeable viewer.

The Indian Pacific makes few stops along the way, although we pass through many towns. Some consist merely of a shed beside the line, leftovers of settlements that had failed to endure this testing environment.

Nullarbor is not, as it might sound, an Aboriginal name; a Latin derived title, it simply means treeless. Parts of the Nullarbor have extremes of temperature that range from freezing to 50 degrees Celsius, the steel rails of the railway line crossing this sunburnt land can reach a searing 90 degrees. In the air-conditioned train, there is fortunately no experience of the temperatures outside. On the journey's first night, we saw a fierce storm, with cracking thunder and whips of lightening that bleached out the black sky. The next day there was water on the desert, soft pools of rain lying on top of hard ground.

The only place during the transit of the Nullarbor where we can leave the train is at the desolate town of Cook. Once a railway settlement home to 300 people, now just three live here. All 200 passengers got out and walked quietly around the dead Outback town, the only sign of life a few persistent clinging flies. There are some trees here, planted by some determined souls who tried greening a tiny part of the desert. The inhabitants were busy selling drinks and souvenirs in the crowded station. As we moved out, cocooned in our small city on wheels, there was nobody to wave goodbye.

Australia's great red spaces have long attracted prospectors to its rich mineral resources and other interests keen to take advantage of its emptiness and isolation. Prisoner-of-war camps stocked with Italian soldiers were set up during the Second World War, and in the 1950s, a British nuclear weapons testing site near Maralinga had deadly effects on local Aborigines and military personnel who witnessed the blasts. A rocket-testing range at Woomera – an Aboriginal word for 'throwing stick' – was active in the 1970s.

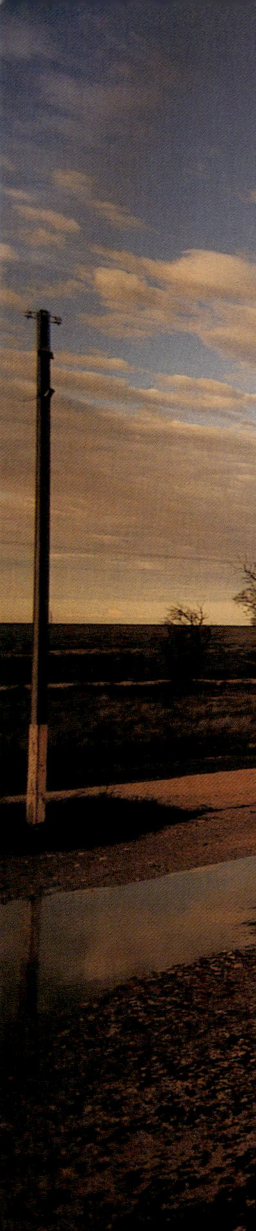

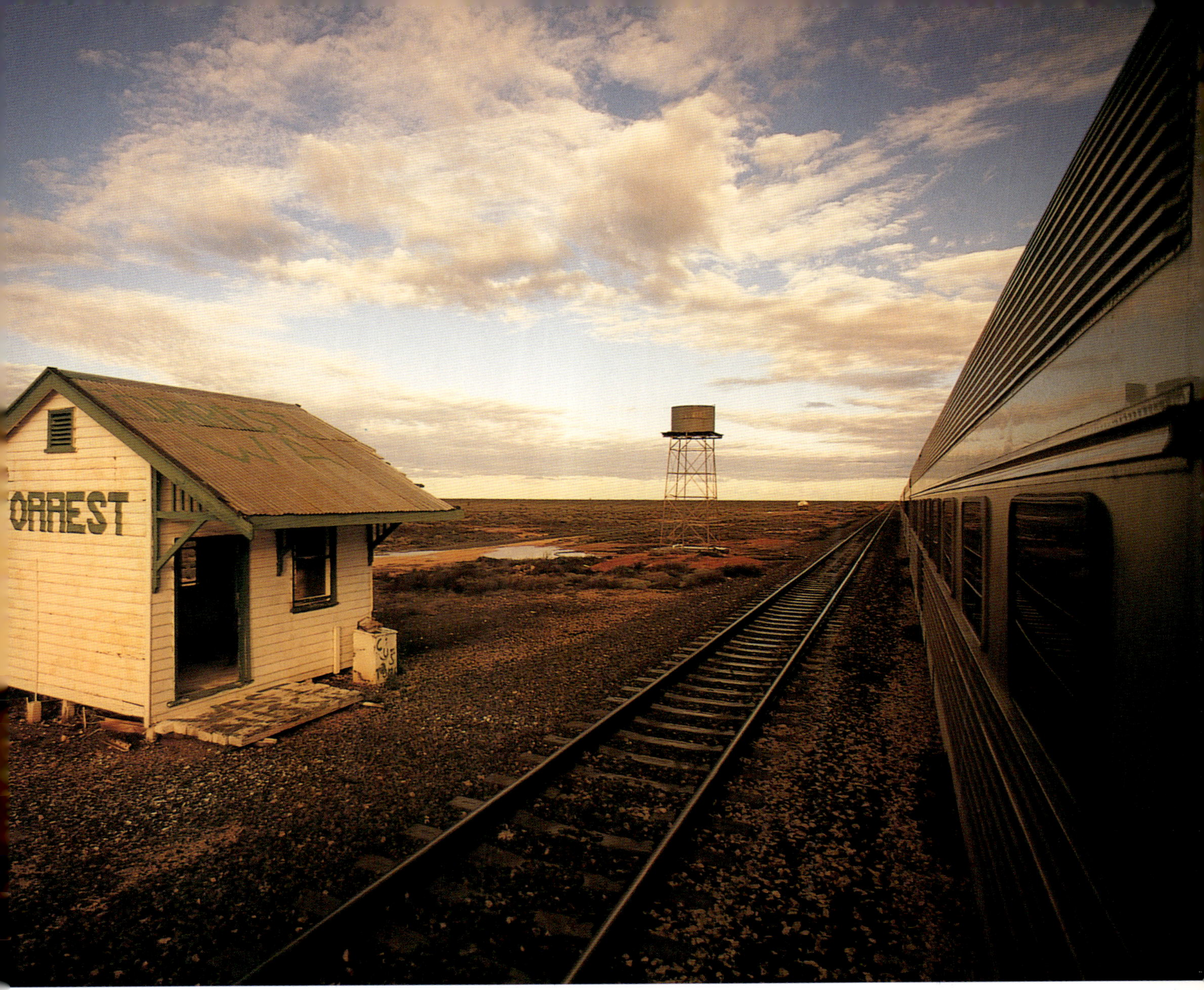

A modest station commemorates John Forrest, a surveyor and statesman who led a number of expeditions into the uncharted wilderness of Western Australia. Nearby is an emergency landing strip for jet aircraft, should they ever need to descend into the desert.

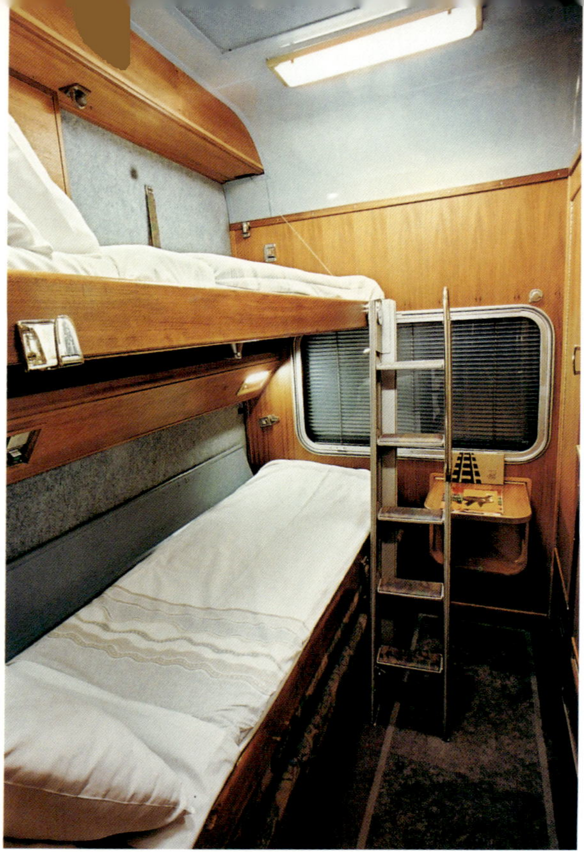

The deluxe compartment shown prepared for the evening.

Travelling Gold Kangaroo Service provided us with a first class 'twinette', a two-berth compartment panelled in Tasmanian oak, and a restful colour scheme. A comfortable capsule by day and night, it has a cleverly constructed bathroom, with facilities that fold out from the walls – another space-saving feat in stainless steel.

Gold rush fever gripped the country in the 1850s, sparking a flurry of emigration to Australia – over half a million people shipped themselves here, lured by the potential for infinite wealth. On the fringe of the Nullarbor, the gold town of Kalgoorlie was no 'flash in the pan'. A thriving city, it is the site of the world's largest single open-cut mining operation, which recovers gold day and night. We arrived late on Friday night in this once frontier town, and although most of its interesting old buildings were not well illuminated, the many pubs were well 'lit up' inside.

The next morning the train is well and truly in the Nullarbor, riding on the longest straight section of track in the world – a line stretching 478 kilometres through a vast lonely plain.

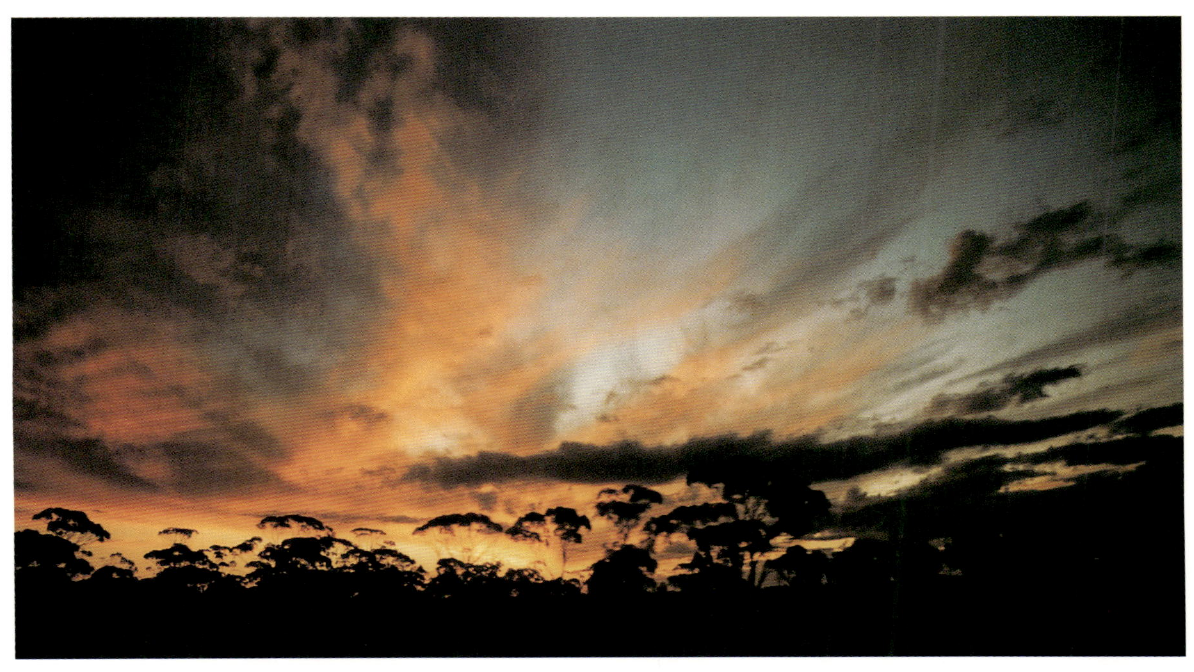

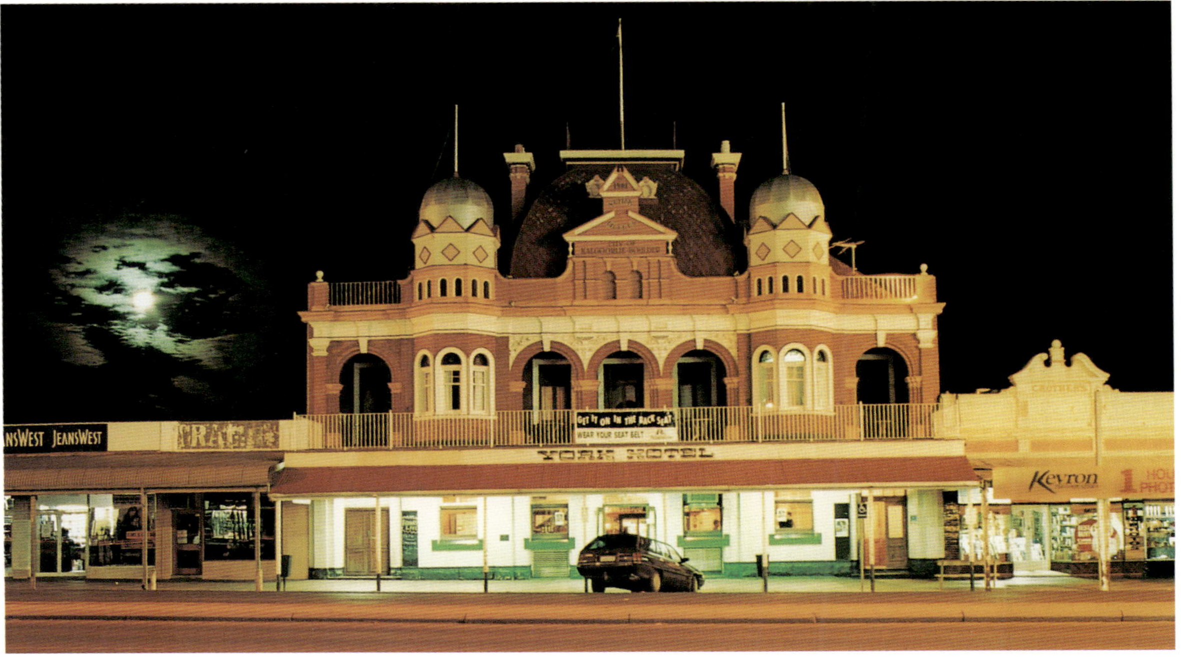
JEANSWEST
GET IT ON IN THE BACK SEAT
WEAR YOUR SEAT BELT
YORK HOTEL
Kevron

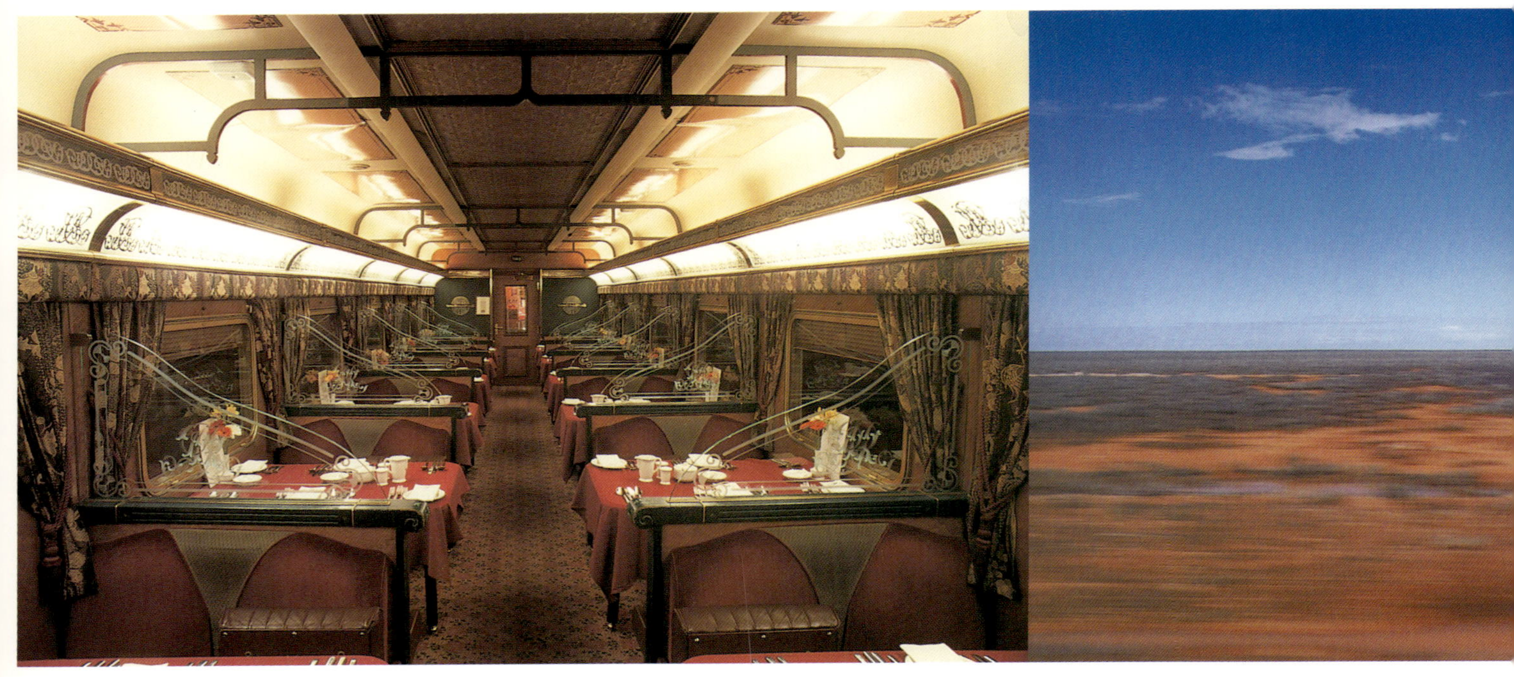

The desert was actually rather colourful, coated with red and orange earth, clumps of grey green and blue bushes dotted close together. It was an interesting wilderness to watch, surprisingly green and varied, and quite fascinating in its vastness. There were few signs of living creatures. I scanned the window for the great Australian wedge-tail eagle, but the recent laying of fibre optic cables alongside the track has removed one of their favourite resting places, the telegraph poles, so they are not seen as often now.

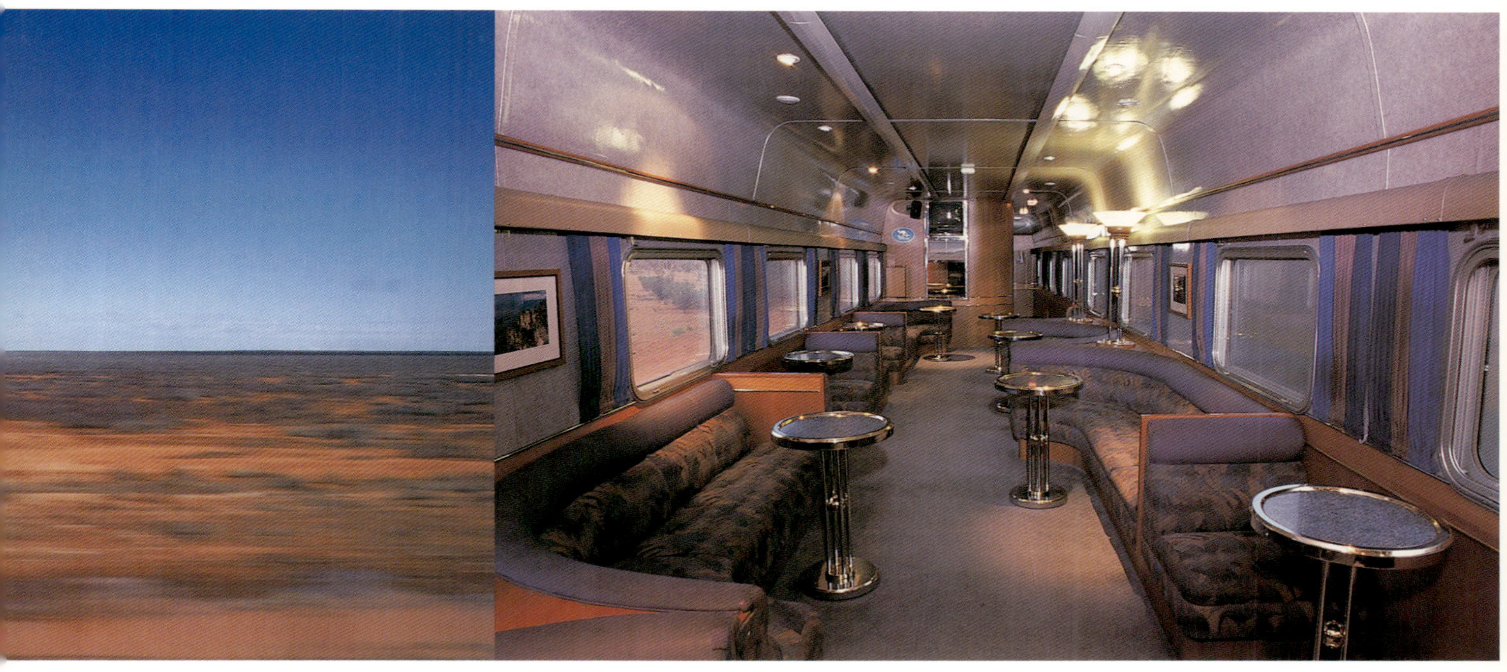

For our desert lunch, we chose a simple meat pie, quintessential casual fare, but this was more formal – a lamb and lemon myrtle pie that was a tasty start to sampling the simple good menu and Australian wines. At the dining room's shared tables, we had an interesting changing mix of co-diners; some more used to menu examples of Australian native cuisine like Kangaroo fillets. I expressed reservations about eating such an icon, when I was hoping to see them outside the window rather than on a plate, inspiring our petite octogenarian companion to tell me how she had longed to shoot a kangaroo when she first arrived from Scotland many years ago. When she did, she felt sorry about it.

'No worries' was our waiter's usual response to any requests – and certainly there were none for us all, being carried along through the Nullarbor in comfort, happily watching both sides of it from the Observation car.

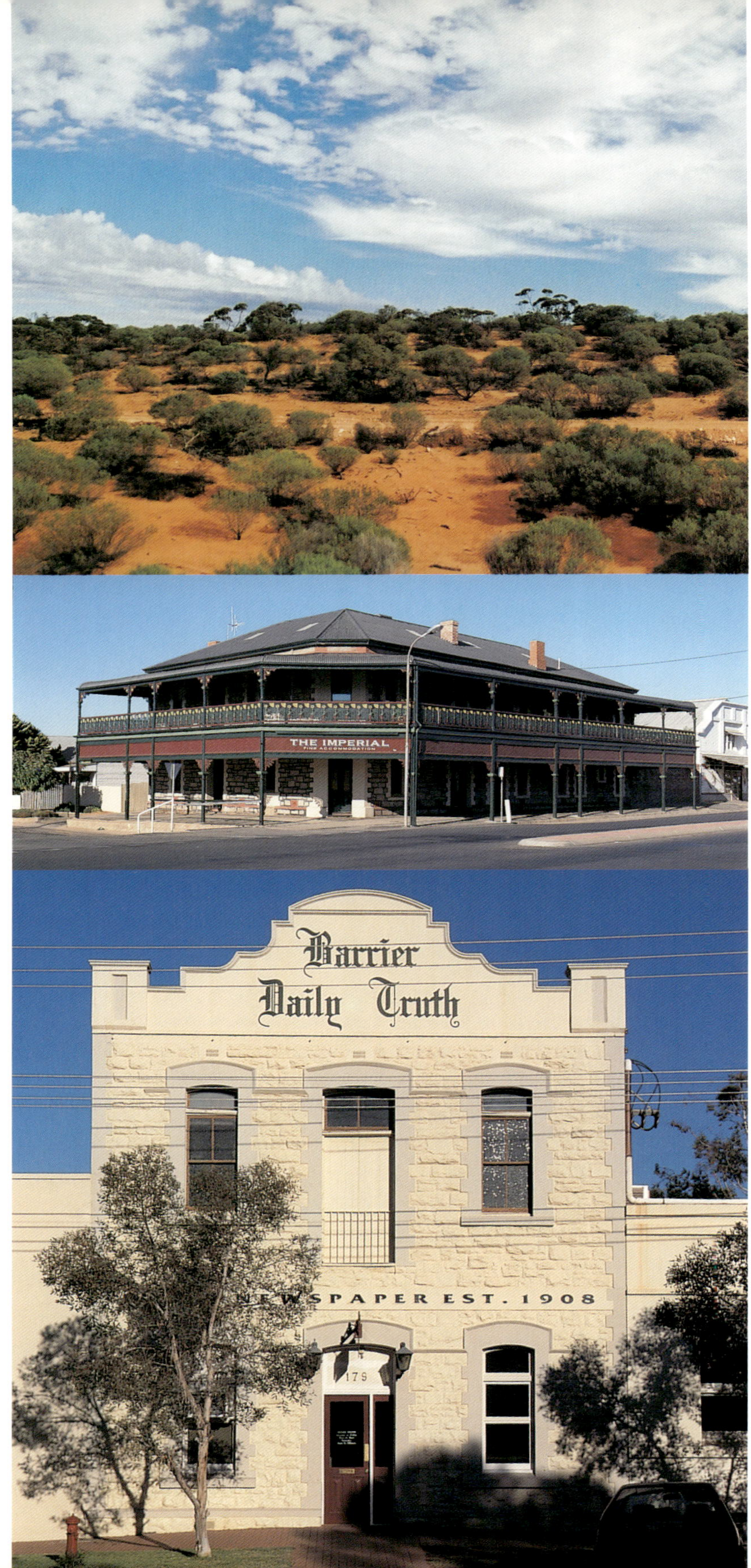
THE IMPERIAL
Barrier
Daily Truth
NEWSPAPER EST. 1908
179

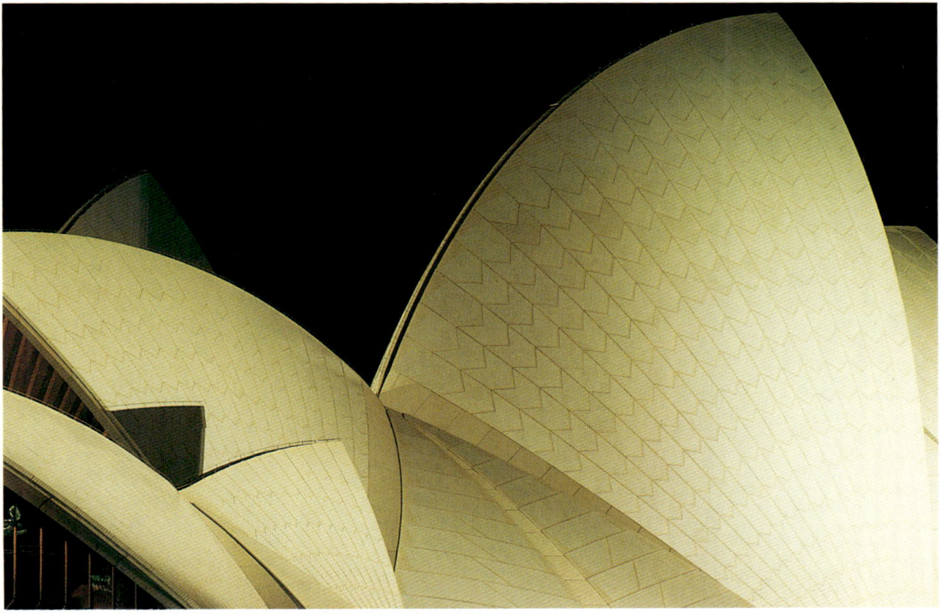

Out of the Nullarbor, we crossed into the dry arid zone of New South Wales, and stop at the Outback town of Broken Hill, where Australia's greatest-ever mineral bonanza began in 1883. The 'Silver City' sits on the world's richest deposit of silver, lead and zinc, and has yielded minerals worth over $1.5 billion Australian dollars over its mining lifetime. Mountains of mining waste edge the town, numerous galleries showcase outback art. This is a base of the Royal Flying Doctor Service; airborne medics whose territory is over 7 million square kilometres of outback Australia.

In the late afternoon, we saw clusters of kangaroos standing in the distance, as if they were watching the train going by, and setting their clocks by it.

The train's first real climb is up to the top of the aptly named Blue Mountains and downhill to the coast. After so much red flatness the sight of massed eucalyptus trees and hills comes as rather a shock, as does the sight of urban sprawl – a reminder that this is a nation of coastal and city dwellers. After our arrival at Sydney's quite grand Central Station, we walk down to the harbour and the stunning Opera House, its swan wings gleaming in the sun. Its vertical white form and the horizontal red plain of the Nullarbor are both remarkable Australian icons.

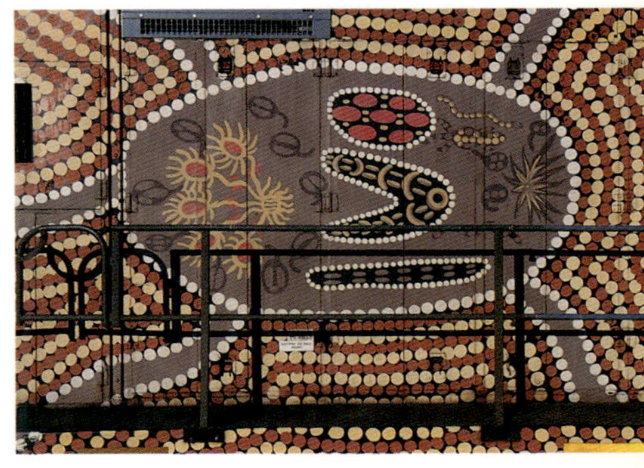

Great Southern Railway | *The Indian Pacific train leaves Perth for Sydney every Friday (arriving Monday) and Tuesday (arriving Friday)*

Leaves Sydney for Perth every Monday (arriving Thursday) and Friday (arriving Monday) | *www.gsr.com.au*

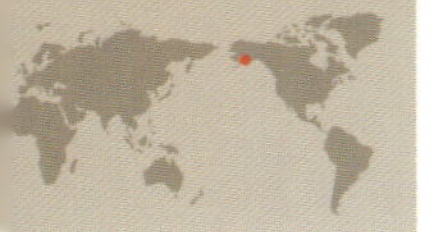

North, to Alaska...

The Spirit of Endeavour cruise ship, the Inside Passage, Alaska

'Going north, the rush is on...' the old song that musician Johnny Horton struck gold with goes part way toward capturing the surge of interest that the very mention of Alaska arouses. It's a place that many people want to visit, and thousands have journeyed here to seek their fortune or just to see the dramatic landscape, much of it lying beneath snow and ice.

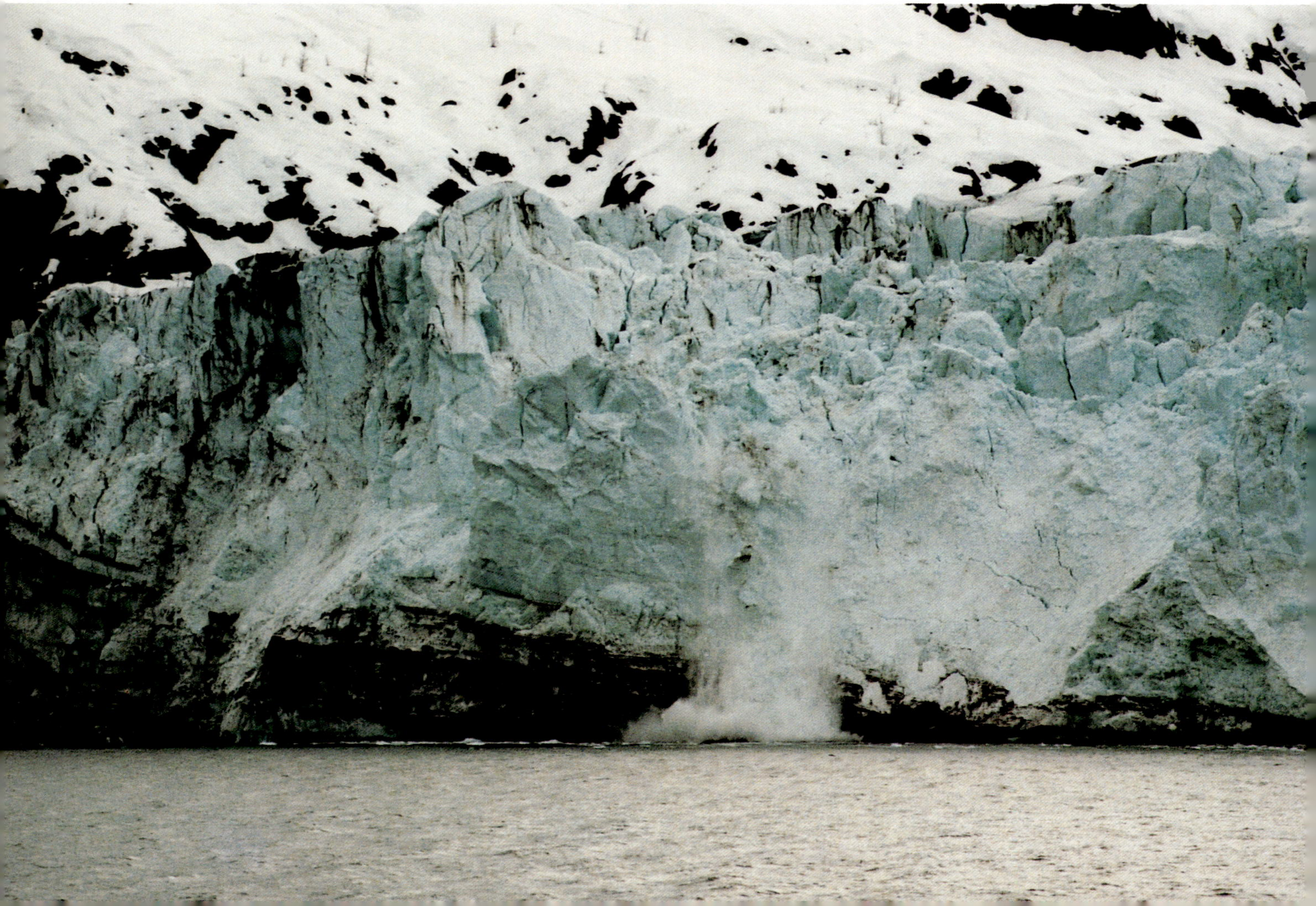

Glaciers once covered half of Alaska; grand masses of ice engraving deep gashes in what the native Aleut people called *Alyeska*, the Great Land. This panoramic curtain of ice, a craggy white cliff face seemingly mottled with blue dye, is the spectacular South Sawyer Glacier, some 20 miles long. From the deck of our ship, less than a quarter of a mile away, we could hear cracking and crashing noises, chilling sounds of nature at work.

The giant glacier is calving, great chunks falling from its frozen façade, crumbling and crashing into the sea beneath. It is a display so powerful that it takes your breath away – and what's left of it the cold air seizes, giving double meaning to the word breathtaking.

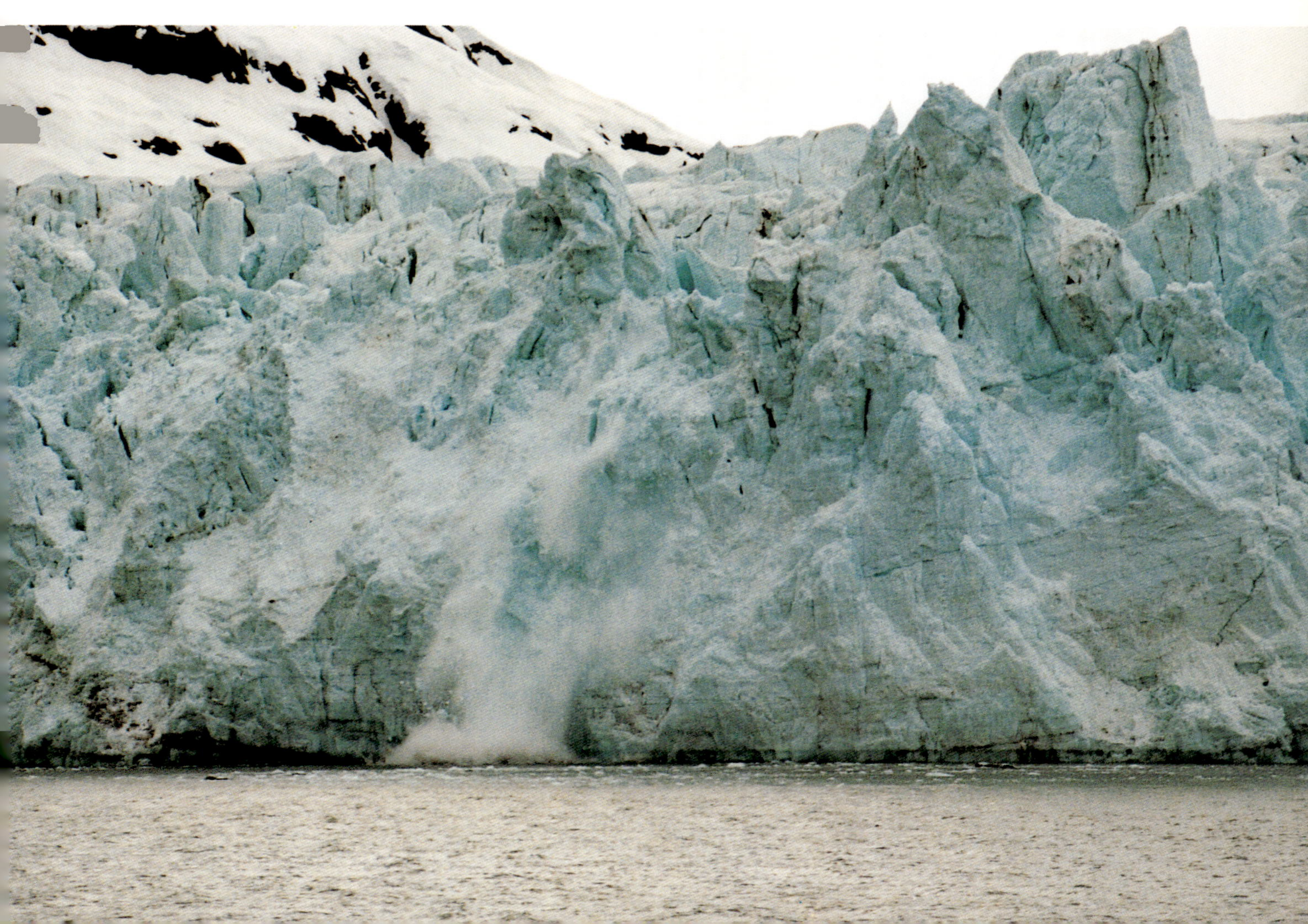

Opposite: St. Michaels' Cathedral at Sitka, the crown jewel of Russian Alaska.

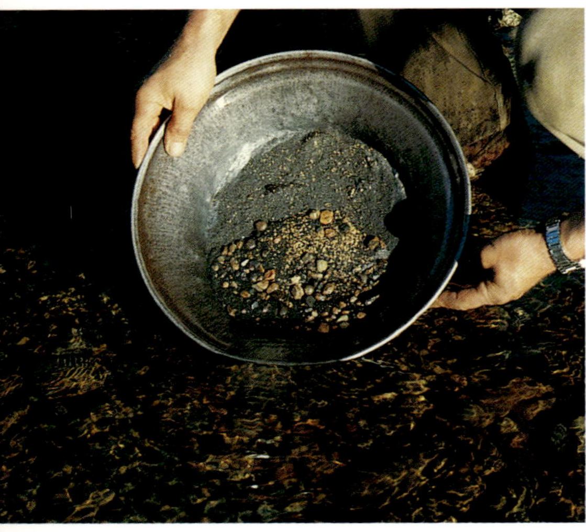

*'What is fame? an empty bubble;
Gold? A transient, shining trouble.'*

James Grainger

Remote, a raw wilderness, this is one of the harshest environments on earth. People speak of Alaska as though it is a realm apart, and somehow it seems to have an existence of its own, more like a separate country than a state within a country. Although it is the 49th and largest of the 51 states that constitute the United States of America, Alaska is a virtual subcontinent. The comparatively few inhabitants of its 365 million acres of land generally refer to the rest of the United States as the 'lower forty-eight', and the remainder of the world as 'outside'.

Despite its extreme conditions, Alaska has always attracted treasure hunters, searching for valuables that might be wrested from the vaults of the vast expanse. Siberian huntsmen came across the icy land bridge that linked Alaska to Siberia in prehistoric times, stalking food, and venturing beyond their borders. Centuries later, soon after Russian explorers had first sighted the Alaskan mainland in 1741, ships carrying the tough promyshlenniki - Russian fur hunters - arrived to mine 'soft gold', the precious velvety fur of the sea otter, whose pelts fetched astronomically high prices in the courts of Russia and China.

A hundred years afterwards, the traders had cut great swathes through the seal otter and fur seal colonies of Alaska's southern and southwest coasts. New Archangel was established as the Russian capital of Alaska - later renamed Sitka - and the Russian-American Company, set up with a royal warrant from the Czar, monopolised the fur trade and controlled activities in the new territory.

Contact with the Russians had a mostly disastrous effect on the native population. Warfare, disease and starvation dramatically reduced the numbers of Aleut Eskimo and Indians. Russian customs, language and religion impacted on their way of life and beliefs. The missionaries left a lasting imprint on the native culture, and the distinctive onion-shaped domes of their Russian Orthodox churches are still visible in Southern Alaska.

Fur revenues waned as the traders near exhausted the once-rich resource. This decline, and the inability to support her distant territory, led to Russia selling Alaska in 1867, for the sum of $7.2 million, about two cents an acre, to the United States. Just thirty years later, gold, that 'shining trouble', was discovered, and the next great rush was on, north to Alaska.

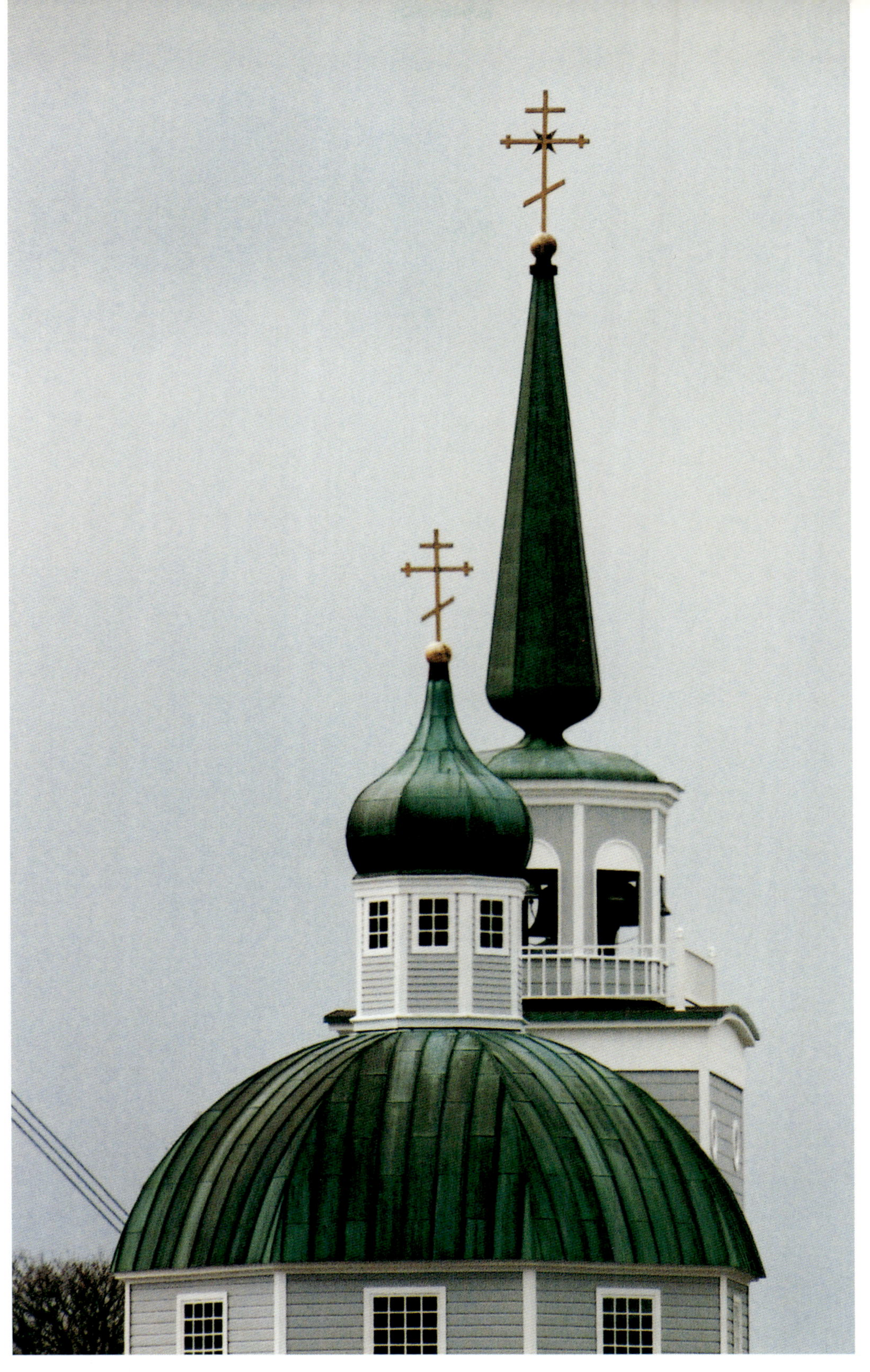

The Inside Passage, an inland waterway of fjords sheltered from ocean winds and waves, begins at Seattle. It was from here in 1897 and 1898 that thousands of fortune hunters headed north on an armada of ageing steamers bound for the Alaskan and Klondike goldfields.

We embarked from here too; as sightseers on the sleek cruise ship Spirit of Endeavour, travelling up the Inside Passage, to Juneau, the capital city of Alaska. The small ship takes a maximum of 102 passengers, and only half of that number was on this trip, the very first of the official tourist season. We had all chosen to go small-ship cruising, so we could draw closer to the shorelines and sights, and by virtue of our ship's size, be as least of an invasive presence as possible.

The impact and management of tourism is hotly debated here, with the number and size of cruise ships visiting Alaska increasing exponentially. Large ships, some carrying thousands of passengers, disgorge crowds into small streets and outnumber the residents when in port. Some of the loneliest places are now starting to become crowded, and what drew people to them at first – the sense of wilderness – is in danger of being overwhelmed.

It seems fitting that it takes two days journeying north through Puget Sound and British Columbia before we reach the green islands, misty fjords, and rain forests of Alaska's southeastern 'panhandle'. Such an uncompromising land deserves a less than immediate approach, and somehow it makes the anticipation of our arrival sharper – an odd feeling when everywhere is usually quite instantly accessible.

Most of Alaska is 'bear beware' country and there is plenty of advice on commonsense behaviour. Three species live here, the black bear, brown grizzly bear and the polar bear, all large, free-range, untamed and forever hungry. My favourite of the bear etiquette tips advised not to surprise bears at close distance, to avoid crowding them, and to respect their 'personal space'. Fast runners, bears can easily climb trees and rock faces, and they tackle the water for more than a spot of salmon fishing. We were surprised to see a bear swimming vigorously towards the ship, as was the Forest Service park ranger on board for that day, who remarked it as being an unusual sight.

It looked a very purposeful bear, and although it turned back to shore, we were glad of our own 'personal space' well above the waterline.

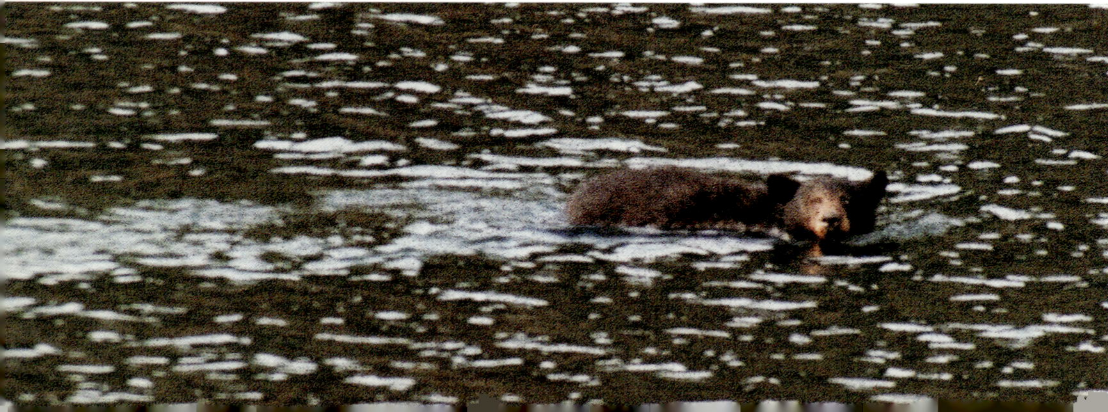

The swimming bear eyeballs the boat.

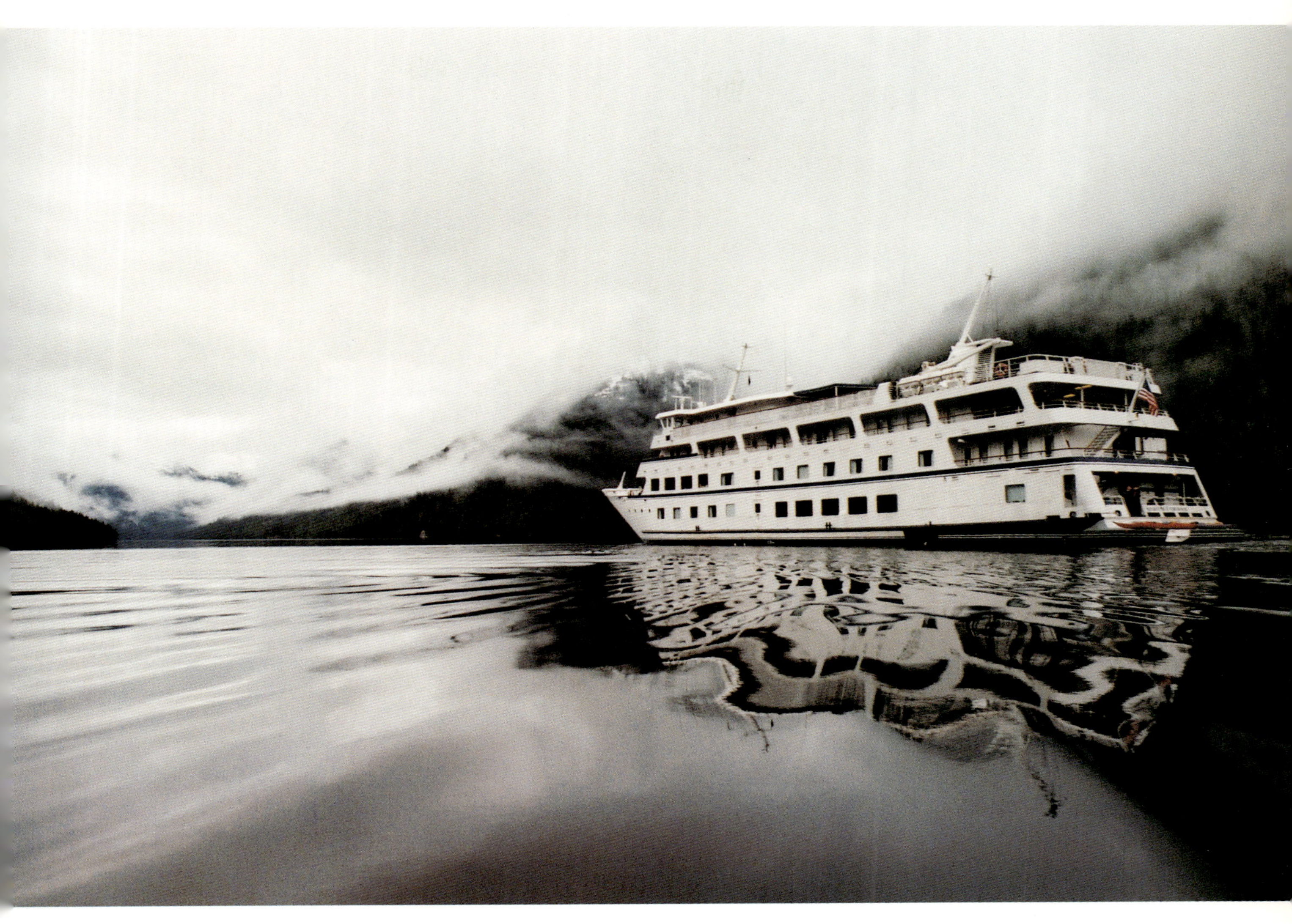

The Spirit of Endeavour cruising on the mirror waters of Misty Fjords National Monument.

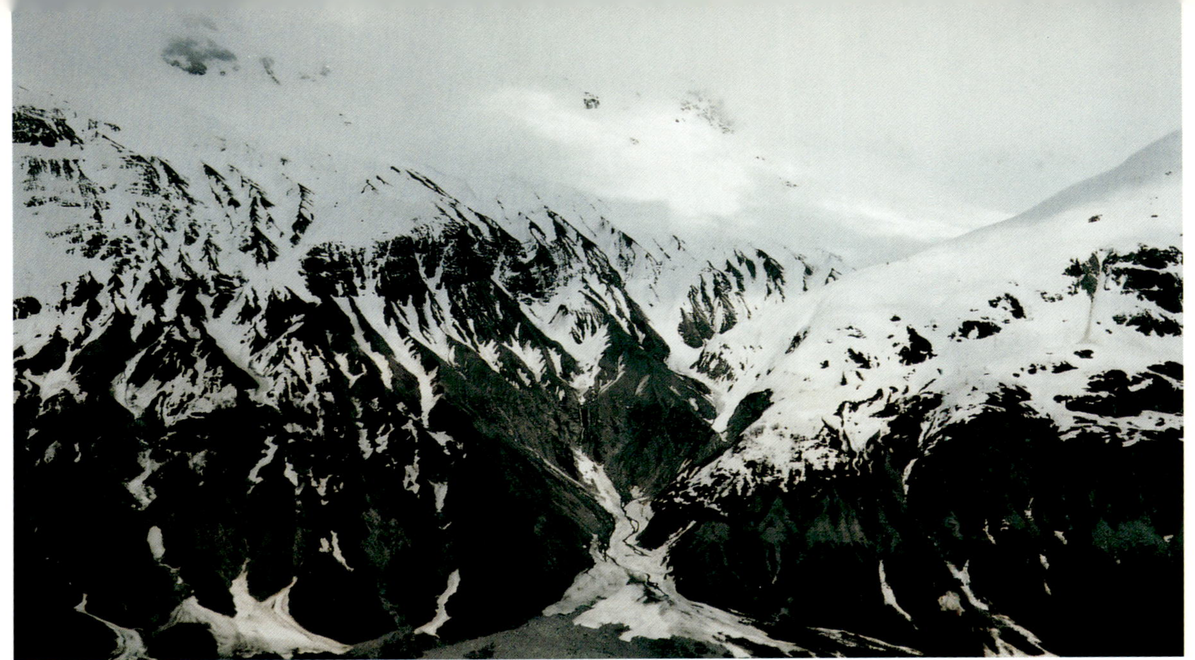

The Spirit of Endeavour is easily manoeuvred; as we discover when she noses up to a spectacular waterfall, near enough for those on deck to get wet from its spray. Our vessel's compact size means that the captain can bring the bow right up to a waterfall, close to a glacier or turn almost instantly to follow a pod of orca whales. Binoculars are at hand, in the large comfortable observation lounge, the staterooms and even taken to the dining room. We are on constant 'creature patrol'. Everyone rushes to the windows and on deck armed with cameras when the on-board naturalist or a scanning passenger spots anything.

The fresh air sharpens our appetites. Every evening the hip young chef, a whip-thin 'dude' from New Orleans, cruises into the lounge to describe the dinner menu he has prepared for us, and ask how our day has been. We look forward to sampling the light and innovative food that follows his entertaining performance.

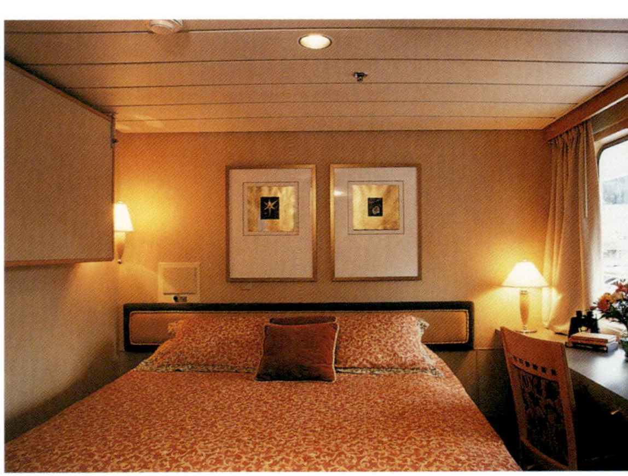

A deluxe stateroom on the Spirit of Endeavour.

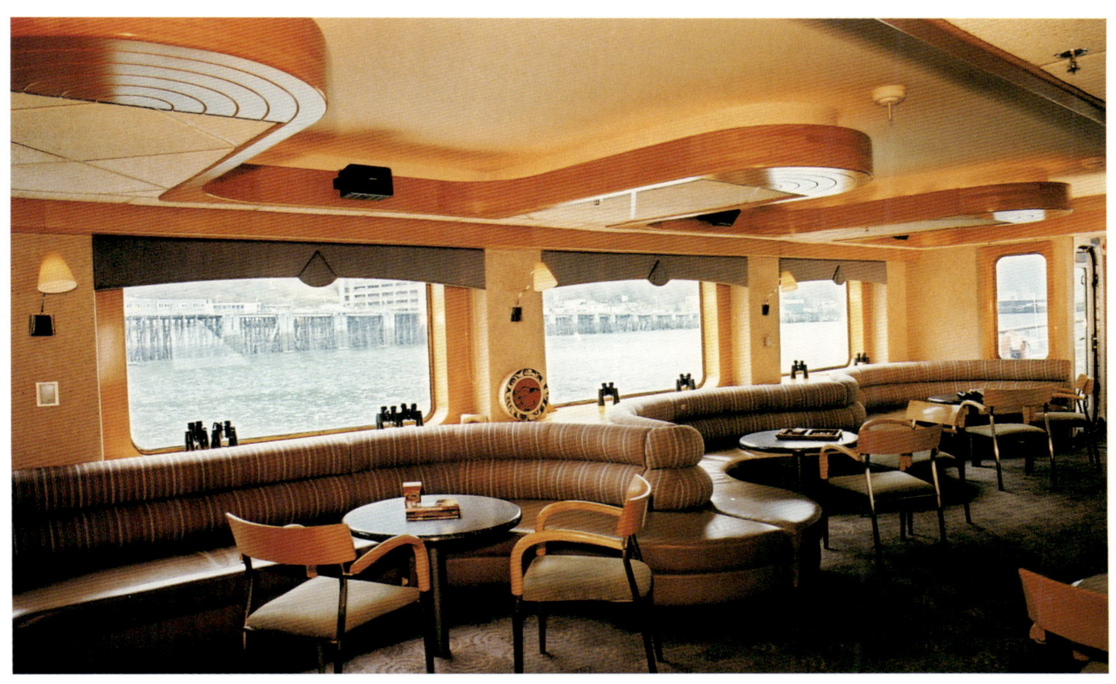

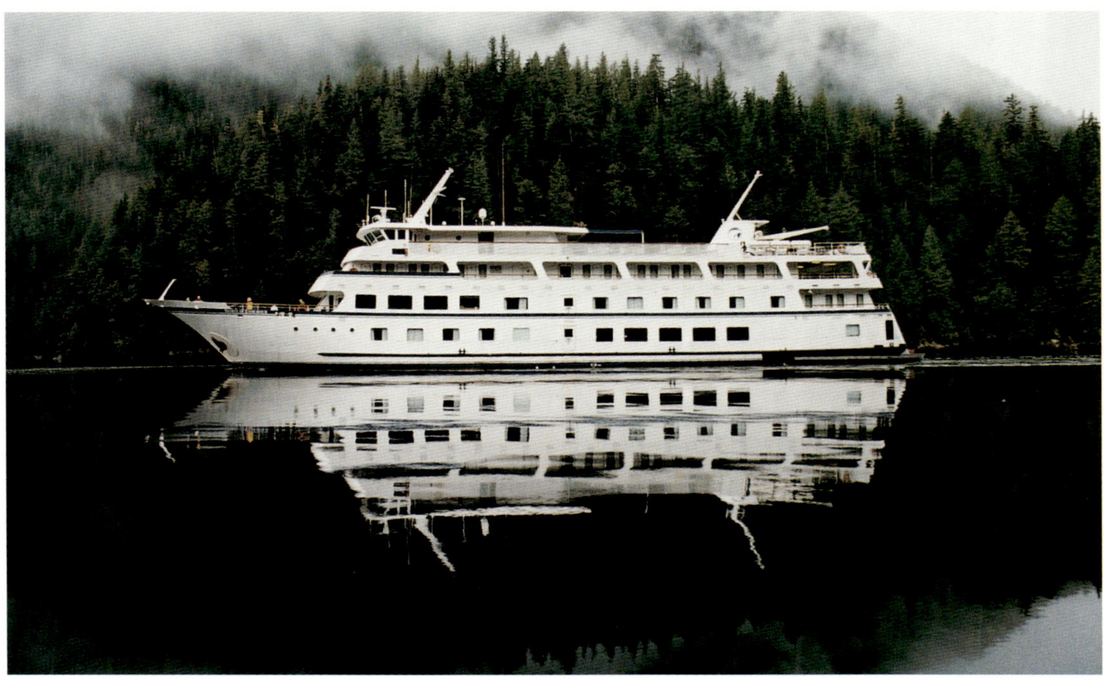

Stunning scenes are on view from the big windows of the spacious Observation Lounge.

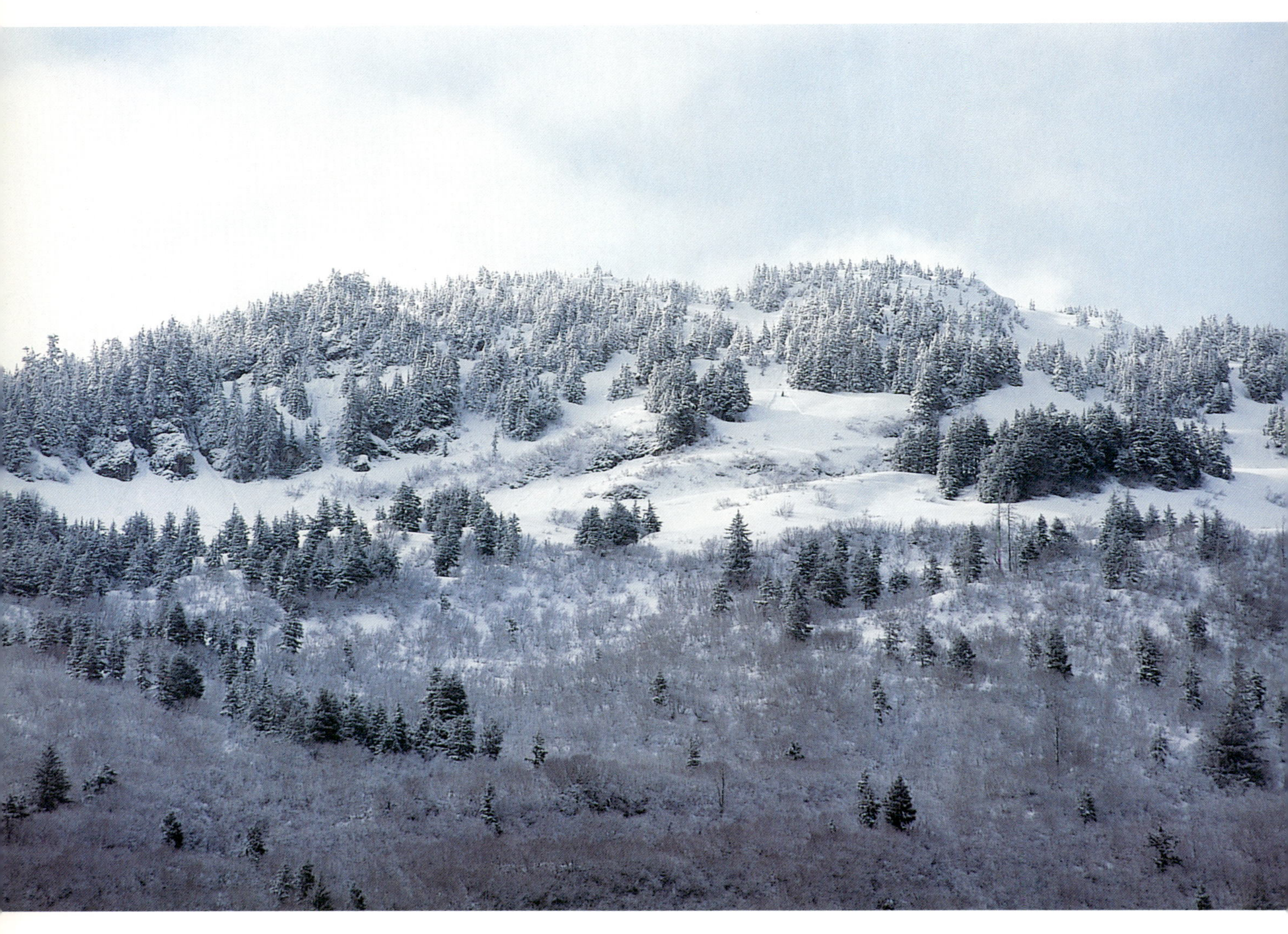

A third of Alaska is covered in forests, these spruce trees temporarily coated with snow.

At times, there is a steely grey sky on show, and in late April, the still, sharp cold air outside hints at the chance of snow. Cosseted inside our centrally heated ship, the contrast between warmth and cold is most obvious out on the decks. From the restful lounge, we look out at high snow-covered mountains passing by, and although it is warm indoors, the sight of the frozen landscape causes us to pull the curtains across the windows in our cosy stateroom even so.

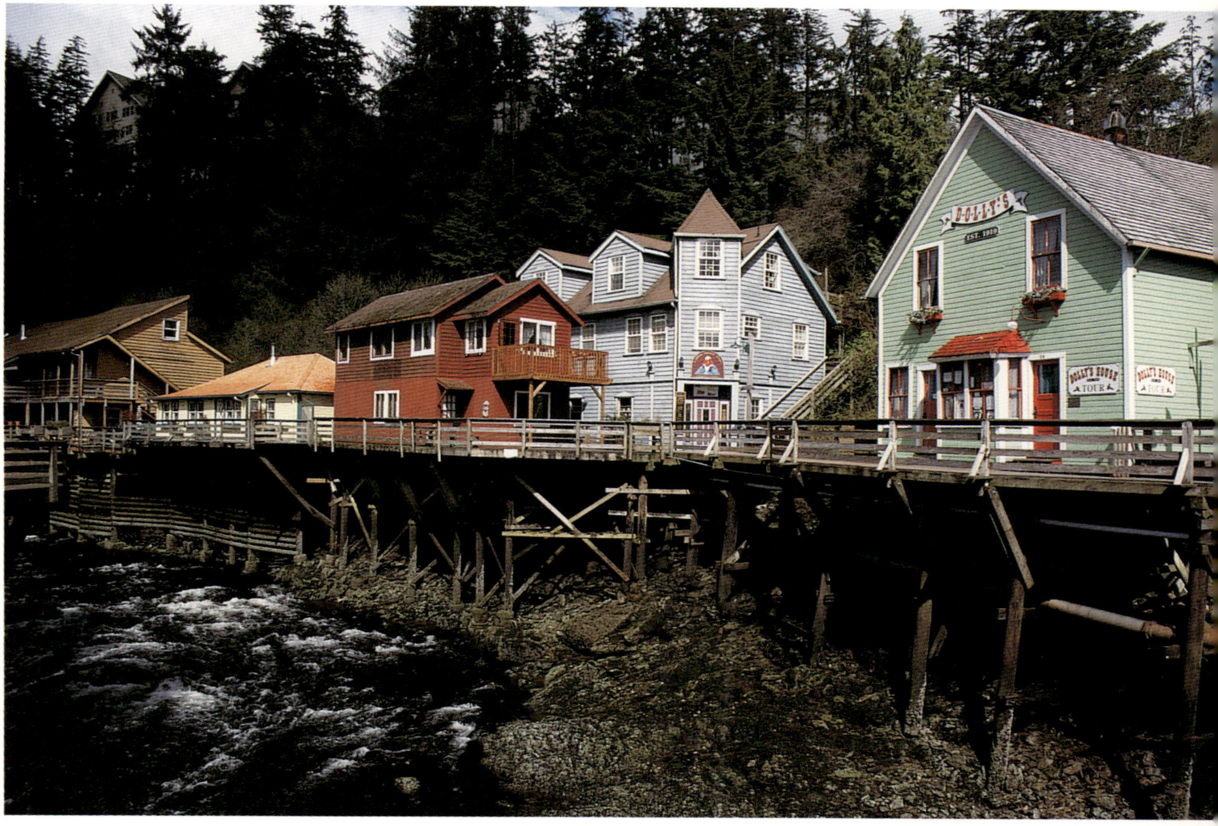

Ketchikan's historic Creek Street.

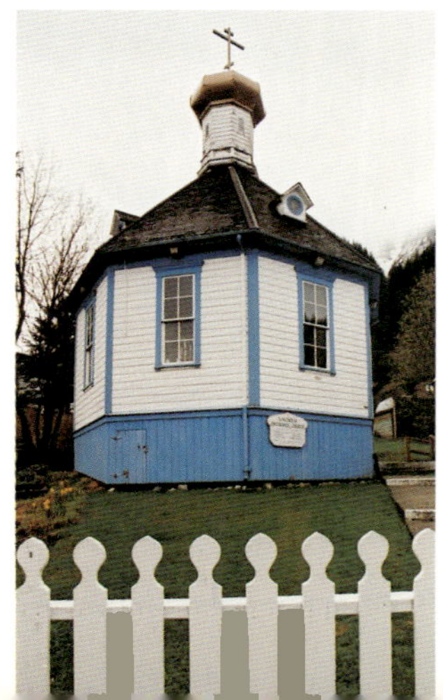

Alaska's waters yielded up another rich treasure – salmon. Fishermen rushed to exploit the still abundant runs that earned the city of Ketchikan title of 'Salmon Capital of the World'. Running literally through the centre of town is Fish Creek, where all five species of salmon spawn each year. The historic old district is built on pilings right above the fertile waterway. In the frontier town's early days, brothels put out welcome mats here for the fishermen, loggers and hunters. Now genteel art galleries and craft shops greet the street's visitors.

Like most southeast Alaskan towns, Ketchikan has a few miles of roads that are not connected to anywhere else. Numerous floatplanes are parked down at the wharf, aircraft often being the only practical way to reach many of the rural areas.

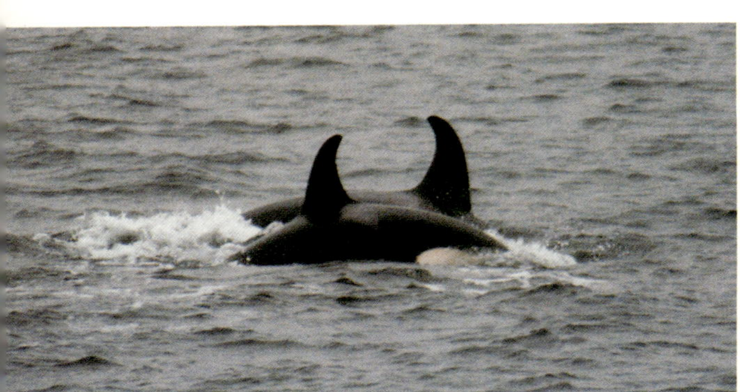

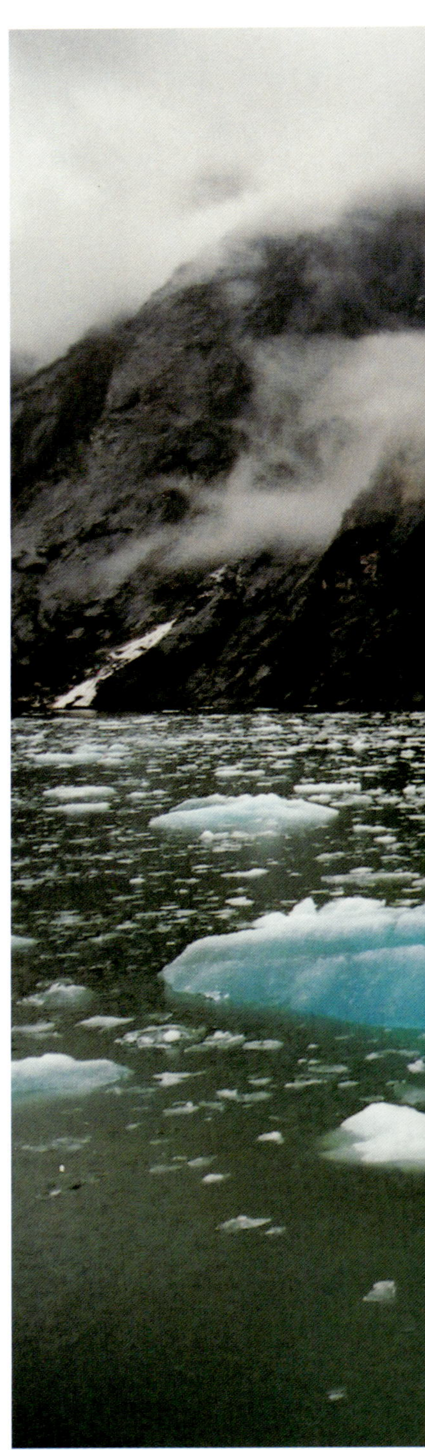

The Tlingit people are a predominant Indian tribe of southeast Alaska. In their mythology, Orcas – killer whales – are a symbol of good luck and fortune to those who see them. We caught sight of two, cruising together in Glacier Bay. Jet black, emblazoned with a brilliant white oval patch around each eye, they curved neatly just out of the water, crossing opposite each other as though part of a synchronized swimming team.

We found ourselves moving slowly through a sea of crushed ice. Many of the floating pieces we saw were like huge jagged jewels, some glittering such a startling blue-green and so highly polished that they could mistaken for hundreds and thousands of temporary emeralds and sapphires.

The ship forged ahead, grinding against the ice, as we all stood on deck, oblivious to the cold, watching mesmerized as the many-faceted shards, resembling broken bits of coloured glass or rejects from a sculptor's studio, sailed past.

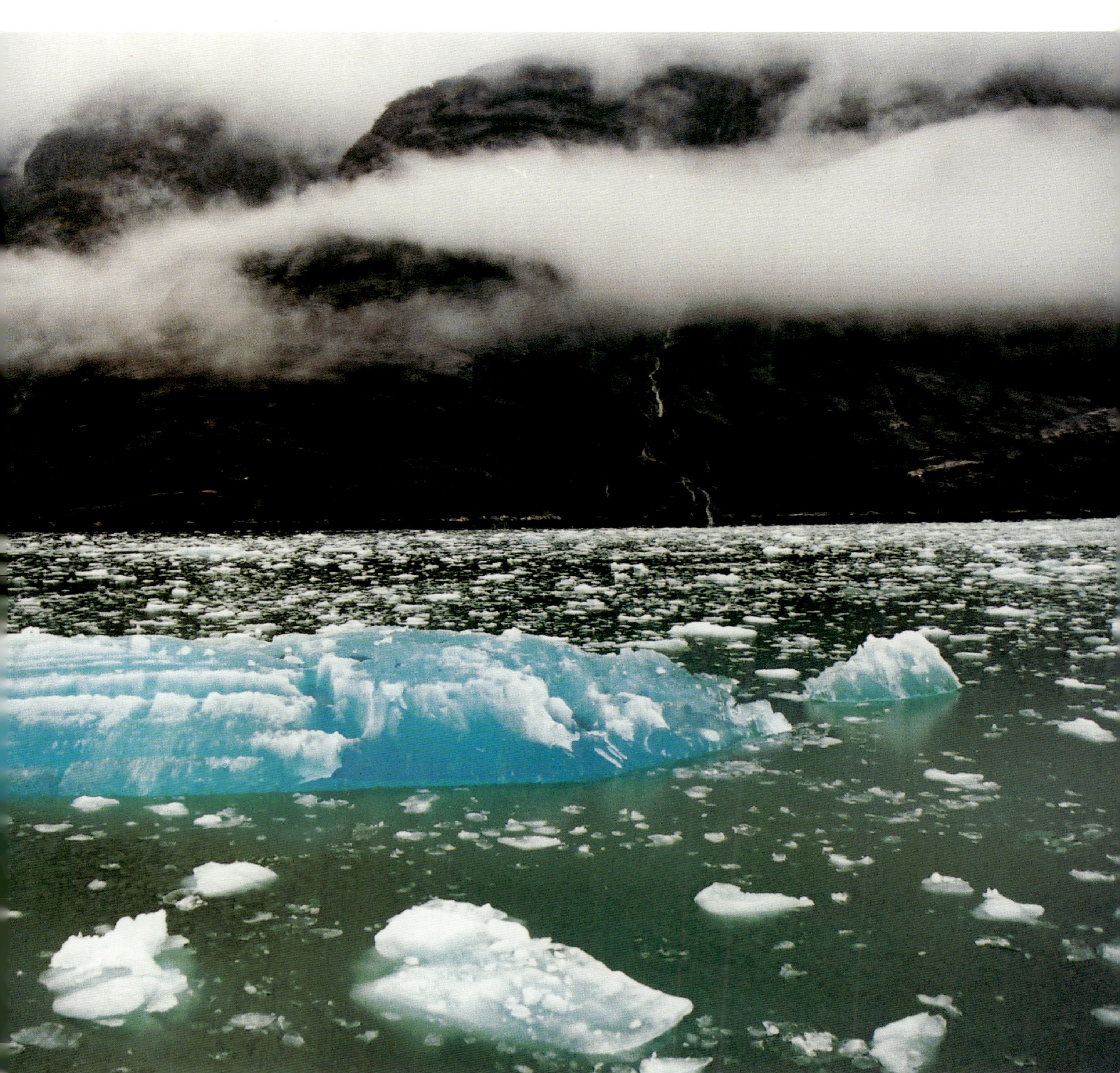

Humpback whales spouted, surfaced, and flicked their great fluke tails, like a giant's paddle, as we cruised Frederick Sound. Once hunted almost to extinction by commercial whalers, now the chance just to watch the whales draws eager onlookers. Another creature we all wanted to see was the great bald eagle, with its distinct white head, actually a respectably feathered skull, and massive 7-foot wingspan. More of these impressive birds of prey live in Alaska than elsewhere in North America. The fishing is good here, and as fish is the raptor's favourite food, we saw many of them.

According to traditional Tlingit legend, people and animals are relatives, who can cross into each other's worlds. Animals have the ability to appear before people in human form, interacting with them in important ways; similarly, humans can be transformed into animals in supernatural encounters and experience life in the animal world. The Bear epitomizes this relationship between humans and animals, behaving in nature like a human. Competing for the same resources, it can walk on its hind legs, fish for salmon and use its paws to eat nuts and berries.

In this intriguing mythology, the Raven also moves between the human and creature world, but has a dual personality. A culture hero and transformer, shaping much of the world, Raven is also a trickster, driven by selfishness, greed and hunger to bizarre adventures. He must be in his element here. The rushes to Alaska for fur, gold, copper, salmon, and oil have so far resulted in enough exploits and escapades to keep an army of Ravens perpetually on the wing.

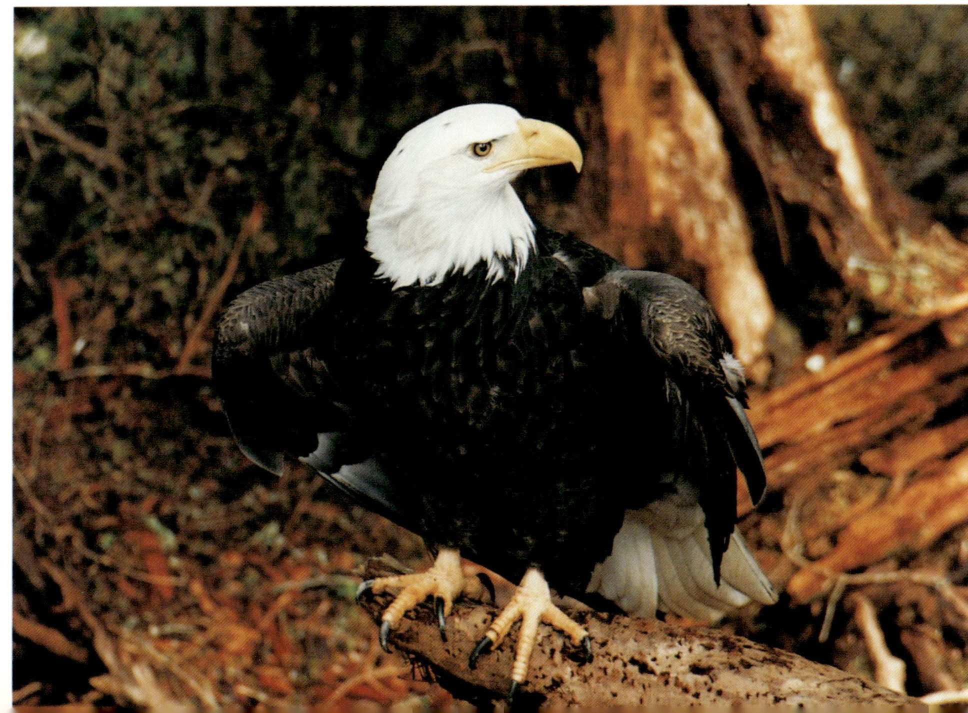

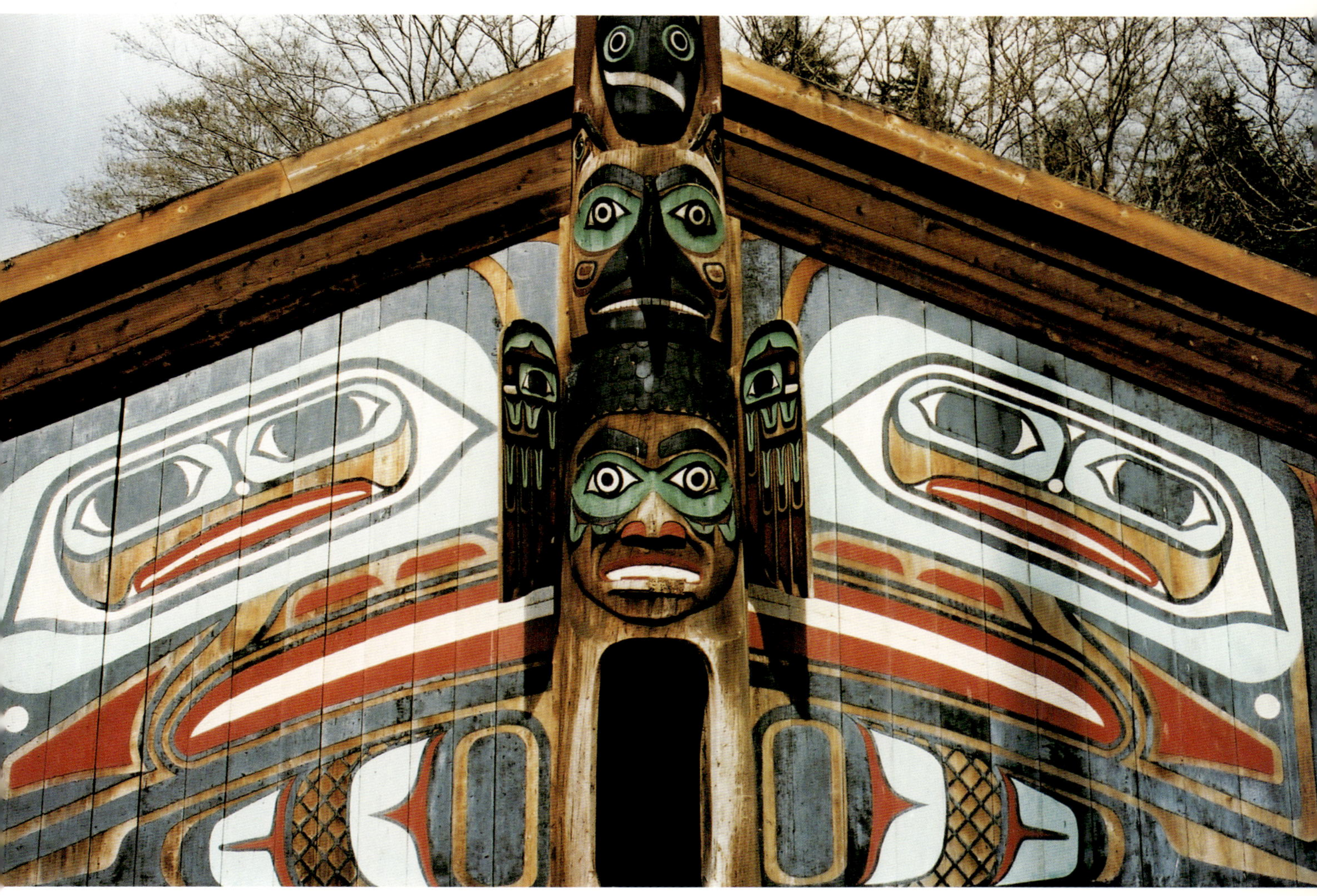

The exterior of this Tlingit winter house is a stylised painting of the Raven, and each of the carved house-posts inside tell the story of a man from the Raven clan. There are not enough pages left here to show and tell any more of Alaska, but we will go back to see more of this visual treasure trove.

Cruise West	*The Spirit of Endeavour and her sister ships cruise north to Alaska, from April to August*	*www.cruisewest.com*